UK countries

England

Capital:	London
Population:	53 million
Area:	130,400 km²

Scotland

Capital:	Edinburgh
Population:	5.3 million
Area:	78,800 km²

Wales

Capital:	Cardiff
Population:	3.1 million
Area:	20,800 km²

Northern Ireland

Capital:	Belfast
Population:	1.8 million
Area:	14,100 km²

Not part of the UK

Republic of Ireland

Capital:	Dublin
Population:	4.6 million
Area:	70,300 km²

THE BRITISH ISLES

Orange Line 3

für Klasse 7

Das Lehrbuch versteht sich als Gesamtangebot. Welche Texte und Aufgaben verpflichtend sind, wird durch die schulinternen Curricula festgelegt.

Zusatzmaterial für Schülerinnen und Schüler:
Orange Line 3 Workbook mit Audio-CD und Übungssoftware (ISBN 978-3-12-548083-4)
Orange Line 3 Workbook mit Audio-CD (ISBN 978-3-12-548283-8)
Orange Line 3 Vokabellernheft (ISBN 978-3-12-548093-3)
Orange Line 3 Vokabeltraining aktiv (ISBN 978-3-12-548243-2)
Orange Line 3 Grammatiktraining aktiv (ISBN 978-3-12-548303-3)
Orange Line 3 Klassenarbeitstraining aktiv (ISBN 978-3-12-548103-9)

1. Auflage 978-3-12-548073-5 (fester Einband) 1 10 9 8 7 | 24 23 22 21
1. Auflage 978-3-12-548273-9 (flexibler Einband) 1 9 8 7 6 | 24 23 22 21

Alle Drucke dieser Auflage sind unverändert und können im Unterricht nebeneinander verwendet werden.
Die letzte Zahl bezeichnet das Jahr des Druckes.

Herausgeber: Dr. Frank Haß, Kirchberg
Autorinnen und Autoren: David Brimage, Brighton; Geraldine Greenhalgh, Hamilton; Wolfgang Hamm, Marktredwitz; Melanie Ku, Hanau; Howard Rayner, London; Clare Treleaven, Castellón sowie Andrew Cowle, Glasgow; Jo Cummins, London; Dr. Andrea Jessen, Tamm; Michael Meisenzahl, Karlstadt; Leonie Pohl, Gütersloh; Katharina Saal, Fürstenfeldbruck; Karen Seekings, London; Nadine Uesbeck, Dortmund; Anna Zagermann, Hattingen; Konstanze Zander, Großenehrich

Beratung: Brunhilde Biek, Leonberg; Karin Braun, Dortmund; Wilma Brings, Bedburg; Amanda Chisnell, Lollar; Ulf Degen, Braunschweig; Tanja Frank, Ulm; Sandra Haberland, Recklinghausen; Wolfgang Hamm, Marktredwitz; Ulrike Heringhaus, Altheim; Michael Herrmann, Ludwigsfelde; Christa Kathmann-Fuhrmann, Bonn; Dr. Margitta Kuty, Greifswald-Eldna; Grit Machut, Berlin; Michael Meisenzahl, Karlstadt; Beatrix Pierce, Eppingen; Annegret Preker-Franke, Bielefeld; Dr. Hubert Schwandt, Parchen; Christian Straukamp, Nordhorn; Ines van Hove, Oldenburg; Dieter Vilimek, Helmstadt-Bargen

Redaktion: André Schmitt, Cornelia Schaller, Lektorat Editoria, Fellbach; Birgit Piefke-Wagner, Korntal-Münchingen
Herstellung: Ulrike Wursthorn

Umschlaggestaltung und Gestaltungskonzept: know idea, Freiburg; Koma Amok, Stuttgart
Umschlagfoto: Avenue Images GmbH (Image Source), Hamburg; Getty Images RF (Vetta/John Madden), München
Fotografen: Thomas Weccard, Ludwigsburg
Illustrationen: Marek Blaha, Offenbach; Kirill Chudinskiy, Köln; Marcus Wilder, Hamburg; sowie Friederike Ablang, Berlin; Lars Benecke, Hannover; Thomas Binder, Magdeburg; Gilles Bonotaux, Paris; Vera Brüggemann, Bielefeld; Christian Dekelver, Weinstadt; Thorsten Droessler, Leipzig; Andreas Florian, Lübeck; Anke Fröhlich, Leipzig; Josef Hammen, Trierweiler; Christian Hansen, Berlin; Susann Hesselbarth, Leipzig; Carmen Hochmann, Bielefeld; Martin Hoffmann, Stuttgart; Hendrik Kranenberg, Drolshagen; Cleo-Petra Kurze, Berlin; Dorothee Mahnkopf, Berlin; Karin Mall, Berlin; Helga Merkle, Albershausen; Pawel Miedzinki, Kozieglowy; David Norman, Meerbusch; Katrin Oertel, Münster; Liliane Oser, Hamburg; Sven Palmowski, Barcelona; Katja Rau, Berglen; Bettina Reich, Zwenkau; Sandra Schmidt, Berlin; Carolin Ina Schröter, Berlin; Jaroslaw Schwarzstein, Hannover; Studio 100 Media GmbH, Claudia Schweiger, München; Manfred Tophoven, Straelen; Jacqueline Urban, Eisenach; Ulrike Vetter, Leipzig; Aurel Voigt, Waiblingen; Martina Vollhardt, Kamenz; Sylvia Wolf, Wiesbaden; Steffen Wolff, Brohl-Lützing; Dorothee Wolters, Köln

Satz: Satzkiste GmbH, Stuttgart
Reproduktion: Schwabenrepro GmbH, Stuttgart
Druck: PASSAVIA Druckservice GmbH & Co. KG, Passau

Printed in Germany
ISBN 978-3-12-548073-5 (fester Einband)
ISBN 978-3-12-548273-9 (flexibler Einband)

9 783125 480735

9 783125 482739

Orange Line 3

Herausgeber: Dr. Frank Haß

Ernst Klett Verlag
Stuttgart • Leipzig

Inhalt

L = Listening S = Speaking R = Reading W = Writing V = Viewing I = Intercultural

L = Listening S = Speaking R = Reading W = Writing V = Viewing I = Intercultural

Inhalt

L = Listening S = Speaking R = Reading W = Writing V = Viewing I = Intercultural

L = Listening S = Speaking R = Reading W = Writing V = Viewing I = Intercultural

So lernst du mit Orange Line

Hier zeige ich dir, wie du dich in deinem Buch gut zurechtfindest. Das Buch hat fünf Units (Kapitel). Jede Unit ist gleich aufgebaut.

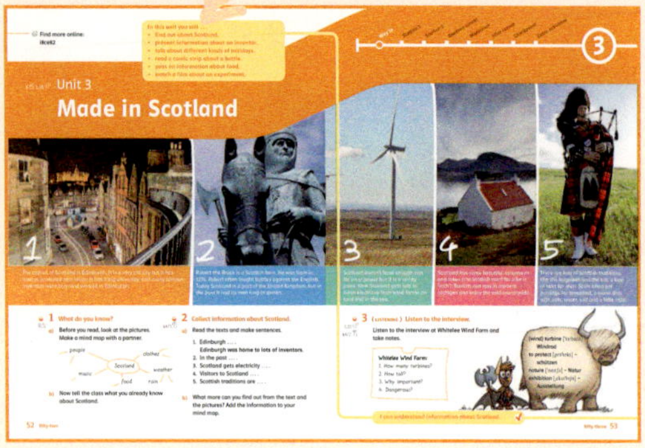

Way in

Hier steigst du in das neue Thema ein. Dazu gibt es auch einen kurzen Film.

Im gelben Kasten siehst du, was du in der *Unit* lernst.

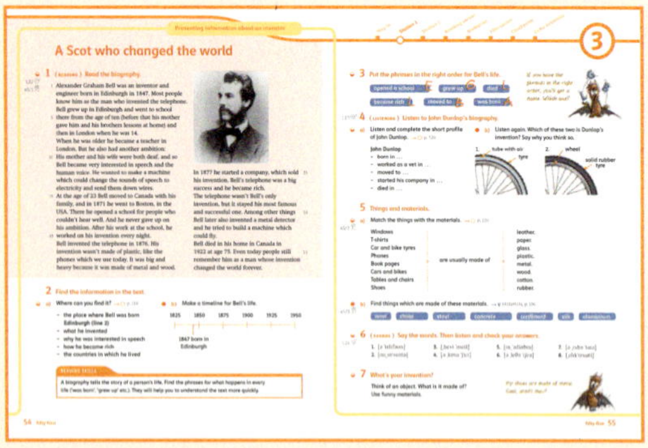

Stations

In jeder *Unit* gibt es zwei *Stations*, in denen du viele neue Dinge lernst. Diese Symbole zeigen dir, wie schwer die Übung ist und ob es im Anhang eine leichtere Variante gibt:

◒ → ○ p. 137, ●

In der *Your turn*-Aufgabe kannst du zeigen, dass du alles verstanden hast, und deine eigenen Ideen einbringen.

Reading corner

In der *Reading corner* gibt es verschiedene Geschichten, Dialoge und andere Texte.

Mediation/Film corner

Auf der linken Seite geht es darum, englische Informationen auf Deutsch weiterzugeben oder umgekehrt.

In der *Film corner* geht es um einen englischen Film.

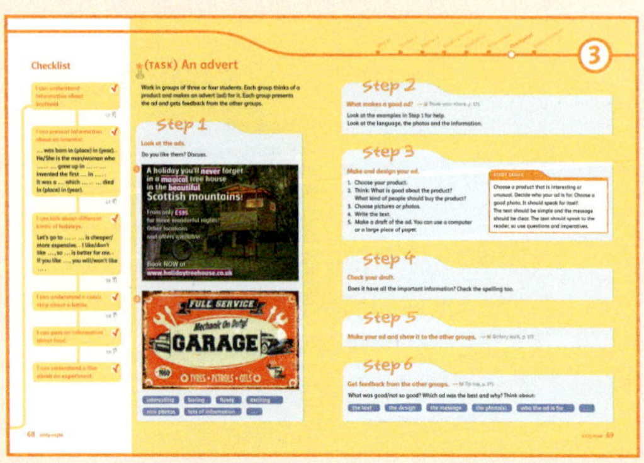

Checkpoint

Auf dieser Seite kannst du überprüfen, ob du in der *Unit* alles verstanden hast.
In der *Checklist* sind alle Lernziele noch einmal aufgelistet.

Die Abschluss-Aufgabe (*task*) sollt ihr zu zweit oder in der Gruppe lösen.

Extra activities

Hier findest du zwei Seiten mit Zusatz-Aufgaben, z. B. zur Vorbereitung auf die Klassenarbeit.

Skills

Auf einige *Units* folgt eine Doppelseite, auf der ihr eine bestimmte Fertigkeit (*skill*) besonders trainieren könnt, also z. B. das Lesen, Schreiben, Sprechen oder Wörterbucharbeit.

More about

Hier findest du interessante weiterführende Informationen zur Region der Unit.

Im Anschluss an die fünf *Units* gibt es noch weitere nützliche Seiten:

Extra: Hier erwarten dich weitere Lesetexte: eine Geschichte, ein Theaterstück und vieles mehr.

Grammar: Hier findest du alle Regeln und Erklärungen zur Grammatik sowie weitere Übungen.

Methods: Manche Übungen könnt ihr auf eine bestimmte Art und Weise bearbeiten.
Das erkennt ihr an diesem Symbol: → M
Wie es genau funktioniert, kannst du hier nachlesen.

Vocabulary: Im *Vocabulary* findest du alle neuen Wörter in der Reihenfolge, in der sie in der *Unit* auftauchen, und die wichtigsten Arbeitsanweisungen.
Im *Dictionary* sind die Wörter noch einmal alphabetisch aufgelistet: zuerst Englisch–Deutsch und dann Deutsch–Englisch.

Am Schluss des Buches findest du noch
- Sätze, die du im Unterricht sagen kannst, z. B. bei der Gruppenarbeit
- eine Liste mit den unregelmäßigen Verben

Symbol	Erklärung
○ ◒ ●	leicht/mittel/schwer (Niveaudifferenzierung)
✿	individualisierende Aufgabe (natürliche Differenzierung)
→ ○ p. 131	Verweis auf leichtere Parallelübung auf der *Diff corner*-Seite
OR	Aufgabe zur Auswahl (Wahldifferenzierung)
(Schlüssel)	Entwicklung von Schlüsselkompetenzen
P	Hier entsteht ein Produkt für das Portfolio.
4/1	Verweis auf eine Übung im *Workbook*
→ G13, p. 172	Verweis auf den Grammatikanhang (*Grammar*)
→ M	Verweis auf die Methodenseite (*Methods*)
→ V	Verweis zum Wortfeld im Vokabular (*Vocabulary*)
(Partner)	Partnerarbeit
(Gruppe)	Gruppenarbeit
(CD)	Verweis auf die Lehrer-CD (Audio)
(DVD)	Verweis auf die Lehrer-DVD (Film)
Find more online:	Code auf www.klett.de eingeben und Zusatzinformationen erhalten

Zoom in – The British Isles

The British Isles

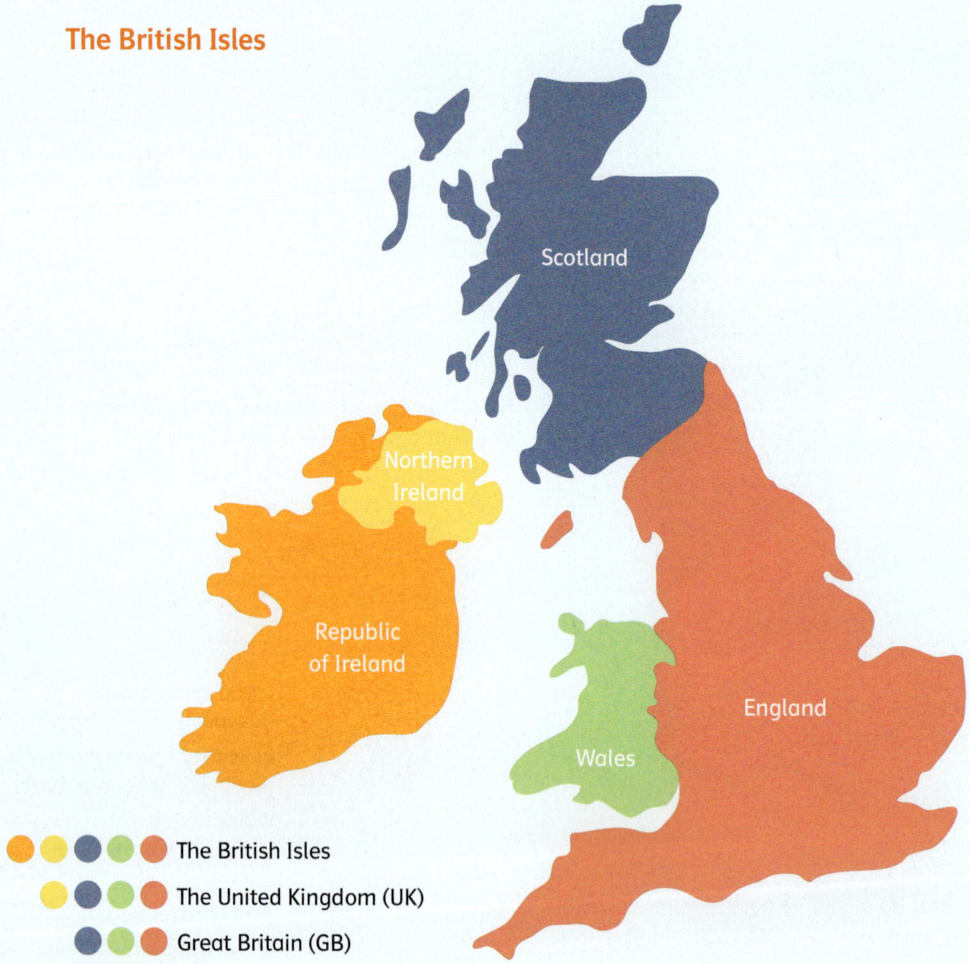

1 Do the British Isles quiz with a partner.

1. What are the names of the five countries of the British Isles?
2. Which is the biggest country in the United Kingdom (UK)?
3. Which is bigger, Northern Ireland or the Republic of Ireland?
4. Which is bigger, Scotland or Wales?
5. Which country is in the UK but not in Great Britain (GB)?
6. Which country has more people, Wales or Scotland?
7. Which is the biggest city in the UK?
8. Which country is not in the UK?
9. The Channel Tunnel goes from France to which country?

Look at the map at the front of the book for help. You can check your answers on page 287.

England

Wales

Scotland

Northern Ireland

Ireland

1,1 **2** (LISTENING) **Listen to five teenagers from the British Isles.**

Make a table. Then listen and take notes.

Name	From?	Age?	Hobbies?	Plans?
Emily 				
Dylan 				
Lewis 				
Sophie 				
Patrick 				

CULTURE

The five teenagers are from different countries of the British Isles and they have different accents. Which accents did you find easiest or most difficult to understand?

Find more online:
i8ce82

In this unit you will ...
- find out about historical places in England.
- give and understand directions.
- talk in more detail about where you live.
- read a story from the past.
- pass on information about the history of a sport.
- understand a film about Greenwich now and in the past.

1 1,2

Unit 1
England now and then

Stonehenge is a very old circle of stones in the south of England. It may be more than **4,000 years** old. No one knows why it is there.

The Romans started to build **Hadrian's Wall** in the north of England in the year **122** to mark the border of their empire. It took six years to build the wall from the east to the west of England.

1 What's the oldest building or sight that you know? Tell the class about it.

2 Fill in the table.

2/1-2

a) Copy the table and put in information from this page.

Where	When	What	Who	Why
Stonehenge	4,000 years ago	circle of stones	?	no one knows
...	...	...	the Romans	...
...	866			

b) What more can you find out to complete the table? Use the internet or books.

In **866** the Viking army under Ivar the Boneless invaded the English city of **York**. They came from Denmark, Norway and other northern countries. Some stayed and York became their home.

In **1066** the Normans came across the sea from France. They fought a battle against the English near **Hastings** and won. The leader of the Normans became the new king of England.

There was lots of industry in **Manchester** during and after the Industrial Revolution (**1780–1840**). Now lots of tourists visit Manchester and there are shops, cafés and parks in the city.

3 (LISTENING) Listen to information about Stonehenge.

1,3 · 2/3

Finish the sentences.

1. The biggest stone weighs … .
2. That's the same as … .
3. Some of the stones came from … .
4. Maybe the circle was a clock and told the time with … .
5. Today Stonehenge is one of England's … .
6. More than a million tourists visited Stonehenge … .

These words will help you to understand the listening text.

I can understand information about historical places in England. ✓

Around York

1 Look at the pictures of York. What do they tell you about the city?

2 (READING) Read the dialogue.

1,4
3/1

Sam: Excuse me. I'm here on holiday. Do you know the way to the tourist information centre?

Mrs Jenkins: I do, but maybe *I* can help you. I come to York almost every day, so I know my way around here. What are you interested in?

Sam: I would like to learn more about the history of the city.

Mrs Jenkins: Well, we are near the Viking Centre. It's a museum and lots of tourists visit it every year. You can see it from here, you just have to cross the road. It's really worth a visit, it shows what the city was like about a thousand years ago. After that you can go to the tourist information centre. The people there are always friendly. Walk past the post office and turn right at the end of the road. Then take the first road on the left.

Sam: I like shopping too but I don't have that much time. Do you know a good clothes shop?

Mrs Jenkins: Yes, I do. The best shops are on the Shambles. I often go there too. Why don't you go to the souvenir shop there? It sometimes sells Viking helmets at a special price.

Sam: Brilliant! I want one of those. How do I get there?

Mrs Jenkins: That's easy. Turn right and walk down the road … it's on the left.

Sam: Is it far away?

Mrs Jenkins: No, not at all. It really doesn't take long. It's just a five-minute walk.

Sam: Oh good. Thank you.

Mrs Jenkins: No problem. You're very welcome

3 Answer the questions.

1. Why is Sam in York?
2. What is he interested in?
3. What is the Viking Centre?
4. Where is the best place to go shopping in York?
5. How long does it take to walk from the Viking Centre to the souvenir shop?

4 (WRITING) Where can you buy these things?

a) Match the things with the right shops. → ○ p. 114

3/2a)

You can buy jeans at the clothes shop.

A 
B 
C 
D 

E 
F 

shoe shop | clothes shop ✓ | card shop | souvenir shop | baker's | sports shop

b) Explain what you can buy at these places. → V Shops, p. 178

3/2b)

jeweller's | newsagent's | greengrocer's | butcher's | pet shop | …

A jeweller's is a shop where you can get jewellery.
At a newsagent's you can buy …

5 (LISTENING) Find the way to the card shop.

1,5
3/3

a) Listen to the dialogue. Find the way on the map. Tell it to a partner.

turn left | turn right | go straight on | walk past …

b) What's the fastest way to the card shop? Tell a partner.

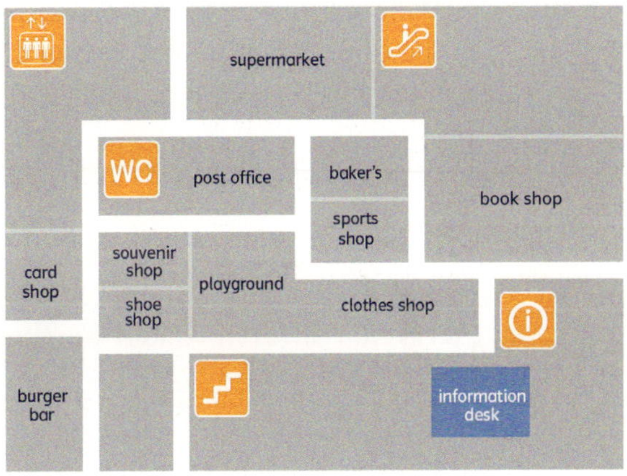

6 (SPEAKING) Plan your own shopping trip.

What do you want to buy and where can you get it? Talk to a partner.

A: I need a new shirt. Can we first go to … ?
B: All right. But after that I would like to …

7 (SOUNDS) How quickly can you say this tongue twister?

1,6

Sharon sells shoes in the shoe shop. The shoes in the shoe shop aren't Sharon's size.

[s] [ʃ]

Language → G1, p. 154

I often go to the Shambles.
I don't have much time.

Is it far away?
Do you know a good clothes shop? – Yes, I do.

Look at the sentences. Which tense is it? How do we form this tense?

8 Make sentences.

4/4-5

a) Complete the sentences with these verbs. → ○ p. 114

know | be (2x) | not arrive | have | take | sell | wait | go ✓ | not like | meet | prefer

1. I sometimes go shopping with my friends at the weekend.
2. We always — in town at 11 a.m.
3. My best friend usually — before 11:30, but we always — for him, because he — all the places to find a bargain.
4. In the afternoon we often — something to drink at a café.
5. My favourite shop — The Busy Bookworm. It — the best books.
6. My friends — it. They — the sports shop.
7. The oldest shops in York — on the Shambles.
8. After that I usually — the bus to get back home.

4/6

b) What do you or your friends usually do on Saturdays? What don't you do?

I don't get up early. I usually get up late. My friend always sleeps until …

5/7

9 (SPEAKING) Interview your partner. → M Double circle, p. 171

a) Ask a partner questions. He or she gives short answers. → ○ p. 114

Do Does	+ you your friends they your dad he	+ usually sometimes often	+ buy … go to … do … play … watch …	+ on Saturdays? on Sundays? …

A: Do you often do the shopping on Saturdays? B: Yes, I do. / No, I don't.

b) Ask more questions. Your partner gives short answers and reasons. Take turns.

buy clothes online ✓ | look for bargains | spend money on … | get comics at a newsagent's | …

A: Do you sometimes buy clothes online? B: No, I don't. They don't usually fit. Do you often …?

10 (WRITING) Make questions and answers.

a) Complete the dialogue. → ○ p. 115

5/8

1. (know) Do you know where the football stadium is? – Yes, I do.
2. How (get) —— I —— there? – You can walk or ... .
3. (take) —— it —— long to get there? – Yes, ——. But ... .
4. Where (be) —— the nearest bus stop? – It's ... .
5. When (leave) —— the buses —— ? – I think ... .
6. (be) —— bus tickets expensive? – No, ...
7. Where (can) —— I buy a ticket? – ... .

b) Make three more questions and answers. Use the words for help.

6/9

toilets | food stalls | ...

11 (YOUR TURN) Directions → V Directions, p. 184

a) You are at X on the map. Work with your partner. Ask for directions to:

6/10

post office | swimming pool | baker's | ...

A: Excuse me, please. Do you know where there is a shoe shop near here?
B: Yes, I do. Go past the church. Then walk down the second street on the left. After that turn left. The shoe shop is opposite the cinema.
A: Is it far away?
B: No, it isn't. It doesn't take long.
A: OK. That's great. Thanks for your help.
B: You're welcome.

turn right | go straight on | cross the road | ...

on the left / right | next to the ... | ...

Can I walk there? | Are there buses? | ...

is just a five minute walk | isn't far | is only five minutes away | ...

b) Draw a simple map of your village/town/city. A is a tourist and B lives in the place. Make a dialogue and act it in a role play.

I can give and understand directions. ✓

Manchester and Bramford

1 (READING) Read about where Hannah and Tom live.

1,7
7/1

Hi! I'm Hannah and I'm from Manchester, in the northwest of England. It's a large city with more than half a million inhabitants. And it's a busy city with lots of traffic, so it's noisy too – that can get on your nerves sometimes! But then again there are always buses, so it's very easy to get around the city and to all the fun places. Just think of all the museums, parks, cinemas, …

In the past Manchester had lots of industry and there were many dirty factories. There were coal mines near Manchester too.

I live in a flat with my mum and my little sister. Our flat is not far from the city centre. It's very small! Mum works in a supermarket in the city. She often has to work in the evening.

The best thing about Manchester? Football! Manchester City are the best team ever!

My name is Tom and I live on a farm in Bramford. That's a small village in the north of England, near Hadrian's Wall. Bramford is about 40 miles from Newcastle. We used to live in Newcastle, but my parents didn't like the city. They wanted to live in the countryside. Did they ask me? No, they didn't!

It's hard work on the farm. Still, I enjoy it because I like our animals. There are two goats, Bert and Daisy, and a lot of cows. I get up at six o'clock most days to help milk them.

It's quiet in the village. Only about 400 people live here. Dad likes the country – I call it boring!

The worst thing about our village? There are only two buses a day. It's difficult to see friends at the weekend! It's so unfair!

2 Take notes about where they live.

a) Make a table and put in the information. → ○ p. 115

Name of place? | Town/city/village? | Where in England? | Good/bad things? | In the past? | Number of inhabitants?

Hannah	Tom
- Manchester	- Bramford
- …	- …

b) What more can you remember? Close your book and write two more sentences about Hannah and two about Tom.

3 Sort the words into groups. → M Peer correction, p. 173

7/2 a) Put the words and phrases into the right list. → ○ p. 115

- sorts of places: village, …
- size of places:
- where?

in the centre of | village ✓ | town | miles away from | big | small | near | in the north/south/east/west of | city | in the mountains | large | on the border with

7/3 b) Complete the sentences with the right words. → V Talking about places, p. 179

1. You need good public transport to get around the city.
2. London is a —— city with more than 10 million inhabitants.
3. The —— from London to Brighton is about 53 miles.
4. There are —— villages in the north of England with only a hundred inhabitants.
5. Liverpool is —— Manchester.
6. Brighton is —— of England.

Check the map at the front of the book.

tiny | distance | to the north/south/east/west of | good public transport ✓ | on the coast | huge

4 (SPEAKING) City or country? → M Think-pair-share, p. 175

7/4 a) Collect adjectives to describe the places.

city	country/village
exciting	…

b) City or country, which do you prefer? Discuss it with a partner.

A: I'd like to live in a big city. Cities are exciting.
B: Yes, but they are … too! I think it's better to live in …, because … .
A: Really? That's … .

5 (SONG) The city

1,8 Listen to the song. What does the singer think about the city?

This city never sleeps
I hear the people walk by when it's late
Sirens bleed through my windowsill
I can't close my eyes
Don't control what I'm into
This tower is alive
The lights that blind keep me awake
With my hood up and lace untied
Sleep fills my mind
Don't control what I'm into
London calls me a stranger
A traveller
This is now my home, my home
I'm burning on the back street
Stuck here sitting in the backseat
I'm blazing on the street
What I do isn't up to you
And if the city never sleeps
Then that makes two

Language → G2, p. 155

My parents wanted to live in the countryside.
They didn't like the city.

There were many dirty factories.
Did they ask you?

Look at the sentences. Which tense is it? How do we form this tense and when do we use it?

8/5-6
6 (WRITING) Make Tom's story.

a) Complete the sentences. → ○ p. 116

1. Last Saturday morning things got (get) a little crazy on our farm.
2. I ___ (hear) a noise in the garden and I ___ (get up).
3. I ___ (see) my dad in the garden. He ___ (want) to catch Bert and Daisy, our goats.
4. Suddenly he ___ (fall) in the mud, head first. It ___ (be) so funny.
5. I just ___ (have) to laugh, but my dad ___ (not be) very happy.

b) Work with a partner. Make up a short story like in a). Answer the questions *who? when? where? what? why?* in your text. Present it in class.

7 What did they do on Saturday?

a) Look at the pictures. Correct the sentences. → ○ p. 116

9/7a)

1. Hannah walked to the baker's in the morning.

2. Hannah sat in the living room at two o'clock.

3. Hannah did her homework in the afternoon.

4. She and her sister made jewellery at five o'clock.

5. Later she wrote a text message.

6. Hannah and her sister were at the cinema in the evening.

1. Hannah didn't walk to the baker's in the morning. She watched TV.

b) Look at the pictures again. What did Hannah's dog, Kilkenny, do?

9/7b)

Kilkenny didn't watch TV. He played with a ball.

8 (SPEAKING) Talk with a partner about the weekend. → M Milling around, p. 172

9/8-9
10/10

a) Make questions about last weekend.

1. nice weekend • ? – Did you have a nice weekend?
2. how • weather • ?
3. all weekend • stay at home • ?
4. do anything nice • with your family • ?
5. what • together • do • ?
6. what time • back home • ?
7. on Sunday evening • your parents • tired • ?

b) Talk with a partner about last weekend.

9 (YOUR TURN) A short talk → V Where I live, p. 185

10/11
11/1-2

Give a short talk about where you live.

name of place: Hamburg / …
size: small village/large town/city …
where: in the northeast of … /in the southwest of …/ in the centre of … / …
how far away: near/100 kilometres from/…
number of inhabitants: 5,000/50,000/a million / …
history: there was …/there were … / we didn't have …/people worked in … / …
favourite place: cinema/…
what I can do there: play football / …

CULTURE

English people usually talk about miles and not kilometres when they say how far it is from one place to another. One mile is 1.6 kilometres. How far is it from your home to your school in miles?

I can talk in more detail about where I live.

A deadly silence

1 What do you know about Manchester – now and in the past? → M Think-pair-share, p. 175

2 (READING) Read the story.

1,9

The Rushy Park Coal Mine, near Manchester. September 1850

1.

My name is Jonas Fox and I'm twelve years old. I work in the mines and my job is to sit near a door in the tunnel every day. I must open the door when the coal arrives. Then, after it's gone, I quickly close the door again. Every day I sit in the dark, but I'm never scared. That's because my friend Billy is always there with me. Billy sings all day long. He's yellow with little black eyes which look like they are made of glass. Billy is a canary, you see? It's never boring with Billy around. I would love to sing too, but I can't even talk.

2.

Sometimes there is gas in the mine. And when gas touches a flame, it explodes. Last year a terrible gas explosion in a mine killed 30 miners and ten boys. A canary notices gas much sooner than a man. So when the canaries sing, the tunnels are OK. But if they go quiet, you know that there's gas in the mine. Their deadly silence tells you that you must hurry. You only have a few minutes to leave the tunnels.

READING SKILLS

This is a longer text, but each section is quite short. Read each section quickly and try to understand the main idea (the gist) of this part of the story. Then look at the section again more carefully and ask **Wh**-questions: **Who** is in this part of the story? **Where** are they, **what** happens and **when**?

3.

My brother, Bart, worked in the mine too. We always ate bread and laughed together on the way to the mine. One day Bart started to cough and he never stopped coughing after that. Then one night my brother coughed so badly that he died. That was when I stopped talking. I don't know why, really. I still had words in my head and I opened my mouth, but I couldn't speak. The men in the mine started to call me 'Silent Jonas' after that. They probably thought I was a bit strange.

4.

The day when things got really bad started like any other. Billy was singing like he always did. I heard the people in the tunnels and the noise of the coal trucks. I opened the door and I felt a cold wind in the tunnel. I closed the door again. Billy stopped singing. For a moment I didn't understand. But then, suddenly, I did: There was gas in the mine! And it could explode any second. I didn't have time to run down the tunnel to warn the men. If only I could talk, if only I could shout!

5.

I knew I had to warn everyone in the mine. So I opened my mouth and tried to say it: "Gas." But there was no sound. Nothing came out. I closed my eyes and opened my mouth again. Nothing. I panicked. We could die in here – I had to speak! I tried again. This time the sound was quiet, but I made a sound. At last! I opened the door and shouted, "Gas. Gas. GAS!" A moment later I heard the sound of the miners' boots in the tunnels. I took Billy's cage and ran too.

6.

I ran through the tunnel as fast as I could. But my head hurt and I couldn't breathe in the gas. Suddenly I heard a voice. I couldn't tell where it was coming from. "Come on, boy!" it said. Somebody picked me up. I turned around and saw that it was one of the miners. He took me out of the mine. All this time I still had Billy's cage with me, but I was sure he was dead. I couldn't just leave him in there, could I? He was my friend, you know. At last we were outside and I could breathe again.

7.

BOOM! The sound of the explosion was awful. My ears hurt. I closed my eyes because they were sore too. Then I opened them again and looked around. I saw that the men and boys from the mine were all safe outside. Somebody asked, "Who warned us?" "Me!" I said. They were so surprised; they all looked at me with their mouths open. When they could speak again, everyone said thank you. "Silent Jonas found his voice!" a miner shouted. But how could I feel happy? My friend Billy had died. I looked in his cage to say goodbye to him. Suddenly I heard a small 'Tweet'. Billy was alive! I opened the cage …

There were canaries in mines until 1987. Today miners use machines to find out if there is gas in the mine.

3 Talk about the story.

Did you like the story? Say why or why not. What surprised you?

4 Make up a heading for each section of the story.

1. Meet Jonas Fox – and Billy!
2. …

5 Talk about the ending of the story with a partner.

What do you think happened to Billy?
What happened to Jonas?

6 (WRITING) Collect facts about Jonas.

a) Look at the story again and make notes about Jonas.

how old? · job? · family? · problems?

READING SKILLS

You have already read the story so you don't need to read every word this time. Look at each section quickly, but read more carefully when you find information about Jonas and write the information in a short note (3 – 4 words).

b) Compare your notes with a partner. Do you have the same facts?

c) Use your notes to write a text about Jonas.

Jonas is twelve years old and …

7 Choose one of these tasks.

12/1
13/2-4

a) Write a poem or a chant about working in a coal mine. This is the first verse:

I'm working in a coal mine, I'm always tired,
I have to work hard, don't want to get fired!

Make up more verses like this. Here are some ideas:

- only eat bread/soon be dead
- gas smell/don't feel well
- coal mine - dirty/get old? - be thirty
- Billy - my friend/the end
- …

OR

b) Write Billy's story. Start like this:

My name is Billy. I'm a canary and I work in a mine near Manchester. Jonas is my friend … .

- play with Jonas
- nice boy - never speak
- sing every day
- then one day …
- …

WRITING SKILLS

Mistakes checklist:
- more than one? Check the s!
  miners, problems, …
- short form? Check the apostrophe!
  I'm, he's, don't
- end of a sentence? Check the full stop.
- small words can have mistakes too! (*and* not *und*!)

I can understand a story from the past.

The history of football

INTERNET

Football now and then

Some people think the English invented football, but they didn't. More than 2,500 years ago the Chinese played a game with many similarities to football. Its name was cuju. The English did do one thing though: they wrote down the first rules for the game.

Football was a popular sport in 19th-century England. When players from different schools played, there was one big problem: they all had different rules! For example, the players from Rugby School carried the ball; others used only their feet. Players often disagreed about who won the game.

To make the game fair for everyone, they wrote down the rules. They were called the Cambridge Rules. The Football Association (FA) used these to make their own rules in 1863. This is when Association Football (called football in England and soccer in the USA) and rugby became two different sports.

Nowadays, it isn't just boys who play football in England. Many of the big English football clubs such as Arsenal, Liverpool and Chelsea have their own female teams and the Women's National Team is one of the best in the world.

1 Beantworte die Fragen.

14/1-2

1. In welchem Land spielte man eine frühe Form von Fußball?
2. Warum wurde es nötig, die Fußballregeln niederzuschreiben?
3. Wie nennt man den Sport Fußball in Amerika?
4. Was erfährt man aus dem Text über Frauenfußball in England?

2 Write about a sport from where you live.

What would you tell an English person about a sport from where you live? Write a short text.

sports? | clubs? | how old? | teams for men and women? | ...

I can pass on information about the history of a sport.

Girl from the past

1 How did children live in Germany or England about 150 years ago?

→ M Think-pair-share, p.175

Think about these things.

children: school, work, home

CULTURE

Queen Victoria was the British queen from 1837 until 1901. We call this the 'Victorian era', and lots of buildings in London are from this time. (One of the most important train stations in London is Victoria Station.)
Which queens do you know?

Now watch the film. Was there anything new to you?

2 (VIEWING) Watch the film.

2

a) Which summary is correct?

1. Laura reads about the Victorian era in a book. Then she and Marley travel back in time.
2. Marley falls asleep in the library. He dreams that he meets a girl from the past.
3. Violet meets Laura in the library. Laura tells her about life in the 21st century.

b) Who says it?

1. I'd rather work than go to school.
2. I wish I could go to school!
3. You see, we've just travelled through time.
4. You've been asleep almost an hour.

Laura

Marley

Violet

3 (SPEAKING) Talk about the film.

a) Watch the film again from 1:30 to 3:25

How does Marley feel?
First he is … .
Later he is … .
At the end he is … .

surprised | confused | happy | …

VIEWING SKILLS

The words in a film are important, but you should also look at the faces and the body language of the people. They can tell you what is happening and give you information about the mood.

b) Would you like to travel back in time? Where would you like to go? Who would you like to meet?

I can understand a film about Greenwich now and in the past. ✓

Checklist

I can understand information about historical places in England. ✓

15

I can give and understand directions. ✓

Excuse me. • Is there a baker's near here? • Go past the church. • Then walk down the second street on the left. • It's opposite the cinema. • Thanks for your help. • You're welcome.

15

I can talk in more detail about where I live. ✓

I live in .... • It is a town/city/village. • It is in the north/south/... of Germany. • It has about ... inhabitants. • In the past there was ....

16

I can understand a story from the past. ✓

16

I can pass on information about the history of a sport. ✓

17

I can understand a film about Greenwich now and in the past. ✓

(TASK) A film project

Work in groups of four to six students. Each group makes a short film about a sight in your home town or village.

Step 1

Collect ideas. → M Placemat, p. 173

First collect ideas and make a mind map of the sights you can film.

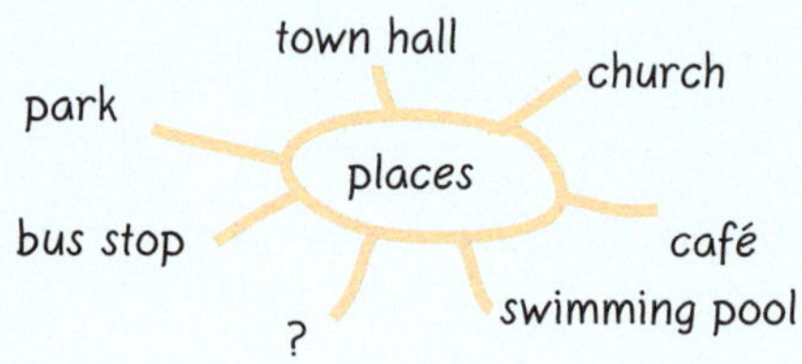

Talk about the ideas. Choose a sight.
You can choose an old or a new sight or building.

Step 2

Find people for the different film jobs.

Who can:
- write 2–3 sentences about the sight?
- say the sentences (presenter)?
- film the presenter and the sight?
- be the director?

STUDY SKILLS

Give each person the chance to say which job he or she wants or doesn't want to do. Try to agree on the ideas in your group.

Step 3

Write the script and get ready.

a) Write two or three sentences about your sight.

b) Check the sentences and correct them if you need to.

c) The presenter must read the sentences in a clear voice. Practise this.
→ M Read and look up, p. 174

Step 4

Make your film.

Use a phone or a camera. Go to the sight and film the presenter there.
Wait until everyone is ready before you start, then say “Action!”
Make two or three versions (‘takes’) of the film. Keep cool if the presenter makes a mistake.

Step 5

Present your film.

Watch all the films together. Then make new groups. The new group has one student from each film group.

Ask for feedback. Make a checklist like this.

Go back to the film group and look at the checklists. What would you do differently in your next film?
→ M Tip top, p. 175

Feedback checklist
The film is

O exciting
O informative
O fun
O easy to understand
O interesting
O not very interesting.

I like
O the presenter
O the …

What's the story?

This is the **Uffington White Horse**. It's a big picture of a horse on a hill not far from Oxford. The horse is cut into the grass and filled with broken white chalk. It's over 100 metres long. That's why you can only see it well from above.

The Uffington White Horse is one of the oldest pictures in the world. People made it about 3,000 years ago. But why did they make it and why did they choose a horse? What is the story behind the Uffington White Horse?

Have a guess!

Here are three different stories.
What do you think: Which story is true?

A) Even in the past, people were very creative. They drew a horse that looked like our modern unicorn. But thousands of years ago, these people didn't have enough paper for drawing. That's why they used hills for their pictures too.

B) About 3,000 years ago, people in Britain believed in many gods. One of these gods rode on a horse and could do magic. So the people near Oxford decided to make the horse as a symbol of this god.

C) When people travelled around thousands of years ago, they didn't have satnav, maps or street names. That's why they painted pictures on trees or hills. This way the people always knew where they were and where they had to go next.

Your guess.

Your idea is as good as the others:
Make up your own story about why the horse is there and tell it to your partner.

SOLUTION

Well, even experts do not really know why the people of the past made the Uffington White Horse. Most experts think that it is a symbol of their god and their tribe (solution B).

Design your own symbol.

a) Horses were very important for people in the past. What is important for you today? Which symbol will people find from you in the future? Draw this symbol on a piece of paper.

b) Now print your symbol on a T-shirt.

You need:

a white T-shirt

a large potato

a kitchen knife

fabric paint

a brush

1. Carefully cut out your symbol from a). Put the rest of the piece of paper on a T-shirt. (You can put an old newspaper inside your T-shirt to keep it clean while you print it.)

2. Wash your potato and cut it in half. Cut a pattern into the potato. This is your stamp.

3. Dip the side of your potato with the pattern in your paint. Then press it onto your T-shirt for a few seconds. Carefully take the potato off the T-shirt. Repeat until the cut-out part (on your T-shirt) is full of colour.

4. Carefully take the piece of paper off the T-shirt. Let your T-shirt dry. Make sure your symbol stays on your T-shirt: Read the instructions on the paint pot.

You can find out about different types of reading here.

1,10 A bike tour of London

A

Come on a bike tour to discover London with us!

Duration: 3 hours
Costs: £20 (adults) and £15 (children)
Times: every Friday and Saturday

Meeting time: 10 a.m.
Meeting point: South Kensington station

We will meet at South Kensington station and rent a bike. First stop – the Science Museum!

The Science Museum has six floors of more than 300,000 science things to see. It is a great place to find out about technology from all over the world. You can see the world's oldest train, some space rockets and learn about the history of flying. You can even do some experiments yourself! There is also a 3D cinema where you can watch science films.

B

Next, we will ride through Hyde Park to the Portobello Road Market. This is a great place to find a souvenir, lots of antiques and old and new clothes. The market is always busy with tourists and people from London looking for bargains. There are also food stalls selling lots of different types of food, from fruit and vegetables to curries and burgers.

C

Our next stop is the world famous Madame Tussauds. This wax museum is where you can meet and take a photo with stars from films, music or sport, and even members of the Royal Family. If you are brave, you could also visit the scary 'Chamber of Horrors'.

D

Finally, we will ride over Oxford Street and into Green Park. This is where Buckingham Palace is. It is one of the homes of the Queen of England. The first king or queen to live there was Queen Victoria in 1837. If the Queen is at home there is a royal flag flying on the palace. You can go inside the palace to visit some rooms, but only a few days every year.

1 Skim the text.

a) What type of text is it? Why?

An e-mail? A brochure?
A story? A song?
It's a … because there is / there are …
It has …. / It doesn't have ….

To say what type of text it is that you are reading you have to look at the structure of the text. Each type of text has its own features. When you know them, you also know where to find certain information.

b) What is the text about?

1. Look at the photo and the highlighted words in part A. What do you think this text is about?
2. Skim part B of the text. Write down the main words. Compare with a partner.

While skimming a text, concentrate on the heading first. It tells you what the text will be about.
Photos pick up the main topic too. So look at them closely.
Then search for keywords in the main text or in other places like lists.
The keywords in part A have already been marked for you.

21/1-3
2 Scan the text.

a) Answer the questions about part C.

1. What type of museum is Madame Tussauds?
2. What can you do at this museum?
3. What's a special part of this museum?

When you scan a text, you look for specific single pieces of information. Look at the questions closely and scan the text. So, if a question asks "How many…?", you need to look for a number. For a question with "Who…?", look for a name.
The main ideas have already been marked for you in part C.

b) Answer the questions about part D.

1. Where is Buckingham Palace?
2. Who was the first king or queen to live there?
3. What happens when the Queen is inside Buckingham Palace?

Find more online:
i8ce82

In this unit you will …
- find out about free-time activities in Wales.
- present information about a sport.
- make an emergency call.
- read a report from a school website.
- pass on information about a free-time activity.
- watch a film about an adventure in Wales.

3 1,11

Unit 2
Adventures in Wales

Learn a language. Are you going to Wales? Learn Welsh! Lots of people speak this very old language. We will read menus and road signs in our course, and you will learn how to get to know people and have a short conversation in Welsh.

Ride down a mountain. Mount Snowdon is the high mountain in Wales (1,085 metres). The longest zip lin in Europe is near here. It's a mile long and you travel at over 60 miles an hour! You can do skiing here too.

1 Look at the pictures.

a) Which activities do you do? Which activities would you/wouldn't you like to do?

I'd like to …
I wouldn't like to …

b) Which activities do you do in your free time?

I often/sometimes/… , because … .

2 Right or wrong?

22/1

1. There is only a small number of rivers in Wales.
   That's **wrong**.
2. Water sports aren't very popular in Wales.
3. Cardiff is the Welsh capital.
4. Cardiff Castle is more than 3,000 years old.
5. In Wales they have road signs in Welsh.
6. The people on lifeboats do the job in their free time.
7. Mount Snowdon is over 1,000 metres high.
8. The zip line there is the longest in Wales.

3

Visit Cardiff Castle. The capital city of Wales is Cardiff. Why not visit Cardiff Castle? It's located in the middle of a beautiful park in the city centre. The castle is almost 2,000 years old! People often make films here too.

4

Try a water sport. Wales has a very long coast and many rivers, so you can try many different water sports. Canoeing, rafting and surfing are very popular activities.

5

Be a volunteer. Lifeboats are very important in Wales. Every year, the lifeboats help thousands of people in trouble at sea. The people on lifeboats are usually volunteers.

3 (LISTENING) What's the word?

1,12
22/2

a) Complete the sentences.

1. Teenagers in Wales must learn Welsh until they are … .
2. People in Wales also speak … .
3. More people speak Welsh in the north and … .
4. There are Welsh computer games and Welsh … .
5. The Welsh word 'plant' means … .

b) Listen to the end again and write down the Welsh word for "Goodbye!" → M Peer correction, p. 173

guest [gest] – Gast
fluent ['flu:ənt] - fließend
all the time [ɔ:l ðə 'taɪm] – die ganze Zeit
plant [plɑ:nt] – Pflanze
to mean [mi:n] – bedeuten

I can understand information about free-time activities in Wales.

Outdoor activities

1 (READING) Read the information.

1,13

INTERNET

BLACK MOUNTAIN ACTIVITY CENTRE, POWYS, WALES

SUMMER ACTIVITIES

Take a relaxing canoeing trip down the River Wye. We go slowly and the trip takes six hours. You can borrow special clothes and a picnic lunch is included.

If you like fast and tough sports, you should try rugby! It's a popular sport in Wales. We play in teams of girls and boys. You can learn the rules quickly.

The Welsh country is great for horse riding. You'll ride on quiet roads and in the woods. Our instructors are friendly, and the horses are too!

We do outdoor rock climbing and we also have an indoor wall – very useful in wet Wales! You can borrow helmets and other equipment to keep you safe.

2 Name the activities.

23/1

a) Which activity is it?

1

2

3 

4 

b) Make up questions like this and do a quiz with a partner:

A: Which activity can you do on a wall? B: Is it climbing? A: Yes, that's right.

3 (READING) Read the dialogue.

1,14
23/2

Beth: I tried rugby at this activity centre last week and it was really good fun. Why don't you come with me next time?

Mark: Rugby? That's cool. But isn't it a tough sport? Are you big and strong enough to play it?

Beth: Don't be so cheeky! I may be small, but I'm fit, you know that. I can run fast and I'm strong. I really enjoyed myself!

Mark: See that? Rock climbing is fun too. I can climb quite well already. It isn't dangerous if you are careful – and you wear a helmet!

Beth: No, thanks, that's not for me. I'm scared of heights. But I'd like to try horse riding. Horses are cute. Just look at their big eyes!

Mark: Horse riding? I did that last year and I hurt myself! That horse was dangerous! No way am I doing that again.

Beth: You're joking, right? Don't tell me you are afraid of horses. Well anyway, you can go rock climbing and I'll try horse riding. We'll tell each other about it later! I hope that won't scare you too much.

Language tip → G 3, p. 156

I hurt **myself**.

4 What is it?

a) Which sport is it?

1. Mark thinks it's a tough sport.
2. Beth is scared of heights so she won't try this.
3. Mark hurt himself when he did this.

b) Which sports do Mark and Beth finally choose?

5 Find the right words. → M Bus stop, p. 170

The dictionary on pages 221-286 can help you!

23/3 a) What are the opposites? → ○ p. 117

1. small
2. slow
3. difficult
4. unfriendly
5. weak
6. dangerous
7. dry
8. unpopular
9. loud
10. boring

24/4 b) Finish the sentences. → V Adjectives for sportspeople, p. 187

1. She can wait. She's really —.
2. He always wants to win. He's very —.
3. He's very tired. He's —.
4. She has won lots of prizes. She's very —.
5. He's going to be a star. He's young and —.

competitive | patient | talented | successful | exhausted

6 (WRITING) Copy the text. Add adjectives. → M Peer correction, p. 173

Rafting is a(n) — sport for people from 12 to 99. You will have — fun at our activity centre. Spend a(n) — day on the — river and meet — people. Rafting is — to learn but it's still a water sport, so you probably won't stay —. But don't worry, our — instructors will make sure that nothing bad can happen: Rafting at our activity centre is very —. You'll love our — trips!

WRITING SKILLS

Adjectives make a text more interesting. When you write a draft of a text, think: Where can you add adjectives to describe the things or people in your text?

You can use adjectives from pages 34 and 35.

7 (SOUNDS) Listen, read and say.

1,15 Make a chart. Put the words into groups.

popular ✓ | canoeing | adventure | difficult | equipment | interesting | instructor | horse riding

Ooo	oOo
popular	...

Language detectives → G4, p. 157

Rugby is a popular sport.
You can learn the rules quickly.
We go slowly down the river.

When do you need the -ly?

8 How did they do it?

a) Complete the sentences. → ○ p. 117

24/5-6a)

1. I climbed the wall slowly. (slow)
2. We arrived at the stadium ––– . (safe)
3. The instructor called to us ––– . (loud)
4. The rugby team played ––– . (brilliant)
5. The tennis player won his match ––– . (easy)
6. We rode our bikes ––– . (careful)

Be careful with words like 'careful' and 'easy'!
carefully
easily

b) Make sentences.

24/6b)

open / quiet

shout / angry

smile / happy

watch / nervous

25/7-9

9 Complete the report.

a) Choose: adjective or adverb? → ○ p. 117

Last month Class 9G went on an **exciting** • **excitingly** camping trip to Wales. We climbed Mount Snowdon on Saturday. It started to rain **heavy** • **heavily** so we had to find a dry place **quick** • **quickly**. At lunchtime we ate our picnics **hungry** • **hungrily**. Then the sun came out and the weather was **nice** • **nicely** again. On Sunday we went canoeing at Llanberis. We went down the river **slow** • **slowly**. Everything went **good** • **well** and no one fell in the water. Phew! You could see that our teacher, Mrs Kent, was **happy** • **happily** about that too.

GRAMMAR → G4, p. 157

a good song – they sing well
a fast game – she runs fast
a hard day – he works hard

b) What does a rugby coach tell his team before a match? Write sentences with adjectives or adverbs.

play/throw/be/kick/think/run/…
quick/good/clever/careful/fast/hard/…

You have to throw the ball quickly! …

10 (WRITING) Adjective or adverb?

a) Complete the dialogue. → ○ p. 118

6/10a)

Mark: Beth, how was horse riding today?
Beth: It was — (awful). It was — (wet) and it rained — (heavy).
Mark: So, I guess you had to ride — (careful)?
Beth: Yes, and there were some — (crazy) people on bikes too. Most of them rode really — (fast) and — (dangerous).
Mark: Was your horse — (nervous) because of them?
Beth: No, it wasn't. You know, Holly is a really — (cool) horse. Look, here's a photo. — (nice), isn't it?

b) Take notes about a sports star. Use adjectives and adverbs. Then talk to a partner. Can he or she guess who it is?

6/10b)

small English
play football well
run fast ...

11 (YOUR TURN) A poster about your favourite activity or sport → V Sports and activities, p. 193

→ M Gallery walk, p. 172

26/11

a) Make a poster about your favourite sport or activity: Make notes. Find more information. Add pictures.

- What's the sport like?
- What do you do?
- What must you be like?
- What equipment do you need?

b) Talk about your poster.

Skiing is an exciting and popular sport.
It's quite easy. You can ski fast on beautiful mountains, but you must be fit and you must be careful. You can usually borrow equipment and special clothes.

STUDY SKILLS

Write your notes on cards. Practise what you want to say before you show your poster.
Speak slowly and clearly when you present it.
Check that the listeners have understood and ask: "Do you have any questions?" at the end.

I can present information about a sport. ✓

Emergency on the beach

1 What do you do if you need help? Which number do you call?

2 (READING) Read the dialogue.

1,16

Operator: Hello, Emergency Services, which service?
Dylan: Hello, it's an emergency. I need an ambulance now! Please hurry! We need help!
Operator: OK, please wait a moment.
Janet: Hi, this is Janet from North Wales Ambulance Service. What's the problem?
Dylan: There's a man on the beach. His head is bleeding and his leg is too.
Janet: Tell me slowly what has happened.
Dylan: He has just had an accident. Maybe he fell over on the rocks, I'm not sure. I think he has broken his leg. It looks awful! He's hurt his head too. It is bleeding badly, he probably has a serious injury.
Janet: OK, where are you?
Dylan: I'm on the north beach in Llandudno, near the Glenbow Hotel.
Janet: Good, the ambulance is coming. I've already told them where you are. Is the man awake right now?
Dylan: Yes, he has just opened his eyes.
Janet: Can you give me your name and your phone number, please?
Dylan: Right, I haven't told you yet. It's Dylan Adams. 07810 460 228.
Janet: Listen, Dylan. Stay with the man. The ambulance should arrive very soon. You've done the right thing.
Dylan: All right, I'll wait here. Thanks. Bye.

3 Correct the wrong sentences.

1. Dylan needs the police.
   That's **wrong**. He needs an ambulance.
2. The man has hurt his head.
3. He has a problem with his leg too.
4. Dylan is on the south beach.
5. Dylan's family name is Thomas.
6. Dylan should go back to the hotel.

4 (LISTENING) Look at the list and listen.

1,17

Which of these things does the caller *not* say?

A good emergency call
1. Say which service you need. ☑
2. Say what has happened. ☐
3. Say where you are. ☐
4. Give your name and phone number. ☐

CULTURE

The number for all emergency calls (police, fire brigade, ambulance or coastguard) is 999 in the UK but you can also call 112. Which number do you call in Germany?

5 (WRITING) Match the sentences. Look at the pictures for help.

27/1-2

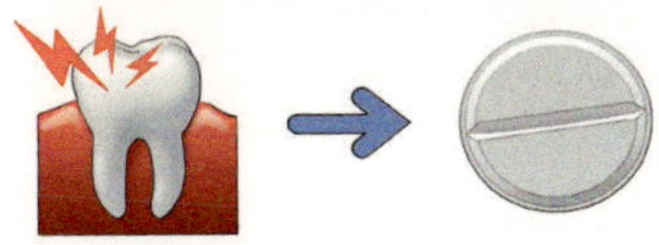
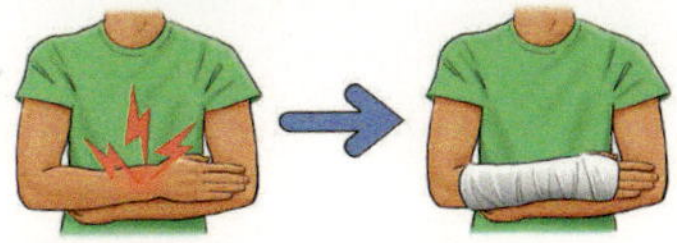

1. I've cut my finger. ✓
2. My tooth hurts.
3. You've broken your arm.

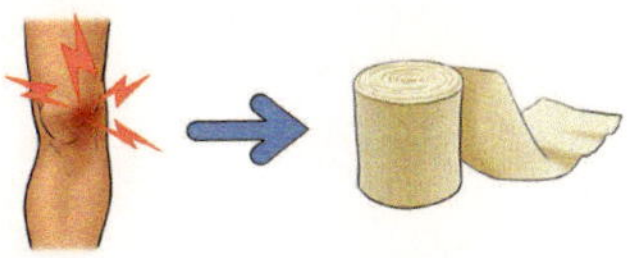
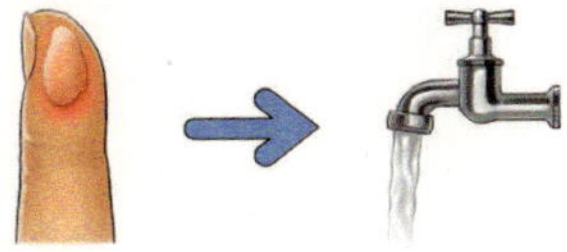
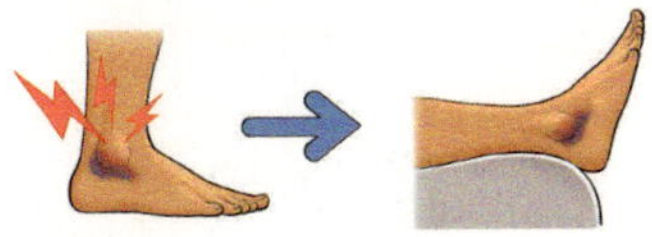

4. I've twisted my knee.
5. She's burnt her finger.
6. He's sprained his ankle.

A You need a cast.
B I'll put a bandage on it.
C Cool it with water.
D Take this tablet.
E Don't move it.
F Here's a plaster. ✓

6 (SPEAKING) Make excuses.

27/4

a) Why can't you do PE? Tell your teacher. → ○ p. 118

27/3a)

I'm so sorry but I really, really can't do PE today. My head hurts terribly. And I have a sore throat too. You know, I've also twisted my knee …

I've cut … | I've burnt … | I've … | My … hurts/hurt | My … is/are bleeding

SPEAKING SKILLS

When you speak, you can use your voice, your face and your hands. They can help you to say what you want to say.

b) What do you need? Make sentences. → V Health and medicine, p. 189

27/3b)

Ooooh, I'm so ill. I think I need … / Please bring me … / I can't live without … / Let me have …

an injection | an operation | some sleep | some medicine | a day off | a cuddly toy

Language → G5, p. 158

He has had an accident.
He has broken his leg.

You've done the right thing.
What has happened?

Which tense is it?
How do you form this tense?
How and when do you use it?

28/5-6

7 What has happened? Make sentences.

1. burn • hand

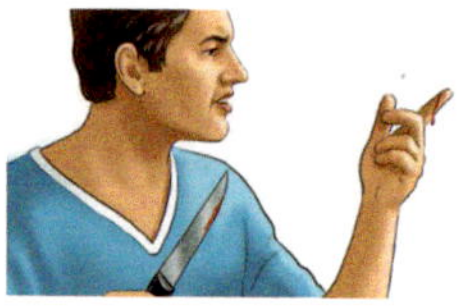

2. cut • finger

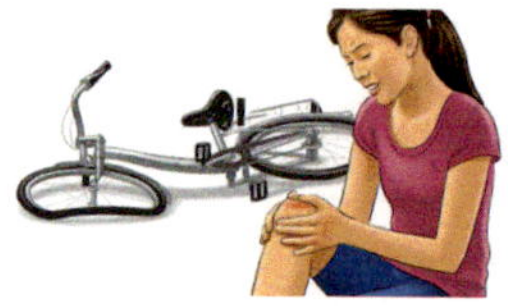

3. fall off • bike

4. twist • ankle

5. break • leg

6. hit • head

7. have • accident

8. hurt • foot

1. He has burnt his hand.

29/8

8 (SPEAKING) What has Megan already done? What hasn't she done yet?

29/7a)

a) Find the differences. Talk with a partner. Make questions and answers. → ○ p. 118

put on her uniform | write a message | have lunch
open the door | collect bandages | drink tea

A: Has Megan already put on her uniform in picture 1?
B: Yes, she has. And in picture 2?

29/7b)

b) Look at the pictures again. Make more questions and answers.
Use already and not yet and the words from the box.

A: Has she already put her boots on in picture 1?
B: No, she hasn't yet.

put on boots • close the window • put on the helmet • get a torch

9 (SPEAKING) Make dialogues.

a) Make sentences. Then act the dialogue with a partner. → ○ p. 119

0/9-10

Kim: Hey, I/not see/your brother/at football training last Monday. What's wrong with him?
Jamie: He/be/in hospital/last week.
Kim: Oh, I'm sorry to hear that. He/already/hurt/his leg many times, right?
Jamie: Yes, he/… . Last time, he and his friend/want/ to try/some new cool skateboard tricks.
Kim: When/he/come/home?
Jamie: My parents/just/bring/him/back from the hospital.
Kim: That's great. His friend/already/hear/the good news?
Jamie: No, he/not … . I/not phone/him/yet.

You need to choose between the simple past and the present perfect. The signal words can help you.

b) Make notes to answer the questions. Then talk with a partner.

30/11

A: Have you ever been in hospital?
Have you ever had an operation?
Have you ever had a cast?
When did it happen?
What happened? Where did it happen?
What was the problem?
…

B: Yes, I have. / No, I haven't.
It happened in … on … .
…

10 (YOUR TURN) A role play: Emergency! → V Emergency, p. 194

31/1-2

1. Work with a partner. Write a list like this. Add your own ideas.
2. Exchange your list with another pair.
3. Practise the emergency call. Use page 38 for help.
4. Act the role play.
5. Give feedback to the other pairs. → M Tip top, p. 175

Who? Lena
Where? In the swimming pool
How? Fell over on the wet floor
What's the problem? Arm, cut, bleeding
What do we need? Ambulance

I can make an emergency call. ✓

A trip to Caldicot Castle

1 Have you ever been to a castle? What castles do you already know?

2 (READING) Read the report.

1,18

INTERNET

YEAR 9'S CRAZY CASTLE TRIP

Story by school reporter Richard 'the Lionheart' Smith.

Castle of history

On a sunny Tuesday morning Year 9 visited Caldicot Castle in Wales. It was a one-hour trip to get there. When we arrived we saw that Caldicot Castle is a big building. It is a stone castle and it was built in the year 1100 AD. It's over 900 years old! Can you believe that? I couldn't, so I said, "Wow, this castle is even older than Mr Yeates, our History teacher!" Everyone laughed, except Mr Yeates ☹.

Castle of adventure

We jumped when the gate opened loudly. A knight appeared in a cloud of smoke! He said, "My name is Lancelot – I am a knight of the castle. I have travelled in time to the future to tell you kids about the castle." So we had a knight as a guide for the day - how cool is that? (But I must say, Lancelot really wasn't a very convincing knight from the past – I saw him with a mobile phone later!)
The castle was very exciting. It had dark corridors and tall towers and it was a real adventure to walk around in it.

3 Find the information.

1. Who went on the trip?
2. Where did they go?
3. When did they go?
4. Who was their guide?
5. What did they like best?
6. What did they do in the end?

READING SKILLS

Before you start, look at the two pages and think: What sort of text is it? What sort of person wrote the text? Who did he/she/they write it for? Can the photos and the titles help you to understand the text?

'Joust' a bit of fun …

The best part of the day was when we learned how to joust. Lancelot showed us how to put on armour and how to hold a sword (not a real one but still very heavy!). It made you feel like a real knight.
The jousting was super cool and we all tried it. Even Ellie could do it in her wheelchair. In the old days there used to be a 'knight school' at the castle, and the knights learned how to joust there. Why isn't our school a bit more like that? Well, one thing is the same: they had cheeky students too. When they were naughty, the knights had to go to the stocks. After that Lancelot did some real jousting. That was cool!

Lancelot goes back to the past

Our time at the castle was coming to an end. At four o'clock Lancelot said it was time for him to go back to the past. He said goodbye and then he left. (I hope he remembered to take his phone!)
But before we left, Mr Yeates wanted to see the stocks where they put the naughty knights. Why did he want to see them? Did he want something like that at our school? We soon found out …

That is me in the stocks. No, of course Mr Yeates didn't put me in the stocks - even if I was a bit cheeky. Phew! But he said we could try them out for fun and we took this photo as a souvenir. Anyway, I got out again quickly, just to be sure … ☺
We all loved the trip and learned lots about Caldicot Castle!

4 Choose one of these tasks.

P
32/1
3/2-4

a) Make a sound diary for the castle trip. Collect, make and record the sounds.

Play the recording to your class – can they guess the sounds?

OR

b) Draw a plan of a castle that you know. Label it in English and add some information (how old?, who lived there?, … ?)

I can understand a report from a school website. ✓

The ride of your life

Dos and Don'ts at Zip World

Zip World in Snowdonia has the fastest zip line in the world and the longest in Europe. And YOU can ride it! Get ready for the ride of your life!

DO wear the equipment we give you. It keeps you safe. The helmet and goggles protect your head and eyes, and the red suit protects your skin, but also makes you travel more quickly!

DO listen to what your instructor says. You will get important information.

DO wear warm clothes and bring some gloves. Even if the weather is sunny, you will feel very cold on the zip line.

DO check the website before you come. If the weather is bad (for example if it is raining heavily or is very windy), the zip line may not be safe and we may close it. You will get your money back.

DO book a place. If you don't, you may have to wait a long time.

DON'T wear sandals or flip flops. If you lose a shoe, we will not find it for you!

DON'T be afraid if you change your mind. We want you to have fun, so if you change your mind and don't want to ride, just let us know.

1 Beantworte die Fragen.

34/1-2

Du bist mit deiner Familie in den Ferien in Wales und willst „Zip World" besuchen.
Du zeigst deinen Eltern diesen Flyer, um sie zu überzeugen, und sie stellen dir diese Fragen.

1. Welche Sicherheitsausrüstung gibt es?
2. Welche Kleidung solltest du tragen?
3. Was passiert bei schlechtem Wetter?
4. Was passiert, wenn du doch nicht mehr damit fahren willst?

2 Would you like to try an activity like this?

Would you like to try it? Say why or why not.
Have you ever done an activity like this (hot air balloon? roller coaster?) Talk about it.

I can pass on information about a free-time activity.

The briefcase

1 Look at the photo and guess.

Why are Laura and Alicia at the beach?
What time of the year is it?
Why is there a briefcase?
What's in it?

Now watch the film and check. Were you right?

2 (VIEWING) Watch the film. Right or wrong?

4

1. After the girls and Mr Becket had lunch, the girls go shopping.
2. A man answers his phone and then leaves his briefcase on the beach.
3. The girls cannot open the briefcase.
4. The man from the beach runs after the girls.
5. The girls find out that the briefcase is only a prop for a film.

CULTURE

You can find a lot of different types of beaches in Wales – if you are a surfer, you will find perfect conditions in the west. But there are also beaches where you can watch seals and even dolphins! Would you like to go to Wales and see the beaches?

3 (SPEAKING) Talk about the film.

Watch the last part of the film again (from 2:56).
Do you like the ending? Give reasons.

☺	☹
I like the ending because it's funny/… . *I expected … .* *I thought … .*	*I don't like the ending because it's boring … .* *I expected something different.* *I thought … .*

VIEWING SKILLS

Every good film script has a turning point. That is the moment when the story suddenly changes. What is the turning point in this film?

I can understand a film about an adventure in Wales. ✓

Checklist

I can understand information about free-time activities in Wales.

35

I can present information about a sport.

… is an exciting sport. • It's quite easy. • You can learn the rules quickly. • You must wear a helmet.

35

I can make an emergency call.

It's an emergency! • I need an ambulance. • I think he has broken his leg. • His head is bleeding. • She's burnt her hand.

36

I can understand a report from a school website.

36

I can pass on information about a free-time activitiy.

37

I can understand a film about an adventure in Wales.

(TASK) A photo story

Work in groups of three or four students. Each group makes a photo story. The groups can use the computer to make their stories as posters. Each group presents its story and gets feedback from the other groups.

Step 1

Find a good story.

Collect ideas and pictures. Your story can be about:

- a sport
- an emergency
- a trip
- …

Your pictures should have the same style. Don't mix comics with real life pictures. (You can also take your own photos.)

STUDY SKILLS

If you work with a computer, save all your files in one folder. Choose the names of the files carefully.

Step 2

Make a plan.

Put the pictures in a good order.
Remember:
Your story must have a beginning, a middle and an ending.

STUDY SKILLS

There are special computer programmes that can help you put your pictures together to make a story. Ask your IT teacher if you need help.

Step 3

Add texts to your pictures.

You can have speech bubbles and / or captions.

The next day …

Step 4

Check your draft. → M Peer correction, p. 173

Does it have all the important information? Check the spelling.
Ask a friend to read the story. What advice can he or she give you?

Step 5

Write the clean copy of your draft.

The clean copy should have no mistakes. Write or type as carefully as you can!

Step 6

Present your story to the other groups and get feedback. → M Tip top, p. 175

Which story was the best and why?

A Welsh message?

On a tour of a castle you find an old-looking piece of paper next to a stone …

1 Decoding the note.

The key to the message are the arrow and the number. The arrow means 'move to the right' and the number '2x' means 'two times'. So the letter 'A' stands for the letter 'C'.

the code	X	Z	A	B	C	D	E	F	G	H
2x				1	2			1	2	
the message	Y	Z	A	B	C	D	E	F	G	H

Can you decode the message?

Take a piece of paper and write the alphabet in the first line. Write the letter that each letter stands for in the next line. This will help you to decode the message faster.

A	B	C	D	E	F	G	H	I	J	K	…
↓	↓	↓	↓	↓	↓	↓	↓	↓	↓	↓	↓
C	D	E	F	G	H	I	J	K	L	M	…

2 Decode the notes.

What's the secret message? Decode the other notes in the right order. Start with the first note and then follow the directions.

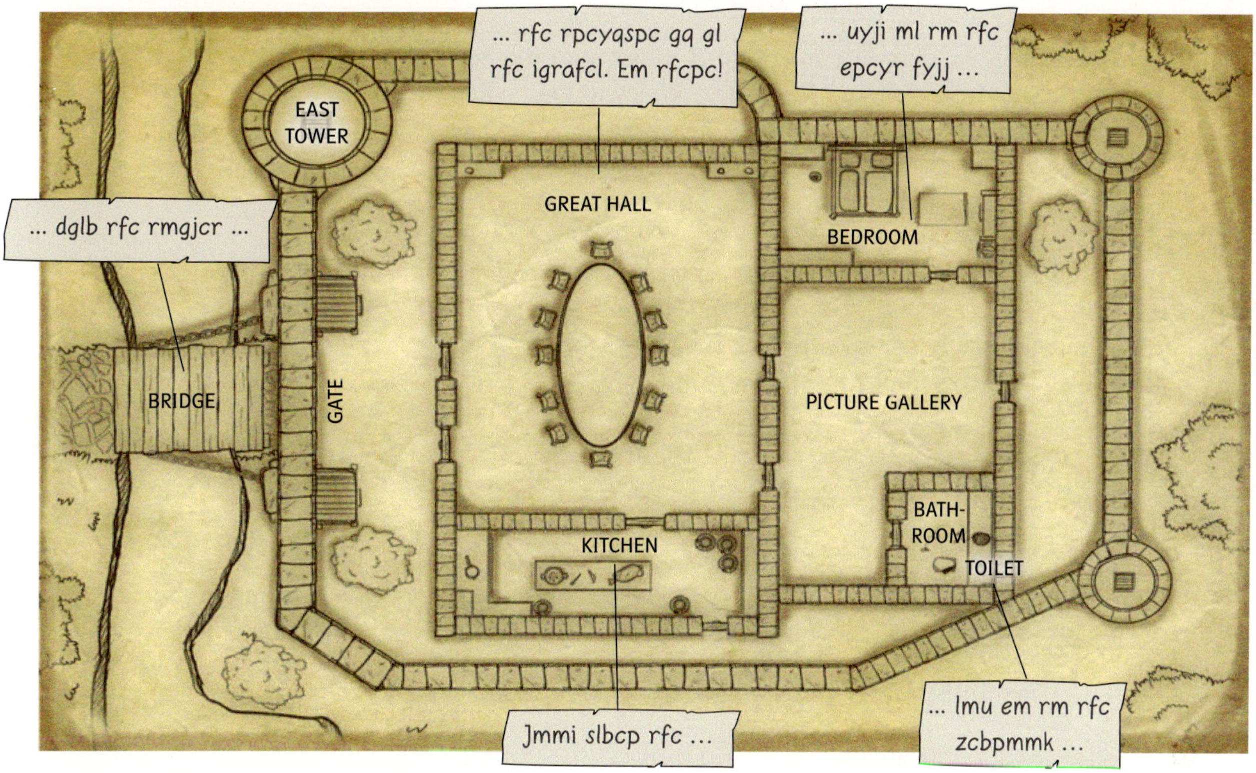

3 Write a secret message.

The treasure is in the ______ of the castle, but where exactly? Write the last message which gives the exact hiding place. Write two or three sentences in code. Don't forget to make the paper look old!

4 A paper chase around the classroom.

a) Create your own secret code. Use the table on p. 48. Choose four places in your classroom where you can hide the notes, for example the cupboard, the blackboard or the teacher's desk. Write a note for each place.

b) Hide the notes in the right places.

c) Tell the other pair or group where they have to start. Can they find and decode your secret message?

You can learn how to write a film review here.

The Baker – an interesting film?

1,19

Review 1 ★★★★☆

I really enjoyed *The Baker.* → 1. Introduction

This comedy has an interesting story about a murderer who runs away from London. He goes to Wales to hide when he has some problems. He becomes the town's new baker so he quickly has to learn how to make cakes and bread. No one knows his secret until his enemy arrives. The film finishes with a big, funny fight. → 2. Content

The stars are brilliant. The actors who play the Welsh people in the town are really funny. The location is very beautiful. There is also a great love story in the film. → 3. The writer's opinion

Go and see this film! I give it four stars. → 4. Conclusion

Review 2 ★☆☆☆☆

The Baker is one of the worst films I have ever seen.

It is the story of a murderer who gets a job wrong, so he moves to a small town in Wales and becomes a baker. Of course, he falls in love with a beautiful Welsh woman and doesn't want to be a murderer again, but the other people in the town find out his secret.

It is a really boring story and the film is very slow. The actors aren't very good and the ending is awful. It is a comedy, but it is more silly than funny.

Give this film a miss! I only give it one star.

Giving your opinion:

+

I really enjoyed this film.
This is one of the best films I've ever seen.
Go and see this film!
I give it four or five stars.

–

I didn't enjoy this film.
This is one of the worst films I've ever seen.
Give this film a miss!
I give it one or two stars.

1 Look at the first review.

Match these sentences with the parts of the review.

A The writer gives reasons why he or she likes the film.
B The writer rates the film and gives advice.
C The writer talks about the story of the film.
D The writer says which film he or she is writing about.

Reviews give a writer's opinion. The reviews always have the same structure. Look at the example on the left.

2 Read the second review.

1. Does the writer like the film or not? Why?
2. Find the parts of the structure in review 2.

To find out the writer's opinion look at the rating and the words (adjectives …).

40/1
41/2-3

3 Write a film review.

a) Think about the last film you saw. Make notes about the story, actors and location.

The actors are … . The stars are … .
This film is a comedy / drama / romance.
The story / location / start / ending is … .

Collect ideas and words about the film you chose before you start to write.

b) Write a draft of the review. Give the film a star rating.

Pay attention to the right structure when you write your draft. A checklist can help you. Use the simple present.

c) Look at the review again. Where can you add some adjectives?

Add adjectives to make your review more interesting.

d) Write a clean copy of the review.

e) Read a partner's review and give feedback. Would you like to see the film he or she has written about?

Read your partner's work and give him or her tips. Was the structure of his or her review OK? Did it explain the film and the writer's opinion well?

Find more online:
i8ce82

In this unit you will …
- find out about Scotland.
- present information about an inventor.
- talk about different kinds of holidays.
- read a comic strip about a battle.
- pass on information about food.
- watch a film about an experiment.

5 1,20 Unit 3

Made in Scotland

The capital of Scotland is Edinburgh. It is a very old city but it has always produced new ideas: It has a big university, and many famous inventors were born and worked in Edinburgh.

Robert the Bruce is a Scottish hero. He was born in 1274. Robert often fought battles against the Engli Today Scotland is a part of the United Kingdom, bu the past it had its own king or queen.

1 What do you know?

a) Before you read, look at the pictures. Make a mind map with a partner.

b) Now tell the class what you already know about Scotland.

2 Collect information about Scotland.

44/1

a) Read the texts and make sentences.

1. Edinburgh … .
   Edinburgh **was home to lots of inventors.**
2. In the past … .
3. Scotland gets electricity … .
4. Visitors to Scotland … .
5. Scottish traditions are … .

b) What more can you find out from the text and the pictures? Add the information to your mind map.

Scotland doesn't have enough sun for solar power but it is a windy place. Now Scotland gets lots of clean electricity from wind farms on land and in the sea.

Scotland has some beautiful mountains and lakes (the Scottish word for lake is 'loch'). Tourists can stay in modern cottages and enjoy the wild countryside.

There are lots of Scottish traditions, like the bagpipes and the kilt, a kind of skirt for men. Scots often eat porridge for breakfast, a warm dish with oats, water, salt and a little milk.

3 (LISTENING) Listen to the interview.

1,21
44/2

Listen to the interview at Whitelee Wind Farm and take notes.

Whitelee Wind Farm:

1. *How many turbines?*
2. *How tall?*
3. *Why important?*
4. *Dangerous?*

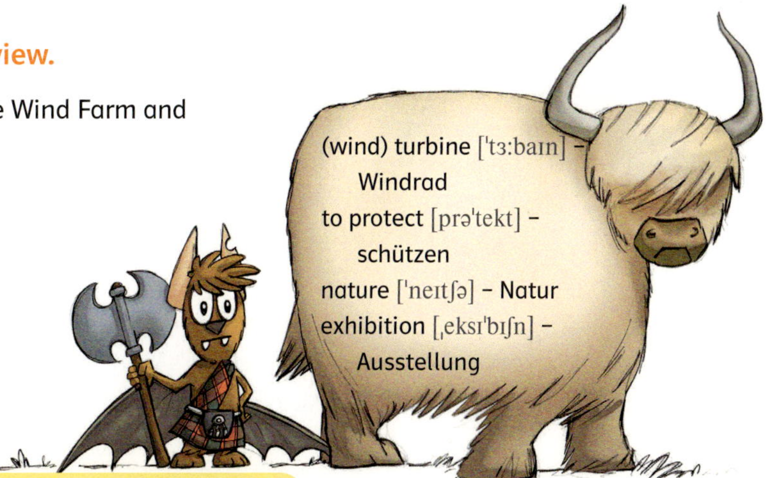

(wind) turbine [ˈtɜːbaɪn] – Windrad
to protect [prəˈtekt] – schützen
nature [ˈneɪtʃə] – Natur
exhibition [ˌeksɪˈbɪʃn] – Ausstellung

I can understand information about Scotland. ✓

A Scot who changed the world

1 (READING) Read the biography.

1,22
45/1

Alexander Graham Bell was an inventor and engineer born in Edinburgh in 1847. Most people know him as the man who invented the telephone.

Bell grew up in Edinburgh and went to school there from the age of ten (before that his mother gave him and his brothers lessons at home) and then in London when he was 14.

When he was older he became a teacher in London. But he also had another ambition: His mother and his wife were both deaf, and so Bell became very interested in speech and the human voice. He wanted to make a machine which could change the sounds of speech to electricity and send them down wires.

At the age of 23 Bell moved to Canada with his family, and in 1871 he went to Boston, in the USA. There he opened a school for people who couldn't hear well. And he never gave up on his ambition. After his work at the school, he worked on his invention every night.

Bell invented the telephone in 1876. His invention wasn't made of plastic, like the phones which we use today. It was big and heavy because it was made of metal and wood. In 1877 he started a company, which sold his invention. Bell's telephone was a big success and he became rich.

The telephone wasn't Bell's only invention, but it stayed his most famous and successful one. Among other things Bell later also invented a metal detector and he tried to build a machine which could fly.

Bell died in his home in Canada in 1922 at age 75. Even today people still remember him as a man whose invention changed the world forever.

2 Find the information in the text.

a) Where can you find it? → ◯ p. 119

- the place where Bell was born
  Edinburgh (line 2)
- what he invented
- why he was interested in speech
- how he became rich
- the countries in which he lived

b) Make a timeline for Bell's life.

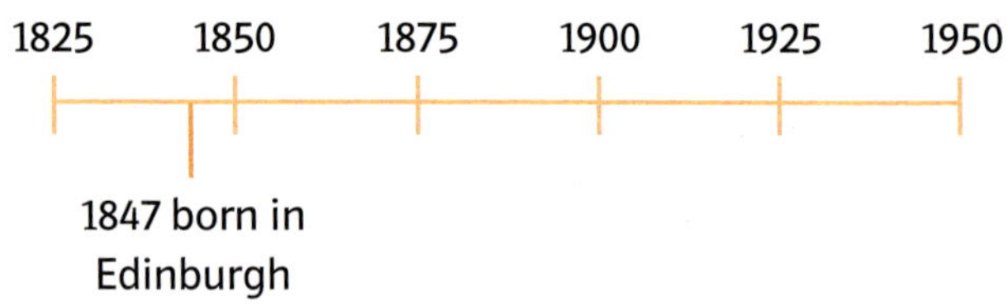

READING SKILLS

A biography tells the story of a person's life. Find the phrases for what happens in every life ('was born', 'grew up' etc.). They will help you to understand the text more quickly.

3 Put the phrases in the right order for Bell's life.

opened a school E | grew up G | died L
became rich L | moved to B | was born A

If you have the phrases in the right order, you'll get a name. Which one?

1,23

4 (LISTENING) Listen to John Dunlop's biography.

a) Listen and complete the short profile of John Dunlop. → ○ p. 120

John Dunlop
- born in …
- worked as a vet in …
- moved to …
- started his company in …
- died in …

b) Listen again. Which of these two is Dunlop's invention? Say why you think so.

1.
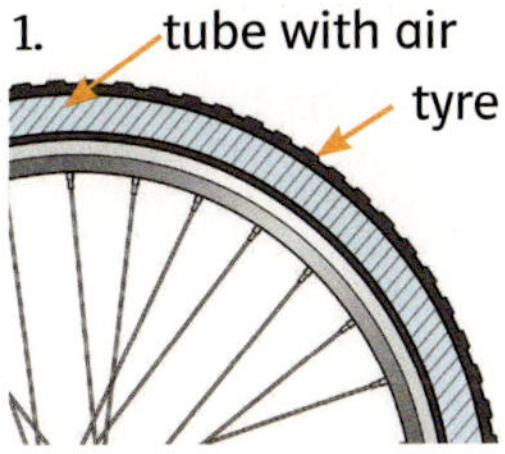

2.
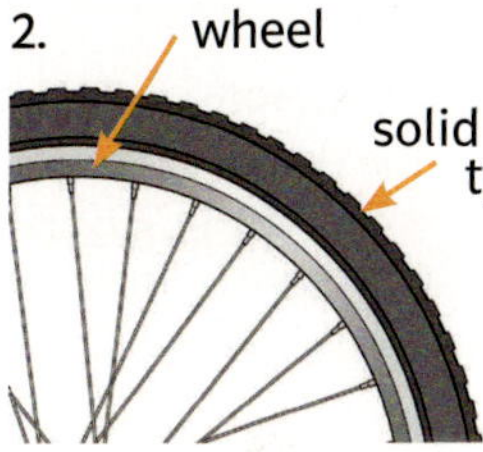

5 Things and materials.

a) Match the things with the materials. → ○ p. 120

45/2

Windows T-shirts Car and bike tyres Phones Book pages Cars and bikes Tables and chairs Shoes	are usually made of	leather. paper. glass. plastic. metal. wood. cotton. rubber.

b) Find things which are made of these materials. → V Materials, p. 196

45/3

wool | china | steel | concrete | cardboard | silk | aluminium

6 (SOUNDS) Say the words. Then listen and check your answers.

1,24

1. [ə 'telɪfəʊn]
2. [ən‿ɪn'ventə]
3. [ˌhevi 'metl]
4. [ə ˌkɒtn 'ʃɜ:t]
5. [ɪn‿'ədinbrə]
6. [ə ˌleθə 'tʃeə]
7. [ə ˌrʌbə 'taɪə]
8. [ˌelɪk'trɪsəti]

7 What's your invention?

Think of an object. What is it made of? Use funny materials.

My shoes are made of metal. Cool, aren't they?

Language detectives → G6, p. 159

Bell is the man who invented the telephone.
The school was for people who couldn't hear well.
His telephone wasn't like the phones which we use today.
He also tried to build a machine which could fly.

When do you use who, when do you use which?
Can you find the rule?

46/4 ## 8 Describe people and things.

a) Match the sentence parts to describe these people and things. → ○ p. 121

1. T-shirts and jeans are clothes		has had a lot of inventors.
2. An inventor is a person		are made of rubber.
3. A plane is a machine		made a successful tyre with air in it.
4. A metal detector is a machine	which	come from Scotland.
5. Scots are people	+ who +	are usually made of cotton.
6. Scotland is a country		finds metal.
7. Cars and bikes have tyres		has ideas and makes new things.
8. Dunlop was an inventor		can fly.

b) Make four sentences with 'who' or 'which' about Alexander Graham Bell and his invention.

Bell was a man who …. **His telephone is (not) ….** **…**

9 (SPEAKING) Do you know the answers? → M Bus stop, p. 170

a) Ask your partner. Can he or she guess the person or thing? → ○ p. 121

46/5
47/6a)

1. person / helps when your pet is ill
   A: It's a person who helps when your pet is ill.
   B: Is it a vet?
   A: That's right!
2. thing / makes electricity with the wind
3. person / cooks meals in a restaurant
4. city / is famous for its inventors
5. inventor / was born in Scotland
6. animal / has big ears
7. singer / comes from Germany

You can also use 'that' in sentences like these:
It's a thing that … .
It's a person that … .

b) Can your partner guess what or who you are thinking of? Use your own ideas.

47/6b)

a person … a material …
an animal … a thing …

10 Match the sentences and use whose.

a) Match the sentences. Then use whose to make one sentence out of two. → ○ p. 121

47/7
48/8

1. Dunlop was an inventor. ✓
2. He was a vet.
3. Bell was a teacher.
4. He was one of many Scottish inventors.

A His mother and wife were both deaf.
B His invention made the bike better. ✓
C Their work made Scotland famous.
D His trips to farms were often on bad roads.

GRAMMAR → G6, p. 159

Dunlop was an inventor whose invention made the bike better.

1. Dunlop was an inventor whose invention made the bike better.

b) Choose who or whose?

48/9

1. Bell was a Scot —— family moved to another country.
2. There are lots of Scots —— don't live in Scotland.
3. People —— inventions are successful often become rich.

11 (YOUR TURN) A short biography → V Inventors and inventions, p. 201

48/10

a) Here are some inventions. Choose one and find information in the library or on the internet about the person who invented it. Write a short biography for the inventor. Add photos. → M Writers' conference, p. 175

1 windscreen wipers

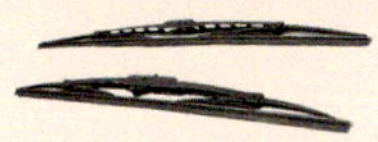

2 blue jeans

3 trolley suitcase

4 steam engine

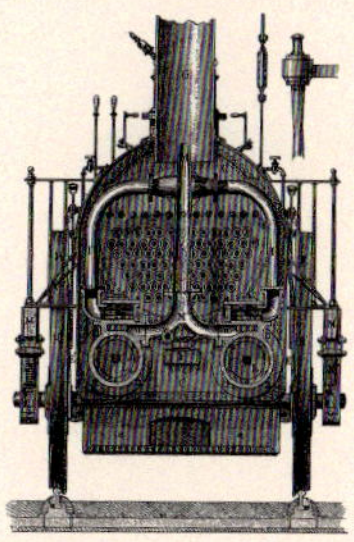

5 light bulb

Use these phrases when you write the biography:

- ... was born in (*place*) in (*year*).
- He / She is the person who invented ....
- ... grew up ...
- It was a ... which ....
- ... moved to ...
- It was made of ....
- ... died in (*place*) in (*year*)?

WRITING SKILLS

A short biography gives the most important facts about a person's life. When you write your text, put them in chronological order. Also say what makes the person special. Use the simple past.

b) Present your biographies. What information surprised you? → M 1-minute-presentation, p. 170

I can present information about an inventor. ✓

Where can we stay?

1 (READING) Read the dialogue.

1,25

Mum: Katie, Jake, Harry. Can you all come to the living room, please? You know our next family holiday is coming up. It's time to plan our trip to the Highlands. For a start we'll have to decide where we want to stay. Here's my idea: I'd love to stay at this cosy bed and breakfast in Inverness. Look, it's on this website. So, what do you think?

Dad: Oh, please, Abby. I thought we could go camping this year. It's a simple and cheap way to spend our holidays. You know I love hiking. If we stay at a campsite, we'll be outside all day. Isn't that great?

Jake: That's a terrible idea, Dad! No way! We'll freeze if we go camping. And there'll be insects too, and you know how much I hate them.

Katie: Are you serious, Dad? I agree with Jake. I don't want to go camping! How about staying at a hotel? If we go to a hotel, there won't be any insects. And we'll have our own bathroom.

Jake: Katie is right. A hotel sounds much better to me too. It's more comfortable and the hotel buffets are fantastic. If we don't stay at a hotel, we won't get nice food!

Mum: I don't want to go camping either but I'm sorry, it won't be a hotel, kids. That's too expensive. But we could rent a holiday cottage. Or maybe we will stay at a B&B if you really want a good breakfast. Spending a few days at a B&B is a good idea. Maybe the people there can also give us some tips about local food and about things to see and do.

Dad: Yes, I think so too. If nobody wants to go camping, that's fine. But let's go to Loch Ness. Maybe we'll see Nessie, the Loch Ness monster …

CULTURE

British people often stay at a B&B (bed and breakfast). That's a family home with extra bedrooms. Have you ever stayed somewhere like this?

2 Find the most important information. → M Bus stop, p. 170

49/1

a) Copy and complete the table.

Who?	Where?	Why?
Abby (Mum) Harry (Dad) Katie Jake	B & B	

b) Where do you think they will stay? Say why you think so.

Language tip → G 7, p. 160

I love **hiking**.
Spending a few days at a B&B is a good idea.

3 Where do people stay on their holidays?

a) Match the words with the definitions. There are more definitions than you need. → ○ p. 122

49/2
49/3a)

1. hotel
2. campsite
3. bed and breakfast
4. youth hostel
5. caravan
6. holiday cottage

A It's a place where you go camping.
B It's a small home which a car can pull from place to place.
C It has many rooms and often a swimming pool and large buffets.
D It's a place with no bathrooms but with a museum.
E It's a small house which you can rent for your holidays.
F It's a place that is almost like home. You stay at a family's place.
G It's a big train with beds.
H It's usually a cheap place where young people stay. Often there is only one kitchen for everyone.

b) Put the steps in the right order. → V Going on holiday, p. 197

49/3b)

check out | ask about prices | pay the bill | make a reservation | check in

1,26
50/4

4 (LISTENING) Which picture is it?

a) Listen to Jim and Dianne and look at the pictures. Where did they stay? → ○ p. 122

hotel

bed and breakfast

hostel

LISTENING SKILLS

Look at the pictures before you listen, and think:
What words do you know about the three places to stay?
Listen carefully for these words when you listen to the dialogue.

b) Why did you choose the picture? Give reasons.

I chose the picture of the … because … . And … .

Language detectives → G8, p. 161 G9, p. 162

If we go to a hotel, there won't be any insects.
If we don't stay in a hotel, we won't get nice food!
We'll freeze if we go camping.

What do you express with this kind of sentence?
What are the two parts of these sentences?
Which tenses are the verbs in each part?

5 Complete the sentences. → M Peer correction, p. 173

50/5-6

1. If Jake goes (go) to Edinburgh, he — (go) shopping.
2. If Dad — (have) time, he — (visit) the castle.
3. If I — (see) a nice souvenir, I — (buy) it.
4. If we — (stay) at a campsite, maybe we — (get) cold.
5. I — (take) a photo of the Loch Ness monster if I — (see) it.
6. We — (become) famous if we — (find) Nessie.
7. Katie — (get) a local breakfast if we — (decide) to stay at a B & B.

6 Make sentences about a holiday in a hotel.

a) Make sentences. → ○ p. 122

51/7

1. If everyone / agree, we / stay / at a hotel
   If everyone agrees, we'll stay at a hotel.
2. If we / stay / at a hotel, we / have / a TV
3. It / not be / so boring / if we / have / a TV
4. You / not meet / other kids / if you / watch / TV all day
5. If we / go / to a good hotel, we / have / internet too
6. If we / have / internet, we / look for / information about things to see and do
7. We / ask / at the Tourist Information Centre / if we / not find / anything interesting online

b) Make more sentences with 'if'.

51/8

1. get up early → go swimming before breakfast
2. be hungry → eat at the hotel restaurant
3. rain → not go horse riding
4. try porridge → like it
5. visit museum ← be open
6. legs get cold ← wear a kilt
7. hear the bagpipes → put hands over ears

Be careful! Which part of the sentence should have the 'if'?

51/9

7 What will we do if … ?

a) Look at the pictures. Make sentences. → ○ p. 123

1. We'll go hiking in the mountains if … .

2. If we leave the hostel after ten o'clock, … .

3. If there's a party at the campsite, … .

4. If we go to the Highlands, … .

5. We'll have a problem with insects if … .

6. We won't stay at that hotel if … .

b) What will happen if …? Make a chain of sentences.

If we have a party at the hostel, we'll go to bed late. If we go to bed late, …

8 (SPEAKING) Persuade your teacher. → M Round robin, p. 174

Oh please don't give us any homework today! If we don't have homework today, I …

9 (YOUR TURN) A role play → V Places to stay, p. 202

52/10
53/1-3

Act a role play with two others. Use the cards and the phrases to talk about where you can go and stay. In the end agree on the place that you want to go to together.

A MacGowan Hotel
Place: Glasgow
Activities: museums, food, theatre, shopping
Price: £275 for 2 people for 2 nights

B Nessie's Nest (B & B)
Place: Inverness
Activities: walking, canoeing, cycling, Loch Ness
Price: £420 for 4 people for 3 nights

C No Tree Hostel
Place: Isle of Skye
Activities: bird watching, boat trips, beach walks
Price: £25 for 1 person for 1 night

Let's go to … .
… is cheaper/more expensive.
I like/don't like … , so … is better for me.
If you like …, you will/won't like … .

I would like to … .
I prefer … .
I think so too. / I agree/disagree.
That's (not) a good/bad idea.

I can talk about different kinds of holiday. ✓

Robert the Bruce

1 What do you already know about Robert the Bruce and the history of Scotland and England?

2 (READING) Read the comic strip.

1,27

1 Welcome to the 14th century! At this time there are lots of battles between Scotland and England.

2 In 1306 …

3 Edward I, King of England, has a strong army …

4 After the sixth battle …

READING SKILLS

Use the pictures to help you read the story. If you don't know a word, look at the picture carefully.
Who is speaking and what is the situation?
What does the person's face tell you? You don't always need to know the word.

5 Robert the Bruce sees something in the cave.

6 A few days later …

7 The Scots and the English fight a lot in the years after this. Robert the Bruce loses some battles, but he also wins some. Edward I, the English king, is angry …

3 Talk about the story.

Did you like the story? Talk about it with a partner and say why (or why not).

4 Who is it?

1. His army lost the battle in 1314.
2. He lost six battles.
3. He died before an important battle.
4. He became king in 1306.

5 Answer the questions.

1. Explain why Robert the Bruce decided to never give up.
2. Who fought whom at Bannockburn?
3. Who won at Bannockburn and why did they win?

11 After two days …

12 In the years after this Robert is a good king and the Scots are proud.

13 In 1329 …

Under Robert the Bruce there was peace in Scotland and it was a free country. He was a brave man and a great leader. He was Scotland's most successful king.

6 Choose one of these tasks.

54/1
55/2-3

a) A short biography of Robert the Bruce.

Search the internet about the life of Robert the Bruce. Then write a short biography. Add pictures. → M Peer correction, p. 173

STUDY SKILLS

When you look for information on the internet, only look for the most important facts and dates ('born', 'grew up', 'invented … in …' etc.) in the person's life. Write these as notes. Then use your notes to write the biography.

OR

b) It's 1329 and Robert has just died. What does an old Scottish soldier tell his son or daughter about the Battle of Bannockburn? Write a dialogue and act it. Give the people names.

A: I'll never forget it, that battle!
B: Tell me more! …
A: Well, …

When … ? | What … ? | Why … ? | …

→ M Dramatic reading, p. 171

I can understand a comic strip about a battle. ✓

Some Scottish and German dishes

Deep fried chocolate

If you like chocolate, you'll love this snack! A fish and chip shop in Scotland put a bar of chocolate in the same batter it used to cover the fish and then fried it in hot oil. Lots of people thought that this gooey, sticky treat that is crisp on the outside was fun to eat.

Haggis

Haggis is a famous Scottish dish. It's a kind of meat pudding which can include the heart, liver and lungs of a sheep, together with onions and oatmeal. Sometimes it's even served in the sheep's stomach.

Kirschmichel

Kirschmichel ist eine traditionelle Süßspeise, die vor allem im Süden Deutschlands serviert wird. Älteres Brot oder Brötchen werden mit Butter, Eiern, Milch und Zucker vermengt. Dazu kommen Kirschen. Alles wird im Ofen gebacken und noch warm serviert.

Himmel und Erde

Himmel und Erde ist ein beliebtes Gericht in einigen Teilen von Deutschland, z. B. im Rheinland. Kartoffeln und Äpfel werden gekocht, gestampft und miteinander vermischt. Dazu wird Bratwurst oder traditionell Blutwurst serviert.

1 Beantworte die Fragen.

56/1

Eine Deutsche und ein Schotte haben diese Texte gesehen, aber sie verstehen sie nicht ganz. Beantworte ihre Fragen in der jeweiligen Sprache.

1. Schokolade gibt es bei uns auch. Was ist da so besonders?
2. Ich bin Vegetarierin. Kann ich das traditionelle Haggis essen?
3. What's 'Kirschmichel'? I can see the word 'Brot'. Is it a kind of sandwich?
4. 'Äpfel' means 'apple', doesn't it? Is 'Himmel und Erde' a cake with apples?

2 What do you think?

Do you like trying different types of food? Is there anything that you wouldn't eat? Say why.

I can pass on information about food. ✓

The old phone

1 Talk about old phones.

Have you ever seen or used a phone like this?
Can you send text messages with it?
What's a pay phone? Where can you find them?

2 (VIEWING) Watch the film.

6

a) Which summary is correct?

1. Alicia helps her grandmother with the shopping and her video chat. After that, her neighbour Alva gives her an old TV.
2. Marley gets an old phone from Alicia. She repairs it and her friends are proud of her.
3. Alicia helps her neighbour, who gives her an old phone. Marley knows how to use it as a radio.

b) Who says it?

1. "I've never had a video chat before."
2. "I have an idea!"
3. "I want to see what you're up to!"
4. "Wow! It looks interesting! What is it?"
5. "It's amazing what you can do with an old telephone!"

CULTURE

Neighbours in the UK often use first names. How would you talk about an older neighbour like Alva? Would you use his or her first name?

3 (WRITING) Write about the film.

Watch the last part of the film again (from 3:20). Describe what happens. Use these words for help:

attach | pipe | antenna | connect | signal

You can start like this:

Marley took an old phone. Laura and Alicia were very .... Marley .... They heard .... It was ....

VIEWING SKILLS

Suspense makes a film more exciting. Sounds, music, lighting and the camera angle can all create suspense.
How does this film make the story more interesting?

I can understand a film about an experiment.

Checklist

I can understand information about Scotland. ✓

57

I can present information about an inventor. ✓

... was born in (place) in (year). • He/She is the man/woman who .... • ... grew up in .... • ... invented the first ... in .... • It was a ... which .... • ... died in (place) in (year).

57

I can talk about different kinds of holidays. ✓

Let's go to .... • ... is cheaper/ more expensive. • I like/don't like ..., so ... is better for me. • If you like ..., you will/won't like ....

58

I can understand a comic strip about a battle. ✓

58

I can pass on information about food. ✓

59

I can understand a film about an experiment. ✓

(TASK) An advert

Work in groups of three or four students. Each group thinks of a product and makes an advert (ad) for it. Each group presents the ad and gets feedback from the other groups.

Step 1

Look at the ads.

Do you like them? Discuss.

1

2

interesting | boring | funny | exciting | nice photos | lots of information | ...

Step 2

What makes a good ad? → M Think-pair-share, p. 175

Look at the examples in Step 1 for help.
Look at the language, the photos and the information.

Step 3

Make and design your ad.

1. Choose your product.
2. Think: What is good about the product?
   What kind of people should buy the product?
3. Choose pictures or photos.
4. Write the text.
5. Make a draft of the ad. You can use a computer or a large piece of paper.

STUDY SKILLS

Choose a product that is interesting or unusual. Decide who your ad is for. Choose a good photo. It should speak for itself.
The text should be simple and the message should be clear. The text should speak to the reader, so use questions and imperatives.

Step 4

Check your draft.

Does it have all the important information? Check the spelling too.

Step 5

Make your ad and show it to the other groups. → M Gallery walk, p. 172

Step 6

Get feedback from the other groups. → M Tip top, p. 175

What was good/not so good? Which ad was the best and why? Think about:

the text | the design | the message | the photo(s) | who the ad is for | ...

Nessie's underwater world

Loch Ness – home of Nessie

In the north of Scotland, in the heart of the Scottish Highlands, there is a big lake called Loch Ness.
Some people believe that a huge, green monster called Nessie lives in this lake.

Nessie's home is about 37 km long, 1.5 km wide and 230 m deep.

People tried to find the swimming dinosaur and some even took photos to prove that Nessie is in the lake. But nobody has ever seen it on land or in its underwater world …

The experiment

Create Nessie's underwater world and see how it comes to life with an experiment in a bottle.

Maybe you can take or draw a picture of it to prove that Nessie is there.

Prepare yourself

You need:

a small plastic bottle (0.5l PET)

transparent paper

scissors

glue stick

waterproof felt-tips

small stones

a peanut, a cork or polystyrene

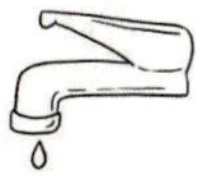
water

blue ink

sunflower oil

a funnel

a fizzy tablet

Prepare the underwater world

Step 1: Design the outside of your bottle

- With transparent paper create small fish, underwater plants and flowers.
- Glue them on the bottle.
- You can also draw on the bottle with waterproof felt-tips.

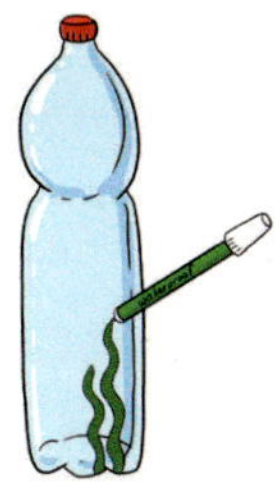

Step 2: Create Nessie

- Create a Nessie monster that can swim in the water.
- Use a peanut, a cork or a piece of polystyrene.

Step 3: Fill the bottle

- Use a funnel to fill ½ of the bottle with water.
- Put some ink into it.
- Fill ¼ of the bottle with sunflower oil.

Step 4: Nessie moves in

- Put Nessie in its new home.

Start the experiment

- Divide the fizzy tablet in two pieces.
- Throw one piece into the bottle.
- Don't close the bottle during the experiment.

You can take your bottle home and do the experiment as often as you want.

Here you can learn how to find the right word in a dictionary.

1,28 On Ben Nevis

INTERNET

Avalanche hits rock climbers

10:35 published Monday 8th January

Four rock climbers who set off an avalanche in the Scottish highlands on Sunday 7th January were very lucky to escape with their lives.

The four young men, all from London, were climbing Ben Nevis, the highest mountain in the UK. At about 2 p.m. a huge wave of snow swept them 300 metres down the mountain.

In an interview later that day one of the men said, "I fell for a very long time. I didn't believe that I would survive. My friends and I, we all had safety equipment like red coats and red helmets. But still we were really lucky to walk out. It was a very scary adventure. The rescue helicopter had already started to look for us. It took us to hospital, but we were all OK. Only one of my friends had a twisted ankle."

Next year, the climbers will climb the highest mountain in Europe, Mont Blanc.

1 Look at the dictionary entry.

Use the entry for 'hit' to find the right German word(s) in these sentences:

1. The avalanche hit the climbers.
2. The car hit a tree.
3. The musical *Cats* is a real hit.
4. The boy hit the ball very hard.
5. There were 143 hits for this search.

hit hɪt **I.** *n* ❶ Schlag *m* ❷ *(shot)* Treffer *m*; **to suffer a direct ~** direkt getroffen werden ❸ *(success)* Hit *m*; **to be a [big] ~ with sb** bei jdm gut ankommen ❹ INET Besuch *m* einer Webseite ❺ COMPUT *(match)* Treffer *m* **II.** *vt* <-tt-, hit, hit> ❶ schlagen ❷ *button* drücken ❸ *(collide)* **to ~ sth** gegen etw *akk* stoßen; *car* gegen etw *akk* krachen *fam* ❹ *(shoot)* **to be ~** getroffen werden ❺ *(occur)* **to ~ sb** jdm auffallen **III.** *vi* ❶ **to ~ hard** kräftig zuschlagen; **to ~ at sb** nach jdm schlagen ❷ *(attack)* **to ~ at sb** jdn attackieren *a. fig*

◆**hit back** *vi* zurückschlagen; **to ~ back at sb** jdm Kontra geben

◆**hit off** *vt* **to ~ it off [with sb]** *(fam)* sich prächtig [mit jdm] verstehen

The words in a dictionary are in groups or 'entries'. Each entry has a root word. Look for the root word first.

This part tells you how to say the word.

Here you can see if the word is a verb, a noun, an adjective, …

In the entry you can find useful phrases.

Many words have more than one meaning. There is a number for each meaning.

These words help you find the right meaning.

62/1
63/2-4

2 Work with a dictionary.

a) Find the right German meaning for the underlined words in the text. Use an English-German dictionary.

b) What do the same words mean here?

1. The man waved wildly from the window.
2. A tornado swept through the town.
3. Can I have a look at that magazine?
4. The man escaped from prison in the night.
5. The plane went into a steep climb.

You can also use online dictionaries. But be careful, don't just take the first meaning you find. It's always good to double-check the translation you choose in a German-English dictionary.

Find more online:
i8ce82

In this unit you will ...
- find out about Northern Ireland.
- give advice to a friend.
- buy things and have a conversation in a small shop.
- read a newspaper report about a disaster.
- pass on information about a B & B.
- watch a film about a conflict.

7 2,1

Unit 4
In Northern Ireland

Belfast is the capital of Northern Ireland. You can see a lot of big murals on the buildings of the city. Most of them are still there from the time of 'The Troubles', when there were problems between the Protestant and Catholic parts of the population.

My friend Julie and I visited the Giant's Causeway in the summe That's on the north coast of Northern Ireland. It was great! Look at the stones, they're spectacular! They look like giant steps. You can even walk on ther

1 Look at the pictures and find titles for them.

1. A city near the sea

2 Read the texts and give the reasons.

70/1

1. Why are there murals on the walls of houses in Belfast?
2. Why did Sarah like the Giant's Causeway?
3. Why are Sarah's parents busy?
4. Why does Sarah like going to Maggie's shop?
5. Why was her grandad's uncle not on the Titanic?

My dad lost his job in Belfast about four months ago and so we have just moved to a town near Lough Neagh. My mum and dad have opened a bed and breakfast here, and a lot of tourists come to stay here. My parents are very busy!

My aunt Maggie runs a shop in Randalstown, a small town northwest of Belfast. You can buy almost everything in her shop. Or you can just chat with her for a little bit. And the best thing is that I always get free sweets when I visit her!

Belfast used to be famous for ships. Did you know that the Titanic was built here? That was in 1912. My grandad's uncle George even got a job as a waiter on it. But then he was sick on the day the ship left, so he didn't travel. Phew!

3 (LISTENING) Answer the questions.

2,2
70/2

1. Where does the tourist want to go?
   He wants to go to the **Giant's Causeway**.
2. How can he get there?
3. How often do the buses go?
4. How much does an adult ticket cost?
5. What kind of ticket does the tourist buy and why?

visitor centre [ˈvɪzɪtə ˌsentə] – Besucherzentrum
giant [dʒaɪənt] – Riese
to cost [kɒst] – kosten
adult [ˈædʌlt] – Erwachsene/r
probably [ˈprɒbəbli] – wahrscheinlich

I can understand information about Northern Ireland. ✓

I'm really fed up!

1 (READING) Read the e-mails.

2,3
71/1

E-MAIL

Hi Julie,

I need your advice. I'm really fed up.

Mum and Dad never have any time for me any more because they're so busy with their new B & B. They work hard all day. And in the evenings they're always too tired to do anything.

We had so much fun together when we lived in Belfast. But now?

At the weekends Mum always nags me to tidy up the dining room. Why do I have to do all this work? It's not my B & B, is it? But at least Ashley helps me a lot. Well, that's really nice of him, I have to say. Sometimes little brothers can be useful. ☺

I don't like the B & B and sometimes I get fed up with the people who come to stay at it too. We have new guests every day and they always ask the same questions. "Where's this? Where's that? How do we get there? Blah blah blah … ." It drives me crazy! I miss you so much! If you were here, I wouldn't be so lonely.

See you,
Sarah ☹

E-MAIL

Hi Sarah,

I miss you too. It's so boring here without you. Can't you talk to your parents? Maybe you can find a quiet moment? I think they would understand if you told them how horrible the place is for you. If I were you, I would speak to your dad first. He seems like somebody who would listen. Who knows, maybe you can get more free time and do some more fun things?

If I lived in a B & B, I'd probably hate it too. But stop complaining - think positive! You can meet people from lots of different places, even other countries. Maybe they can tell you interesting stories or teach you funny words in their language?

If I visited you in our next holidays, you could show me Lough Neagh. I would probably ask the same silly questions as the tourists. But I have to go to Dublin with my family.

Can you come to Belfast again soon? If you were here now, I would take you to the cool new milkshake place in town.

I'll call you tomorrow.
Julie XOX

2 Find the answers.

1. Which things does Sarah complain about?
2. What is nice of her brother?
3. What is Julie's advice for Sarah?
4. What's a good thing about the B & B?

3 What's your opinion? → M Think-pair-share, p. 175

1. What do you think about Sarah's complaints?
   In my opinion she is right/wrong, because …
2. What is your opinion on Julie's advice?

4 (LISTENING) Listen to the phone call. Choose the right answer.

2,4

1. Who called Sarah?
   Ashley • Julie • her aunt
2. When was Sarah so fed up?
   yesterday • last week • two days ago
3. Who will she try to talk to later that week?
   her brother • her dad • her mum
4. When will the girls talk again?
   tomorrow morning • tomorrow afternoon • tomorrow evening

5 Work with adjectives.

71/2

a) Make a chart. Sort the adjectives. → ○ p. 123 → M Bus stop, p. 170

sad ✓ · honest · furious · smart · confident · horrible · optimistic · cautious

You need your dictionary for some of these. There are tips on how to work with a dictionary on page 73.

☺	☹
…	*sad*

71/3

b) Find words with the same meaning. Match the new words with the words from a).
→ V Adjectives for feelings, p. 203

1. down – sad
2. dreadful
3. hopeful
4. intelligent
5. straightforward
6. very annoyed
7. sure of oneself
8. guarded

6 (WRITING) Describe an important person in your life.

72/4-5

a) Choose a person (family or friend) and make notes.

Who? Why is the person important?
Which adjectives (from Ex. 5) can you use?

b) Write your text. → M Peer correction, p. 173

My best friend always listens to me. He's smart and knows a lot of things. He also … . But he's often late. That really makes me furious. Sometimes he …

7 (SONG) Let your tears fall

2,5

Listen to the song. What advice does the singer give?

Watch your tears fall, let them fall, falling now,
Make the seas calm, take you in my arms, you
cry. (Let your tears fall …)
It's not a crime to fall apart sometimes,
It's not a crime to ask why, to ask why, you cry.
(Let your tears fall …)
I will come, no, I won't run,
I'm not scared, to care.
Come to me when you're in need,
Set it free, let the truth breathe.
(Chorus): Tell me all your secrets,
tell me your fears,
I'm gonna push you away,
then I'll pull you near,
No, I won't judge you, I'm gonna help
you through.

Language detectives → G10, p. 163

If I lived in a B & B, I would hate it too.
If you were here, we'd go to the new place.
They would understand if you told them how you feel.

Look at the verbs. What is different from the if-sentences that you already know?
Are the sentences about something that really happens?

72/6 73/7

8 (WRITING) Complete the sentences.

a) What would Sarah do if she was ten years older? Complete the sentences. → ○ p. 124

If Sarah was 10 years older …

1. move / Belfast

2. find / job

3. work / office

4. live / flat

5. meet / Julie

6. visit / parents

b) Finish these sentences with your own ideas.

1. If Sarah invited a new friend to her place, … .
2. If Sarah's parents didn't come to Belfast, … .
3. If Sarah's brother was older, … .
4. If her parents didn't work in the B & B any more, … .

9 What would happen?

a) Put in the verbs. → ○ p. 124 → M Peer correction, p. 173

73/8

1. If Sarah went (go) to a sports club, she would make (make) new friends.
2. If Sarah — (speak) to her parents about her problems, they — (understand) her better.
3. Sarah and her friend Julie — (be) happier if they — (meet) each other more often.
4. If Julie — (not live) in Belfast, Sarah — (see) her best friend more often.
5. Sarah — (spend) more time in Ashley's room if he — (not listen) to that awful music.
6. If her mum and dad — (not work) so hard, they — (not be) so tired.

b) In what situation would you do it?

73/9

move to Belfast | eat ten sausages | sing for a big crowd | kiss a spider

I would move to Belfast if all my friends came with me.

74/10 **10** (SPEAKING) **What would you do in this situation?** → M Double circle, p. 171

a) Make and answer questions with a partner. → ○ p. 125

Here are some ideas:
- you lose your phone
- you own an elephant
- you have a year without school
- you are the only person in the world
- you can only eat one sort of food

ask | travel | choose | go to | play | show | …

A: What would you do if you lost your phone?
B: I would ask a friend: "Can you call my number, please?"
Maybe then I would hear it and find it.

b) Read the headlines. What would you do in each situation?

School boy finds 200 year old coins in garden!

Woman wins big prize in art competition!

Engineer invents time travel machine!

11 (YOUR TURN) **An e-mail with advice** → V Giving advice, p. 208

a) Read the e-mail. What is Steve's problem?

74/11

E-MAIL

Hi Julie,
I've got a big problem, please help me. You know that 'The Spectacular Tigerboy III' is in cinemas now.
My mum hates the 'Tigerboy' movies and she told me: "You can't see that horrible movie!"
But I really wanted to see it.
So yesterday I told her: "I have to do homework with Seb tonight." But really Seb, Carol and I went to watch the movie together. And you already know what happens next. We walk into the building and look who's there: my mum's best friend. And of course she sees me. What should I do now? Mum will be furious … . Maybe it's a good idea to look for my mum's friend? But she's a very honest person. If I talked to her, what do you think she would do?
Any ideas? I'm really worried. You're the smart one here. Please help!
See you,
Steve

b) Write an e-mail to Steve and give advice. These phrases can help:

That sounds awful. / That's bad news. / That's …
Think positive. / I have a good idea. /
Why don't you … / Maybe you should …
If I were you, … / If you told your mum, … /
If you talked to your mum's friend, … / If you …
Call me later. / Let's speak soon. / …
→ M Writers' conference, p. 175

WRITING SKILLS

Follow these steps:
- Start the e-mail correctly.
- Show that you understand the problem.
- Say two things the person can do.
- Finish the e-mail correctly.

I can give advice to a friend. ✓

Buy one, get one free

1 (READING) Read the dialogue in Maggie's shop in Randalstown.

2,6
75/1a)

Maggie: Hello! You're Ian Thompson's son, aren't you? How are you today?

Dan: Yes, that's right! I'm fine. Thanks for asking. And how are you?

Maggie: I'm good, thank you. How can I help you? What would you like?

Dan: Actually, I have to buy some things for my dad. I'd like some raspberry jam, please.

Maggie: Oh dear, we don't have any raspberry jam. But we have the strawberry kind. Look, this one is the cheapest, but it's as tasty as the others. There's a special offer. Buy one, get one free! Why don't you try that?

Dan: Strawberry is fine too. OK, I'll have two jars then. Do you have any brown bread?

Maggie: Yes, we do. There is some sliced bread over there, and we have farmer's bread too. It's more expensive than the sliced one, but it's healthier. All our customers love it.

Dan: How much does a loaf cost?

Maggie: It's only £1.20.

Dan: I'd like one loaf of farmer's bread, please. And I almost forgot, I have to post a letter for my dad too. Can I have four stamps, please?

Maggie: Of course. Where is the letter for? Oh, Ballyronan? My niece Sarah lives there.

Dan: Really? Well, er, … how interesting.

Maggie: Yes. She's about your age. Her family moved there from Belfast. They have a B & B there now. Of course, Ballyronan isn't as big as Belfast, and it's less exciting than the big city, but I hope Sarah likes it there.

Dan: Well, I'm sorry, but I think I really have to get going. How much do I owe you?

Maggie: Let's see, that's £2.52 for the stamps. Anything else? Would you like any sweets?

Dan: Er, no, thanks. I think I have everything.

Maggie: OK. That will be £5.27 all in all, please.

Dan: Excuse me, but can you repeat that, please? I didn't get that.

Maggie: Yes, of course. £5.27, please.

Dan: Sorry, I've only got a twenty pound note in my wallet.

Maggie: Don't worry, that's OK. So that's £14.73 change for you. Here you are.

Dan: Thanks a lot. Bye now.

Maggie: You're welcome. Bye!

2 Find out about the shopping trip.

a) What is on Dan's shopping list? What does he really buy?

Dan's shopping list:	What Dan really buys:
raspberry jam …	…

b) How much does the jam cost?

3 Find the phrases in the dialogue.

What can you say …

1. to check that somebody is OK?
2. when you want to say thanks?
3. when you don't hear or understand?
4. when you give something to somebody?

4 Work with shopping phrases.

a) Put the phrases in the right order to make a shopping dialogue. → ○ p. 125 → M Peer correction, p. 173

75/1b)

Shop assistant:
A That will be £3.63.
B Goodbye!
C That's £1.37 change.
D Anything else?
E Hi!
F What would you like?

Customer:
u Yes, … . / No, thanks.
v Hello!
w I'd like … .
x Here you are.
y See you.
z Thank you.

b) Who can say these phrases, the customer or the shop assistant?

75/1c)

Sorry, we've run out of that. | Do you have another brand? | I don't have any money left. | Do you have the exact change? | Sorry, I can't change a twenty pound note. | Sorry, I've changed my mind. | I can order some for you.

5 (LISTENING) Listen to three more customers in Maggie's shop.

2,7
75/2
76/3

a) Look at the things and listen. Who buys which thing(s)?

Customer 1 buys …

tissues

mineral water

peanut butter

b) Listen again. How many do the customers buy and how much do they pay?

jar(s) of | packet(s) of | bottle(s) of

6 (PUZZLE) Which is more money, A or B?

A

B

CULTURE

All British coins and notes have a picture of the queen or king on one side. What people or things are on the money you use every day, or that you know from holidays?

Language → G11, p. 164

Do you remember how to compare things in English?

It's more expensive than the sliced bread.
It's healthier.
This one is the cheapest.
It's as nice as the others.
Ballyronan is less exciting than Belfast.

When do we use more / most and when do we use -er / -est?
What does the word than mean?
How do we say that two things are the same?

7 Compare the things on the shelf.

76/4a)

1. sliced bread — brown bread (big)
   The sliced bread is bigger than the brown bread.
2. brown box of tea — red box of tea (cheap)
3. raspberry jam — peanut butter (expensive)
4. jar of jam is — the jar of peanut butter (big)
5. tissues in the green packet — tissues in the blue packet (cheap)
6. water from Northern Ireland — the Scottish water (expensive)

8 (SPEAKING) What do you think? Talk with a partner.

a) Which do you prefer? Say why. → ○ p. 126

76/4b)
77/5-6

1. Giant's Causeway or Stonehenge?
   A: I think the Giant's Causeway is more interesting than Stonehenge because it's more spectacular. Do you agree?
   B: Yes, you're right.
2. chocolate or strawberry?
3. winter or summer?
4. dogs or cats?
5. doing homework or tidying up your room?
6. speaking any language or talking to animals?

as … as | not as … as | -er than | more … than | less … than

b) Compare these things with your partner. Do you agree?

77/7

books or films? football or tennis? small shops or big shops?

Language detectives → G12, p. 165

I have to buy some things for my dad.
Oh dear, we don't have any raspberry jam.
Do you have any brown bread?

When do we use some and when do we use any? Find more examples in the text on page 80.

9 Some or any?

a) Put in some or any. → ○ p. 126

78/8

1. I'd like to buy some comics.
2. Sorry, we don't have — tissues.
3. Do you have — sweets in your bag?
4. There is — chocolate over there.
5. Oh dear! We don't have — change!
6. Maggie has — farmer's bread in her shop.
7. Let's eat — cake!
8. Sorry, I didn't buy — orange juice. I forgot!

b) Make the second sentence. Use the ideas on the right.

78/9

1. I can't go out today. I have to do some homework.
2. I can't buy those jeans. …
3. I'm very hungry. …
4. Are you thirsty? …
5. Oh dear, my nose! …

be / sandwiches in the kitchen ?
have / tissues ?
have / homework + ✓
have / money –
give you / mineral water +

10 (YOUR TURN) A shopping dialogue → V Shopping, p. 209

a) Write notes for a shopping dialogue with a partner. You can use the phrases from Ex. 4 on page 81. Here are some more ideas:

79/1

Assistant:
Ask friendly questions. (How are you? / … ?)
Say what is cheaper, healthier, more / less …
Say that there is a special offer.
Say that you have some new / cool / …

Customer:
Answer the assistant's questions. (Be friendly!)
Say that you need some … and why.
Ask: "Do you have any … ?"
Say: "No thanks, I don't need any … ."

SPEAKING SKILLS

Listen to your partner when you have the conversation. Show interest in what he or she says. (You can say "Really?" or "That's interesting.") If you don't understand something, say: "Sorry, can you repeat that, please?" Try to help if the other person gets stuck.

b) Practise and act the dialogue. → M Read and look up, p. 174

I can buy things and have a conversation in a small shop. ✓

The Titanic disaster

1 What do you already know about the Titanic? → M Think-pair-share, p. 175

2 (READING) Read the newspaper report.

2,8

The Belfast News

Wednesday, 17th April 1912

Titanic hits iceberg and sinks

TWO DAYS AFTER – MORE FACTS

The giant ship Titanic, which was built here in Belfast's shipyard, hit an iceberg on 14th April, shortly before midnight. Water filled the ship until it sank two hours and forty minutes later at 2:20 a.m. It was on its way from Southampton to New York, on its very first voyage. There were more than 2,200 passengers and crew on board. The people who were not in lifeboats when the ship sank did not survive in the cold sea. About 1,500 people died.

WORLD'S LARGEST SHIP

The Titanic was the largest and most expensive ship in the world. It had a swimming pool, Turkish baths, a gymnasium and two libraries. The ship's builders, The White Star Line company, were sure that their ship was safe and could not possibly sink, so the Titanic only had 20 lifeboats. Those were only enough for 1,178 people, which is a bit more than half of the people on board the ship.

3 Talk about the report.

Which pieces of information about the disaster were new to you?

4 Find the facts.

1. number of people on board?
2. from where to where?
3. time and date of accident?
4. number of lifeboats?
5. number of people who survived?
6. number of crew members from Northern Ireland?

READING SKILLS

You can guess the meaning of some English words if you know a similar one in German. Try it for *iceberg*, *optimistic* and *passenger*. Can you find more examples in the text?

LOCAL MEN DIE AT SEA

Twenty of the crew were from Northern Ireland. The ship's doctor, Dr John Simpson, 37, was born in Belfast. His mother was optimistic when a letter from him arrived at her home yesterday. However, we have found out that he posted the letter during the ship's last stop. We now know that Dr Simpson did not survive.

Dr John Simpson

DOG SAVES LIVES

Some were lucky and the ships which came to save the passengers of the Titanic found their lifeboat. According to a passenger, one of the dogs on board saved the lives of the people in one lifeboat. A ship only found this lifeboat in the dark night and the foggy weather because they heard the dog when it barked.

HOW COULD IT HAPPEN?

After the sinking of the Titanic a number of questions still need answers. Why did no one see the iceberg? Why did the ship break? Why were there only 20 lifeboats for 2,200 people on board? Why did lifeboats leave the ship when they were not yet full? And how can we make sure that an accident like this will never happen again?

About 700 people survived the accident.
Some ships today have over 6,500 passengers and crew. After the Titanic's accident there were laws that ships must have one lifeboat place for every person on board.
Dr Simpson's last letter to his mother is now in the Belfast Titanic museum.

5 Choose one of these tasks.

80/1
1/2-5

a) Write the diary for 15th April 1912 of a person who survived the disaster (100 words). Think about these questions:

- Where are you now?
- How do you feel?
- What was it like on the lifeboat?
- ...

OR

b) Interviews: You are the reporter. Take notes. What are your questions for ...
- a person from the White Star Line company?
- Dr John Simpson's mother?
- the passenger who told the story of the dog?

Interview three students in your class. They play your interview partners.

I can understand a newspaper report about a disaster. ✓

At a bed and breakfast

1 Beantworte die Fragen.

82/1-2

Du übernachtest mit deiner Familie im Browns Bed & Breakfast in der Nähe von Lough Neagh. Dort siehst du diese Schilder.

1. Wer darf hier parken? Was passiert mit Falschparkern?
2. Wann soll man die Klingel betätigen? Was meinst du, warum wurde der Text auf dem Schild geändert?
3. Bekommen die Gäste im B & B wirklich Frühstück ans Bett?
4. Was müssen die Gäste bei der Ankunft machen?
5. Was machst du mit den nassen Handtüchern, wenn du dieses Schild im Bad siehst?
6. Was bedeutet dieses Schild?

CULTURE

British B & Bs often have signs that are funny. Which of the signs at Sarah's B & B are funny? Have you ever seen any funny signs?

2 What rules would you have?

If you ran a B & B, what rules would you have? Make signs for two of them.

I can pass on information about a B & B.

The cousin from Northern Ireland

1 Talk about the photos.

Nathan and Laura are with their cousin, Sean. Look at the photos from the film.
What do you think is happening?

2 (VIEWING) Watch the film.

8

a) Right or wrong? Correct the wrong sentences.

1. Sean is very good at sport.
2. There are some good basketball teams in Northern Ireland.
3. Nathan is not very good at computers.
4. Sean can't help Nathan with his computer problems.
5. The boys want to cook a meal together.

b) Watch for details.

1. What colour is Sean's shirt?
2. What's behind the basketball court?
3. How many bottles of water are there?
4. What colour is the bench that they sit on?

CULTURE

A lot of Irish and Northern Irish people moved to the UK in the past. Today about 6 million people in the UK have at least one Irish or Northern Irish grandparent. Do you have family in other countries?

3 (SPEAKING) Talk about the film.

Watch the film again from the start to 1:00.
How do the kids feel? Match the feelings with the names and tell your partner.

Sean | Nathan | Laura | Marley | angry | proud | unhappy | sorry | ...

VIEWING SKILLS

To make a film, you need a lot of people, for example the scriptwriter, a director, a camera operator and make-up artists. Would you like to work on a film production?

I can understand a film about a conflict.

Checklist

I can understand information about Northern Ireland. ✓

83

I can give advice to a friend. ✓

Think positive. • I have a good idea. • Why don't you …? • Maybe you should … • If I were you, … . • If you told …, … .

83

I can buy things and have a conversation in a small shop. ✓

How are you today? • I'd like … . • This … is less expensive than that one. • Anything else? • Here's your change.

84

I can understand a newspaper report about a disaster. ✓

84

I can pass on information about a B & B. ✓

85

I can understand a film about a conflict. ✓

(TASK) A newspaper report

Work in groups of three or four students. Each group thinks about an interesting, fun, or scary event during their last school year. Each group writes a report about it.

Step 1

Collect ideas.

Choose an event. Collect ideas. Make a mind map.

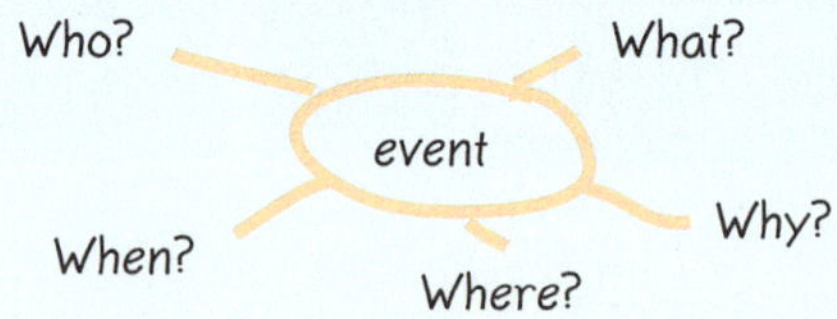

Step 2

Look at the example.

It shows the most important features of a newspaper report.

1 Headline
2 Date, author
3 Introduction
4 Main part
5 Ending

1 **Film crew visits local school**

2 **7th April 2016, by Jamie Smith**

3 **A film crew was at Hollywell School on Saturday. But nobody knows what the film will be!**

4 Students heard the news yesterday from the headteacher, Lucy Green. Mrs Green told us: "A film company came to the school on Saturday and they filmed in the morning and the afternoon. We are all very excited, but we don't know the name of the film yet." "No children or teachers were at the school. The caretaker opened the doors at 9 o'clock but left after that," she added.

5 Film companies often work in Northern Ireland, of course, but Hollywell School has never been in a film before.

Hollywell School

Step 3

Write the introduction, the main part and the ending.

a) Introduction:
Write one or two sentences.
Answer the Wh-questions.

It took place in … on … . • … were there. •
… because … .

b) Main part:
Write more details about the event.

First …
Then … • After that … • …

c) Ending:
Write one or two sentences to finish your report.

In the end … . • Finally … . • …

Step 4

Find one or two photos.

Write captions for the photos.
Find a headline.
Headlines are always very short.
Use about five words only.
Say who wrote the report and when.

Step 5

Check your report. → M Writers' conference, p. 175

Are there any spelling mistakes?
Did you write clearly?
Do you have a headline?
Did you add a date?
…

WRITING SKILLS

If you use a computer, the spell check can help you to avoid mistakes.
Make your reports more fun to read. Use connectives (but, and, after that). Add adjectives.

Step 6

Present your report. Give feedback to other groups. → M Tip top, p. 175

Battleships game

1. Work with a partner.
   You need (each):
   a sheet of checked paper (size A4),
   a pen or pencil, a ruler

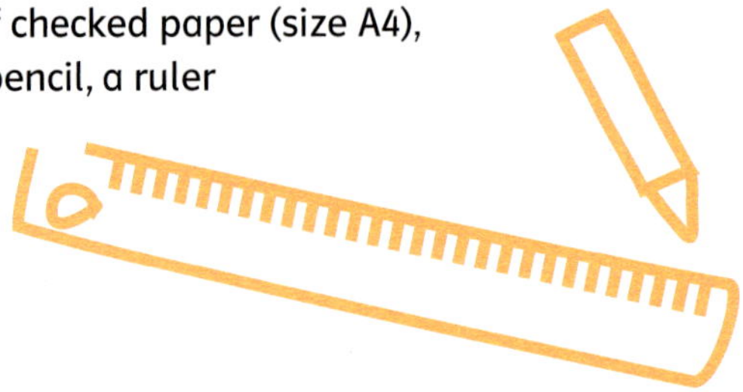

2. Draw two grids of 10x10 squares.

3. Label the grids.

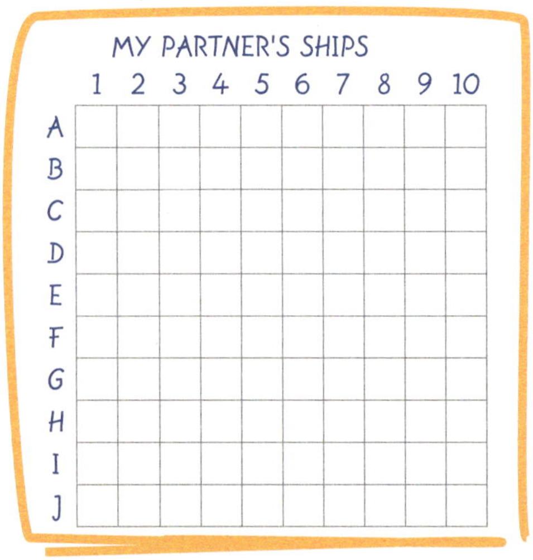

4. Choose **one word from each category.**
Write the words across → or down ↓ into your grid 1. But don't show them to anybody!

Titanic (= ship with 7 letters)
ANNOYED SURVIVE BELFAST CAPITAL FURIOUS

Motor ship (= ship with 5 letters)
COAST ADULT MURAL SMART VISIT

Sailing ships (= ship with 4 letters)
LOAF SHIP MOVE THAN LESS

Boat (= ship with 3 letters)
HIT DIE JAR ASK SAD

	1	2	3	4	5	6	7	8	9	10
A		C								
B		O				S	H	I	P	
C		A								
D		S		S	U	R	V	I	V	E
E		T								
F					H	I	T			

5. Start playing:
Partner A: call out a certain box, for example "B2".
Partner B: answer "miss" (box with no letter in it) or "hit" (box with a letter in it; say the letter).

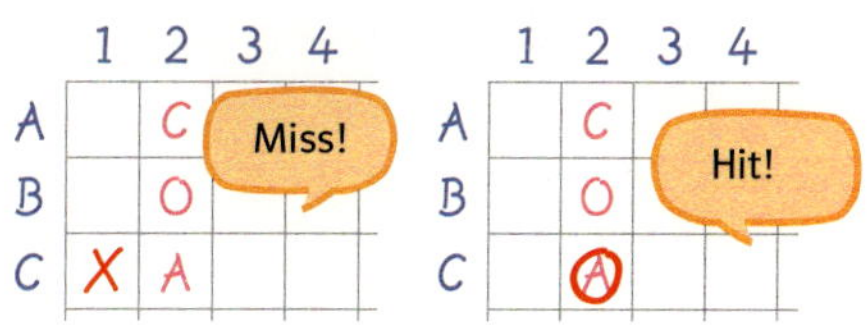

6. Draw a circle "O" for a miss or an "X" for a hit into grid 2. Take turns.

MY PARTNER'S SHIPS

	1	2	3	4	5	6	7	8	9	10
A					O					
B					O	X	X			
C										
D										
E										

Winner of the game: the player who shot all their partner's ships first

You can find out how to describe pictures here.

A day in Lisburn

1 What, who, where?

Answer the questions about the picture.

1. What can you see?
2. Who can you see?
3. Where is it?

Look at the photo closely before your start talking about it in a general way. Answer the three questions in only one or two sentences.

2 Describe the picture.

a) Add more details.

In the upper left corner there is ... .
On the left (side) I can see ... .
In the lower left corner there are ... .
In the background I can see ... .
In the middle there is ... .
...

Choose where to start. You can start from the upper left corner and then go to the lower right corner, for example.

b) Look at the picture again.
Where are the people or the things?

In front of the ice cream van there is ... .
Next to the book shop there are ... .

Say where the person or thing is with these prepositions:
next to, between, behind, over, in, on, in front of, under.

3 What are the people doing?

Look at the people and say what they are doing.

In front of the café some people are having lunch.
The dog is eating the boy's ice cream.

Say what the people are doing at the moment. Use the present progressive.

88/1-2
89/3-5

4 Describe your own picture.

Choose a picture or photo and describe it.

Find more online:
i8ce82

In this unit you will …
- find out about Ireland.
- talk to people in a host family.
- plan a journey by public transport.
- read a story about moving to another country.
- pass on information about an actor.
- watch a film about music lessons.

9 2,9

Unit 5
Welcome to Ireland

The green republic

Welcome to Ireland! The Republic of Ireland is in the European Union and it uses the euro. Unlike Northern Ireland, the Republic isn't a part of the United Kingdom.

Music has a special place in the hearts of the Irish. There are many famous Irish rock and pop bands, and people often play music in pubs. Classical music is also popular, and many cities have a youth orchestra.

1 Talk about the pictures.

a) Describe the pictures.
You can use these phrases:

- In the foreground …
- In the middle …
- In the background …
- …

b) Which picture would you like to learn more about? What would you like to know about it?

92/1-2

2 Correct the wrong sentences.

1. Ireland has the same money as the United Kingdom.
   That's **wrong**. Ireland has the euro.
2. Rock music is popular in Ireland.
3. Keith Hanley was second in a competition for dancers.
4. In Dublin you can take courses in film making.
5. People only have St Patrick's Day parades in Cork and Dublin.

Keith Hanley is a young Irish singer from a small town near Cork. He is the surprise winner of 'The Voice of Ireland' singing competition. Keith's favourite musical style is hip hop.

Dublin, the capital of Ireland, has lots of arts programmes for young people. In workshops they can learn how to dance and make films. There are also courses in music and acting.

Every year on 17th March, the Irish celebrate St Patrick's Day. There are many parades and parties, not just in Ireland but all around the world. Most people wear green, the Irish colour.

3 (LISTENING) Listen to the information about Keith Hanley.

2,10

Choose the right answer.

1. Keith Hanley's age is 17 • 19 • 29.
2. The morning after he won, Keith stayed in bed • called his mum • went to work.
3. He works with old people • a rock band • children.
4. He knows sign language from his aunt • brother • uncle.
5. Keith soon wants to write his own songs • a book about his life • a letter to his biggest fan.

to care for [tə 'keə ˌfɔː] – sich kümmern um
sign language ['saɪn ˌlæŋgwɪdʒ] – Zeichensprache
with special needs [wɪθ 'speʃl ˌniːdz] – mit Behinderung
guitar [gɪ'tɑː] – Gitarre

I can understand information about Ireland. ✓

At home with the O'Brians

1 (READING) Read the dialogue. → M Dramatic reading, p. 171

2,11 93/1

Leo Kurz (14), from Hanau in Germany

Conor O'Brian (14), from Cork in Ireland

Conor: Here we are. I'll show you the house. Just leave your bags here in the corridor. And you don't have to take off your shoes. … Right, here's the kitchen and there's the fridge. You just help yourself with the food and drinks. You don't have to ask, feel completely at home. … What else? We don't usually have breakfast together during the week but we all meet for dinner around 6:30 in the evening.

Leo: Do you think we could have a traditional Irish breakfast one day, please? I've heard that an Irish breakfast is very different from a German one.

Conor: No problem. We can have it at the weekend. I'll tell dad. He makes the best scrambled eggs in the world. But on weekdays I often just have cereal or toast with jam.

Leo: That's fine. Some people like bread with ham or cheese, but I prefer a sweet breakfast.

Conor: So, this is the bathroom. Mum put some towels for you over there on that shelf. You can use the shampoo too, but please don't take the blue bottle. That's my sister Maddy's. I'll introduce you to her later. At the moment she's practising with her school band. … So, are you nervous about your own concert?

Leo: Yes, a little. It's my first concert with our orchestra in another country.

Conor: I'm sure it'll be grand. OK, where were we? You can put your toothbrush and other things over here. Did you bring an adaptor?

Leo: Err, I think I didn't.

Conor: Don't worry about that. We always have one at home, because we often have guests from different places. You can use ours.

Leo: Great. Thanks.

Conor: Oh, the phone is ringing. Just a second.

Conor: That's Maddy's bedroom, and that's Jamie's. I'll share my room with you. Here we are. Just make yourself at home. Are you hungry? Would you like some tea?

Leo: No, thanks. I don't drink tea.

Conor: Ha. I don't mean the drink, but the meal. Mum's preparing a snack in the kitchen right now. We call that 'tea' here. Just come down when you're ready and join us.

Leo: Thanks a lot.

2 Work with the text.

a) Describe the situation: Where are Leo and Conor? Why is Leo there? What are they doing?

b) Answer the questions.

1. When is the family's dinner time?
2. Why hasn't Leo had an Irish breakfast yet?
3. Who is Maddy?
4. Why is Maddy not at home?
5. Why is Leo nervous?
6. What does 'tea' mean for Conor?

CULTURE

Most British and Irish people have a hot meal in the evening. Some people call this meal 'tea', others use the word 'dinner'. What time do you eat?

2,12

3 (LISTENING) Listen and find out.

What's the problem with …
- … the window?
- … dinner?
- … the time?

93/2

4 Make a mind map with things for a trip. → M Think-pair-share, p. 175

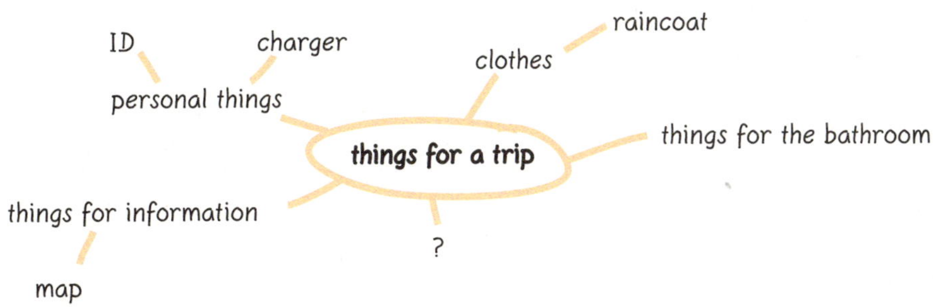

5 What would you take on a trip?

93/3

a) Match the things for a trip with the words. Add them to your mind map. → ○ p. 126

1. nail scissors
2. comb
3. toothpaste
4. hairdryer
5. shower gel
6. body lotion

93/4

b) Say when you need these things. → V In the bathroom, p. 211

hair gel | soap | perfume | mirror | hairbrush | …

1. You need it when your hair is a mess.

94/5

6 (SPEAKING) Play the game: I'm going to take …

A: I'm going to take a toothbrush.
B: I'm going to take a toothbrush and an umbrella.
C: I'm going to take a toothbrush, an umbrella and … .

SPEAKING SKILLS

When you can't think of a word fast enough, use little words like "Well … / I think … / Uhm …" to win some extra time.

Language detectives → G13, p. 166

I often have cereal or toast with jam.
Mum is preparing something in the kitchen now.

What is the difference between the two situations?
Find more examples in the dialogue on page 96.

Die Signalwörter helfen dir, die richtige Zeitform zu finden.

7 Choose the right form. → M Peer correction, p. 173

94/6
95/7-8

1. Conor: Hi Leo, what **do you do** • **are you doing** right now?
2. Leo: I **listen** • **I'm listening** to some new songs.
3. Conor: What kind of music are they? I usually **listen** • **am listening** to rock music. What do you like?
4. Leo: I always **enjoy** • **am enjoying** hip hop music a lot. This is Torch OneTwo, a new German rapper. He usually **has** • **is having** interesting things to say. He often **writes** • **is writing** about his own life.
5. Conor: The music sounds OK to me. What **does he talk** • **is he talking** about now?
6. Leo: He **sings** • **is singing** about his town, Heidelberg.
7. Conor: Well, this is really something new for me. We never **hear** • **are hearing** about German hip hop around here.

8 Complete the text messages.

a) Simple present or present progressive? → ○ p. 127

95/9

1 Leo Germanguy
I'm in the bathroom right now and I —— (look for / towels). Where are they?

2 Conor O'Brian
We always —— (put / in cupboard). Let me know if you can't find them there.

3 Little Bro Conor
I am still at school and I —— (finish / Art project). I'm going to be home late. Will u tell mum?

4 Mad O'Brian
Sure, I'll tell her. But she —— (hate / it) when you're late.

5 Mad O'Brian
I'm here and I —— (wash / hair). And now my shampoo isn't here. Grrrrrh!!! M

6 Conor O'Brian
Boy, Maddy is angry. She never —— (share / shampoo). Did you take it???

b) Write Leo's text messages for these situations.

96/10

- at bus stop / no school bus
- dinner with family / like the food

9 Complete the sentences.

a) Complete the answers. Use possessive pronouns. → ○ p. 127

6/11a)

1. Is this Dad's raincoat?
   – Yes, this is his. Where did you find it?
2. Is this Maddy's tea cup?
   – No, —— is on the kitchen table.
3. Is that your shirt?
   – Yes, that's ——. Can you give it to me, please?
4. Spike is your family's cat, is that right?
   – Yes, he's ——. Why, what did he do this time?
5. Is that your chocolate pudding? – No, —— is already in my stomach.
6. And this is your parents' room, right? – Yes, it's ——. Don't go in there, please.
7. That's Conor's bike, isn't it? – No, I'm sure it isn't. —— is red.

GRAMMAR → G14, p. 167

my – mine	your – yours
his – his	her – hers
our – ours	their – theirs

b) Leo has forgotten many things. Who can he borrow things from?

6/11b)

Mr O'Brian
Conor
Mr and Mrs O'Brian
Jamie
Maddy

1. Jamie has a phone charger. I can borrow his.

10 (YOUR TURN) A text message dialogue → V Things for a trip, p. 215

96/12

You are staying with a host family: Your partner is in town and you are at home. Write a text message dialogue.

A (at home)

1. Say hi. Ask what your partner is doing and where he or she is.
3. Answer. Say that you have forgotten … / you can't find … / you would like to borrow ….
5. Answer: It's a good / bad idea because … .

B (in town)

2. Answer your partner. Ask: Is he or she OK?
4. Answer your partner. Ask: Can he or she meet for an ice cream (where, when)?
6. Finish the dialogue.

WRITING SKILLS

When you are writing in CAPITAL letters, you are "SHOUTING" at the other person. Stay polite.

I can talk to people in a host family. ✓

Getting around in Dublin

1 (READING) Read the flyer and the dialogue. → M Read and look up, p. 174

2,13
97/1

Jamie: I can't wait to go to the Striking Moves workshop tomorrow. I'm sure they will teach us some new moves there.

Lisa: That's why I want to talk to you. We should plan our journey.

Jamie: Where is the workshop, anyway?

Lisa: It's in Sackville Place. I've been there before. It's not too far from The Spire on O'Connell Street.

Jamie: So how do we get there? I don't often use public transport!

Lisa: Here, I've brought the timetables for the bus and the tram. You really needn't try the homepages for public transport, they're not helpful at all. All right, let's see what we can find out. We can take the number 9 bus to Goldenbridge. We must get off the bus there and change to the tram. Then it's ten stops on the Red Line. Our stop is Abbey Street.

Jamie: How long do you think the journey will take?

Lisa: About an hour. Maybe longer. The bus may not be on time, you know that they usually aren't.

Jamie: Fair enough. Well, the workshop starts at 10 a.m., so we must leave by 8:30 a.m. We really mustn't be late. Why don't we meet at the bus stop near my house? There's a bus at 8:25.

Lisa: OK, that sounds good to me.

Jamie: Good. How much is the fare?

Lisa: We can get tickets from the bus driver that are valid all day for three euros and fifty cents each. But we needn't spend that much money. A single ticket only costs one euro and forty cents each. And then it's the same for the way back.

Jamie: Right, let's do that. See you tomorrow, then! I won't be late …

STRIKING MOVES
Dance and drumming worksho

Take part in our dance and drumming project:
Practise great rhythms and lear the coolest moves!
Perform with us at the Big Bang Festival!

Saturdays 21st, 28th June and 5th, 12th July
10 a.m. – 5 p.m.

14 Sackville Place, Dublin

For ages 15 – 35

2 Find the information. → M Think-pair-share, p. 175

a) What can you find out about the Striking Moves workshop? Answer the questions *what? when? where? who?*

b) Read the dialogue again and say what the numbers mean.

1. 9
2. ten
3. one forty
4. 8:30
5. three fifty
6. 8:25

c) When would you choose a day ticket and when single tickets?

CULTURE

You can travel by bus or tram in Dublin. There are two different systems and there are two different maps. What public transport is there where you live?

3 Find the odd one out.

a) Which word doesn't go with the others? Why? → ○ p. 128

97/2

1. train • bus • ticket • taxi
2. fare • price • receipt • present
3. stop • line • station • museum
4. on time • sure • late • early
5. clock • date • timetable • map
6. plan • change • get on • get off

b) What are these tickets valid for? → V Public transport, p. 212

97/3

daily · weekly · monthly · single · return · annual · adult

A daily ticket is valid for one day.

4 (SPEAKING) Find the way. → M Milling around, p. 172

98/4

a) Look at the map and find the best way to get from James's to … → ○ p. 128

- George's Dock
- Connolly train station
- Milltown
- Blackhorse

To get from James's to George's Dock, take the Red Line. Stay on the tram for eight stops. Get off the tram and you're there.

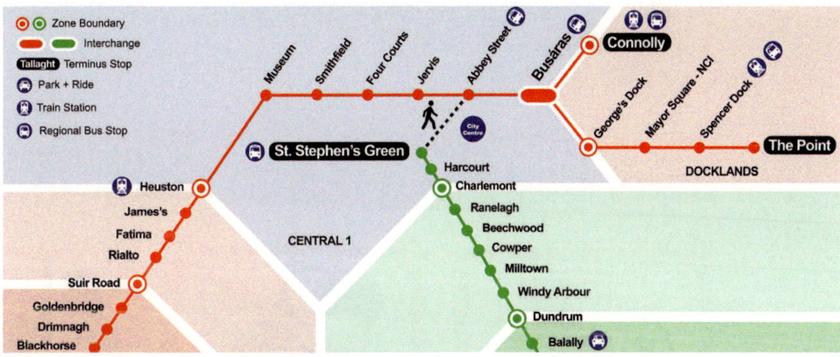

b) Make a list with four places. Partner A's list has starting points and partner B's list has places to go. Give each other directions.

5 (SONG) Luminous

2,14

Listen to the song by the Irish group, Jedward: What will the singer always know, and why?

We see the day, tryin' to fight it.
It's all in vain, 'cause we know the night wins,
But we don't care,
We're lighting up like a flare.

It's so unreal,
The light that you're shining.
You make me feel like
The darkness won't matter,
'Cause you and I,
Don't care where the day has gone.
We don't need the break of dawn,
We don't need the break of dawn.

(Chorus): And I will always know
where you are,
'Cause I can see you glow in the dark.
We got the stars, and moon in us,
We're always gonna be luminous.

Language detectives → G15, p. 168

We must get off the bus.
We needn't buy tickets for the journey back.
We mustn't be late.
We can take the number 9 bus.
The bus may not be on time.

Must, mustn't, needn't, can and may, may not are special verbs.
In which situations do you use them?

6 Fill in can or mustn't.

98/5

1. The kids at the workshop mustn't be late. The teachers really don't like that.
2. They —— eat during the dance classes. There is a lunch break, when they can eat.
3. They —— stop dancing when they need a break. That isn't a problem.
4. They —— talk when the teachers dance, or they won't hear what the teachers say.
5. They —— drink water when they are thirsty. There's a drinks machine outside.
6. They —— learn new dance steps.

7 (SPEAKING) What must you do on a bus? What mustn't you do?

a) Explain these school bus rules. → ○ p. 129

99/6a)

1 

show

2 
eat

3 
talk

4 
sit

5 
bring

6 
leave

7 
listen

8 
push

b) Talk with a partner about these bus rules. Do you think they are good rules? Why or why not? Then make three rules that you would like to see.

99/6b)

- You must talk quietly!
- You mustn't eat chewing gum!
- You mustn't put your feet on the seats!

8 Match the parts of the sentences and choose must or needn't. → M Peer correction, p. 173

99/7

1. I have two tickets. So you	must	take our coats? It's a warm day!
2. Do you really think we	needn't	talk so loudly.
3. It's already four o'clock! We		call her. We can meet her at the station.
4. Alan is at the workshop. So we		buy one. You can have one of mine.
5. I can hear you very well. You		go now or we won't get our bus.
6. Do you know where Kate is? We		get off the bus here.
7. That's our stop. We		wait for him at the bus stop.

9 Must, needn't or mustn't?

a) Choose the right verb in these rules for dogs. → ○ p. 129

99/8
100/9

1. Dogs travel free. You **must** • **needn't** • **mustn't** buy an extra ticket.
2. Your dog **must** • **needn't** • **mustn't** be with you all the time.
3. Your dog **must** • **needn't** • **mustn't** hurt people.
4. It **must** • **needn't** • **mustn't** be nice to other people.
5. You **must** • **needn't** • **mustn't** carry a small dog in a bag. It's OK to hold it.
6. You **must** • **needn't** • **mustn't** play with your dog when you're on the bus.

b) Find rules for a pet at home. Write a list.

0/10-11

sleep · eat · play · go out · sit · drink · ...

10 (YOUR TURN) A journey by public transport → V Public transport, p. 216

a) Find out how to get from the airport or train station to your house on public transport.

101/1

b) Write an e-mail to a friend from another country. Give him or her advice how to get to your house from the airport or train station.

E-MAIL

Hi Helen,

Let me tell you how to get to my house from the airport. You should take the train ...

You should take ... .
Then ... .
It's ... stops.
The journey takes ... .

You must buy ...
You needn't ...
It costs ...
...

I can plan a journey by public transport. ✓

A different kind of gold

1 Have you ever moved to another place? How did you feel?

→ M Think-pair-share, p. 175

2 (READING) Read the story.

2,15

It was St Patrick's Day yesterday and I only wished I was back home in Ireland. You see, my Dad and I moved here two months ago and I still miss my Irish friends and our nice little home in Donegal.

Oh, I should introduce myself to you. My name is Niamh. That's an old Irish girl's name. You say it like it rhymes with 'leave'. I always have to explain it to people here in England. That's where we moved, Northampton in England.

Dad used to work in a factory in Donegal in the northwest of Ireland until it closed last year. He tried to find another job in the area, but there weren't any because lots of other factories were closing too. Finally my Dad found a new job – in England. And that meant that we both had to move to here.

So yesterday it was my favourite holiday. St Patrick's Day is the holiday of the Irish. Back home we have lots of parades and parties on that day. Everyone wears green clothes. In fact the whole city is green. We send cards with shamrocks and rainbows on them and give each other sweets in gold paper. The shamrock is our national flower. The rainbows and the sweets go back to an old Irish story. It says that at the end of a rainbow there is a pot of gold and that you can go there and find it.

Here in Northampton there were parties too. That almost felt like being back home. But I still don't know a lot of people and places here, so I stayed at home. That's why the day just made me feel very lonely and homesick. I got even sadder because the netball girls Sonya, Billy and Nisha, who I really like, didn't answer any of my calls.

3 Make notes about St Patrick's Day.

Write down the pieces of information about St Patrick's Day which are new to you.

4 Talk about feelings.

a) Make a list of adjectives and verbs that describe how Niamh feels. Compare with a partner.

b) How do Niamh's feelings change? Say why.

5 Explain the title of the story.

Read the poem again and explain what the 'different kind of gold' is.

READING SKILLS

In some stories the reader has to use clues to find out for himself or herself how the people feel, and even what really happened. We call this kind of reading 'reading between the lines' of the text.

When Dad came home from work that afternoon, I was just sitting there, staring out of the window.
"Are you OK, Niamh?" he asked me.
"Yes," I said.
Dad tried to cheer me up with this old poem (don't ask me where he got that one from):

At the end of the rainbow is a pot of gold,
My dad would say to me.
We packed our bags, our house was sold,
We crossed the Irish Sea.
But until the fable once foretold
Actually comes to be,
The wealth of friends and family old
Is gold enough for me.

He wasn't very successful, though: I still felt miserable and I just wanted to feel sorry for myself. I thought that nothing could cheer me up. Do you know what I mean?

Later that day, in the late afternoon, our doorbell rang. Dad sent me to open the door. I couldn't believe my eyes. There they were, standing in front of me: the netball girls. All three dressed in green clothes and big green party hats on. And Billy had a green shamrock on her face. I couldn't help but laugh.
"Surprise!" they screamed together. "Your dad says it's OK to take you to a St Patrick's Day party in our youth centre. Do you want to join us?"
You bet I did. I rushed into my room and grabbed my Paddy's Day outfit as fast as I could, and off we went.

So I went to my first Paddy's Day party in England. And I went there together with the girls. Maybe this was the beginning of something wonderful.

6 Choose one of these tasks.

02/1-3
03/4-5

a) Some singers and bands have left Ireland to become successful in Britain or the USA. Others come from a family which moved to these countries a long time ago.

Find information and photos on the internet for a short presentation about one of them.

→ M 1-minute-presentation, p. 170

OR

b) Write your own poem like this. Choose one of these titles:

Friends | Summer | Without you | I'm angry!

			F	I	N	D
	P	A	**R**	T	Y	
		M	**I**	S	S	
		H	**E**	L	P	
	F	U	**N**			
G	U	I	**D**	E		
			S	A	F	E

I can understand a story about moving to another country. ✓

A German star

INTERNET

Emilia Schüle

Die Schauspielerin Emilia Schüle kam als Einjährige 1993 aus Russland nach Deutschland. Bereits mit acht Jahren begann sie, Ballettstunden und Unterricht in Hip-Hop und Street Dance zu nehmen. Mit 13 Jahren nahm sie am Theaterworkshop „Talents Getting Started“ teil und beeindruckte die Jury mit ihrem Können. Danach erhielt sie erste Rollen als Schauspielerin und spielte auch in einigen Werbefilmen mit.

Emilia Schüle

Ihre erste Hauptrolle hatte sie 2007 in dem Film „Manatu – Nur die Wahrheit rettet dich“, in dem es um ein magisches Brettspiel geht. Auch in der bekannten Serie „Tatort“ spielte sie schon mit. Bekannt wurde sie schließlich durch die beiden Filme „Freche Mädchen“ und „Freche Mädchen 2“, in denen sich alles um Teenagerfreundschaften und erste Liebesprobleme dreht.

Emilia hat in dieser kurzen Zeit ihrer Schauspielerkarriere schon einige Preise verliehen bekommen: Im Jahr 2014 erhielt sie die „Goldene Kamera“ und den „Deutschen Schauspielerpreis“ in der Kategorie „Beste Schauspielerin Nachwuchs“. Trotz dieser frühen Erfolge war es ihr sehr wichtig, die Schule abzuschließen. Während des letzten Schuljahres arbeitete sie sogar nebenher als Schauspielerin.

1 Talk about Emilia Schüle.

104/1-2

You are on an exchange visit in Ireland. Your exchange partner sees the article and is interested in acting. Tell her about Emilia Schüle. Say:

1. who she is
2. how she became an actor
3. what TV and film work she has done

2 And you?

Would you like to be an actor? Say why or why not.

I can pass on information about an actor. ✓

The guitar lesson

1 Talk about music. → M Think-pair-share, p. 175

What is music good for?
What can you do with music?
Collect words.

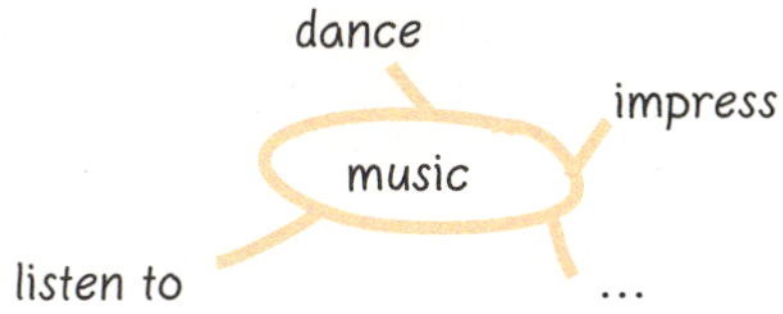

CULTURE

Music plays in important role in many people's lives all over the world. Most countries have special instruments. Some of the traditional instruments in Ireland are the harp and the bodhran (a kind of drum). Can you find more traditional instruments from other countries?

2 (VIEWING) Watch the film.

10 a) Watch the film from the beginning to 1:45. Find the right answer.

1. Where does Ciara (the music teacher) want to go?
   a) Victoria Station b) Greenwich
2. Where did Hayley work?
   a) in a café and on a pineapple farm b) at a restaurant and on a wind farm
3. What does Hayley mean when she says, "I go wherever the wind takes me."
   a) She'll go to a very windy place next. b) She doesn't know where she'll go next.

b) Watch the film from 1:45 to the ending.

1. Where does Marley find out about the guitar lessons?
2. What does Alicia think about Marley's idea at the end?
3. Why does Marley want to have guitar lessons?

3 (SPEAKING) Talk about the film.

a) Which places are not in the film?

bus station | café | supermarket | streets in Greenwich | music school

b) What do you think: why did the film makers choose the places to shoot the film?

VIEWING SKILLS

It is difficult to shoot a film outside. When you shoot in a busy street, people may walk by and there may be background noise. And of course the weather may change too. But shooting in small rooms is not easy either. So film companies often shoot scenes in a studio.

I can understand a film about music lessons. ✓

Checklist

I can understand information about Ireland. ✓

105

I can talk to people in a host family. ✓

I didn't pack any … . • You can put your … here. • We usually eat at half past six.

105

I can plan a journey by public transport. ✓

You can take the number 9 bus to … . • You must change at … . • The journey takes … minutes. • The tickets cost … .

106

I can understand a story about moving to another country. ✓

106

I can pass on information about an actor. ✓

107

I can understand a film about learning to play an instrument. ✓

(TASK) A quiz

Work in groups and write questions for a quiz about the five countries of the British Isles. Each group writes eight questions for one country. The groups are the teams when you do the quiz.

Step 1

Collect ideas and decide on your questions.

a) Collect ideas for questions about your country.

England

Northern Ireland

Wales

Scotland

The Republic of Ireland

Here are some ideas for questions (you can ask about things that were in the units in this book):
- food?
- sport?
- town?
- famous person?
- flag?
- transport?
- …

CULTURE

This is the flag that is usually connencted with Northern Ireland. It is called the St Patrick's Cross. (Officially, Northern Ireland doesn't have its own flag.) It uses the Union Flag.

b) Make a long list with everyone's ideas. Then look at all the ideas together and agree on a short list.
→ M Placemat, p. 173

STUDY SKILLS

Listen to all the ideas carefully and give everyone the chance to say something. Agree on the ideas you want to use for the questions.

Step 2

Write your questions and check the answers.

a) Each student writes a card with one question and the answer on the back.

b) Another student checks the English. A third student checks that the answer is correct.

c) Each student in the team has to read one or more questions. Decide on the order of the questions and practise before you do the quiz.

Step 3

Get ready for the quiz.

1. When can you do the quiz?
2. Who can be the umpire and start/finish the quiz?
3. Which team reads its questions first?

Each team can make a flag. You can also bring a mascot! Good luck!

Step 4

Do the quiz.

Each team reads its questions. The other teams write the answers.

SPEAKING SKILLS

Read the question in a loud and clear voice. Look at the other teams when you read. If you don't understand a question, ask politely. (If you know the answer, keep quiet!)

- Can you say that again please?
- Sorry, I didn't understand that!
- Can you speak louder, please?

One student from each team checks the answers at the end and gives the results to the umpire. The umpire says who the winner is.

Step 5

Talk about the quiz. → M Round robin, p. 174

Did you enjoy the quiz? What was good/not so good about it?

Let's dance ... the Irish way

CULTURE

Irish Dancing has a very characteristic style: You keep your arms close to your body and let your legs do all the work. One possible reason for that is that people used to put a door on the ground to dance on it. That way there wasn't much room to move.

Learn how to do skips in Irish dancing

Partner A and B face each other
A: look at the pictures and give instructions to B
B: close your book and follow the instructions

Before you start: Find the basic position

A says:

- Stand straight.
- Look to the front.
- Relax your shoulders and arms: you only need your feet.
- Place your right foot in front, pointing to the right.
- Place your left foot at the back, pointing to the left.

A sees:

Getting started: Rising onto the toes

- Rise onto your toes.

Don't give up!
Try again!
That was excellent!
Wow! You look like an Irish dancer!

Step 1: Shift your weight to the front

- Shift your weight to the front.
- The foot at the back goes up a little bit.

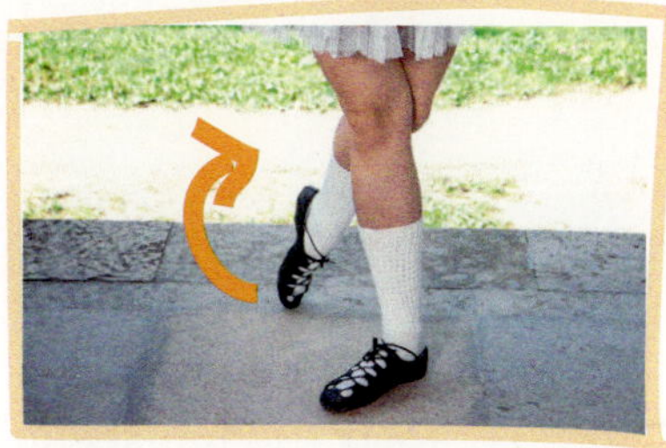

Step 2: Shift your weight to the back

- Shift your weight to the back.
- The front toe goes up a little bit.

Step 3: Hop and leg shift

- Shift your weight to the front again, do a HOP on your right toes and lift the left leg.

Step 4: Get ready for the next round

- Now place the left foot in front and do it again: front-back-front-HOP.

Practice

Let's find a rhythm and do it again and again:
- right foot in front: front-back-front-HOP.
- left foot in front: front–back-front-HOP.
- right foot …

Now B gives instructions and A dances.

You can learn how to write the ending of a story here.

2,16 The magic water stone by Clare Treleaven (2014)

A visitor

"You can keep it until we find its owner," said Max's mum. She didn't want any more pets. The dog died two months ago and Max was very sad. The cat didn't look like a stray. It was fat and clean. Max took a photo with his mobile and started to make a poster to put up around the village. It was a beautiful black cat. It looked intelligent, too. It followed Max into his bedroom and sat on the bed.

"You should sleep in the kitchen," said Max, but he really wanted the cat to stay. He missed his dog.

It was late and Max had a maths exam the next day so he decided to go to bed early. He was asleep in minutes.

Max started to dream instantly. He was following the cat through a dark forest. He didn't know the forest. It wasn't like anywhere he knew around his village, Kingskerswell, because it looked too big and old. He didn't know any of the trees either.

The cat moved very easily through the dark night but it was difficult for Max to keep up because there were big branches on the forest floor and he had to climb over them. He wanted to look at the trees. They were very tall and had lots of very odd leaves. There was a strange, horrible smell and suddenly Max knew that he wasn't in his village or even in Devon. He wasn't in England.

"Where am I?" he asked himself.

Out of nowhere a voice replied: "Don't think about that now, follow, quick!"

Max was confused. He couldn't see anyone near him. The voice was inside his head! That wasn't possible. The cat was running very fast as if it had something very important to do. It looked back at Max and then jumped into a small hole. Max heard the voice again.

"Quick! Get in the hole with me."

Setting

1. Ask yourself, how does the writer present the information and why does she do it this way?
   Often the important pieces of information are right there in the text. But sometimes you also have to read between the lines.
   Here you can find out that the beginning of the story takes place at Max's home.

Characters

2. In the text it says that Max's dog has died.
   The text doesn't tell you directly, but you can find out this: Max must be a boy, because he still lives with his mum and goes to school. He wants to help to find the owner of the cat, so he seems to be nice.

1 Read the text.

a) Answer these questions.

1. What does the writer tell you about the setting and how does she do it?
   Check the example on page 112 for the setting at the beginning. Then find out about the setting in the rest of the text.

2. What does the writer tell you about the characters and how does she do it?
   Check the example on page 112 for Max. Then find out about the cat.

b) Make a timeline for the events in the story.

110/1 ## 2 How does the story go on? Write an ending for the story in 150 words.

a) Prewriting

1. Collect ideas for your text.
2. Plan your text.

b) Drafting

Write down your story.

c) Revising

Read and check your text.

d) Editing

1. Correct the mistakes.
2. Check the punctuation.
3. Check the spelling.

e) Write a clean copy.

Making a mind map or a list can help you with this. You can also exchange ideas with other people.

Make decisions for your text:
- Characters: Who is in the story? (How do they look? What kind of personality do they have? What happened in their past?)
- Setting: Where does your story take place?
- Plot: What happens in your story? Make a timeline for the events.
- How does your story end? There are many ways you can end your story. You can write a happy ending, for example. Or an open ending, which doesn't give all the answers. Or a surprise ending, in which something unexpected happens or the reader finds out something new.

Concentrate on the message when you write your draft, correct mistakes later.

Does your story make sense? Do you need more details? Or can you leave out pieces of information which are not important for the story?

Diff Corner

Unit 1, p. 13

○ **4** (WRITING) **Where can you buy these things?**

Complete the sentences.

A You can buy jeans at the clothes shop.
B You can get bread at the … .
C You can buy a football at the … shop.
D You can find a birthday card at the … shop.
E When you want shoes you go to the … shop.

card · clothes ✓ · sports · shoe · baker's

Unit 1, p. 14

○ **8** **Make sentences.**

1. I sometimes **have** • **go** shopping with my friends at the weekend.
2. We always **meet** • **know** at 11 a.m. in town.
3. My best friend usually **doesn't arrive** • **doesn't like** before 11:30, but we always **wait** • **sell** for him, because he **has** • **knows** all the places to find a bargain.
4. In the afternoon we often **have** • **are** something to drink at a café.
5. My favourite shop **is** • **has** The Busy Bookworm. It **is** • **sells** the best books.
6. My friends don't **wait** • **like** it. They **know** • **prefer** the sports shop.
7. The oldest shops **are** • **have** on the Shambles.
8. After that I usually **go** • **take** the bus to get back home.

Unit 1, p. 14

○ **9** (SPEAKING) **Interview your partner.** → M Double circle, p. 171

Ask a partner questions. He or she gives short answers.

A:				B:
Do you Do your friends Do they Does your dad Does he	+ usually sometimes often	+ buy clothes go to the cinema? do your homework? play football? watch TV?	+ on Saturdays? on Sundays?	Yes, I do. No, I don't. Yes, he / she does. No, he / she doesn't. Yes, they do. No, they don't.

A:
Do you do the shopping on Saturdays?

B:
Yes, I do. / No, I don't.

Unit 1, p.15

○ 10 (WRITING) Make questions and give answers.

1. Do you know (know) where the football stadium is? – Yes, I do. …	turn right / go straight on
2. How do I — (get) there? – You can walk or …	take / bus
3. Does it — (take) long to get there? – Yes, it — . But … .	nice trip
4. Where — (be) the next bus stop? – It's … .	three minutes / down the road
5. When do the buses — (leave)? – I think, … .	every five minutes
6. — (be) bus tickets expensive? – No, …	90p
7. Where — (can) I buy a ticket? – … .	on the bus

Unit 1, p.16

○ 2 Make a table and put in the information.

Hannah: I'm from Manchester, in the north-west of England. It's a large city with more than half a million inhabitants. We have lots of traffic here. So it's noisy, but it's easy to get around the city.
In the past Manchester had lots of industry, there were dirty factories and coal mines.
Our flat is not far from the city centre. It's very small.
The best thing about Manchester? Football!

Tom: I live on a farm in Bramford. That's a small village in the north of England, about 40 miles from Newcastle. We used to live in Newcastle, then we moved to the country.
It's hard work on the farm, we have two goats and many cows. And it's quiet in the village.
Only about 400 people live here. I think the country is boring, but I like the animals.
There are only two buses a day. It's difficult to see friends at the weekend!

Name of place | Town / city / village | Where in England
Good / bad things | In the past | Number of inhabitants

Unit 1, p.17

○ 3 Sort the words into groups. → M Peer correction, p. 173

Copy the table. Put the words and phrases into the right groups.

size of places	where?	sorts of places

in the centre of | village | town | miles away from | big | small | near
in the north/south/east/west of | in the mountains | large | on the border with

Unit 1, p. 18

6 Make Tom's story.

Complete the sentences.

got ✓ | wasn't | fell | got up | wanted
heard | was | had | saw

1. Last Saturday morning things got (get) a little crazy on our farm.
2. I —— (hear) a noise in the garden and I —— (get up).
3. I —— (see) my dad in the garden. He —— (want) to catch Bert and Daisy, our goats.
4. Suddenly he —— (fall) in the mud, head first. It —— (be) so funny. I just —— (have) to laugh.
5. Dad —— (not be) very happy.

Unit 1, p. 18

7 What did they do on Saturday?

Look at the pictures. Correct the sentences.

1. Hannah walked to the baker's in the morning.

2. Hannah sat in the living room at two o'clock.

3. Hannah did her homework in the afternoon.

4. She and her sister made jewellery at five o'clock.

5. Later she wrote a text message.

6. Hannah and her sister were at the cinema in the evening.

1. Hannah didn't walk to the baker's in the morning. She watched TV.

didn't sit … / sat in the garden | didn't walk … / watched TV ✓
didn't do … / played computer games | didn't make … / they cooked a meal
didn't write … / listened to music | weren't … / they were at a shoe shop

Unit 2, p. 35

5 Find the right words. → M Bus stop, p. 170

Match the words with their opposites.

1. small – …
2. slow – …
3. difficult – …
4. unfriendly – …
5. weak – …
6. dangerous – …
7. dry – …
8. unpopular – …
9. loud – …
10. boring – …

friendly · strong · wet · easy · quiet · safe · quick · big · popular · exciting

Unit 2, p. 36

8 How did they do it?

Complete the sentences

1. I climbed the wall slowly. (slow)
2. We arrived at the stadium —— . (safe)
3. The instructor called to us —— . (loud)
4. The rugby team played —— . (brilliant)
5. The tennis player won his match —— . (easy)
6. We rode our bikes —— . (careful)

Add -ly to the adjectives to make adverbs.
Be careful with words like 'careful' and 'easy'!
carefully
easily

Unit 2, p. 36

9 Complete the report.

Choose: adjective or adverb?

Last month Class 9G went on an **exciting • excitingly** camping trip to Wales. We climbed Mount Snowdon on Saturday. It started to rain **heavy • heavily** so we had to find a dry place **quick • quickly**. At lunchtime we ate our picnics **hungry • hungrily**. Then the sun came out and the weather was **nice • nicely** again. On Sunday we went canoeing at Llanberis. We went down the river **slow • slowly**. Everything went **good • well** and no one fell in the water. Phew! You could see that our teacher, Mrs Kent, was **happy • happily** about that too.

GRAMMAR → G4, p. 157

a good song - they sing well
a fast game - she runs fast
a hard day - he works hard

Use adjectives with nouns and forms of 'be'

Unit 2, p. 37

forms of 'be' → adjective

○ 10 (WRITING) Adjective or adverb?

Complete the dialogue.

Mark: Beth, how was horse riding today?
Beth: It was awful • **awfully** (1). It was **wet** • **wetly** (2) and it rained **heavy** • **heavily** (3).
Mark: So, I guess you had to ride **careful** • **carefully** (4)?
Beth: Yes, and there were some **crazy** • **crazily** (5) people on bikes too. Most of them rode **dangerous** • **dangerously** (6).
Mark: Was your horse **nervous** • **nervously** (7) because of them?
Beth: No, it wasn't. You know, Holly is a really **cool** • **cooly** (8) horse. Look, here's a photo. **Nice** • **nicely** (9), isn't it?

Unit 2, p. 39

○ 6 (SPEAKING) Make excuses.

Why can't you do PE? Tell your teacher. Use the words in the box.

I'm so sorry. I can't do PE today.
My head hurts terribly. I have a sore throat too.
I've also twisted my knee. …

- I've burnt my finger / hand / arm / … .
- I've cut my finger / hand / … .
- I've broken my finger / hand / arm / foot / leg …
- My knee / ankle / stomach / … hurts.
- My … is bleeding …

Unit 2, p. 40

○ 8 (SPEAKING) What has Megan already done? What hasn't she done yet?

Find the differences. Talk with a partner. Make questions and answers.

Has Megan …
- put on her uniform
- opened the door
- written a message
- collected bandages
- had lunch
- drunk tea?

Yes, she has. / No, she hasn't.
A: Has Megan already put on her uniform in picture 1? – B: Yes, she has. And in picture 2?

Unit 2, p. 41

9 (SPEAKING) Make dialogues.

Complete the dialogue. Use the simple past (last) or the present perfect (already, yet, just).

Kim: Hey, I — your brother at football training last Monday. (not see) What's wrong with him?
Jamie: He — in hospital last week. (be)
Kim: Oh, I'm sorry to hear that. He — already — his leg many times, right? (hurt)
Jamie: Yes, he — (have). Last time, he and his friend — to try some new cool skateboard tricks. (want)
Kim: When — he — home? (come)
Jamie: My parents — just — him back from the hospital. (bring)
Kim: That's great. — his friend already — the good news? (hear)
Jamie: No, he — (have). I — him yet. (not phone)

Unit 3, p. 54

2 Find the information.

Alexander Graham Bell was an inventor and engineer born in Edinburgh in 1847. Most people know him as the man who invented the telephone. Bell grew up in Edinburgh and went to school there from the age of ten (before that his mother gave him and his brothers lessons at home) and then in London when he was 14.

When he was older he became a teacher in London. But he also had another ambition: His mother and his wife were both deaf, and so Bell became very interested in speech and the human voice. He wanted to make a machine which could change the sounds of speech to electricity and send them down wires.

At the age of 23 Bell moved to Canada with his family, and in 1871 he went to Boston, in the USA. There he opened a school for people who couldn't hear well. And he never gave up on his ambition. After his work at the school, he worked on his invention every night.

Bell invented the telephone in 1876. His invention wasn't made of plastic, like the phones which we use today. It was big and heavy because it was made of metal and wood.

In 1877 he started a company, which sold his invention. Bell's telephone was a big success and he became rich.

The telephone wasn't Bell's only invention, but it stayed his most famous and successful one. Among other things Bell later also invented a metal detector and he tried to build a machine which could fly.

Bell died in his home in Canada in 1922 at age 75. Even today people still remember him as a man whose invention changed the world forever.

p. 120

Where can you find it?

- the place where Bell was born
  Edinburgh (line 2)
- what he invented
- why he was interested in speech
- how he became rich
- the countries in which he lived

Unit 3, p. 55

4 (LISTENING) Listen to John Dunlop's biography.

1,23

Listen to the short profile. Choose the right answer.

John Dunlop
- was born in a) 1850 • b) 1840
- worked as a vet in a) Boston • b) Edinburgh
- moved to a) Ireland • b) Germany
- started his company in a) 1876 • b) 1889
- died in a) 1912 • b) 1921

Unit 3, p. 55

5 Things and materials.

What is the right material?

1. Windows are usually made of **glass** • **rubber.**
2. T-shirts are usually made of **cotton** • **wood.**
3. Car and bike tyres are usually made of **paper** • **rubber.**
4. Phones are usually made of **wood** • **plastic.**
5. Book pages are usually made of **metal** • **paper.**
6. Cars and bikes are usually made of **metal** • **paper.**
7. Tables and chairs are usually made of **wood** • **cotton.**
8. Shoes are usually made of **leather** • **paper.**

Unit 3, p. 56

○ 8 Describe people and things.

Choose 'who' or 'which'.

1. T-shirts and jeans are clothes who • which are usually made of cotton.
2. An inventor is a person who • which has ideas and makes new things.
3. A plane is a machine who • which can fly.
4. A metal detector is a machine who • which finds metal.
5. Scots are people who • which come from Scotland.
6. Scotland is a country who • which has had a lot of inventors.
7. Cars and bikes have tyres who • which are made of rubber.
8. Dunlop was an inventor who • which made a successful tyre with air in it.

Unit 3, p. 56

○ 9 (SPEAKING) Talk about people and things. → M Bus stop, p. 170

Ask your partner. Can he or she find the person or thing?

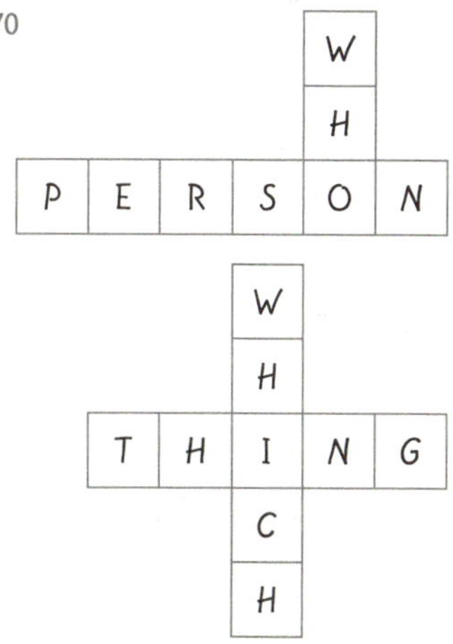

1. person / helps when your pet is ill
   A: It's a person who helps when your pet is ill.
   B: Is it a vet?
   A: That's right!
2. thing / makes electricity with the wind
3. person / cooks meals in a restaurant
4. city / famous for its inventors
5. inventor / was born in Scotland
6. animal / has big ears
7. singer / comes from Germany

elephant? | Edinburgh? | chef? | wind turbine? | vet? ✓ | Bell? | ?

Unit 3, p. 57

○ 10 Make sentences about Bell and Dunlop.

Make sentences with whose.

1. Dunlop was an inventor
2. He was a vet
3. Bell was a teacher
4. He was one of many Scottish inventors

\+ whose +

mother and wife were both deaf.
invention made the bike better.
work made Scotland famous.
trips to farms were often on bad roads.

Unit 3, p. 59

○ 3 Where do people stay on their holidays?

Match the words with their definitions. There are more definitions than you need.

1. hotel
2. campsite
3. bed and breakfast
4. youth hostel
5. caravan
6. holiday cottage

A It's a place where you go camping. (c ...)
B It's a small home which a car can pull from place to place. (c ...)
C It has many rooms and often a swimming pool and large buffets. (h ...)
D It's a place with no bathrooms but with a museum.
E It's a small house which you can rent for your holidays. (h ...)
F It's a place that is almost like home. You stay at a family's place. (b ...)
G It's a big train with beds.
H It's usually a cheap place where young people stay. Often there is only one kitchen for everyone. (y ...)

Unit 3, p. 59

○ 4 (LISTENING) Which picture is it?

1,26 Listen to Jim and Dianne and look at the pictures. Where did they stay?

Look at the chairs, shelves, pictures and lamps.

hotel

bed and breakfast

hostel

Unit 3, p. 60

○ 6 Make sentences about a holiday in a hotel.

Complete the sentences.

1. If everyone agrees, we / stay / at a hotel.
2. If we stay at a hotel, we / have / a TV.
3. It / not be / so boring if I have a TV.
4. You / not meet / other kids if you watch TV all day.
5. If we go to a good hotel, we / have / internet.
6. If we have internet, we / look / for information about interesting things to see and do.
7. We / ask / at the Tourist Information Centre if we don't find anything interesting online.

Unit 3, p. 61

○ 7 What will we do if …?

Look at the pictures. Make sentences.

1. We'll go hiking in the mountains if … .

2. If we leave the hostel after ten o'clock, … .

3. If there's a party at the campsite, … .

4. If we go to the Highlands, … .

5. We'll have a problem with insects if … .

6. We won't stay at that hotel if … .

we'll have a barbecue | we'll take a photo | we stay in a tent
we'll pay fifty pounds extra | there's no swimming pool | the weather is nice / sunny

Unit 4, p. 77

○ 5 Work with adjectives. → M Bus stop, p. 170

Make a chart. Sort the adjectives.

sad ✓ | honest | furious | smart
confident | horrible | optimistic | cautious

☺	☹
h…	sad
s…	f…
c…	h…
o…	c…

You need your dictionary for some of these. There are tips about how to work with a dictionary on page 73.

Unit 4, p. 78

○ 8 (WRITING) Complete the sentences.

If Sarah was 10 years older …

1. move to Belfast

2. find a job

3. work in an office

4. live in a flat

5. meet Julie

6. visit her parents often

Unit 4, p. 78

○ 9 What would happen?

Put in the verbs. → M Peer correction, p. 173

didn't work | spoke | didn't live | went ✓ | didn't listen | met

1. If Sarah — (go) to a sports club, she — (make) new friends.
   If Sarah went to a sports club, she would make new friends.
2. If Sarah — (speak) to her parents about her problems, they — (understand) her better.
3. Sarah and her friend Julie — (be) happier if they — (meet) each other more often.
4. If Julie — (not live) in Belfast, Sarah — (see) her best friend more often.
5. Sarah — (spend) more time in Ashley's room if he — (not listen) to that awful music.
6. If her mum and dad — (not work) so hard, they — (not be) so tired.

Unit 4, p. 79

○ 10 (SPEAKING) What would you do in this situation?

Make and answer questions with a partner. → M Double circle, p. 171

What would you do if …
- you lost your phone?
- you owned an elephant?
- you had a year without school?
- you were the only person in the world?
- you could only eat one sort of food?

I would …
→ ask friend
→ play / show
→ travel
→ go to / …
→ choose

A: What would you do if you lost your phone?
B: I would ask a friend: "Can you call my number, please?" Maybe then I would hear it and find it.

Unit 4, p. 81

○ 4 Work with shopping phrases.

Put the phrases in the right order. → M Peer correction, p. 173

E Hi! – Hello! (v)
F …
D Anything else? – Yes, … . / No, thanks. (u)
A …
C That's £1.37 change. – Thank you. (z)
B …

That'll be £3.63. – Here you are. (x)

Goodbye! – See you. (y)

What would you like? – I'd like … . (w)

Unit 4, p. 82

8 (SPEAKING) What do you think? Talk with a partner.

Which do you prefer? Say why.

1. Giant's Causeway or Stonehenge?

A: I think Giant's Causeway is more interesting than Stonehenge because it's more spectacular. Do you agree?

B: Yes, you're right.

2. chocolate or strawberry? (tasty)
3. winter or summer? (good)
4. dogs or cats? (funny)
5. doing homework or tidying up your room? (boring)
6. speaking any language or talking to animals? (exciting)

as … as | not as … as | -er than | more … than | less … than

Unit 4 p. 83

In verneinten Aussagen und Fragen steht „any"!

9 Some or any?

Put in some or any.

1. I'd like to buy some comics.
2. Sorry, we don't have — tissues.
3. Do you have — sweets in your bag?
4. There is — chocolate over there.
5. Oh dear! We don't have — change!
6. Maggie has — farmer's bread in her shop.
7. Let's eat — cake!
8. Sorry, I didn't buy — orange juice. I forgot!

Unit 5, p. 97

5 What would you take on a trip?

Match the things with the words.

1. nail scissors
2. comb
3. toothpaste
4. hairdryer
5. shower gel
6. body lotion

Unit 5, p. 98

○ 8 Complete the text messages.

Simple present or present progressive?

1 Leo Germanguy
I'm in the bathroom right now and I … (look for / am looking for) towels. Where are they?

2 Conor O'Brian
We always … (put / are always putting) them in the cupboard. Let me know if you can't find them there.

3 Little Bro Conor
I'm going to be home late. I am still at school and I … (finish / am finishing) my Art project. Will u tell mum?

4 Mad O'Brian
Sure, I'll tell her. But she … (hates / is hating) it when you're late.

5 Maddy O'Brian
I'm here and I … (wash / am washing) my hair. And now my shampoo isn't here. Grrrrrh!!! M

6 Conor O'Brian
Boy, Maddy is angry. She never … (shares / is never sharing) her shampoo. Did you take it???

Unit 5, p. 99

○ 9 Complete the sentences.

Complete the answers. Use possessive pronouns.

1. Is this **Dad's** raincoat? – Yes, this is his. Where did you find it?
2. Is this **Maddy's** tea cup? – No, — is on the kitchen table.
3. Is that **your** shirt? – Yes, that's — . Can you give it to **me**, please?
4. Spike is **your family's** cat, is that right? – Yes, he's — . Why, what did he do this time?
5. Is that **your** chocolate pudding? – No, — is already in **my** stomach.
6. And this is your **parents'** room, right? – Yes, it's — . Don't go in there, please.
7. That's **Conor's** bike, isn't it? – No, I'm sure it isn't. — is red.

GRAMMAR → G14, p. 167

my – mine	your – yours
his – his	her – hers
our – ours	their – theirs

Unit 5, p. 101

○ 3 Find the odd one out.

Which word doesn't go with the others? Why?

1. train • bus • ticket
2. fare • receipt • present
3. stop • line • museum
4. on time • sure • late
5. date • timetable • map
6. plan • change • get off

Unit 5, p. 101

○ 4 (SPEAKING) Find the way. → M Milling around, p. 172

Look at the map and find the best way to get from James's to …

- George's Dock
- Connolly train station
- Milltown
- Blackhorse

To get from James's to George's Dock, take the Red Line. Stay on the tram for eight stops. Get off the tram and you're there.

Take the Red Line to … .

Stay on the tram for … stops.

Change at … and walk to … .

Take the Green Line.

…

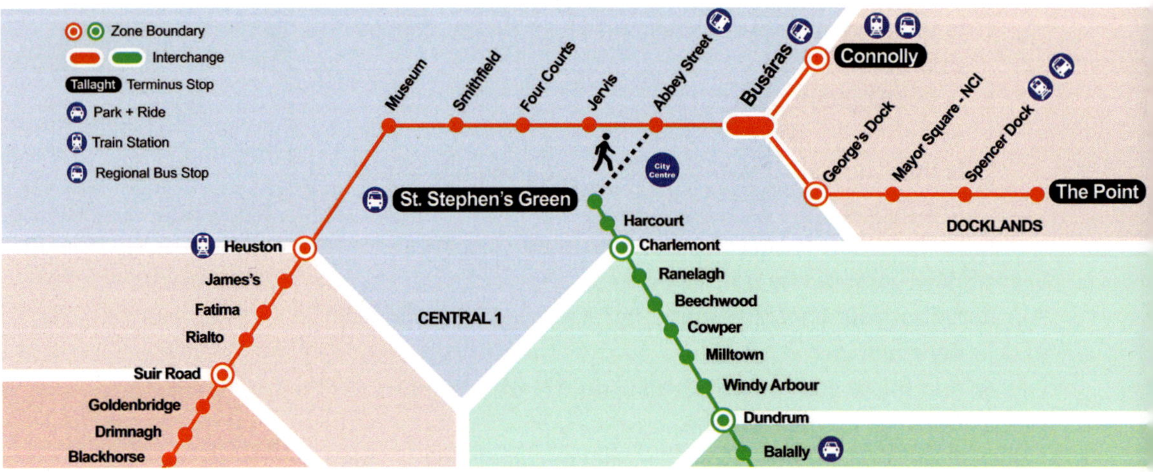

Unit 5, p.102

7 (SPEAKING) What must you do on a bus? What mustn't you do?

Explain these school bus rules.

show your ticket

eat ice cream

talk to bus driver

sit when bus moves

bring pets

leave rubbish

listen to music

push other students

Unit 5, p.103

9 (WRITING) Must, needn't or mustn't?

Put in the right verb.

1. Dogs travel free. You **must** • **needn't** • **mustn't** buy an extra ticket.
2. Your dog **must** • **needn't** • **mustn't** be with you all the time.
3. Your dog **must** • **needn't** • **mustn't** hurt other people.
4. It **must** • **needn't** • **mustn't** be nice to other people.
5. You **must** • **needn't** • **mustn't** carry a small dog in a bag. It's OK to hold it.
6. You **must** • **needn't** • **mustn't** play with your dog when you're on the bus.

2,17 The Norman conquest

1

The old king of England, Edward, died in 1066. He had no children and both his Anglo-Saxon brother-in-law, Harold, and his French cousin, William, Duke of Normandy, wanted to be the next king of England. Harold made himself king, and William was very angry. So what did he do next? He sailed to England with his army ...

2

Harold and William fought the battle on Senlac Hill, near Hastings. William's men were knights and they were better trained. They fought on horses and were good archers. Harold's men fought on foot and they were already tired from an earlier battle at Stamford Bridge, 200 miles away in the north of England. (Yes, they had to walk those 200 miles!)

conquest – *Eroberung*
the Anglo-Saxons – *die Angelsachsen (das Volk, das schon vor 1066 in England lebte)*
brother-in-law – *Schwager*
duke – *Herzog*
army – *Heer; Armee*
knight – *Ritter*
archer – *Bogenschütze; Bogenschützin*
tapestry – *Wandteppich*
surname – *Nachname; Familienname*

3

How do we know what happened during the Battle of Hastings? Well, we have the 70-metre long Bayeux Tapestry to tell us! The tapestry is like a comic and it tells the story of the battle. It tells us that Harold died when he got an arrow in his eye, but we don't know if this really happened.

4

William won the Battle of Hastings and he became king of England on Christmas Day 1066. Today we know him as William the Conqueror. He was a big castle fan and built lots of them in England, including part of the Tower of London. He also took land from the Anglo-Saxons and gave it to his Norman friends.

5

Did the Normans change England? Yes, of course they did! For example, they brought many new words to the English language. Words like 'pork' and 'garden' come from this time. Guess what? There are still many English people who have Norman surnames, like Archer or Darcy. Before the Normans came to England, most people didn't even have surnames. They lived in small villages, so a first name or a nickname was often enough.

1 What did you find most interesting in the texts? Talk about it with a partner.

2 Sum up the text.

Sum up the most important information of each paragraph in one or two sentences.

When the king of England died in 1066, Harold made himself the new king. His cousin William was angry because he wanted to become king too. ...

Unit 2, More about ...

The RNLI: Volunteers on the coast

Did you know?

- The RNLI is the Royal National Lifeboat Institution. It's a charity and it saves lives at sea.
- The RNLI has 237 lifeboat stations and about 4,600 crew members in the UK and Ireland.
- The RNLI rescues about 8,000 people per year.
- The RNLI has saved about 140,000 lives since 1824.
- Many of the lifeboat crew members are volunteers.
- The RNLI gets money from fundraising.

2,18 A rescue – boys in trouble

18th June 2016, by Simon Spade.

Yesterday the RNLI rescued two teenage boys who got into trouble when they were kayaking off the coast near Llandudno.

The two 14-year-old boys went out too far in their kayaks and could not get back to the beach because of strong winds. They tried to get back for more than two and a half hours, then shouted for help and waved. A tourist spotted the boys and made an emergency call to the RNLI. The lifeboat crew left their station at 1:40 p.m. and got to the kayaks in only a few minutes. The RNLI crew picked up the boys and gave them blankets and hot drinks to keep them warm. Lifeboat helm Howard Link called the ambulance to meet them on the beach. Both boys were very weak and seasick. They both spent the night in Llandudno hospital but are back home now.

The lifeboat crew got back to their station at 3:25 p.m.

Rules to remember

There are some rules to remember when you go to the beach:

Spot the dangers.

Always go with a friend or adult.

Find and follow the safety signs and flags.

Emergency – put up your hand and shout or call 999/112.

RNLI profiles

Most lifeboat crew members are volunteers. Let's meet some.

Name: Howard Link
Job: Postman

Lifeboat helm
I lead the rescue. It is my job to make sure that everyone on the boat stays safe while we are at sea.

Name: Susan Merchant
Job: Teacher

Lifeboat crew member
I grew up in Wales near the sea, so I have been in boats for many years. I help during the rescue and look after the rescued person.

Name: John Taylor
Job: Student

Lifeboat youth volunteer
I'm only 16 so I'm too young to join the lifeboat crew, but I work at the station. I look after the equipment and help at fundraising events.

Fundraising Calendar, Llandudno RNLI

January 25th:
10k run around Llandudno

March 17th:
Cake sale at the lifeboat station

April 4th:
Talent show at Llandudno High School

September 13th:
Fun boat race at West Beach

charity – *Wohltätigkeits-organisation*
to save – *retten; bergen*
crew – *Crew; Besatzung*
to rescue – *retten*
fundraising – *Spendenaktionen*
to join – *Mitglied in / bei etwas werden*

1 Talk about the RNLI.

1. Does Germany have a charity like the RNLI?
2. Would you join the RNLI? Why? Why not?

2 Write an adventure story.

Write the story behind the article 'A rescue' on page 132 from the point of view of Susan Merchant of the RNLI. Make up pieces of extra information and add quotes to make your story more interesting.

Yesterday seemed like a quiet day. But then we had an emergency call. "Come on, we have to be quick," Howard shouted. …

Unit 3, More about ...

2,19 The Highland Games

History

Legend says that in the 11th century the Scottish king Malcolm III wanted to find the strongest and fastest men in the land. So he organized a competition. The winners became his bodyguards or they ran across the country with messages from the king. Later large families or 'clans' met every year to compete against each other.

Today

People come from around the world every summer to watch the Highland Games.
The Games take place in towns and villages all over Scotland. The 'heavy' events for the strongest and fittest people are the most popular.
All the competitors who take part in the 'heavy' events must wear kilts. There's also lots of music and dancing.
And there are children's Highland Games too, for young people from 5–18.
In Scotland there are up to 100 Highland Games every year.

Caber toss

The most famous 'heavy' event is the caber toss.
A caber is a pole that is made from a tree.
It's five metres long and very heavy (about 45 kg).
People hold the caber at one end and throw it so that it lands on the other end. It's not important how far it goes.

the Highlands – *Berge im Norden Schottlands*
bodyguard – *Leibwächter*
to compete (against) – *gegeneinander antreten*
caber – *(Baum)stamm*
pole – *Pfahl*
to let go – *loslassen*
complete – *vollständig*

Hammer throw

Competitors swing a heavy ball which is on the end of a long chain around their heads. Then they let go and throw it as far as they can. Haggis hurling is very similar: you have to throw a haggis as far as possible. After that the haggis must still be OK to eat. This sport started as a joke in 1977.

Stone put

There are two ways to throw or 'put' the stone: you can stand (then you use a heavier stone) or you can run with it (then it's not so heavy). In the first competitions, men chose a stone from a river.

Music and dance

No Highland Games are complete without the sounds of bagpipes and Highland dancing. Pipe bands march and play together and they also compete against each other. One of the most famous dances is the Sword Dance.

1 Talk about the Highland Games.

Would you like to go to the Highland Games? Are there sports like this in your country? Talk with a partner.

2 Give your opinion.

Is it better to be really strong or to be a very good musician? Write a text of 100 words in which you give your opinion and the reasons why you think so.

In my opinion it is much better to be … . Because if you are … you can …

The Troubles and after

Murals

If you go to Belfast, you'll see lots of large pictures on the sides of the buildings. These are called murals. They show events and people from the past which are important to people who live in the city. A lot of these murals are from the time that we call 'The Troubles'.

Different schools

Catholic and Protestant children in Northern Ireland often go to separate schools. Even in small towns there are often two schools – one for the children of each religion.

The background

Many Scottish and English Protestant people arrived and settled in what is now Northern Ireland about 400 years ago. Since then, there have often been problems between the Catholic and Protestant people who lived there. Some people (usually Protestants) want Northern Ireland to stay part of the UK. Others (usually Catholics) want it to be part of the Republic of Ireland. This disagreement has often caused fighting.

'The Troubles' (late 1960s – 1998) were a very violent time in Northern Ireland's history. There was a lot of terrorism and more than 3,500 people died. When British soldiers came to help in 1969, people welcomed them, but many Catholics soon felt the soldiers were not on their side.

D

Belfast - then and now

During the Troubles, high walls were built to separate Protestants and Catholics. These walls were called 'peace walls'. A lot has changed since the time of the Troubles. Now everyone is working for a future without violence. Today Belfast is a very friendly city for tourists. Many of the walls are still there, but now you can walk from one side to the other. And you can write your own message of peace on one of the 'peace walls'. More 'mixed' schools, for children from Protestant and Catholic families, open every year too.

New chances

Did you know that 30,000 people worked in Belfast's shipyards in the past? When we didn't need as many ships, many people lost their jobs. During the Troubles, not many businesses wanted to come to Northern Ireland and unemployment was high. This has changed and there are new jobs now in making films and TV series.

to settle (in) – *besiedeln*
to cause – *verursachen*
violent – *gewaltsam, gewalttätig; brutal*
separate – *getrennt; verschieden*
to separate – *trennen*
peace – *Frieden*
business – *Unternehmen*
unemployment – *Arbeitslosigkeit*

1 Talk about the texts.

What did you find most surprising and interesting in the texts? Talk about it with a partner.

2 Read and explain.

Read the text again and explain: Why were there walls in Belfast? Why were they called 'peace walls'? How has their purpose changed since the time of the Troubles?

Highlights of Irish history

About 500 BC

I'm a Celt. The Celtic people were early settlers on the island of Ireland. We came from Central Europe.

9th century

I'm a Viking from Denmark. We invaded Ireland and our people lived here for about 300 years!

12th century

I'm Henry II, King of England. I invaded Ireland with a huge army and then built lots of castles there.

16th century

I'm Henry VIII, King of England and Ireland. The English own 90% of Ireland now. Many Irish people don't like me.

Saint Patrick

Saint Patrick is the patron saint of Ireland. He lived about 1,500 years ago and brought Christianity to Ireland. There are many stories about his life. One of the most famous is that he drove all the snakes in Ireland into the sea, where they drowned. St Patrick's Day is on 17th March every year.

settler – *Siedler, Siedlerin*
century – *Jahrhundert*
to own – *besitzen*
famine – *Hungersnot*
to emigrate – *auswandern*
to split – *teilen; spalten*
to sign – *unterschreiben; unterzeichnen*
patron saint – *Schutzheiliger, Schutzheilige*
to drive – *treiben*
economy – *Wirtschaft*
financial crisis – *Wirtschaftskrise*

D

1845

was the year of the Great Famine. One million people died and one million emigrated. Many went to America. I am one of them.

20th century

We split Ireland into Northern Ireland and the Republic of Ireland. There were many problems after this, like 'The Troubles' in Northern Ireland.

1998

I'm Bertie Ahern, prime minister of Ireland. I signed the Good Friday Agreement which was a big step in the peace process.

2002

I'm the euro! Ireland began to use me in 2002. Ireland has been a member of the European Union since 1973.

Celtic Tiger

When the Republic of Ireland joined the EU in 1973, it was a poor country. Between 1995 and 2000, Ireland's economy grew very quickly and people said it was as strong as a tiger. Many companies moved their European offices to Ireland. After the European financial crisis in 2008, however, people said that the 'Celtic Tiger' was dead.

1 Talk about the texts.

What did you find most surprising and interesting in the texts about Ireland? Talk about it with a partner.

2 Find out more.

Search the internet for information about these people. Write short texts like the ones above for them.

WWW

Grace O'Malley (1530–1603)
Michael Collins (1890–1922)
Bram Stoker (1847–1912)
Nano Nagle (1718–1784)
Phil Lynott (1949–1986)

Extra

Be a better photographer[1].

1 Do you take a lot of pictures? How many pictures do you take a day?

Taking pictures is a fun hobby for many people. You probably take pictures almost every day with your phone too. Some people are professional photographers. They have very good cameras and know all the tricks. But even with your own phone you can get better results.

2 Look at the pictures. Do you think they are OK? Why? Why not?

☺ I like picture 1 because it is … .
☺ I think picture 1 is great/OK because it has … .
☹ I don't like picture 1 because it is … .
☹ I think picture 1 isn't OK because … .

nice colours • funny • interesting • great • …
too light • too dark • blurred[2] • boring • …

You have the perfect subject and the light couldn't be better. Just when you press the shutter[3], somebody jumps into the picture and makes a funny face. That's what's called a **photobomb**.

3 Find funny photobombs on the internet and show them to the class. What's funny about them?

1 photographer [fə'tɒgrəfə] – *Fotograf/Fotografin*; 2 blurred [blɜ:d] – *unscharf*; 3 shutter ['ʃʌtə] – *Auslöser*

Three simple tips for better pictures

1. Be creative. Change perspectives and angles[1]. Sometimes the world looks different then.

A front

B low angle

C birds-eye view

2. Always check the background. Sometimes the picture might be embarrassing[2] for someone.

That's wrong.

That's right.

3. Try to zoom with your camera. Or just move forward a foot or two. Sometimes details can be more interesting than the whole person or thing.

A Medium shot

B Close up

B Extreme close up

4 Choose an interesting subject and take three pictures. Use the tips. Show your pictures to the class and discuss them.

1 angle [ˈæŋgl] – *Winkel;* 2 embarrassing [ɪmˈbærəsɪŋ] – *unangenehm*

How the heart works

1 Look at the sentences. Do you know any German sayings with the word 'heart'?

I know the words by heart.

I have a broken heart.

He has a heart of stone.

Follow your heart.

You're close to my heart.

2 Read the facts about the heart. What do you find most interesting?

The heart begins beating four weeks after conception[1] and does not stop until death[2].

Every day, the heart produces[3] enough energy to drive a truck 20 miles (about 32 km). In a lifetime, that is like driving to the moon[4] and back.

During an average[5] lifetime, the heart will pump nearly 1.5 million tons of blood[6] – enough to fill 200 wagons.

Take a tennis ball and squeeze[7] it tightly[8]: that's how hard the beating heart works to pump blood.

The heart beats 100,000 times a day.

The heart has its own electrical impulse[9]. It can beat even when it is outside of the body. But it must get enough oxygen[10].

3 What keeps your heart healthy?

A healthy heart is a happy heart. But what can you do to keep it happy? Make sentences.

1 conception [kən'sepʃn] – *Empfängnis;* 2 death [deθ] – *Tod;* 3 produce [prə'dju:s] – *erzeugen;* 4 moon [mu:n] – *Mond;* 5 average ['ævrɪdʒ] – *durchschnittlich;* 6 blood [blʌd] – *Blut;* 7 squeeze [skwi:z] – *drücken;* 8 tight [taɪt] – *fest;* 9 impulse ['ɪmpʌls] – *Impuls;* 10 oxygen ['ɒksɪdʒən] – *Sauerstoff*

4 Read about the anatomy[1] of the heart

The heart is your strongest muscle. It's a little to the left in your chest[2] and about the size of your fist[3]. Your heart pumps blood through your body to provide you with oxygen and other useful things. Your blood moves through tubes (arteries[4] and veins[5]). Your heart has four different chambers[6] – two chambers in each side. The chambers on top are called atria[7], the ones on the bottom ventricles[8].

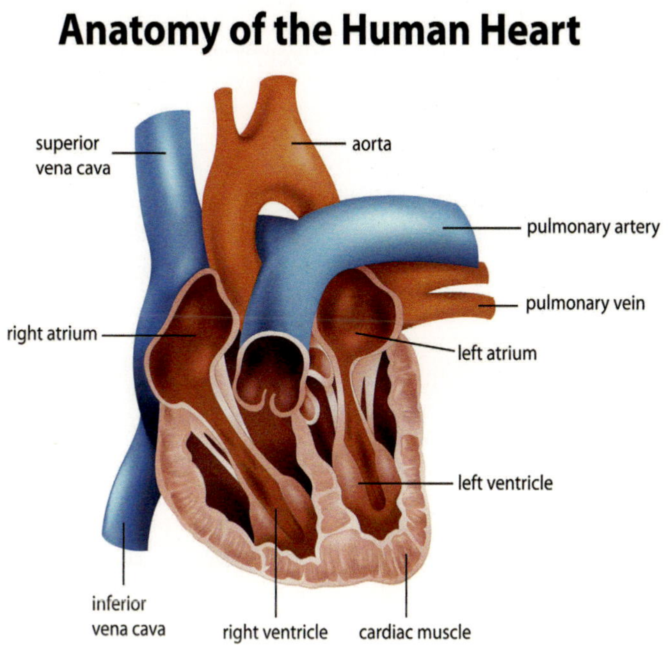

5 Find out your pulse[9].

Check your pulse in different situations.
Count the beats for one minute.

What's your pulse when you are sitting?
What's your pulse when you have just run for a minute?

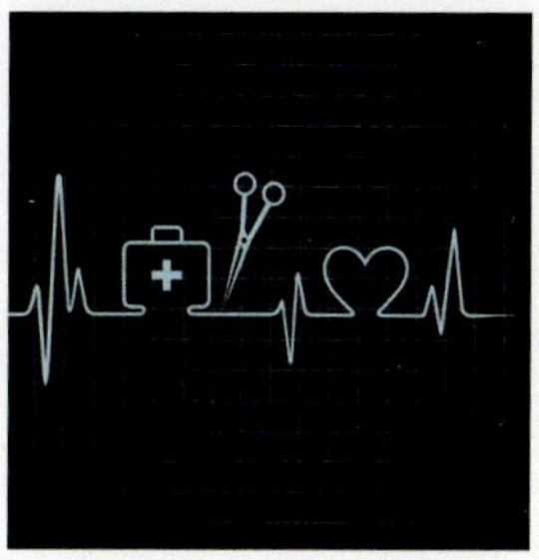

1 anatomy [ə'nætemi] – *Anatomie (Lehre vom Aufbau der Organismen);* 2 chest [tʃest] – *Brust;* 3 fist [fɪst] – *Faust;* 4 artery ['ɑːtri] – *Arterie;* 5 vein [veɪn] – *Vene;* 6 chamber ['tʃeɪmbə] – *Kammer;* 7 atrium ['eɪtriəm] – *Vorhof (des Herzens);* 8 ventricle ['ventrɪkl] – *Herzkammer;* 9 pulse [pʌls] – *Puls*

2,21

The London Eye Mystery by Siobhan Dowd (2007)

Ted is different. His hobby is looking at the weather. He isn't good at reading other people's feelings and body language. Then his cousin Salim and his mum, Ted's Aunt Gloria, come to stay. They want to see Ted and his family before they go to live in New York. During the visit Salim rides on the London Eye. Ted and Kat, his sister, wait for him. But the pod[1] comes down again and Salim isn't in it any more.
What has happened to Salim?

"Let's lie[2]," said Kat. "About taking that ticket from a stranger[3]." She grabbed[4] my arm so hard it hurt.
"Lie," I repeated[5]. "Uhm. Lie."
"We could say Salim got lost in the crowds, say he …" She let my arm go. "Oh, forget it," she said. "I know you can't lie. And stop looking at me like that!"
We walked over to the table where Aunt Gloria and Mum sat talking in the café.
We stood by them in silence[6]. But a pounding[7] started up in my ears.
"There you are," Aunt Gloria said. "Have you got the tickets?"
Kat waited for me to say something.
I waited for Kat to say something.
"Where's Salim?" asked Mum. "Not still in the queue?"
"Uhm," I said. "No."
"Where then?"
"We don't know!" Kat said. "This man – he came up and gave us his ticket. For free. He bought it, he said, but didn't want to go on the ride."
"He had claustrophobia[8]," I said.
"That's right. And the queue was awful. So we took the ticket. And gave it to Salim. And Salim went up alone. And he didn't come down."
Aunt Gloria looked up at the London Eye. "So he's still up there," she said.
Kat had a hand to her mouth and a strange look on her face. "No," she said. "He went up some time ago. Ted and I watched his pod. But when it came down – he wasn't on it."
Mum's face scrunched up[9], so I knew she was a) confused[10] or b) angry or c) both[11]. "What is it you're trying to say: He wasn't on it?!"
"He went up, Mum," I repeated. "But he didn't come down." Mum's mouth became like an O. "He went against the law of gravity[12], Mum. He went up but he didn't come down. Uhm."

1 pod [pɒd] – *Gondel;* 2 lie [laɪ] – *lügen;* 3 stranger ['streɪndʒə] – *Fremder;* 4 grab sth. [græb] – *nach etw. greifen;* 5 repeat [rɪ'pi:t] – *wiederholen;* 6 silence ['saɪləns] – *Schweigen;* 7 pounding ['paʊndɪŋ] – *Pochen;* 8 claustrophobia [ˌklɔ:strə'fəʊbiə] – *Platzangst;* 9 scrunch up ['skrʌnʃˌʌp] – *verziehen;* 10 confused [kən'fju:zd] – *verwirrt;* 11 both [bəʊθ] – *beides;* 12 against the law of gravity [ə'genst ðə lɔ:‿əv 'grævəti] – *gegen das Gesetz der Schwerkraft*

Mum looked more angry than confused now. But Aunt Gloria looked calm[1].

"I think I know what happened," she said.

"What?" we all said."I bet he went around one more time."

Yes, that's it, I thought, it was really that easy.

"That's it," said Kat like she could read my thoughts. "He just stayed on."

I looked at the big clock on the wall. "So … he'll land at … twelve thirty-two."

We went back to the Eye with Mum. Aunt Gloria stayed at the café so Salim would find her if he came back while we were away.

We watched a lot of pods open and close, but no Salim. 12:32 came and went. No Salim.

Mum asked a woman from customer services[2] but she just said children mustn't ride on the Eye without a parent. So, sorry, she couldn't help.

"Kat," Mum said, "I relied[3] on you. It was wrong to take that ticket and let Salim go up alone."

Something awful happened then. Kat started crying[4]. Not something she usually does. "It's always my fault[5]. Never Ted's. Ted never does anything wrong."

"You're older, Kat. But really not much wiser." Mum stared[6] angrily at Kat and Kat stared back.

"Why don't we call his mobile?" I said.

Suddenly Mum's face cleared[7]. (I like this phrase because it's like with the weather: A face can clear just like the sky after a dark cloud[8] has passed over and the sun comes out again.)

"Of course! Ted," Mum said, "You're a genius. Why didn't we think of that before?"

Back with Aunt Gloria in the café, there was no sign[9] of Salim.

"You've got your phone," said Mum. "Call him on his mobile!"

"OK," Aunt Gloria said. "Yes, maybe he's near us."

She called his number and put the phone to her ear with a smile. Then her face became the opposite[10] of 'clear'. It became cloudy.

"The mobile phone you are calling has been switched off," she repeated. "Please try again later."

22 "Why isn't his phone on?" she whispered. "Why?"

We all went to the woman at the London Eye again and she called the police. A police officer took our names and addresses. Could Salim find his way back to our house? he asked. Yes, we said. Then he told us to do three things: a) keep[11] trying his

1 calm [ka:m] – *ruhig;* 2 customer service [ˌkʌstəmə ˈsɜ:vɪs] – *Kundenservice;* 3 rely on sb. [rɪˈlaɪ] – *sich auf jdn. verlassen;* 4 cry [kraɪ] – *weinen;* 5 fault [fɔ:lt] – *Schuld;* 6 stare [ˈsteə] – *anstarren;* 7 clear [klɪə] – *aufhellen;* 8 cloud [klaʊd] – *Wolke;* 9 sign [saɪn] – *Zeichen;* 10 opposite [ˈɒpəzɪt] – *Gegenteil;* 11 keep trying sth. [ki:p ˈtraɪɪŋ] – *etwas immer wieder versuchen*

phone, b) go home and wait and c) try not to worry. And if Salim wasn't home in a few hours, a police officer would visit us.

Kat tried to say Salim went missing[1] some time after getting on the wheel and before getting off. But he just said, "Children don't disappear[2] into thin air!"

So then we did b) and went home to wait. And Aunt Gloria did a): She called Salim again and again. Mum made tea. Kat brought in a plate of my favourite biscuits, chocolate fingers. This was Mum and Kat trying to do c). But no one ate any. We all tried not to worry but it didn't really work.

Mum called Dad and told him what had happened. He said he was on his way home.

I looked at Aunt Gloria.

"What are you staring at?" she cried out. "You wanted to go to the London Eye – now this has happened! You and your silly bike wheel up in the clouds!" She sat down on the sofa.

A bit later she said,"Oh, Ted. I'm sorry. I didn't mean[3] that."

"Glo!" Mum said and sat down next to her. "Calm down, love." She made a sign at me to say she didn't want me in the room.

I went to see Kat, who was in the kitchen, sitting at the table. She had her headphones[4] on and her head on her arms so she couldn't see me or hear me. So I went up to my room.

I got out one or two volumes[5] of my encyclopaedia[6] and sat on my bed, looking at some interesting pages. There was a knock[7] on the door. Kat came in.

"Ted, I need you now," Kat said. She did something strange – she sat on the bed next to me. "You're all I've got. Mum isn't talking to me. Auntie Gloria thinks I'm a really bad girl.

Dad's home from work now, but he just stares at me every time I open my mouth."

I looked up. "The dodo[8] disappeared, Kat," I said.

"What?"

"The dodo. It disappeared from the evolutionary path[9]."

"Right. The dodo. So?"

"Darwin would say it wasn't adaptable[10] enough to survive[11], so it didn't."

"I don't think Salim's disappeared from the evolutionary path, Ted."

"No, I know," I said. "But there's lots more about disappearing in my encyclopaedia."

"Oh, yeah?"

1 go missing [ˌɡəʊ ˈmɪsɪŋ] – *verloren gehen;* 2 disappear into thin air [ˌdɪsəpɪə ɪntə θin‿ˈeə] – *sich in Luft auflösen;* 3 mean [mi:n] – *meinen;* 4 headphones [ˈhedfəʊnz] – *Kopfhörer;* 5 volume [ˈvɒlju:m] – *Band;* 6 encyclopaedia [ɪnˌsaɪkləˈpi:dɪə] – *Lexikon;* 7 knock [nɒk] – *Klopfen;* 8 dodo [ˈdəʊdəʊ] – *Dodo (ausgestorbener, großer, flugunfähiger Vogel);* 9 evolutionary path [ˌi:vəˌu:ʃnri ˈpɑ:θ] – *Evolutionsgeschichte;* 10 adaptable [əˈdæptəbl] – *anpassungsfähig;* 11 survive [səˈvaɪv] – *überleben*

“There was this lord called Lord Lucan. People think he killed his kids’ nanny and then killed himself. Maybe he did. But they never found his body, Kat. Maybe he wanted it to look that way, but really disappeared ... went away, say, to India and became a long-haired hippie.”

“I don’t see what that’s got to do with –” There was a long silence. “That’s not very helpful, Ted.”

“And there was the *Mary Celeste*, a hundred-foot ship from New York. It turned up[1] in the sea near Gibraltar with no one on board, like ... like aliens beamed them up!”

“Ted, I don’t think this is a time for joking.”

I closed my book and looked at Kat.

“OK,” she said. “It wasn’t a joke. I should know you never joke. So what do you mean?”

I didn’t really know what I meant. The only thing that linked[2] the dodo, Lord Lucan, the people on board the *Mary Celeste* and Salim was they all disappeared.

The room was silent except for our breathing[3]. Kat sat there, all hunched[4] up. It was difficult but I did it, I put my hand on her shoulder[5].

“Kat,” I said, “you and I are together in this. People disappear. And things. Most of them reappear.”

Kat put her hand on mine and I saw the tears[6] on her face. Then I felt tears falling onto the hand on her shoulder. For a moment I didn’t know if it was her hand or mine. I hate touching[7] people. With the wet feeling of the tears and the confusion of hands, it was like we didn’t really know where she started and I ended.

“Ted,” she said, shaking[8] her head, “the *Mary Celeste* people never reappeared. Nor[9] the dodo. Nor Lord What’s-His-Name. That police officer was right. People don’t just disappear. Salim must be somewhere[10]. If it’s all my fault, then I have to find him. But I need your help. I need your brain[11], Ted. No one is better at thinking than you.”

That was Kat’s first compliment to me ever. I put my hands into my jacket pockets[12] and stared down at my trainers and went, “Hrumm.” Then I felt something in one of the pockets – something I didn’t expect[13] to find there. I took it out and Kat and I stared at it.

“Salim’s camera!”

How will the story go on? Will Salim return?

1 turn up [ˌtɜːn‿ˈʌp] – *erscheinen;* 2 link [lɪŋk] – *verbinden;* 3 breathing [ˈbriːðɪŋ] – *Atmen;* 4 hunch [hʌntʃ] – *sich krümmen;* 5 shoulder [ˈʃəʊldə] – *Schulter;* 6 tear [tɪə] – *Träne;* 7 touch [tʌtʃ] – *berühren;* 8 shake [ʃeɪk] – *schütteln;* 9 nor [nɔː] – *und auch nicht;* 10 somewhere [ˈsʌmweə] – *irgendwo;* 11 brain [breɪn] – *Grips, Verstand;* 12 pocket [ˈpɒkɪt] – *(Jacken-)Tasche;* 13 expect [ɪkˈspekt] – *erwarten*

Ivanhoe

Characters:
Narrator
Rowena
Cedric
Athelstane
Rebecca
Isaac
Prince John
Three Norman knights
Five Anglo-Saxon knights
Ivanhoe (The Disinherited)
Crowd (5 – 8 people)
King Richard (The Black Knight)
Robin Hood
Robin's men (5 – 8 people)

2,24

Scene 1

NARRATOR: This is a story about brave[1] men and women. It is a story about hate[2], but also about love. It is a story about power, but also great kindness[3]. Our story is old, but hate, love, power and kindness are still a big part of all of our lives today. The date is 1194. The place is England. But at this time the Normans ruled[4] England. The good King Richard is in another country. He was fighting in a war[5], but now he is in prison far from his country. His awful brother, the Norman Prince John, now rules England and the Anglo-Saxons that live there are not happy. *(A trumpet[6] plays)*. Ah! Hear that. It is the start of the famous competition between Norman and Anglo-Saxon knights. Look, there sits Cedric, an Anglo-Saxon. He looks after the beautiful Rowena. Listen, they are having an argument.

(NARRATOR leaves. CEDRIC and ROWENA are sitting in the crowd – a semi-circle[7] of chairs are in front of the audience[8].)

ROWENA: *(Angry)* No, I will not get married to him!

CEDRIC: But Rowena, Athelstane is an Anglo-Saxon and a good man! I am your father and I say you will get married to him!

ROWENA: *(Very angry)* You are not my father!

CEDRIC: But Rowena, I have loved you like my own child. I have looked after you.

ROWENA: Yes, it is true, you have. I had no mother or father, but you took me into your home and looked after me. But what about Ivanhoe, your real child?

CEDRIC: *(Angry now)* Today Ivanhoe is not my child! He went away to fight with the Normans and King Richard. He is not a true Anglo-Saxon and you will not say his name again!

1 brave [breɪv] – *mutig;* 2 hate [heɪt] – *Hass;* 3 kindness ['kaɪndnəs] – *Güte;* 4 rule [ru:l] – *regieren;* 5 war [wɔ:] – *Krieg;* 6 trumpet ['trʌmpɪt] – *Trompete;* 7 semi-circle ['semi 'sɜ:kl] – *Halbkreis;* 8 audience ['ɔ:diəns] – *Zuschauer*

ROWENA: But it is Ivanhoe I love and I will only get married to HIM!

CEDRIC: Stop, girl! Look, Athlestane is here.

ATHELSTANE: *(ATHELSTANE is drunk[1]. He has a bottle in his hand. He walks to CEDRIC and sits next to him.)* Hello Cedric, and lovely Rowena. *(He gives ROWENA's hand a kiss. She looks very unhappy.)*

CEDRIC: Will you fight today in the competition, Athlestane?

ATHELSTANE: I will fight tomorrow. Yes, tomorrow I will fight.

(An old man and a young woman come on stage and sit near ROWENA and CEDRIC).

ROWENA: *(To CEDRIC)* Who is that man and the beautiful woman over there?

CEDRIC: Ah, that is Isaac and his daughter Rebecca. Isaac is a great businessman[2]. He has a lot of money.

REBECCA: *(Speaks to her father)* Father, do you think the Anglo-Saxon knights will win the competition?

ISAAC: I'm not sure, Rebecca. But I know there is a young, good Anglo-Saxon knight who will fight today. He saved me from some very bad men in the forest[3] yesterday. They wanted to take all my money and my horse. He walked with me through the forest until I arrived home safely. I gave him a good horse and some money. I am sure the man was a knight.

(The trumpet plays again; someone who is not on stage calls 'Prince John'. PRINCE JOHN walks to his place in the middle of the semi-circle and sits down. The crowd cheers[4].)

PRINCE JOHN: Let's start the competition!

(Trumpet plays again. Three knights on horses come onto the stage from the right. They are carrying a flag that says 'Normans'. Five knights on horses come on stage from the left. They are carrying a flag that says 'Anglo-Saxons'. All the knights have lances[5].)

PRINCE JOHN: *(Stands up)* Let the first knights start!

(One Norman and one Anglo-Saxon knight attack[6] each other. The Norman hits the Anglo-Saxon with his lance and the Anglo-Saxon falls from his horse. Half the crowd cheer and half boo[7]. PRINCE JOHN is laughing. CEDRIC, ROWENA, ISAAC and REBECCA look unhappy. ATHELSTANE is sleeping and snoring[8]. The next Norman knight wins against the next Anglo-Saxon. The third Norman also wins. The knights who fall leave the stage. Two Anglo-Saxon knights are on stage.)

FIRST NORMAN KNIGHT: Who will fight us next?

(The two Anglo-Saxon knights are scared. Suddenly a new knight comes on stage from the left. He holds a flag that says 'The Disinherited[9]'. This knight wins against each of the three Norman knights. He holds his flag up to PRINCE JOHN.)

PRINCE JOHN: Very good, brave knight. You call yourself the Disinherited, but do you have a real name?

IVANHOE: I am the Disinherited. My father does not want to call me his child. I fought with your brother King Richard in the great war.

(Sounds of surprise from the crowd. PRINCE JOHN looks very unhappy.)

1 drunk [drʌŋk] – *betrunken;* 2 businessman ['bɪznɪsmæn] – *Geschäftsmann;* 3 forest ['fɒːrɪst] – *Wald;* 4 cheer [tʃɪə] – *jubeln;* 5 lance [lɑːns] – *Lanze;* 6 attack [ə'tæk] – *angreifen;* 7 boo sb. [buː] – *jdn. ausbuhen;* 8 snore [snɔː] – *schnarchen;* 9 disinherited [ˌdɪsɪn'herɪtɪd] – *der Enterbte*

PRINCE JOHN: All right, Disinherited. As the winner of the first part of the competition you can choose the woman who you believe is the most beautiful. She will be our competition queen. *(He puts a crown[1] on the end of IVANHOE's lance. IVANHOE walks around and finds ROWENA. He holds the lance so she can take the crown. She puts it on her head. The crowd cheers. IVANHOE leaves the stage.)*

2,25

Scene 2

(Music is playing. The crowd is talking and laughing.)
NARRATOR: *(On stage)* It is the second day of the competition. The knights must now fight with swords[2]. This part of the competition is very dangerous. Some knights may get hurt. Look! The knights are coming. *(Trumpet plays. Narrator leaves.)*
(Three Norman knights come from the right with a Norman flag. Two knights and Ivanhoe come from the left with an Anglo-Saxon flag. All the knights are on horses and have swords.)
PRINCE JOHN: *(Stands up)* Let the second part of the competition start! *(Trumpet plays.)*
(There is a big fight: IVANHOE is hit badly on his left side, but he still fights. Suddenly a knight arrives from the side. The knight is wearing black. The crowd makes sounds of surprise. The black knight fights two of the Norman knights. IVANHOE fights the last Norman knight. Ivanhoe and the black knight get off their horses and walk to each other.)
IVANHOE: *(Whispers[3])* There is only one man in England who can fight like this. Is it really you?
KING RICHARD: *(Whispers back)* Yes, Ivanhoe. I am back. Meet me in the forest in five days and I will be King of England again. *(KING RICHARD leaves the stage on his horse.)*
PRINCE JOHN: Disinherited! Come and get your prize. You are the winner of the competition! And as the winner, I give you this crown, but you must take off[4] your helmet. *(IVANHOE takes off his helmet. Sounds of surprise from the crowd)* Ah, it is you, Ivanhoe! The son of Cedric. *(He puts the crown on Ivanhoe's head. IVANHOE falls.)*
ROWENA: *(Stands up)* We must help him! He is hurt. Come on!
CEDRIC: Sit down, Rowena! He is not part of my family. King Richard can help him.
ROWENA: King Richard is in prison in another country. He cannot help Ivanhoe. We must help him. He is your son and the man I love. *(She starts to leave.)*
CEDRIC: *(Angry)* You will not help him!
ROWENA: But he fought in the competition for the Anglo-Saxons. He was so brave and now he really needs our help. Please, Cedric, let's help him. *(CEDRIC pushes her back into her seat.)*
REBECCA: *(Speaks to her father)* Father! That is the knight who saved you from those bad men. We must help him. Come, father.
ISAAC: Wait, child, be careful! If we help him now, the Prince will hate us.
REBECCA: I don't care[5]! This man saved your life. I will help him. *(She looks at the man next to her.)* Will you help me take that man home? I will give you money. *(The man nods[6] and he and REBECCA go to IVANHOE. ISAAC follows. REBECCA talks to IVANHOE.)* You are a brave man. I can help you. I will take you home and give you medicine[7].
IVANHOE: Thank you.
REBECCA: Here, your money. *(She gives the man money and she, the man and ISAAC carry IVANHOE off stage.)*

1 crown [kraʊn] – *Krone;* 2 sword [sɔːd] – *Schwert;* 3 whisper ['wɪspə] – *flüstern;* 4 take off [ˌteɪk‿'ɒf] – *abnehmen;* 5 I don't care! [aɪ dəʊnt keə] – *Es ist mir egal!;* 6 nod [nɒd] – *nicken;* 7 medicine ['medsn] – *Medizin*

2,26

Scene 3

(In the forest. ROBIN's men are sitting around a fire. They are eating, drinking and laughing. KING RICHARD has no helmet, but is still wearing black. He is talking to ROBIN HOOD.)

ROBIN HOOD: Your plan is good, King Richard. With your army[1], the help of my men and Ivanhoe, we can fight Prince John and win.

KING RICHARD: When Cedric knows that the famous Robin Hood is fighting with me against Prince John, he and the other Anglo-Saxons will join[2] us too.

ROBIN HOOD: Yes, I have sent one of my men to tell Cedric to meet us here. Listen! *(ROBIN's men stop talking and eating and listen carefully.)* I think I hear someone coming.

IVANHOE: *(Just his voice)* This must be the place, my friends.

(ISAAC, REBECCA and IVANHOE come on stage.)

IVANHOE: *(Very happy to see KING RICHARD.)* It is you, my King! *(IVANHOE and KING RICHARD hug.)* I thought I would never see you again.

KING RICHARD: It is good to see you too, my great friend. I escaped[3] from prison and now I am back in England with my brave army. Robin and I have a plan to chase[4] Prince John and his men out of this country and I will rule England again. *(ROBIN's men cheer and start eating and drinking again.)* Who is this man and lovely woman with you? *(He looks at ISAAC and REBECCA.)*

IVANHOE: This beautiful woman is Rebecca. When I was hurt, she gave me medicine and made me well. And this is her father who gave me a horse and money so I could fight.

ROBIN HOOD: Listen, I hear voices again.

CEDRIC: *(Just his voice)* Come! Robin Hood and his men must be here.

(CEDRIC, ATHELSTANE and ROWENA come on stage. ATHELSTANE sits with ROBIN's men.)

ROWENA: *(Suddenly sees IVANHOE)* Oh, Ivanhoe! *(She runs to IVANHOE and they hug.)*

ROBIN HOOD: Cedric, this is King Richard. He was The Black Knight at the competition.

KING RICHARD: Your son, Ivanhoe, is a brave man, Cedric. He was the knight who won the competition. I believe the brave Ivanhoe and the lovely Rowena want to get married.

CEDRIC: *(Looks at his feet)* I … I thought Athelstane …

KING RICHARD: *(Looks at ROBIN's men where ATHELSTANE is eating and drinking and laughing.)* I think Athelstane is already married … *(Everyone looks at ATHELSTANE)* … to food and drink! *(Everyone laughs. ATHELSTANE looks up from his food. He doesn't understand the joke.)*

CEDRIC: *(Looks at IVANHOE and ROWENA and then at KING RICHARD.)* You are right, King Richard. I have a brave son and I am proud of him. He and Rowena WILL get married. *(Everyone cheers and ROWENA and IVANHOE hug again.)*

ROBIN HOOD: Now let's use your plan, King Richard, and take action against the awful Prince John. Cedric, what about your men, the good Anglo-Saxons? Will you join us?

CEDRIC: Of course we will join you, Robin. Long live King Richard! *(Everyone says 'long live King Richard' together.)*

NARRATOR: *(Comes on stage)* Together, these brave men and women chased Prince John and his men out of England. King Richard ruled England once more and the Anglo-Saxons were very happy – so were Rowena and the great Invanhoe. Long live King Richard!

1 army ['a:mi] – *Armee;* 2 join [dʒɔɪn] – *sich anschließen;* 3 escape [ɪ'skep] – *entkommen;* 4 chase [tʃeɪs] – *verfolgen*

Grammar

G4

Mit G sind die Grammatikkapitel gekennzeichnet und der Reihe nach durchnummeriert. Eine Übersicht über alle Themen in diesem Band findest du auf der nächsten Seite.

Language tip G7

Die Seiten kennzeichnen zusätzliche Grammatikkapitel. Du kannst dir die neuen Formen dort wie neue Vokabeln merken oder – wenn du es genau wissen willst – ein paar Regeln dazu lernen.

Hier stehen Besonderheiten und Tipps.

(TEST YOURSELF)

Hier kannst du üben.
Die Lösungen findest du auf S. 169.

(FÜR PROFIS)

Hier findest du knifflige Extras zum Thema.

R = Revision (Wiederholung)

Unit 1 Unit 2 Unit 3 Unit 4 Unit 5

G

	Englisch	Deutsch	Beispiel	Seite
G1	R: simple present	einfache Gegenwart	I (don't) know. • He doesn't know her. • Do you know?	154
G2	R: simple past	einfache Vergangenheit	They worked a lot. • She was in York. • I didn't go. • Did you go?	155
G3	reflexive pronouns, each other	Reflexivpronomen	I have hurt myself. • You should help each other.	156
G4	adjectives and adverbs	Adjektive und Adverbien	slow – slowly	157
G5	R: present perfect	Perfekt	I have already read the book. • He hasn't been to Wales yet. • Have you ever gone skiing?	158
G6	relative clauses	Relativsätze	This is my friend who goes climbing with me. • Edinburgh is a town which is very old.	159
G7	gerund	Gerundium	Swimming is great! • I love running too.	160
G8	R: will-future	Zukunft mit will	The weather will be fine tomorrow. • I'll help you.	161
G9	If-clauses I	Bedingungssätze Typ I	If it's sunny, I'll go swimming.	162
G10	If-clauses II	Bedingungssätze Typ II	If I had a holiday, I would go to the mountains.	163
G11	clauses of comparison	Vergleichssätze	Travelling is more interesting than staying at home. • Water is less expensive than juice. • London is as nice as Paris.	164
G12	some and any	some und any	I must drink some water. • They don't sell any bread.	165
G13	simple present and present progressive	Gegenwartszeiten	They eat porridge every day. • I can't go with you, I'm doing my homework now.	166
G14	possessive pronouns	Possessivpronomen	Is this your pen? Yes, it's mine.	167
G15	modal auxiliaries	modale Hilfsverben	They must / mustn't / needn't / may take the car.	168

Unit 1

G1 R: Die einfache Gegenwart

Revision: The simple present

Wenn du einen Zustand beschreiben möchtest oder sagen willst, dass jemand etwas gewohnheitsmäßig tut oder dass etwas häufig oder regelmäßig geschieht, verwendest du das **simple present**.

Signalwörter	
every Monday	jeden Montag
always	immer
often	oft
usually	normalerweise
sometimes	manchmal
never	nie

I **like** computer games.	Ich mag Computerspiele.
He never **goes** to a fast food restaurant.	Er geht nie in ein Fastfood-Restaurant.
The new shop **sells** Indian food.	Der neue Laden verkauft indisches Essen.

He, **she**, **it** – das **s** muss mit!

Mit **don't** oder **doesn't** (bei he, she, it) kannst du sagen, was man **nicht** macht.

I **don't know** where the best shops are.	Ich weiß nicht, wo die besten Geschäfte sind.
She **doesn't have** much time.	Sie hat nicht viel Zeit.

Und so kannst du fragen und kurz darauf antworten:

Do you sometimes **go** to the cinema?	Yes, I **do**.	No, I **don't**.
Does your brother **read** comics?	Yes, he **does**.	No, he **doesn't**.

Aussagen und Verneinungen mit **be** bildest du so:

I **am** (I'**m**)	I **am not** (I'**m not**)
you **are** (you'**re**)	you **are not** (you **aren't**)
he / she / it **is** (he'**s** / she'**s** / it'**s**)	he / she / it **is not** (he / she / it **isn't**)
we **are** (we'**re**)	we **are not** (we **aren't**)
they **are** (they'**re**)	they **are not** (they **aren't**)

Fragen und Kurzantworten mit **be** bildest du so:

Are you from York?	Yes, I **am**.	No, I'**m not**.
Is the park far away?	Yes, it **is**.	No, it **isn't**.

(TEST YOURSELF) Put the verbs in the simple present.

1. I sometimes —— (buy) clothes online.
2. She —— (do) her shopping every Friday.
3. The buses —— (not go) after 9 p.m.
4. —— you —— (go) to school by bus?
5. The girls —— (be) near the Viking Centre.
6. —— (be) Sam from Bristol?

Do you remember?

G2 R: Die einfache Vergangenheit

Revision: The simple past

Um über Dinge zu sprechen, die in der Vergangenheit passiert und vorbei sind, verwendest du die einfache Vergangenheit (**simple past**).

Signalwörter	
yesterday	gestern
last month	letzten Monat
a week ago	vor einer Woche
in 2015	(im Jahr) 2015

Das simple past bildest du so:
Hänge die Endung **-ed** an das Verb.
Achte auf unregelmäßige Verben, z. B. do → **did**; fall → **fell**; get → **got**; go → **went**; have → **had**; hear → **heard**; make → **made**; see → **saw**; write → **wrote**

Eine Liste der unregelmäßigen Verben findest du auf Seite 219.

I **helped** my aunt last Sunday.	Letzten Sonntag half ich meiner Tante.
Hannah **bought** a coat yesterday.	Hannah kaufte gestern eine Jacke.

Um zu sagen, was in der Vergangenheit nicht passiert ist, setzt du **didn't** (= did not) vor das Verb.

I **didn't watch** TV yesterday.	Ich schaute gestern nicht fern.
Tom's parents **didn't like** Bramford.	Toms Eltern gefiel Bramford nicht.

Und so kannst du im **simple past** Fragen stellen:

Did you **have** a nice weekend?	Yes, I **did**.	No, I **didn't**.
When **did** your sister **visit** you?	At the weekend.	

Im Deutschen gibt es verschiedene Möglichkeiten, Vergangenes auszudrücken:

Tim met Sarah.	Tim hat Sarah getroffen. / Tim traf Sarah.

Aussagen und Verneinungen mit **be** bildest du so:

I **was** in York. I **wasn't** in London.	Ich war in York. Ich war nicht in London.
Sue **wasn't** at the zoo. She **was** at home.	Sue war nicht im Zoo. Sie war zu Hause.
The students **were** at the theatre. They **weren't** at the cinema.	Die Schüler waren im Theater. Sie waren nicht im Kino.

Fragen und Kurzantworten mit **be** bildest du so:

Were you at home?	Yes, I **was**.	No, I **wasn't**.
Was it funny?	Yes, it **was**.	No, it **wasn't**.

(TEST YOURSELF) Put the verbs in the simple past.

1. Hannah — (have) a great time.
2. I — (not hear) a noise.
3. — you — (have) a nice day?
4. What — you — (do) yesterday?
5. Last Friday Tom — (not be) at home.
6. — (be) you in Italy last summer?

Language tip

G3 Reflexivpronomen und each other

Reflexive pronouns and each other

I have hurt myself.

Ich habe mich verletzt.

Im Englischen werden die Reflexivpronomen mit **-self** oder **-selves** gebildet. Im Deutschen werden sie meist mit „mir" oder „mich", „dir" oder „dich", „sich" usw. übersetzt.

I bought **myself** a new T-shirt.	Ich habe mir ein neues T-Shirt gekauft.
Can you make **yourself** dinner tonight?	Kannst du dir heute Abend etwas zu essen machen?
He cut **himself** with a knife.	Er hat sich mit einem Messer geschnitten.
She asked **herself** why it happened.	Sie fragte sich, warum es passiert ist.
The cat hurt **itself**.	Die Katze hat sich verletzt.
We enjoyed **ourselves** very much.	Wir amüsierten uns sehr.
Help **yourselves**!	Bedient euch!
They hurt **themselves** in the accident.	Sie haben sich bei dem Unfall verletzt.

Achtung: Beachte den Unterschied zwischen **themselves** und **each other**.

Ben and his sister are looking at **themselves**.	Ben und seine Schwester schauen sich an (= jeder sich selbst).
Ben and his sister are looking at **each other**. (= Ben looks at his sister and she looks at him.)	Ben und seine Schwester schauen sich gegenseitig an (= jeder den anderen).

(TEST YOURSELF) Put in the correct word.

1. I enjoyed — (myself / himself) very much.
2. Did you buy — a present (itself / yourself)?
3. Grandma cut — (herself / himself) with a knife.
4. We saw — (yourselves / ourselves) on TV.
5. Sam and Ben always tell — (each other / themselves) jokes.
6. The dog cut — (itself / himself).

(FÜR PROFIS)

Du kannst mit den Reflexivpronomen auch betonen, dass jemand etwas selbst gemacht hat:

He made the cake **himself**.	Er hat den Kuchen selbst gebacken.

G4 Adjektive und Adverbien

Adjectives and adverbs

That was easy.
I won the race easily.

Das war leicht.
Ich hab' das Rennen leicht gewonnen.

Ein **Adjektiv** (Eigenschaftswort) beschreibt eine Person oder eine Sache.

Beth is a **good** student.	Beth ist eine gute Schülerin.
Climbing is a **dangerous** sport.	Klettern ist ein gefährlicher Sport.

Ein **Adverb** beschreibt, wie jemand etwas tut oder wie etwas geschieht. Im Englischen erkennt man Adverbien durch ein angehängtes **-ly**.

He ran **slowly**.	Er rannte langsam.
It happened **quickly**.	Es geschah schnell.

Achtung Schreibweise: easy → eas**ily**; careful → careful**ly**

Es gibt aber auch unregelmäßige Adverbien:

That's a **good** song.	(Adjektiv)	Das ist ein gutes Lied.
She can sing **well**.	(Adverb)	Sie kann gut singen.

Manche Adverbien verändern sich nicht:

Rugby is a **fast** game.	(Adjektiv)	Rugby ist ein schnelles Spiel.
Look, the players are running **fast**.	(Adverb)	Schau, die Spieler rennen schnell.
This was a **hard** exercise.	(Adjektiv)	Das war eine schwierige Übung.
Mum works **hard** every day.	(Adverb)	Mama arbeitet jeden Tag schwer.

(TEST YOURSELF) Use adjectives or adverbs.

1. You must always ride —— (careful).
2. Max is a —— (good) tennis player.
3. Lucy speaks English —— (good).
4. Sherlock is a —— (clever) dog.
5. They walked home —— (slow).
6. Don't run so —— (fast).

G5 R: Das Perfekt

Revision: The present perfect

Do you remember?

Wenn eine Handlung in der Vergangenheit beginnt und in der Gegenwart zu einem Ergebnis führt, verwendest du das **present perfect**:
have / has + dritte Form des Verbs (past participle).

Signalwörter	
already	schon
just	gerade
not … yet	noch … nicht
ever (in Fragen)	jemals

Bei den meisten Verben hängst du für die dritte Form ein **-ed** an das Verb: help → help**ed**

I **have** just **played** football.	Ich habe gerade Fußball gespielt.
He **has** already **had** his lunch.	Er hat schon zu Mittag gegessen.

Achtung: Einige Verben haben unregelmäßige dritte Formen, z. B.:
break → broke → **broken**; do → did → **done**; be → was / were → **been**

Eine Liste der unregelmäßigen Verben findest du auf S. 219.

Um die Sätze zu verneinen, benutzt du **haven't** oder **hasn't** (bei he, she, it):

I **haven't called** the hospital yet.	Ich habe das Krankenhaus noch nicht angerufen.
She **hasn't been** to London yet.	Sie ist noch nicht in London gewesen.

Fragen und Kurzantworten bildest du so:

Have you ever **broken** your arm?	Yes, I **have**.	No, I **haven't**.
Has your brother ever **won** a prize?	Yes, he **has**.	No, he **hasn't**.
Have the girls **been** to the party?	Yes, they **have**.	No, they **haven't**.

Bei Fragen mit Fragewörtern stellst du das Fragewort an den Satzanfang.

What **has happened**?	Was ist passiert?
Where **have** you **been**?	Wo bist du gewesen?

(TEST YOURSELF) Put the verbs in the present perfect.

1. Where —— you —— (be), Dylan?
2. Sue —— already —— (do) her homework.
3. We —— just —— (have) an accident.
4. I —— (not ask) him yet.
5. —— you —— (forget) your mobile again?
6. Why —— she —— (not call) the ambulance yet?

G6 Relativsätze mit Relativpronomen

Relative clauses with relative pronouns

This is the coat which is best for tonight.

Das ist die Jacke, die für heute Abend am besten ist.

Wenn du eine Person oder eine Sache genauer beschreiben willst, verwendest du die Relativpronomen **who**, **which** oder **that**.

who → Personen
which → Dinge
that → Personen und Dinge

Bell was **the man who / that** invented the telephone.	Bell war der Mann, der das Telefon erfand.
He invented **machines which / that** changed the world.	Er erfand Geräte, die die Welt veränderten.

Willst du Zugehörigkeit oder Besitz ausdrücken, verwendest du bei Personen und Dingen **whose**.

That's the **boy whose** parents are doctors.	Das ist der Junge, dessen Eltern Ärzte sind.
Edinburgh is a **city whose** centre is very old.	Edinburgh ist eine Stadt, deren Zentrum sehr alt ist.

(TEST YOURSELF) **Put in who, whose or which.**

1. Bell was a man ___ had lots of fantastic ideas.
2. He even built a machine ___ could fly.
3. One day he opened a school for people ___ couldn't hear.
4. The phones ___ people used fifty years ago are in museums now.
5. Many people ___ are famous inventors come from Scotland.
6. This is the girl ___ parents are from India.

(FÜR PROFIS)

Folgt nach who, which oder that ein Personalpronomen wie **I**, **you**, **he**, **she**, **it**, **we**, **they**, kannst du who, which oder that auch weglassen. Diesen Satz nennt man **contact clause**.

The lady (who) **we** saw on TV last night is my cousin.	Die Frau, die wir gestern im Fernsehen gesehen haben, ist meine Kusine.
Scotland is the country (which) **I** want to visit next year.	Schottland ist das Land, das ich nächstes Jahr besuchen möchte.

Language tip

G7 Das Gerundium

Gerund

Spending a few days in Scotland is always a great idea.
I love looking at the sheep.

Ein paar Tage in Schottland zu verbringen ist immer eine tolle Idee.
Ich liebe es, die Schafe anzuschauen.

Ein Gerundium bildet man, indem man **-ing** an ein Verb anhängt. Dadurch wird das Verb zu einem Nomen (Hauptwort). Mit dem Gerundium kann man über Tätigkeiten und Aktivitäten sprechen. Es steht am Satzanfang und ist **Subjekt / Satzgegenstand** des Satzes.

Watching TV can be interesting.	Fernsehen kann interessant sein.
Playing football is my favourite sport.	Fußballspielen ist mein Lieblingssport.

Das Gerundium kann aber auch nach dem Verb stehen und ist dann **Objekt / Satzergänzung** des Satzes. Das gilt besonders für Verben wie **love**, **(not) like** und **hate**.

I like **swimming**.	Ich schwimme gern.
I don't like **cleaning** my shoes.	Ich putze meine Schuhe nicht gerne.
Tim hates **tidying** his room.	Tim hasst es, sein Zimmer aufzuräumen.

Das Gerundium darf man nicht mit dem **present progressive** verwechseln. Vergleiche:

I am walking on the beach.	Ich gehe gerade am Strand spazieren.
I love walking on the beach.	Ich mag es, am Strand spazieren zu gehen.

(TEST YOURSELF) Use the verbs to make the gerund.

1. —— (walk) with a dog can be fun.
2. —— (meet) friends is my favourite activity.
3. Rock —— (climb) can be very exciting.
4. Jane likes —— (stay) on a farm.
5. I hate —— (work) in the garden.
6. I don't like —— (write) tests.

(FÜR PROFIS)

Ein Gerundium kann auch nach Ausdrücken wie **be good at ...** oder **What about ...?** stehen.

I'**m good at playing** frisbee.	Ich bin gut im Frisbeespielen.
What about dancing?	Wie wär's mit Tanzen?

G

G8 R: Die Zukunft mit will

Revision: The will-future

Mit dem **will-future** sprichst du über die Zukunft. Oft drückst du damit Hoffnungen, Wünsche und Vorhersagen aus. Dann beginnen diese Sätze mit **I hope**, **I think**, **I'm sure** oder **maybe**.
Du bildest das **will-future** mit **will** oder **won't** und der **Grundform des Verbs**. Häufig wird die Kurzform verwendet: I **will** go → I'**ll** go

We'll **stay** at a campsite.	Wir werden auf einem Campingplatz übernachten.
Maybe we'**ll see** Nessie.	Vielleicht sehen wir Nessie.
I hope it **won't rain** tomorrow.	Ich hoffe, es wird morgen nicht regnen.

Im Deutschen kann man über Zukünftiges mit der Zukunft oder der Gegenwart sprechen:

We'll **wait** for you.	Wir werden auf dich warten. Wir warten auf dich.

Auch wenn du dich in einer Situation ganz spontan für etwas Bestimmtes entscheidest, verwendest du das **will-future**.

I don't understand this exercise.	Ich verstehe diese Aufgabe nicht.
– Don't worry, I'**ll help** you.	– Keine Sorge, ich helfe dir.
Look, it's sunny. I **won't take** a coat.	Schau, es ist sonnig. Ich nehme keine Jacke mit.

Achtung! Verwechsle **will** (werden) nicht mit **want to** (wollen):

I **will** buy some souvenirs.	Ich **werde** ein paar Souvenirs kaufen.
I **want to** buy some souvenirs.	Ich **will** ein paar Souvenirs kaufen.

(TEST YOURSELF) Complete the sentences.

1. Maybe we — (stay) in a cosy B&B in Inverness this summer.
2. I hope you — (not be) ill on holiday.
3. Look, that's real Scottish food. – Great, I — (have) that.
4. Excuse me, where is the museum? – I — (show) you the way.
5. Can you help us? – We — (do) our best.
6. You can give her the money, she — (not lose) it.

G9 Bedingungssätze Typ I

If-clauses type I

If it stops raining soon, I'll take a photo.

Wenn es bald aufhört zu regnen, mache ich ein Foto.

If-Sätze benutzt man, um Bedingungen und Folgen auszudrücken. Im if-Satz steht das **simple present**. Im Hauptsatz steht das **will-future**. Geht der **if**-Satz voran, steht am Ende des **if**-Satzes ein Komma.

Bedingung	Folge	
If it **rains**,	we'**ll stay** at home.	Wenn es regnet, bleiben wir zu Hause.
If it'**s** too dark,	I **won't take** any photos.	Wenn es zu dunkel ist, mache ich keine Fotos.

Im **if**-Satz steht nie **will / won't**!

Bedingungssätze können auch mit dem Hauptsatz beginnen. Dann entfällt das Komma.

I'**ll be** unhappy if you **don't come** to my party.	Ich werde unglücklich sein, wenn du nicht zu meiner Party kommst.

(TEST YOURSELF) Complete the sentences.

1. If I — (meet) Nancy, I — (tell) her about the new swimming pool.
2. If Jake — (go) to Scotland, he — (not visit) a museum.
3. If Olivia — (have) time on Saturday, she — (go) shopping.
4. If Katie — (not do) her homework, she — (not be) good at Maths.
5. You — (become) famous if you — (take) a good photo of Nessie.
6. We — (be) very unhappy if you — (not visit) us at the weekend.

G10 Bedingungssätze Typ II

If-clauses type II

If I had a lot of money, I would buy a castle.

Wenn ich viel Geld hätte, würde ich ein Schloss kaufen.

Du kennst schon die Bedingungssätze Typ I. Bei Typ I steht die Bedingung im simple present und die Folge im will-future. (S. 162)
Bei Bedingungssätzen Typ II ist eine Bedingung unwahrscheinlich oder nicht erfüllbar. Du verwendest im if-Satz **simple past**. Im Hauptsatz steht **would / wouldn't + Grundform des Verbs**.

Bedingung	Folge	
If I **had** a dog,	I **would go** outside every day.	Wenn ich einen Hund hätte, würde ich jeden Tag nach draußen gehen.
If it **rained**,	I **would take** my umbrella.	Wenn es regnen würde, würde ich meinen Regenschirm mitnehmen.

Im if-Satz steht nie **would / wouldn't**.

Bedingungssätze können auch mit dem Hauptsatz beginnen. Dann entfällt das Komma.

I **would be** very sad if I **didn't find** my mobile again.	Ich wäre sehr traurig, wenn ich mein Handy nicht mehr finden würde.

Achtung Besonderheit: Statt **If I was** … wird oft **If I were** … gebraucht.

If I **were** you, I **would call** her.	Wenn ich du wäre, würde ich sie anrufen.

Im Deutschen verwendet man in beiden Satzteilen **würde**, **wäre** oder **hätte (Konjunktiv)**.

If your mum **didn't work** so hard, she **wouldn't be** so tired.	Wenn deine Mutter nicht so schwer arbeiten **würde**, **wäre** sie nicht so müde.

(TEST YOURSELF) **Complete the sentences.**

1. If I — (have) more time, I — (go) camping with my friends.
2. If Sue — (be) older, she — (understand) the film.
3. If I — (be) in Northern Ireland, I — (visit) the Giant's Causeway.
4. I — (hear) you better if you — (speak) louder.
5. Your grandparents — (be) very sad, if you — (not visit) them.
6. Kate — (not stay) at home if she — (not be) ill.

G11 Steigerung und Vergleiche von Adjektiven

Clauses of comparison

My eyes are bigger than your eyes.

Meine Augen sind größer als deine Augen.

Adjektive mit **einer Silbe** steigerst du mit **-er / -est**:

cheap	cheap**er**	the cheap**est**	billig, billiger, am billigsten

Zweisilbige Adjektive, die auf **-y** enden, wie z. B. **happy**, **easy**, **crazy**, steigert man auch mit **-er / -est**.

happy	happ**ier**	the happ**iest**	glücklich, glücklicher, am glücklichsten

Alle anderen Adjektive **mit zwei und mehr Silben** steigerst du, indem du **more** und **the most** davor setzt.

expensive	**more** expensive **the most** expensive	teuer, teurer, am teuersten

Und so kannst du ausdrücken, dass etwas weniger oder am wenigsten ist:

interesting	**less** interesting **the least** interesting	interessant, weniger interessant, am wenigsten interessant

So kannst du Dinge miteinander vergleichen:

My big sister is **as** nice **as** my little brother.	Meine große Schwester ist genauso nett wie mein kleiner Bruder.
Mineral water is **not as** expensive **as** juice.	Mineralwasser ist nicht so teuer wie Saft.

Achtung: Um ungleiche Dinge zu vergleichen, benutzt du **than**.

London is **bigger than** Berlin.	London ist größer als Berlin.

(TEST YOURSELF) Compare these things.

1. Northern Ireland is — (small) than England.
2. Eating fruit is — (healthy) than eating sweets.
3. Watching a film can be — (interesting) than surfing the internet.
4. Belfast is the — (exciting) city in Northern Ireland.
5. A bike is — (expensive) than a car.
6. Look, the black shoes are as — (nice) as the white shoes.

G12 Some und any

Some and any

I need some milk but I don't need any cheese.

Ich brauche Milch, aber ich brauche keinen Käse.

Some oder **any** bedeuten im Deutschen **etwas**, **einige** oder **ein paar**.

In positiven Aussagen benutzt du **some**. Es muss nicht immer übersetzt werden.

I'd like **some** fruit.	Ich möchte gerne (etwas) Obst.
I must buy **some** carrots.	Ich muss (ein paar) Karotten kaufen.

In verneinten Aussagen und in den meisten Fragen steht **any**. Es wird nicht immer übersetzt.

Do you have **any** milk at home?	Hast du Milch zu Hause?
Sorry, we don't have **any** bread.	Es tut mir leid, wir haben kein Brot.

Wie **some** und **any** werden auch ihre Zusammensetzungen verwendet:

something und **anything**	(irgend)etwas
somebody und **anybody**	(irgend)jemand
someone und **anyone**	(irgend)jemand
somewhere und **anywhere**	irgendwo

He told me **something**.	Er hat mir etwas gesagt.
Did he tell you **anything**?	Hat er dir etwas gesagt?
No, he didn't tell me **anything**.	Nein, er hat mir nichts gesagt.

Achte auf folgende Übersetzungen:
not … anything → nichts; not … anybody / anyone → niemand; not … anywhere → nirgendwo

(TEST YOURSELF) Put in some or any.

1. Do you know ___ facts about Northern Ireland?
2. Look, there are ___ funny dancers in the street.
3. Let's buy ___ food for the party.
4. Mr Taylor asked me ___ questions about Belfast.
5. Do you have ___ strawberries?
6. Sorry, we don't have ___ strawberries today.

Unit 5

G13 Gegenüberstellung: Simple present und present progressive

Simple present and present progressive

I usually don't drink juice, but today I'm drinking green juice because it's St Patrick's Day.

Normalerweise trinke ich keinen Saft, aber heute trinke ich grünen Saft, weil St. Patrick's Day ist.

Present progressive

Wenn du sagen möchtest, was gerade passiert oder was jemand im Augenblick tut, verwendest du das **present progressive**.

Signalwörter	
now	jetzt, nun
at the moment	im Moment

So bildest du Aussagen im **present progressive: am / are / is + Verb + -ing.**
So verneinst du die Sätze: **am / are / is not + Verb + -ing.**
Bei Fragen stellst du **am / are / is** an den Satzanfang.

Listen, your mobile **is ringing**.	Hör' mal, dein Handy klingelt gerade.
We **are not using** the computer at the moment.	Wir benutzen den Computer gerade nicht.
Are you **preparing** a snack?	Bereitest du gerade einen Imbiss vor?

Simple present

Wenn du einen Zustand beschreiben möchtest oder sagen willst, dass jemand etwas gewohnheitsmäßig tut oder dass etwas häufig oder regelmäßig geschieht, verwendest du das **simple present**.

Signalwörter	
every ...	jede / r / s
always	immer
usually	normalerweise
often	oft
sometimes	manchmal
never	nie

He, **she**, **it** – das **s** muss mit!

Mit **don't** oder **doesn't** (bei he, she, it) kannst du sagen, was man **nicht** macht.
Bei Fragen mit Vollverben (z. B. sing, write, play etc.) musst du **do** oder **does** verwenden.

Every year Keith celebrate**s** St Patrick's Day.	Jedes Jahr feiert Keith den St. Patrick's Day.
Sue **doesn't** speak German.	Sue spricht kein Deutsch.
Do you often eat fish?	Isst du oft Fisch?

(TEST YOURSELF) Use simple present or present progressive.

1. Simon often — (help) his grandma.
2. Listen, Maddy — (practise) with her band.
3. — you sometimes — (eat) eggs?
4. Keith — (not listen to) music now.
5. — (you) — (watch) TV at the moment?
6. Leo — (not drink) tea every day.

G14 Possessivpronomen

Possessive pronouns

I found a mobile. Is it yours?

Ich habe ein Handy gefunden. Ist es deins?

Du kennst bereits die Possessiv**begleiter** (**my**, **your**, **his**, **her**, **our**, **their**). Sie stehen **vor** einem Nomen. Mit den Possessiv**pronomen** kannst du sagen, wem etwas gehört, wenn **kein** Nomen **folgt**.

Possessive determiner	Possessivbegleiter	Possessive pronoun	Possessivpronomen
That's **my** umbrella.	Das ist **mein** Schirm.	It's **mine**.	Das ist **meiner**.
Is that **your** coat?	Ist das **deine** Jacke?	Is it **yours**?	Ist das **deine**?
This is **his** toothbrush.	Das ist **seine** Zahnbürste.	It's **his**.	Das ist **seine**.
This is **her** shampoo.	Das ist **ihr** Shampoo.	It's **hers**.	Es ist **ihrs**.
Look at the cat and **its** ball.	Schau dir die Katze und **ihren** Ball an.	It's **its**.	Das ist **ihrer**.
They are **our** bags.	Es sind **unsere** Taschen.	They are **ours**.	Es sind **unsere**.
Are they **your** towels?	Sind das **eure** Handtücher?	Are they **yours**?	Sind das **eure**?
This is **their** new car.	Das ist **ihr** neues Auto	It's **theirs**.	Das ist **ihrs**.

(TEST YOURSELF) Put in the correct word.

1. Your mobile just looks like ___ (my / mine).
2. Have you put ___ (your / yours) scarf in the bag, Leo?
3. Is that Maddy's bag? – Yes, it's ___ (theirs / hers).
4. Their towels are white, ___ (our / ours) are brown.
5. Is this the O'Brians' new car? – No, it isn't ___ (their / theirs).
6. I think it's Conor's bike. – Well, I don't think it's ___ (his / yours) bike.

G15 Modale Hilfsverben

Modal auxiliaries

You mustn't walk.

Du darfst nicht gehen.

Modale Hilfsverben verändern die Art und Weise eines Verbs. **Can**, **can't**, **must**, **needn't**, **mustn't**, **may**, **may not** kommen immer zusammen mit einem anderen Verb vor.

I **can** play tennis.	Ich kann Tennis spielen. (Ich habe es gelernt.)
I **can't** play tennis now.	Ich kann jetzt nicht Tennis spielen. (Ich muss meine Hausaufgaben machen.)
You **must** play tennis with Amy.	Du musst mit Amy Tennis spielen.
He **needn't** play tennis.	Er braucht nicht Tennis (zu) spielen. (Wir sind genug Spieler.)
She **mustn't** play tennis.	Sie darf nicht Tennis spielen. (Sie ist krank.)
We **may** play tennis later.	Wir spielen vielleicht später Tennis. (Jetzt ist der Platz besetzt.)
They **may not** play tennis then.	Sie spielen dann vielleicht nicht Tennis. (Also können wir spielen.)

Aufgepasst bei **mustn't** (nicht dürfen) und **needn't** (nicht brauchen, nicht müssen):

You **mustn't** talk so loud.	Du darfst nicht so laut sprechen.
You **needn't** wait for me.	Du brauchst nicht auf mich (zu) warten. oder: Du musst nicht auf mich warten.

(TEST YOURSELF) Choose the right word.

1. —— (can / mustn't) I use your pen?
2. You —— (mustn't / needn't) eat ice cream in the classroom.
3. Sara —— (must / mustn't) do her homework.
4. You —— (may not / mustn't) have time to come to the party.
5. We —— (must / needn't) go now. It's already 7 o'clock.
6. You —— (can / needn't) worry. The children will be OK.

Lösungen

G

TEST YOURSELF

G1
1. buy
2. does
3. don't go
4. Do … go
5. are
6. Is

G2
1. had
2. didn't hear
3. Did … have
4. did … do
5. wasn't
6. Were

G3
1. myself
2. yourself
3. herself
4. ourselves
5. each other
6. itself

G4
1. carefully
2. good
3. well
4. clever
5. slowly
6. fast

G5
1. have … been
2. has … done
3. have / 've … had
4. have not / haven't asked
5. Have … forgotten
6. has … not / hasn't … called

G6
1. who
2. which
3. who
4. which
5. who
6. whose

G7
1. Walking
2. Meeting
3. climbing
4. staying
5. working
6. writing

G8
1. 'll / will stay
2. won't / will not be
3. 'll / will have
4. 'll / will show
5. 'll / will do
6. won't / will not lose

G9
1. meet, 'll / will tell
2. goes, won't / will not visit
3. has, 'll / will go
4. doesn't do, won't / will not be
5. 'll / will become, take
6. 'll / will be, don't visit

G10
1. had, would go
2. was, would understand
3. were, would visit
4. would hear, spoke
5. would be, didn't visit
6. wouldn't / would not stay, wasn't

G11
1. smaller
2. healthier
3. more / less interesting
4. most exciting
5. less expensive
6. nice

G12
1. any
2. some
3. some
4. some
5. any
6. any

G13
1. helps
2. is practising
3. Do … eat
4. isn't listening to
5. Are … watching
6. doesn't drink

G14
1. mine
2. your
3. hers
4. ours
5. theirs
6. his

G15
1. Can
2. mustn't
3. must
4. may not
5. must
6. needn't

Methods

1-minute-presentation

Step 1
Nimm ein Blatt DIN A4-Papier quer und falte es so, dass das untere Drittel nach hinten wegknickt.

Step 2
Schreibe den Vortragstext auf die oberen zwei Drittel.

Step 3
Streiche nun die wichtigsten Stichpunkte im Text an. Notiere sie noch einmal auf dem unteren Drittel. Das ist dein Spickzettel.

Step 4
In deiner Präsentation verwendest du nur den Spickzettel. Wenn du steckenbleibst, darfst du ihn umknicken und kurz auf den Text oben schauen.

Bus stop

(Lerntempoduett)

Step 1
Bearbeite die Aufgabe zunächst allein. Schreibe deine Lösungen auf.

Step 2
Wenn du fertig bist, gehe zum „bus stop“. Warte dort auf die nächste Person bzw. triff die Person, die dort schon wartet. Vergleicht und korrigiert eure Ergebnisse.

Step 3
Gehe danach wieder zu deinem Platz zurück. Bearbeite die nächste Aufgabe.

Double circle

(Kugellager)

Step 1

Teilt euch in zwei Gruppen A und B.
Gruppe A bildet den inneren Kreis. Gruppe B bildet den äußeren Kreis. Steht dabei so, dass ihr euch anseht.

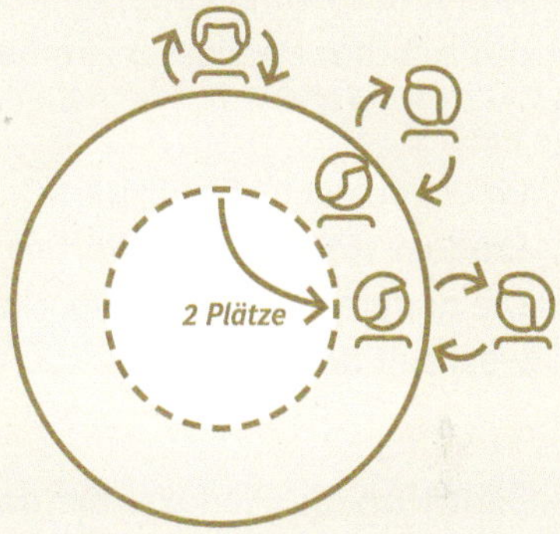

Step 2

Wenn ein Signal ertönt, sprecht ihr mit der Person, die euch gegenübersteht.

Step 3

Beim nächsten Signal rückt der mittlere Kreis zwei Plätze weiter nach links. Wiederholt den Vorgang.

Dramatic reading

(Szenisches Lesen)

Step 1

Verteilt die Rollen innerhalb eurer Gruppe.

Step 2

Lies dir deinen Text lautlos oder ganz leise immer wieder vor, bis du ihn gut kennst.

Step 3

Übt euren Text in der Gruppe mit der Methode „Read and look up" (Seite 174).

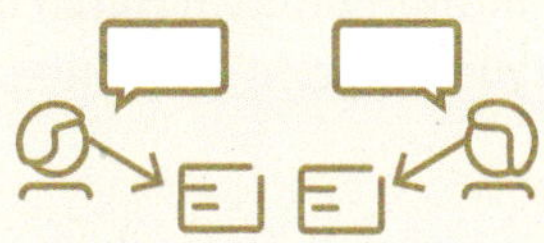

Step 4

Überlegt euch, wie ihr euch in der Rolle fühlt und wie ihr euch bewegen würdet. Tragt euren Text so frei wie möglich vor.

Gallery walk

Step 1

Hängt nach eurer Gruppenarbeit euer Produkt gut sichtbar im Klassenzimmer auf.

Step 2

Einer von euch, der „Experte", bleibt bei eurem Produkt stehen und erklärt es den anderen. Die anderen gehen herum. Nach jedem Durchgang wechselt der Experte.

Step 3

Seht euch die Produkte der anderen an und bewertet sie.

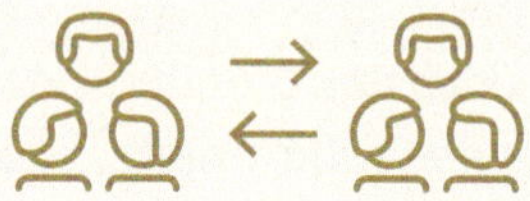

Step 4

Wertet im Anschluss eure Ergebnisse in der Klasse aus.

Milling around

(Marktplatz)

Step 1

Bearbeite die Aufgabe zunächst allein.
Auf ein Zeichen vom Lehrer oder der Lehrerin steht ihr auf und geht durch den Raum.
Nimm die Aufgabe und einen Stift mit.

Step 2

Wenn ein Signal ertönt, bleibt ihr stehen.
Besprecht mit der Person die Aufgabe, die euch am nächsten steht.

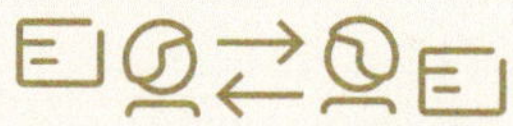

Step 3

Beim nächsten Signal trennt ihr euch und geht weiter durch den Raum. Wiederholt den Vorgang.

Peer correction

(Partnerkontrolle)

Step 1

Bearbeite die Aufgabe zunächst selbstständig.

Step 2

Tausche deine Lösungen mit einem Partner/einer Partnerin. Kontrolliere seine oder ihre Lösungen.

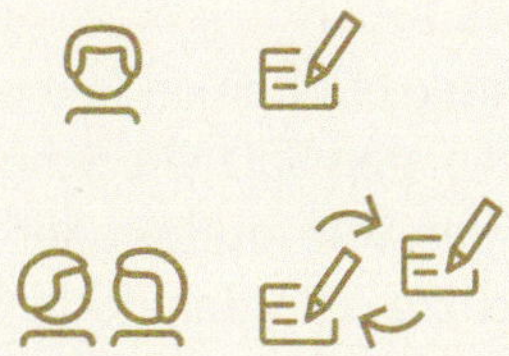

Step 3

Tauscht euch danach zu der Aufgabe aus und korrigiert den Text.

Placemat

(Platzdeckchen)

Step 1

Bildet Vierergruppen.

Step 2

Teilt ein großes Blatt Papier in fünf Bereiche ein.

Step 3

Setzt euch so hin, dass alle in eine Ecke des Blattes schreiben können.

Step 4

Jedes Gruppenmitglied denkt allein über das Thema nach und schreibt Ideen auf seinen Teil des Blattes.

Step 5

Tauscht euch über die Ideen aus. Einigt euch auf die besten Ideen und schreibt diese in die Mitte des Blattes.

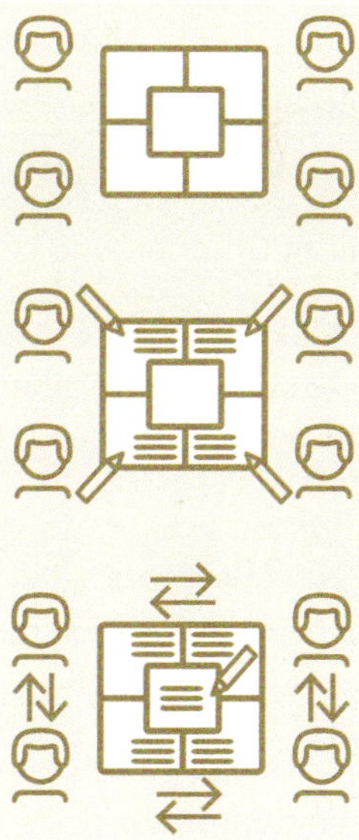

Read and look up

(Lesen und Aufschauen)

Step 1

Schaue auf deinen Text und präge dir die erste Zeile oder den ersten Satz ein. Schaue hoch und sprich deine Zeile/deinen Satz lautlos oder leise vor dich hin. Nimm dir die nächste Zeile/den nächsten Satz vor.

Step 2

Übe nun mit einer Partnerin/einem Partner. Erzähle deinen Text, Zeile für Zeile oder Satz für Satz. Dazwischen schaust du immer wieder nach unten auf deinen Text.

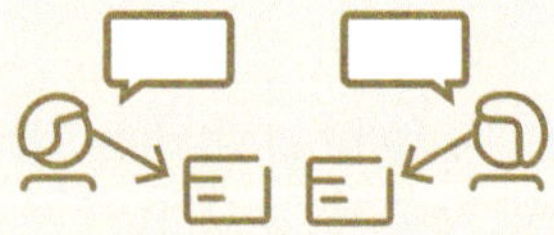

Step 3

Wiederhole alles, bis es gut klappt. Überlege dir, wo du stehen und wie du dich bewegen willst.

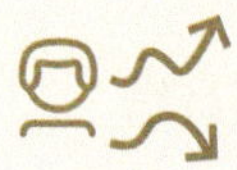

Round robin

(Blitzlicht)

Step 1

Bildet Gruppen und setzt euch in einen Kreis.

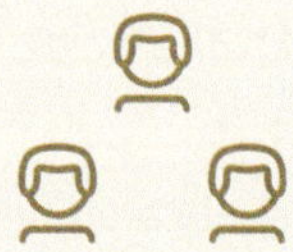

Step 2

Jedes Gruppenmitglied überlegt sich kurz einen Satz, der seine persönliche Meinung zum Thema ausdrückt.

Step 3

Wenn alle bereit sind, sagen die Gruppenmitglieder der Reihe nach ihre Meinung.

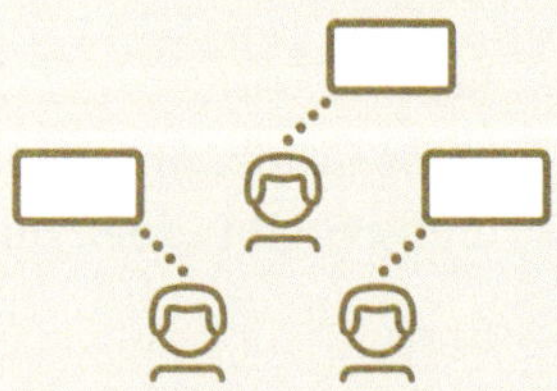

Step 4

Die anderen Gruppenmitglieder dürfen die Sätze nicht kommentieren.

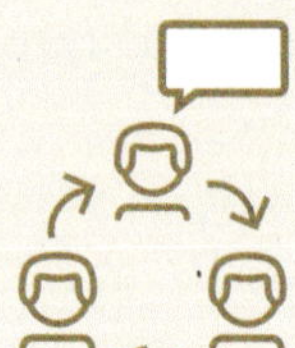

Think – pair – share

Step 1
Schreibe deine Ideen, Gedanken oder Lösungen zur Aufgabe auf.

Step 2
Tauscht eure Notizen zu zweit aus und besprecht sie.

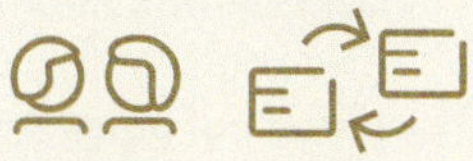

Step 3
Präsentiert euer Ergebnis anderen Paaren oder der gesamten Klasse.

Tip top

Step 1
Sage zunächst, was dir gut gefallen hat – was „top“ war.

Step 2
Sage nun, was noch nicht so gut war, und gib einen Tipp, was man noch verbessern könnte.

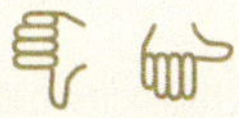

Writers’ conference

(Schreibwerkstatt)

Step 1
Bildet Vierergruppen.

Step 2
Lest euch eure Sätze/Texte gegenseitig vor.

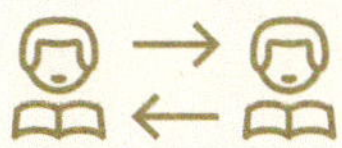

Step 3
Die anderen sagen, was ihnen gefallen hat.

Step 4
Die Zuhörer machen Verbesserungsvorschläge.

Step 5
Jede Gruppe wählt den besten Text aus und liest ihn der Klasse vor.

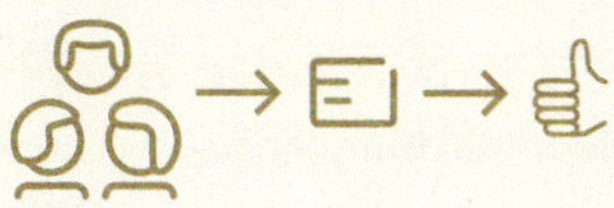

Vocabulary

Das Vocabulary enthält alle neuen Wörter und Wendungen. Sie stehen in der Reihenfolge, wie sie im Buch vorkommen.

Die Wortliste ist in drei Spalten aufgeteilt:

Links findest du das englische Wort mit der Lautschrift in Klammern. (Die Lautschrift wird ganz unten auf jeder Seite im *Dictionary* erklärt.)

In der mittleren Spalte steht die deutsche Übersetzung.

Rechts findest du Beispielsätze, Hinweise und Tipps, die dir beim Lernen helfen.

Die **fett** gedruckten Wörter musst du lernen.
Die blau gedruckten Wörter kannst du lernen, musst du aber nicht.
Die Wörter aus den Checkpoints musst du nicht lernen.

Symbole und Abkürzungen:

(Lippen-Symbol)	Achte auf die Aussprache!	=	entspricht
(Stift-Symbol)	Achte auf die Schreibung!	*(sg)*	Einzahl (Singular)
↔	ist das Gegenteil von	*(pl)*	Mehrzahl (Plural)
→	ist verwandt mit	R	ähnlich wie im Russischen
sth	something	T	ähnlich wie im Türkischen

Die *Word bank*-Seiten helfen dir, die *Your turn*-Aufgaben in den *Units* zu bearbeiten. Du findest dort nützlichen individuellen Wortschatz zum Thema der *Unit*, der dir hilft, über deine eigene Situation zu sprechen oder zu schreiben. Diese Wörter findest du auch im *Dictionary*.

Wenn du ein Wort nicht weißt und im Wörterbuch nachschlagen willst, schau auf den *Dictionary*-Seiten ab S. 221 nach. Oder bei den *Instructions* auf S. 217.

Zoom in – The British Isles

p. 8 **The British Isles** [ðə ˌbrɪtɪʃ ˈaɪlz]	die Britischen Inseln	
Scotland [ˈskɒtlənd]	Schottland	
Northern Ireland [ˌnɔːðn‿ˈaɪələnd]	Nordirland	
The Republic of Ireland [ðə rɪˌpʌblɪk‿əv‿ˈaɪələnd]	Irland	
Wales [weɪlz]	Wales	
The United Kingdom [ðə juːˌnaɪtɪd ˈkɪŋdəm]	Vereinigtes Königreich von Großbritannien und Nordirland	
Great Britain [ˌgreɪt ˈbrɪtn]	Großbritannien	

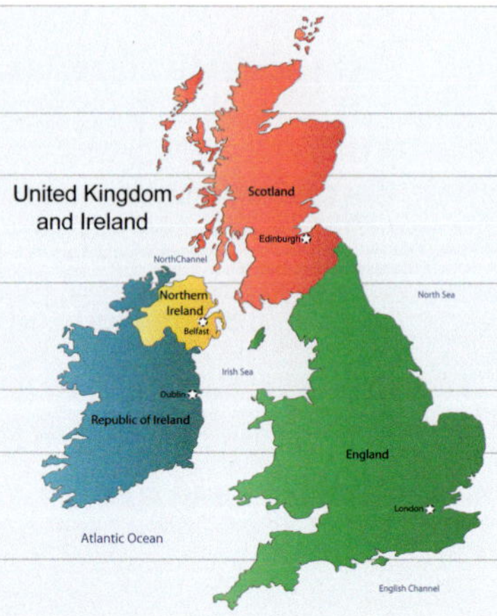

p. 9	**hobby** ['hɒbi]	Hobby	R хобби T hobi

Unit 1 England now and then

p. 10	**then** [ðen]	damals	We lived in Wales **then**.

Way in

	circle ['sɜ:kl]	Kreis; Ring	
	stone [stəʊn]	Stein	
	in the south of [ˌɪn ðə 'saʊθ‿əv]	im Süden von	Stonehenge is **in the south of** England.
	the Romans [ðə 'rəʊmənz]	die Römer	**The Romans** built Hadrian's Wall.
	north [nɔ:θ]	Norden	**north** ↔ south
	to mark [mɑ:k]	markieren; kennzeichnen	Read the text and **mark** the new words!
	border ['bɔ:də]	Grenze	Hadrian's Wall marks the **border**.
	empire ['empaɪə]	Reich; Kaiserreich	The Romans had an **empire** in 122.
	to take [teɪk]	dauern	It **takes** two hours by train.
	east [i:st]	Osten	
	west [west]	Westen	
p. 11	**Viking** ['vaɪkɪŋ]	Wikinger-	The **Viking** army was big.
	army ['ɑ:mi]	Armee; Heer	They had a big **army**.
	to invade [ɪn'veɪd]	einmarschieren (in); eindringen (in)	The Viking army **invaded** York.
	Denmark ['denmɑ:k]	Dänemark	**Denmark** is in the north of Europe.
	Norway ['nɔ:weɪ]	Norwegen	R Норвегия T Norveç
	northern ['nɔ:ðən]	nördlich	They came from other **northern** countries.
	the Normans [ðə 'nɔ:mənz]	die Normannen	In 1066 **the Normans** came from France.
	across [ə'krɒs]	über	They came **across** the sea.
	to fight [faɪt], **fought** [fɔ:t], **fought** [fɔ:t]	kämpfen; (sich) streiten	Achtung Schreibweise! fi<u>gh</u>t
	battle ['bætl]	Schlacht; Kampf	The Normans won a **battle**.
	the English [ði 'ɪŋglɪʃ]	die Engländer	**The English** lost a battle near Hastings.

leader ['li:də]	Anführer; Anführerin; Führer; Führerin	He was the **leader** of the Normans.
king [kɪŋ]	König	
industry ['ɪndəstri]	Industrie	There is lots of **industry** in England.
during ['djʊərɪŋ]	während	I ate my lunch **during** the break.
Industrial Revolution [ɪnˌdʌstriəl revl'u:ʃn]	industrielle Revolution	The **Industrial Revolution** was from 1780 to 1840.
million ['mɪljən]	Million	**1 million** = 1,000,000
sun [sʌn]	Sonne	
sick [sɪk]	krank	She isn't at school because she is **sick**.
grave [greɪv]	Grab	People found **graves** near Stonehenge.

Station 1

Shops

souvenir shop ['su:vnɪə ˌʃɒp]	Souvenirladen	**greengrocer's** ['gri:nˌgrəʊsəz]	Obst- und Gemüseladen
baker's ['beɪkəz]	Bäckerei	**butcher's** ['bʊtʃəz]	Metzgerei
jeweller's ['dʒu:ələz]	Juwelierladen	**pet shop** ['pet ˌʃɒp]	Tierhandlung
newsagent's ['nju:zˌeɪdʒnts]	Zeitschriftenladen		

p. 12 **way** [weɪ]	Weg	Do you know the **way** to the shops?
almost ['ɔ:lməʊst]	fast; beinahe	55 minutes is **almost** an hour.
I know my way around here. [aɪ ˌnəʊ maɪ 'weɪ əraʊnd ˌhɪə]	Ich kenne mich hier aus.	Ganze Sätze am besten als Einheit lernen.
to be interested in [bi: 'ɪntrəstɪd‿ɪn]	sich interessieren für; interessiert sein an	**to be interested in** = to like sth
to learn about sth [ˌlɜ:n ə'baʊt]	etwas erfahren über	I'd like to **learn about** the city.
history ['hɪstri]	Geschichte	[R] история
to cross [krɒs]	überqueren	We have to **cross** the road to get there.
to be worth [bi: 'wɜ:θ]	wert sein	It's really **worth** a trip.

V

visit ['vɪzɪt]	Besuch	**visit** → to visit → visitor
what sth was like [ˌwɒt … 'wəz laɪk]	wie etwas war	It shows you **what the city was like** before.
friendly ['frendli]	freundlich; nett	**friendly** → friend
past [pɑ:st]	vorbei (an)	Walk **past** the cinema, then cross the road.
right [raɪt]	rechts	Turn **right** at the end of the road.
left [left]	links	**left** ↔ right
that [ðæt]	so *(Betonung)*	I don't have **that** much time!
to sell [sel], **sold** [səʊld], **sold** [səʊld]	verkaufen	The souvenir shop **sells** souvenirs.
helmet ['helmət]	Helm	 
How do I get there? [ˌhaʊ du aɪ 'get ðeə]	Wie komme ich dahin?	Ganze Sätze am besten als Einheit lernen.
down [daʊn]	entlang; herunter; hinunter	**down** ↔ up
far [fɑ:]	weit	**far** ↔ near
a five minute walk [ə 'faɪv mɪnɪt ˌwɔ:k]	fünf Minuten zu Fuß	It's just **a five minute walk** from here.
p. 15 **near** [nɪə]	nah	Excuse me, where's the **nearest** book shop?
ticket ['tɪkɪt]	Fahrschein; Eintrittskarte	 
street [stri:t]	Straße	Walk down the second **street** on the left.

Station 2

Talking about places

northwest [ˌnɔ:θ'west]	Nordwesten	**tiny** ['taɪni]	klein; winzig
northeast [ˌnɔ:θ'i:st]	Nordosten	**distance** ['dɪstns]	Entfernung; Distanz
southwest [ˌsaʊθ'west]	Südwesten	**to the north of** [ˌtə ðə 'nɔ:θ‿əv]	nördlich von
noisy ['nɔɪzi]	laut	**on the coast** [ˌɒn ðə 'kəʊst]	an der Küste
quiet ['kwaɪət]	ruhig; leise; still	**huge** [hju:dʒ]	riesig; riesengroß
in the centre of [ˌɪn ðə 'sentər‿əv]	in der Mitte von		
in the mountains [ˌɪn ðə 'maʊntɪnz]	in den Bergen		

p. 16	**half a million** [ˌhɑ:f‿ə 'mɪljən]	eine halbe Million	More than **half a million** people live there.
	inhabitant [ɪn'hæbɪtnt]	Einwohner; Einwohnerin; Bewohner; Bewohnerin	**inhabitants** of a town = people who live in a town
	traffic ['træfɪk]	Verkehr	There's lots of **traffic** in the city.
	to **get on one's nerves** [ˌget‿ɒn wʌnz 'nɜ:vz]	auf die Nerven gehen	Diese Wörter am besten als Einheit lernen.
	then again [ˌðen ə'gen]	andererseits	It's noisy, but **then again** it's a big city.
	to **get around** [ˌget ə'raʊnd]	herumkommen	It's very easy to **get around** the city.
	past [pɑ:st]	Vergangenheit	In the **past** Manchester had lots of industry. 
	factory ['fæktri]	Fabrik; Werk	
	coal [kəʊl]	Kohle	**Coal** is black stones you use on a fire.
	mine [maɪn]	Bergwerk	You get coal from a coal **mine**.
	city centre [ˌsɪti 'sentə]	Stadtzentrum; Stadtmitte	There are lots of shops in the **city centre**.
	village ['vɪlɪdʒ]	Dorf	There are not many houses in a **village**.
	used to (live) ['ju:st tə]	(wohnte) früher	We **used to** live in Newcastle.
	countryside ['kʌntrɪsaɪd]	Land; Landschaft	Tom didn't want to live in the **countryside**.
	still [stɪl]	dennoch	It's hard work, **still** I enjoy it. 
	goat [gəʊt]	Ziege	
	cow [kaʊ]	Kuh	
	to **milk** [mɪlk]	melken	We **milk** the cows at six o'clock.
	to **call** [kɔ:l]	nennen	I **call** it boring, not fun!
	worst [wɜ:st]	schlimmste; schlechteste	That is the **worst** thing about our village.
	unfair [ʌn'feə]	unfair	I can't see my friends. It's so **unfair**!
p. 17	**public transport** [ˌpʌblɪk 'trænspɔ:t]	öffentliche Verkehrsmittel	**public transport**: buses, trams, trains
	to **check** [tʃek]	überprüfen; kontrollieren	Can you **check** my homework, please?
p. 18	**mud** [mʌd]	Schlamm; Matsch	
	head first ['hed fɜ:st]	kopfüber	He fell into the mud, **head first**.

Reading corner

p. 20	**deadly** ['dedli]	tod-; tödlich	It was **deadly** quiet in the house.
	silence ['saɪləns]	Stille; Schweigen; Ruhe	**silence** = no noise
	tunnel ['tʌnl]	Tunnel	R тоннель T tünel 
	after it's gone [ˌɑ:ftə ɪts 'gɒn]	nachdem sie (die Kohle) weg ist	Diese Wörter am besten als Einheit lernen.
	the dark [ðə 'dɑ:k]	Dunkelheit	I sit in **the dark** every day.
	That's because ... [ˌðæts bɪ'kɒz]	Das liegt daran, dass ...	**That's because** my friend is with me.
	to **be made of** [bi: 'meɪd‿əv]	hergestellt sein aus	The house **is made of** stone.
	canary [kə'neəri]	Kanarienvogel	
	gas [gæs]	Gas	R газ T gaz
	to **touch** [tʌtʃ]	berühren	I **touched** him with my hand. 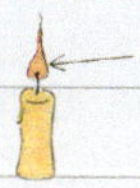
	flame [fleɪm]	Flamme	
	to **explode** [ɪk'spləʊd]	explodieren	When gas touches a flame, it **explodes**.
	explosion [ɪk'spləʊʒn]	Explosion	There was a big **explosion**.
	to **kill** [kɪl]	töten	An explosion **killed** 30 men.
	miner ['maɪnə]	Bergarbeiter; Bergarbeiterin	A **miner** works in a mine.
	to **notice** ['nəʊtɪs]	bemerken; wahrnehmen	A canary **notices** gas sooner than a man.
	to **go quiet** [ˌgəʊ 'kwaɪət]	still werden	The canary **went quiet**. I knew there was gas.
	a few [ə 'fju:]	ein paar; wenige; einige	You only have **a few** minutes to leave.
p. 21	**one day** [wʌn 'deɪ]	eines Tages	**One day** I stopped talking.
	to **cough** [kɒf]	husten	Bart **coughed** all the time.
	badly ['bædli]	sehr; schwer	He was hurt so **badly**.
	that [ðæt]	dass	I saw **that** everyone was OK.
	to **die** [daɪ]	sterben	He was really ill and **died**.
	still [stɪl]	immer noch; noch	I **still** like it here in the mountains.
	could [kʊd]	konnte	I **couldn't** talk.
	silent ['saɪlənt]	schweigsam; stumm	**silent** → silence
	probably ['prɒbəbli]	wahrscheinlich	They **probably** thought I was strange.
	truck [trʌk]	Wagen; Karre	

	any ['eni]	jede	The gas could explode **any** second.
	to warn [wɔ:n]	warnen	I **warned** the men in the mine.
	sound [saʊnd]	Ton; Laut; Geräusch	I opened my mouth, but no **sound** came.
	nothing ['nʌθɪŋ]	nichts	**nothing** ↔ something
	time [taɪm]	Mal	I will go with you next **time**.
p. 22	**to breathe** [bri:ð]	atmen	I couldn't **breathe** in the mine.
	voice [vɔɪs]	Stimme	I could hear the miners' **voices**.
	Come on! [ˌkʌm‿'ɒn]	Komm schon!	**Come on!** Let's go!
	somebody ['sʌmbədi]	jemand	**Somebody** helped me after the explosion.
	to turn around [ˌtɜ:n‿ə'raʊnd]	(sich) umdrehen	I **turned around** and saw the miners.
	dead [ded]	tot	I thought Billy was **dead**.
	safe [seɪf]	in Sicherheit; sicher	The people from the mine were **safe**.
	open ['əʊpn]	offen; geöffnet	They all had their mouths **open**.
	alive [ə'laɪv]	am Leben	**alive** ↔ dead
p. 23	**fired** ['faɪəd]	gefeuert; hinausgeworfen	to get **fired** = to lose your job
	smell [smel]	Geruch	There was a gas **smell** in the tunnel.

Film corner

p. 25	**Victorian era** [vɪkˌtɔ:riən 'ɪərə]	viktorianisches Zeitalter	This was when Queen Victoria was the Queen.
	to fall asleep [ˌfɔ:l‿ə'sli:p]	einschlafen	I **fell asleep** at ten o'clock.
	to dream [dri:m], **dreamt** [dremt], **dreamt** [dremt]	träumen	I **dreamt** that I was a teacher.
	century ['senʃri]	Jahrhundert	a **century** = 100 years
	I'd rather [aɪd 'rɑ:ðə]	ich würde lieber	**I'd rather** eat vegetables than meat.
	to wish [wɪʃ]	wünschen	I **wish** every day was Saturday.
	to be asleep [bi: ə'sli:p]	schlafen	You **have been asleep** all day.
	confused [kən'fju:zd]	verwirrt; wirr	I was **confused**, I didn't know where I was.

Checkpoint

project ['prɒdʒekt]	Projekt	informative [ɪn'fɔ:mətɪv]	informativ
presenter [prɪ'zentə]	Moderator; Moderatorin		

V

Reading skills

p. 31	**type** [taɪp]	Sorte; Typ; Art;	What **type** of text is it?
	brochure [ˈbrəʊʃə]	Broschüre; Prospekt	T брошюра T broşür
	to **be about** [biː əˈbaʊt]	gehen um; handeln von	The text **is about** a bike tour.
	queen [kwiːn]	Königin	
	inside [ˌɪnˈsaɪd]	in; innen in; im Innern	The Queen is **inside** the palace.

Word bank: Directions

on the left

on the right

beside / next to

opposite

on the corner

at the traffic lights

our house is on the right / left

turn right

turn left

go straight on

cross the road

walk down the road

go / walk past (a book shop)

Asking for help:	Getting help:
Excuse me, please.	Can I help you?
Do you know where there is a … ?	Yes, I do.
	No, I don't.
Can I walk there?	Yes, it's just a five minute walk.
	Yes, it isn't far.
	No, I'd take the bus / underground.
Are there buses?	Yes, every five minutes.
	No, there aren't.
Does it take long?	Yes, about 30 minutes.
	No, it doesn't take long.
Is it far away?	Yes, it is.
	No, it isn't.

V

Word bank: Where I live

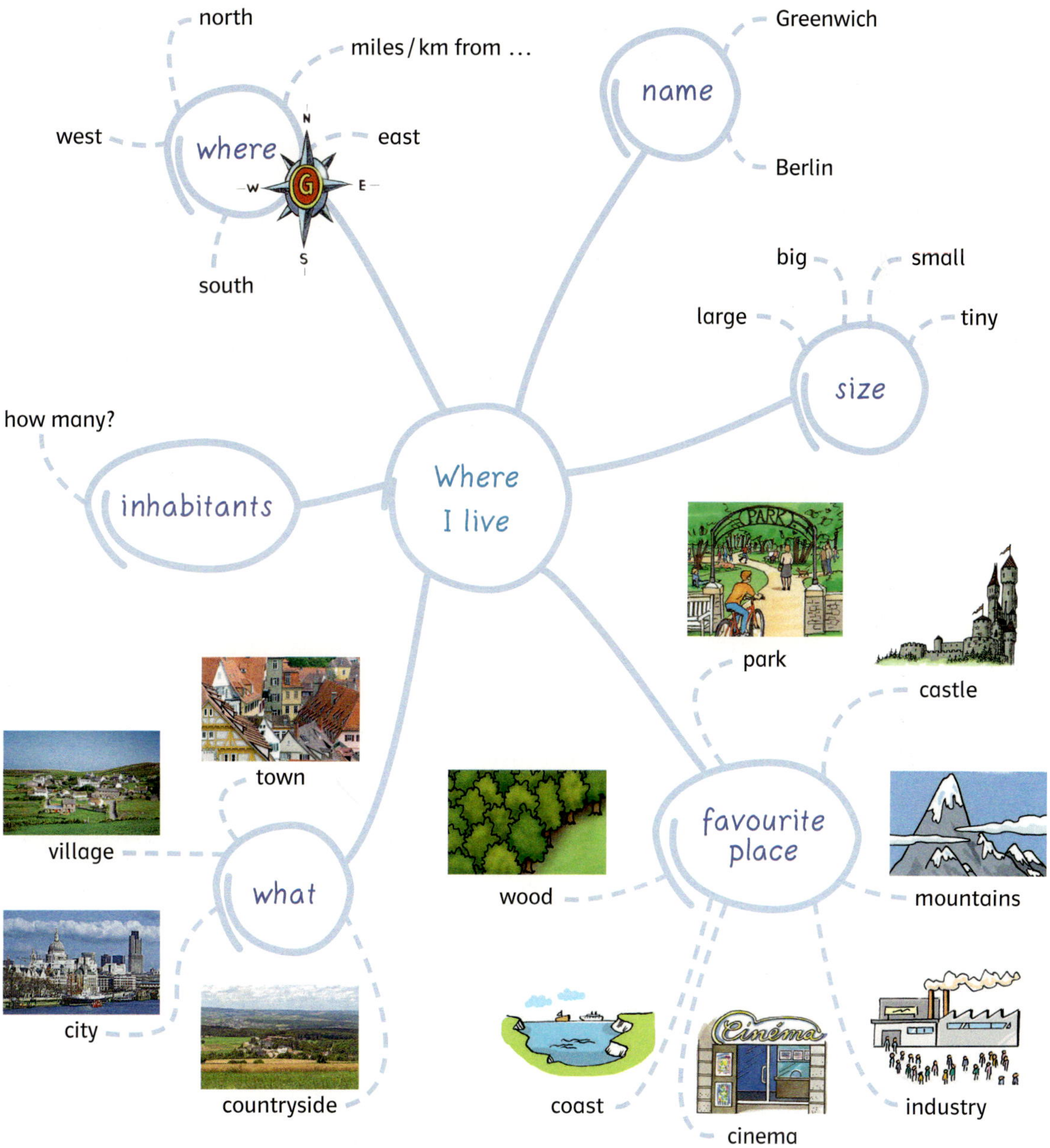

Unit 2 Adventures in Wales

Way in

p. 32	**Welsh** [welʃ]	Walisisch; walisisch; Waliser; Waliserin	**Welsh** is a very old language.
	sign [saɪn]	Schild; Zeichen	✎ Achtung Schreibweise! sign
	course [kɔ:s]	Kurs	We have lots of different **courses**.
	conversation [ˌkɒnvəˈseɪʃn]	Konversation; Gespräch; Unterhaltung	You can have a **conversation** in Welsh.
	zip line [ˈzɪp ˌlaɪn]	Seilrutsche	The longest **zip line** in Europe is in Wales.
	over [ˈəʊvə]	über	You travel **over** 60 miles an hour.
	skiing [ˈski:ɪŋ]	Skifahren	
p. 33	**capital (city)** [ˈkæpɪtl (sɪti)]	Hauptstadt	The **capital** of England is London.
	to **be located** [bi: ləʊˈkeɪtɪd]	liegen	It **is located** in the park.
	middle [ˈmɪdl]	Mitte	**middle** = centre
	sport [spɔ:t]	Sportart	R спорт T spor
	coast [kəʊst]	Küste	England has a lot of **coast**.
	rafting [ˈrɑ:ftɪŋ]	Rafting	You can do **rafting** in the sea or on a river.
	surfing [ˈsɜ:fɪŋ]	Surfen; Wellenreiten	
	popular [ˈpɒpjələ]	beliebt	Canoeing and rafting are **popular** sports.
	volunteer [ˌvɒlənˈtɪə]	Freiwilliger; Freiwillige; ehrenamtlicher Helfer; ehrenamtliche Helferin	**Volunteers** help people and don't get any money.
	lifeboat [ˈlaɪfbəʊt]	Rettungsboot	**Lifeboats** are very important in Wales.
	trouble [ˈtrʌbl]	Schwierigkeiten; Problem; Ärger	They help people in **trouble**.
	teenager [ˈti:neɪdʒə]	Teenager; Teenagerin; Jugendliche; Jugendlicher	**Teenagers** in Wales must learn Welsh.
	guest [gest]	Gast	We have **guests** for the weekend.
	fluent [ˈflu:ənt]	fließend; flüssig	I'm German, but can speak **fluent** English.
	all the time [ˌɔ:l ðə ˈtaɪm]	die ganze Zeit	My grandma speaks Welsh **all the time**.

to **mean** [mi:n], **meant** [ment], **meant** [ment]	bedeuten; meinen	'Wurst' **means** 'sausage' in English.

Station 1

Adjectives for sportspeople

slow [sləʊ]	langsam	**unpopular** [ʌn'pɒpjələ]	unpopulär; unbeliebt
tough [tʌf]	hart	**loud** [laʊd]	laut
strong [strɒŋ]	stark	**competitive** [kəm'petɪtɪv]	wettkampforientiert; leistungsorientiert
fit [fɪt]	fit; in Form	**talented** ['tæləntɪd]	begabt; talentiert
difficult ['dɪfɪklt]	schwierig	**exhausted** [ɪg'zɔ:stɪd]	erschöpft
unfriendly [ʌn'frendli]	unfreundlich	**patient** ['peɪʃnt]	geduldig
weak [wi:k]	schwach	**successful** [sək'sesfl]	erfolgreich
dry [draɪ]	trocken		

p. 34	**outdoor** [ˌaʊt'dɔ:]	Freiluft-; Outdoor-	Kayaking is an **outdoor** sport.
	activity centre [æk'tɪvəti ˌsentə]	Jugendzentrum	The **activity centre** looks really good.
	to **take a trip** [ˌteɪk‿ə 'trɪp]	eine Fahrt machen	We **took** a canoeing **trip** down the river.
	relaxing [rɪ'læksɪŋ]	entspannend; erholsam	We took a **relaxing** trip down the river.
	to **be included** [bi: ɪn'klu:dɪd]	enthalten sein	A picnic lunch **is included** in the trip.
	should [ʃʊd]	sollte	You **should** try something new this year.
	rugby ['rʌgbi]	Rugby	[R] регби [T] rugbi 
	rule [ru:l]	Regel	You can learn the **rules** quickly.
	wood [wʊd]	Wald	You will ride in the **woods**.
	instructor [ɪn'strʌktə]	Lehrer; Lehrerin	All our **instructors** are friendly.
	indoor [ˌɪn'dɔ:]	Hallen-; Innen-	**indoor** ↔ outdoor
	useful ['ju:sfl]	nützlich; hilfreich	The tips were very **useful**.
	equipment [ɪ'kwɪpmənt]	Ausrüstung	**equipment**: helmet, special clothes, ...
	to **keep safe** [ˌki:p 'seɪf]	schützen	Wear a helmet to **keep** you **safe**.
	enough [ɪ'nʌf]	genug; genügend	I'm strong **enough** for it.
	cheeky ['tʃi:ki]	frech	Mark was **cheeky** to Beth.
	to **enjoy oneself** [ɪn'dʒɔɪ]	Spaß haben; sich amüsieren	I **enjoyed myself** at the activity centre.

	myself [maɪ'self]	selbst; selber	It's nice. I often go there **myself**.
	to **climb** [klaɪm]	klettern; steigen; besteigen	✎ Achtung Schreibweise! climb
	quite [kwaɪt]	ziemlich	I can climb **quite** well already.
	dangerous ['deɪndʒrəs]	gefährlich	**dangerous** ↔ safe
	That's not for me. [ˌðæts nɒt fə 'mi:]	Das ist nichts für mich.	Ganze Sätze am besten als Einheit lernen.
	No way am I doing that again! [ˌnəʊ 'weɪ əm aɪ ˌdu:ɪŋ ðæt ə'gen]	Das mache ich auf keinen Fall noch mal!	Ganze Sätze am besten als Einheit lernen.
	to **joke** [dʒəʊk]	Witze machen; scherzen	I'm **joking**. I'm not allergic to cats.
	anyway ['eniweɪ]	trotzdem; jedenfalls	You can go climbing **anyway** and I'll wait.
	each other [ˌi:tʃ‿'ʌðə]	einander; sich; sich gegenseitig	We can tell **each other** about it later!
	self [self]	selbst; sich	**self**: myself, yourself, himself, herself, itself, ourselves, yourselves, themselves
p. 35	**himself** [hɪm'self]	sich (selbst); er selbst	He hurt **himself** on the trip.
	to **make sure** [ˌmeɪk 'ʃɔ:]	dafür sorgen; sich versichern	They will **make sure** nothing bad happens.
p. 36	to **smile** [smaɪl]	lächeln	She **smiled** happily.
	class [klɑ:s]	Klasse	Our **class** went on a trip last week.
	camping ['kæmpɪŋ]	Camping; Zelten	We went on a **camping** trip to Wales.
	to **kick** [kɪk]	schießen; treten	In football you **kick** the ball.
p. 37	**because of** [bɪ'kɒz‿əv]	wegen	I was late **because of** the weather.
	What must you be like? [wɒt ˌmʌst ju 'bi: laɪk]	Wie musst du sein?	Ganze Sätze am besten als Einheit lernen.

V

Station 2

Health and medicine

to **bleed** [bli:d], **bled** [bled], **bled** [bled]	bluten
injury ['ɪndʒri]	Verletzung
finger ['fɪŋgə]	Finger
tooth *(sg)* [tu:θ], **teeth** *(pl)* [ti:θ]	Zahn
knee [ni:]	Knie
to **burn** [bɜ:n], **burnt** [bɜ:nt], **burnt** [bɜ:nt]	verbrennen; brennen
to **sprain** [spreɪn]	verstauchen; verrenken
cast [kɑ:st]	Gips
to **put on** [ˌpʊt‿'ɒn]	anlegen; anziehen
bandage ['bændɪdʒ]	Verband
to **cool** [ku:l]	kühlen
to **move** [mu:v]	(sich) bewegen
plaster ['plɑ:stə]	Pflaster
injection [ɪn'dʒekʃn]	Spritze
operation [ˌɒpr'eɪʃn]	Operation
sleep [sli:p]	Schlaf
medicine ['medsn]	Medikamente; Medizin
a day off [ə ˌdeɪ‿'ɒf]	ein freier Tag

p. 38	**emergency** [ɪ'mɜ:dʒnsi]	Notfall	Help! It's an **emergency**.
	operator ['ɒpreɪtə]	Vermittlung	You get the **operator** when you call 999.
	emergency service [ɪ'mɜ:dʒnsi ˌsɜ:vɪs]	Notdienst; Rettungsdienst	You call 999 for the **emergency services** in the UK.
	service ['sɜ:vɪs]	Dienst	Which **service** do you need? 
	ambulance ['æmbjələns]	Krankenwagen	
	accident ['æksɪdnt]	Unfall	The man has had an **accident**.
	to fall (over) [ˌfɔ:l‿'əʊvə]	fallen; hinfallen; umfallen	I think he **fell** over on the beach.
	rock [rɒk]	Fels; Stein	
	serious ['sɪəriəs]	schwer; ernst	I think she has a **serious** injury.
	awake [ə'weɪk]	bei Bewusstsein; wach	Is the man **awake**?
	right now [ˌraɪt 'naʊ]	jetzt gerade	Yes, he is awake **right now**.
	phone number ['fəʊn ˌnʌmbə]	Telefonnummer	Give me your **phone number**, please!
	to do the right thing [ˌdu: ðə 'raɪt θɪŋ]	das Richtige tun	It's OK. You've **done the right thing**.
	police [pə'li:s]	Polizei	[R] полиция [T] polis
	emergency call [ɪ'mɜ:dʒnsi ˌkɔ:l]	Notruf	The phone number for **emergency calls** is 999.
p. 39	**without** [wɪ'ðaʊt]	ohne	I can't live **without** food.

	cuddly toy ['kʌdli ˌtɔɪ]	Kuscheltier	My little sister has lots of **cuddly toys**.
p. 40	to **fall off** [ˌfɔːl‿'ɒf]	fallen; herunterfallen	I **fell off** my bike and needed help.
	to **hit** [hɪt]	(sich) stoßen; anstoßen	He **hit** his head on the table.
p. 41	**training** ['treɪnɪŋ]	Training	On Friday I have football **training**.
	skateboard ['skeɪtbɔːd]	Skateboard	R скейтборд T skateboard 
	trick [trɪk]	Kunststück	I want to try some skateboard **tricks**.

Reading corner

p. 42	**reporter** [rɪ'pɔːtə]	Reporter; Reporterin	A **reporter** writes stories for magazines.
	to **get there** ['get‿ðeə]	hinkommen	How do they **get there**?
	AD (= Anno Domini) [ˌeɪ'diː]	nach Christus	It was built in the year 1100 **AD**.
	except [ɪk'sept]	außer	We all laughed, **except** the teacher.
	to jump [dʒʌmp]	zusammenzucken; erschrecken	The loud noise made us **jump**.
	gate [geɪt]	Tor	
	knight [naɪt]	Ritter	Achtung Schreibweise! <u>k</u>night 
	to appear [ə'pɪə]	auftauchen; erscheinen	Suddenly the knight **appeared**.
	cloud [klaʊd]	Wolke	
	smoke [sməʊk]	Rauch	
	future ['fjuːtʃə]	Zukunft	past – today – **future**
	convincing [kən'vɪnsɪŋ]	überzeugend	He wasn't a very **convincing** knight.
p. 43	to **joust** [dʒaʊst]	einen Turnierzweikampf austragen; turnieren	We learned how to **joust**. 
	armour ['ɑːmə]	Rüstung	
	to **hold** [həʊld], **held** [held], **held** [held]	halten; festhalten	I **held** the door open for the film star.
	sword [sɔːd]	Schwert	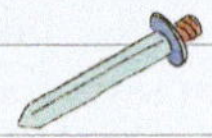
	to make sb feel like sth [ˌmeɪk … 'fiːl laɪk]	jmdm. das Gefühl geben, etw. zu sein	It **made you feel like a real knight**.
	jousting ['dʒaʊstɪŋ]	Turnierzweikampf	The **jousting** was super cool.
	wheelchair ['wiːltʃeə]	Rollstuhl	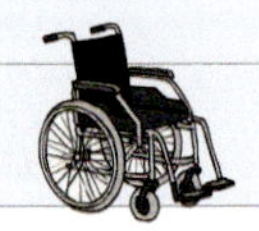

	in the old days [ɪn ði 'əʊld ˌdeɪz]	früher	**In the old days** there was a knight school.
	naughty ['nɔ:ti]	frech; böse	**naughty** ↔ good
	stocks [stɒks]	Pranger	He put me in the **stocks**.
	to **try out** [ˌtraɪ‿'aʊt]	ausprobieren	We **tried out** the stocks.
	for fun [fə 'fʌn]	zum Spaß	We did it just **for fun**.
	to **get out** [ˌget 'aʊt]	herauskommen	I **got out** of the stocks quickly.
	lots [lɒts]	viel; jede Menge	We learned **lots** about Caldicot Castle.

Film corner

p. 45	**briefcase** ['bri:fkeɪs]	Aktenkoffer; Aktentasche	My dad puts things in his **briefcase**.
	to **answer the phone** [ˌɑ:nsə ðə 'fəʊn]	ans Telefon gehen	I **answered the phone** when you called.
	cannot ['kænɒt]	nicht können	The girls **cannot** open the briefcase.
	prop [prɒp]	Requisit	You need **props** for films and plays.
	ending ['endɪŋ]	Schluss; Ende	I didn't like the **ending**.
	to **expect** [ɪk'spekt]	erwarten	I **expected** a happy ending.

Writing skills

p. 50	**review** [rɪ'vju:]	Kritik	Read this **review** about the new book.
	to **enjoy** [ɪn'dʒɔɪ]	*hier:* mögen	I really **enjoyed** the film.
	introduction [ˌɪntrə'dʌkʃn]	Einleitung; Einführung	The **introduction** is very short.
	comedy ['kɒmədi]	Komödie	R комедия T komedi
	murderer ['mɜ:drə]	Mörder; Mörderin	You don't see the **murderer** until the end.
	to **run away** [ˌrʌn‿ə'weɪ]	weglaufen	She was scared and **ran away**.
	to **hide** [haɪd], **hid** [hɪd], **hidden** ['hɪdn]	(sich) verstecken	She ran away and **hid** behind the car.
	baker ['beɪkə]	Bäcker; Bäckerin	
	enemy ['enəmi]	Feind; Feindin	**enemy** ↔ friend
	fight [faɪt]	Kampf; Streit	**fight** → to fight
	content ['kɒntent]	Inhalt	The **content** is about the film.
	location [ləʊ'keɪʃn]	Drehort; Lage	The **location** of the film was beautiful.
	writer ['raɪtə]	Verfasser; Verfasserin; Autor; Autorin	The **writer** of the review liked the book.

	opinion [ə'pɪnjən]	Meinung	I gave my **opinion** and said what I thought.
	star [stɑ:]	Stern	In her review she gave the film four **stars**.
	conclusion [kən'klu:ʒn]	Schlussfolgerung; Schluss	The **conclusion** is at the end.
	to **get a job wrong** [ˌget‿ə dʒɒb 'rɒŋ]	einen Auftrag vermasseln	The murderer **gets a job wrong**.
	to **fall in love (with)** [ˌfɔ:l‿ɪn 'lʌv]	sich verlieben (in)	I **fell in love** with the actor in the film.
	to **give sth a miss** [ˌgɪv sʌmθɪŋ‿ə 'mɪs]	auf etw. verzichten; etw. bleiben lassen	**Give** the film **a miss**.
p. 51	to **give reasons** [ˌgɪv 'ri:znz]	Gründe nennen; Gründe angeben	**Give** the **reasons** for your opinion.
	to **rate** [reɪt]	bewerten; einstufen	The writer **rates** the film.
	advice [əd'vaɪs]	Rat; Ratschlag	Olivia gave me some good **advice**.
	structure ['strʌktʃə]	Aufbau; Struktur	What's the **structure** of the text?
	drama ['drɑ:mə]	Drama	R драма T dram
	romance ['rəʊmæns]	Liebesgeschichte	**Romance** is also a type of film.
	start [stɑ:t]	Start; Anfang	**start** ↔ ending

V

Word bank: Sports and activities

Water sports

swimming

surfing

windsurfing

canoeing

rafting

Ball sports

rugby

football

netball

handball

basketball

Winter sports

skiing

snowboarding

ice skating

Athletics

high jump

long jump

javelin

Racket sports

tennis

badminton

squash

Equipment

boat

racket

paddle

waterproofs

ball

goggles

helmet

Activities

ride a bike

go rock climbing

do skateboard tricks

go jogging

go hiking

Word bank: Emergency

Emergency services

police

ambulance

fire brigade

coastguard

cast

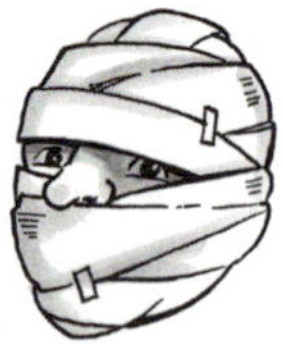
bandage

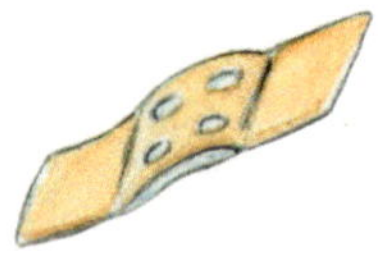
plaster

cut

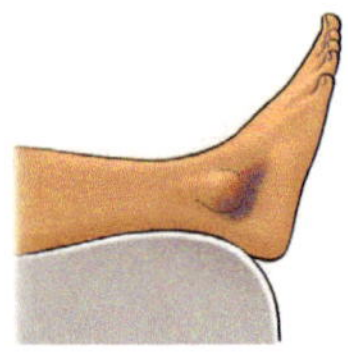
bruise

poison

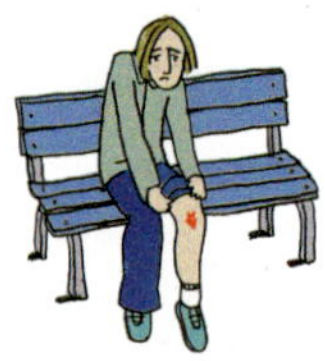
wound

Useful verbs the operator says

to cool

to move

to sit

Useful verbs the caller says

to cut

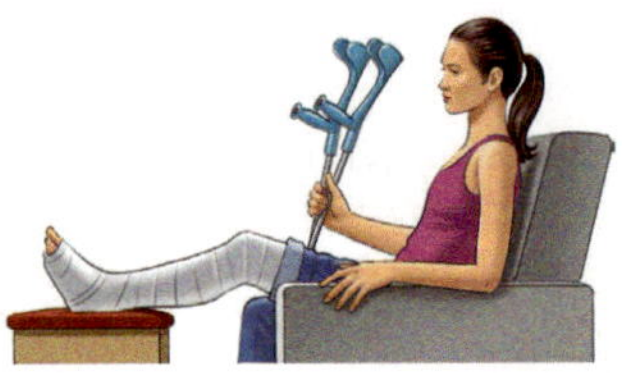
to break

to fall

to hurt

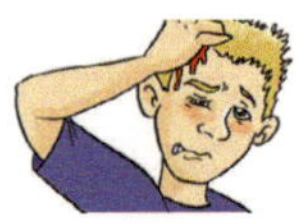
to bleed

to sprain

to breathe

Unit 3 Made in Scotland

Way in

p. 52	**rain** [reɪn]	Regen	**rain** → to rain
	to **produce** [prəˈdjuːs]	hervorbringen; produzieren	Edinburgh has always **produced** new ideas.
	university [ˌjuːnɪˈvɜːsəti]	Universität	It has a big **university**.
	inventor [ɪnˈventə]	Erfinder; Erfinderin	Lots of **inventors** are from Scotland.
	to **be born** [biː ˈbɔːn]	geboren werden	I **was born** in Germany.
	Scottish [ˈskɒtɪʃ]	schottisch	**Scottish** → Scotland
	hero *(sg)* [ˈhɪərəʊ], **heroes** *(pl)* [ˈhɪərəʊz]	Held	He was the **hero** in the story.
	its [ɪts]	sein; ihr	The dog has **its** leg stuck in the mud.
p. 53	**solar** [ˈsəʊlə]	Sonnen-; Solar-; solar	**Solar** things use the sun.
	power [ˈpaʊə]	Energie; Kraft; Macht	There isn't enough sun for solar **power**.
	electricity [ˌelɪkˈtrɪsəti]	Strom; Elektrizität	Scotland has clean **electricity**.
	wind farm [ˈwɪnd fɑːm]	Windpark	A **wind farm** makes lots of electricity.
	lake [leɪk]	See	
	loch [lɒk]	See *(in Schottland)*	'**loch**' is Scottish for 'lake'
	cottage [ˈkɒtɪdʒ]	Häuschen	
	wild [waɪld]	wild	Elephants are **wild** animals.
	tradition [trəˈdɪʃn]	Tradition	There are many **traditions** in Scotland.
	bagpipes *(pl)* [ˈbægpaɪps]	Dudelsack	In Scotland people play the **bagpipes**.
	kilt [kɪlt]	Schottenrock; Kilt	A **kilt** is a Scottish skirt, usually for men.
	kind [kaɪnd]	Art; Sorte	**kind** = sort
	Scot [skɒt]	Schotte; Schottin	**Scot** → Scotland
	porridge [ˈpɒrɪdʒ]	Haferbrei	Scots often eat **porridge** for breakfast.
	oat [əʊt]	Hafer	Porridge is made with **oats**.
	(wind) turbine [(wɪnd) ˈtɜːbaɪn]	Windrad	The **turbines** are very tall.
	to **protect** [prəˈtekt]	schützen	We must **protect** the animals.
	nature [ˈneɪtʃə]	Natur	We help to protect **nature**.
	exhibition [ˌeksɪˈbɪʃn]	Ausstellung	Come and look at the **exhibition**.

Station 1

Materials

wire ['waɪə]	Draht; Kabel	**china** ['tʃaɪnə]	Porzellan
plastic ['plæstɪk]	Plastik; Kunststoff	**steel** [sti:l]	Stahl
metal ['metl]	Metall	**concrete** ['kɒŋkri:t]	Beton
wood [wʊd]	Holz	**cardboard** ['kɑ:dbɔ:d]	Pappe; Karton
rubber ['rʌbə]	Gummi	**silk** [sɪlk]	Seide
leather ['leðə]	Leder	**aluminium** [ˌæljə'mɪniəm]	Aluminium
paper ['peɪpə]	Papier		
cotton ['kɒtn]	Baumwolle		

p. 54	**who** [hu:]	der; dem; den; die	There's the man **who** was in the film.
	to change [tʃeɪndʒ]	verändern; (sich) ändern	He was a Scot who **changed** the world.
	as [æz]	als	They know him **as** the man from Scotland.
	to invent [ɪn'vent]	erfinden	to **invent** → inventor
	telephone ['telɪfəʊn]	Telefon	R телефон T telefon
	to grow up [ˌgrəʊ‿'ʌp], **grew up** [ˌgru:‿'ʌp], **grown up** [ˌgrəʊn‿'ʌp]	aufwachsen	She **grew up** in London.
	before that [bɪ'fɔ: ðæt]	davor	**Before that** his mother gave him lessons.
	ambition [æm'bɪʃn]	Ziel	My **ambition** is to become famous.
	wife *(sg)* [waɪf], **wives** *(pl)* [waɪvz]	Ehefrau	My **wife**'s name is Sarah.
	both [bəʊθ]	beide	We are **both** happy.
	deaf [def]	gehörlos; schwerhörig; taub	She can't hear you. She's **deaf**.
	speech [spi:tʃ]	Sprache; Rede	Bell was very interested in **speech**.
	human ['hju:mən]	menschlich	The **human** voice interested him too.
	which [wɪtʃ]	die; der; dem; den; das	That's the dog **which** ate the food.
	Canada ['kænədə]	Kanada	**Canada** is north of America.
	USA (United States of America) [ju:es'eɪ (ju:ˌnaɪtɪd ˌsteɪts‿əv ə'merɪkə)]	USA (Vereinigte Staaten von Amerika)	Boston is in the **USA**.
	to give up [ˌgɪv‿'ʌp]	aufgeben	He never **gave up** on his ambition.
	invention [ɪn'venʃn]	Erfindung	**invention** → to invent → inventor

	to start [stɑ:t]	*hier:* gründen	In 1877 he **started** a company.
	success [sək'ses]	Erfolg	Bell's telephone was a **success**.
	rich [rɪtʃ]	reich	He has a lot of money. He is **rich**.
	only ['əʊnli]	einzige	I'm the **only** boy in our family.
	successful [sək'sesfl]	erfolgreich	She is a **successful** singer.
	one(s) [wʌn(z)]	*Platzhalter für ein Nomen*	This scarf is nice, but that **one** is nicer.
	among [ə'mʌŋ]	unter; inmitten	**Among** other things, he liked sport.
	detector [dɪ'tektə]	Detektor	He invented a metal **detector**.
	whose [hu:z]	dessen; deren	He is a man **whose** invention saves time.
p. 55	**vet** [vet]	Tierarzt; Tierärztin	A **vet** is a doctor for animals.
	tube [tju:b]	Schlauch; Rohr	There's a **tube** in the tyre.
	air [eə]	Luft	You have to put **air** in the tyres.
	tyre [taɪə]	Reifen	
	solid ['sɒlɪd]	fest	They were made of **solid** rubber.
	tyre [taɪə]	Reifen	**Tyres** are usually black.
p. 56	**material** [mə'tɪəriəl]	Material; Stoff	**Materials:** cotton, rubber, paper, …
p. 57	**windscreen wiper** ['wɪnskri:n ˌwaɪpə]	Scheibenwischer	Cars have **windscreen wipers**.
	trolley suitcase ['trɒli ˌsu:tkeɪs]	Rollkoffer	
	steam engine ['sti:m‿ˌendʒɪn]	Dampfmaschine	
	light bulb ['laɪt ˌbʌlb]	Glühbirne	

Station 2

Going on holiday

bed and breakfast (B & B) [ˌbed‿ən 'brekfəst]	Frühstückspension	to **check out** [ˌtʃek‿'aʊt]	auschecken
campsite ['kæmpsaɪt]	Campingplatz; Zeltplatz	to **pay the bill** [ˌpeɪ ðə 'bɪl]	die Rechnung bezahlen
youth hostel ['ju:θ ˌhɒstl]	Jugendherberge	to **make a reservation** [ˌmeɪk‿ə 'rezəveɪʃn]	reservieren
caravan ['kærəvæn]	Wohnwagen	to **check in** [ˌtʃek‿'ɪn]	einchecken

p. 58	**to come up** [ˌkʌm‿ˈʌp]	bevorstehen	Our next holiday is **coming up**.
	to plan [plæn]	planen	We want to **plan** our holiday.
	trip [trɪp]	Reise	It's time to plan our **trip**.
	for a start [ˌfɔ:r‿ə ˈstɑ:t]	zunächst	**For a start**, where do we want to go?
	to decide [dɪˈsaɪd]	(sich) entscheiden	We have to **decide** where to go.
	I'd love to ... (= I would love to) [aɪd ˈlʌv tə]	Ich würde sehr gern ...	**I'd love to** stay in a hotel.
	cosy [ˈkəʊzi]	gemütlich	This hotel looks nice and **cosy**.
	could [kʊd]	könnten	We **could** go camping.
	simple [ˈsɪmpl]	einfach	**simple** = easy
	way [weɪ]	Art und Weise	It's a good **way** to spend our holidays.
	hiking [ˈhaɪkɪŋ]	Wandern	You know I love **hiking**.
	all day [ˌɔ:l ˈdeɪ]	den ganzen Tag	They work **all day**.
	No way! [ˌnəʊ ˈweɪ]	Auf keinen Fall!; Was?!; Echt?!	**No way!** I'm not going camping.
	to freeze [fri:z], **froze** [frəʊz], **frozen** [ˈfrəʊzn]	frieren; gefrieren	We'll **freeze** in a tent.
	insect [ˈɪnsekt]	Insekt	
	how much [ˌhaʊ ˈmʌtʃ]	wie sehr	You know **how much** I hate insects.
	Are you serious? [ˌɑ: ju ˈsɪəriəs]	Im Ernst?	Ganze Sätze am besten als Einheit lernen.
	to agree (with) [əˈgri:]	einer Meinung sein (mit)	I **agree** with you about the food.
	comfortable [ˈkʌmftəbl]	angenehm; bequem	A hotel is more **comfortable** than a tent.
	buffet [ˈbʊfeɪ]	Büfett	R буфет T büfe
	nice [naɪs]	*hier:* lecker; gut	The food is **nice** in a hotel.
	not ... either [nɒt ... ˈaɪðə]	auch nicht	I **don't** want to go camping **either**.
	to rent [rent]	mieten	We could **rent** a holiday cottage.
	local [ˈləʊkl]	hiesig; lokal; örtlich	I love the **local** food.
	nobody [ˈnəʊbədi]	niemand	If **nobody** wants to go camping, fine.
	monster [ˈmɒnstə]	Ungeheuer; Monster	R монстр 
p. 60	**to get cold** [ˌget ˈkəʊld]	frieren	We will **get cold** if it rains.
p. 61	**walking** [ˈwɔ:kɪŋ]	Wandern	**Walking** in the mountains is fun.

	cycling ['saɪklɪŋ]	Radfahren	My favourite activity is **cycling**.
	bird watching ['bɜ:d ˌwɒtʃɪŋ]	Vogelbeobachtung	**Bird watching** is an activity you can do.
	walk [wɔ:k]	Spaziergang	A **walk** in the afternoon is nice.

Reading corner

p. 62	to **keep out** [ˌki:p ˈaʊt]	draußen halten	I will **keep** the English **out**.
	to beat [bi:t], **beat** [bi:t], **beaten** ['bi:tn]	besiegen; schlagen	We can't **beat** the English.
	soldier ['səʊldʒə]	Soldat; Soldatin	They have so many **soldiers**.
	impossible [ɪm'pɒsəbl]	unmöglich	I think it's **impossible** to win.
p. 63	**spider** ['spaɪdə]	Spinne	
	web [web]	Spinnennetz; Netz	Look at its **web**.
	must not/never [ˌmʌst 'nɒt/'nevə]	nicht/nie dürfen	I **must never** give up.
	brave [breɪv]	tapfer; mutig	We must be **brave**.
p. 64	**son** [sʌn]	Sohn	**son** ↔ daughter
	tactic ['tæktɪk]	Taktik; Vorgehensweise	We have good **tactics**. We can win.
	ground [graʊnd]	Boden; Erdboden	The **ground** is very wet.
p. 65	**peace** [pi:s]	Frieden	There was **peace** in Scotland.
	proud (of) [praʊd (əv)]	stolz (auf)	The Scots are **proud** of Robert the Bruce.
	sad [sæd]	traurig	**sad** ↔ happy
p. 64	**whom** [hu:m]	wen; wem	Who fought **whom** at Bannockburn?

Film corner

p. 67	**pay phone** ['peɪ fəʊn]	Münztelefon	I need some money for the **pay phone**.
	grandmother ['grænˌmʌðə]	Großmutter	
	video chat ['vɪdiəʊ ˌtʃæt]	Video-Chat	We can talk about it on the **video chat**.
	neighbour ['neɪbə]	Nachbar; Nachbarin	Our **neighbours** live next to us.
	to **repair** [rɪ'peə]	reparieren	Alicia **repairs** everything.
	to **be up to** [bi: 'ʌp tə]	vorhaben	I want to see what you'**re up to**.
	to **attach** [ə'tætʃ]	verbinden	You have to **attach** the two wires.

pipe [paɪp]	Rohr	The machine has a water **pipe** in it.
antenna [æn'tenə]	Antenne	The radio has an **antenna** on it.
to **connect** [kə'nekt]	verbinden	**Connect** the wire to the radio.
signal ['sɪgnl]	Empfang; Signal; Zeichen	Have you got a **signal**?

Checkpoint

magical ['mædʒɪkl]	zauberhaft; magisch	on duty [ɒn 'dju:ti]	im Dienst
wonderful ['wʌndəfl]	wunderbar	garage ['gærɑ:ʒ]	Werkstatt; Tankstelle
offer ['ɒfə]	Angebot	since [sɪns]	seit
available [ə'veɪləbl]	erhältlich; verfügbar	petrol ['petrl]	Benzin
full service [ˌfʊl 'sɜ:vɪs]	Komplettservice	free [fri:]	kostenlos
mechanic [mə'kænɪk]	Mechaniker; Mechanikerin	coffee ['kɒfi]	Kaffee
		design [dɪ'zaɪn]	Design; Gestaltung

Word bank: Inventors and inventions

Talking about inventors

… was born in …
… grew up in …
… moved to …
… died in … (place / year)

… invented …
… also invented …
… was rich …
… was famous because …

Talking about inventions

is made of …

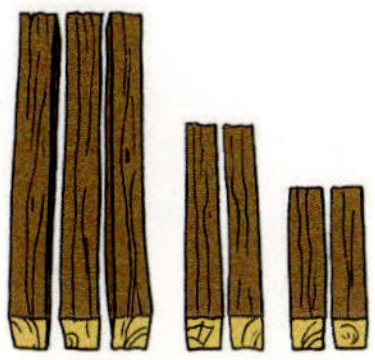
wood

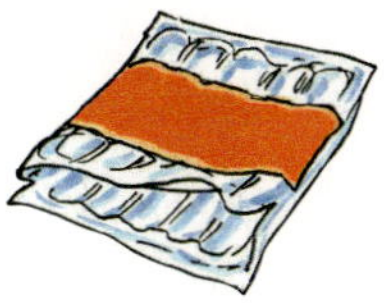
plastic

metal

glass

is used for …

trolley suitcases

tyres

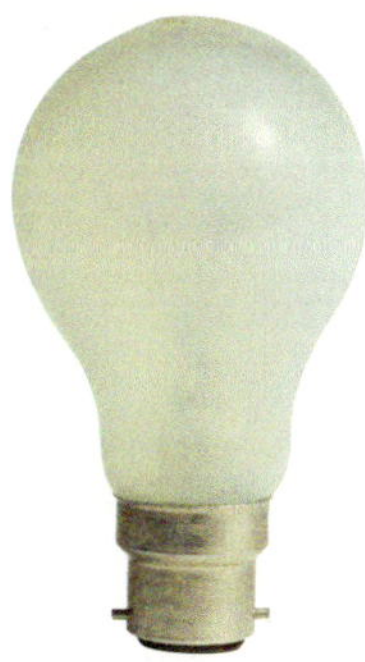
light bulbs

mirrors

tables

… is good because …

it is light
it is heavy
it is fast

it is slow
it is recyclable
it is washable

Word bank: Places to stay

B&B

hotel

guest house

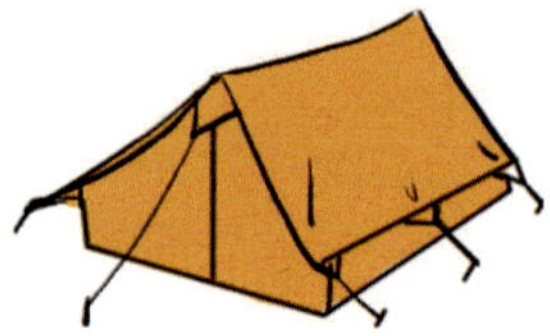
tent

campsite

hostel (youth hostel)

caravan

camper

static caravan

holiday flat

holiday cottage

farm

town

village

city

countryside

Words for describing places to stay

- cheap
- comfortable
- cosy
- big
- small
- clean
- near …
- good for …

V

Unit 4 In Northern Ireland

Way in

p. 74	**mural** ['mjʊərəl]	Wandgemälde	That **mural** on the building is great.
	Protestant ['prɒtɪstnt]	protestantisch; Protestant; Protestantin	There were problems between the **Protestants**
	Catholic ['kæθlɪk]	katholisch; Katholik; Katholikin	and the **Catholics** parts.
	population *(no pl)* [ˌpɒpjə'leɪʃn]	Bevölkerung; Einwohner; Einwohnerzahl	The **population** of Dublin is over 500,000.
	spectacular [spek'tækjələ]	spektakulär	Giant's Causeway is **spectacular**.
	giant [dʒaɪənt]	Riesen-; riesig	The Titanic was a **giant** ship.
p. 75	to **run** [rʌn], **ran** [ræn], **run** [rʌn]	*hier:* betreiben; leiten; führen	My parents **run** a hotel.
	northwest of [ˌnɔ:θ'west‿əv]	nordwestlich	It is a town **northwest of** Belfast.
	free [fri:]	kostenlos	You don't have to pay for it. It's **free**.
	grandad ['grændæd]	Opa	
	adult ['ædʌlt]	Erwachsene; Erwachsener	**adult** ↔ child
	to **cost** [kɒst], **cost** [kɒst], **cost** [kɒst]	kosten	The tickets **cost** a lot of money.
	giant [dʒaɪənt]	Riese	

Station 1

Adjectives for feelings

useful ['ju:sfl]	nützlich; hilfreich
lonely ['ləʊnli]	einsam
horrible ['hɒrəbl]	schrecklich; furchtbar
positive ['pɒzətɪv]	positiv
silly ['sɪli]	dumm; doof
honest ['ɒnɪst]	ehrlich
furious ['fjʊəriəs]	wütend
smart [smɑ:t]	schlau; klug; intelligent
confident ['kɒnfɪdnt]	selbstsicher; selbstbewusst
optimistic [ˌɒptɪ'mɪstɪk]	optimistisch

cautious ['kɔ:ʃəs]	vorsichtig; behutsam
down [daʊn]	deprimiert
dreadful ['dredfl]	furchtbar
hopeful ['həʊpfl]	hoffnungsvoll
intelligent [ɪn'telɪdʒnt]	intelligent; klug; vernünftig
straightforward [ˌstreɪt'fɔ:wəd]	aufrichtig; geradlinig
annoyed [ə'nɔɪd]	verärgert
sure of oneself ['ʃʊər‿əv ˌwʌnself]	selbstsicher
guarded ['gɑ:dɪd]	vorsichtig; zurückhaltend

p. 76	to **be fed up (with)** [bi: fed‿'ʌp (wɪð)]	die Nase voll haben (von); sauer sein	I'**m fed up** with school and homework.
	not … any more [ˌnɒt … eni 'mɔː]	nicht mehr	They aren't friends **any more**.
	in the evenings [ɪn ði 'iːvnɪŋz]	abends	**In the evenings** they don't have time.
	to **nag** [næg]	nörgeln; meckern	They always **nag** me about my jobs.
	at least [ət 'liːst]	wenigstens; mindestens	**At least** Ashley helps me.
	to **drive sb crazy** [ˌdraɪv … 'kreɪzi]	jmdn. verrückt machen	The guests sometimes **drive me crazy**.
	so much ['səʊ ˌmʌtʃ]	so sehr	I miss my friends **so much**.
	without [wɪ'ðaʊt]	ohne	I don't like it **without** you.
	to **seem** [siːm]	scheinen	He **seems** like he would listen.
	somebody ['sʌmbədi]	jemand	**Somebody** helped me with my bag.
	to **complain** [kəm'pleɪn]	sich beschweren; sich beklagen	Stop **complaining** and think positive.
	to **teach** [tiːtʃ], **taught** [tɔːt], **taught** [tɔːt]	beibringen; unterrichten; lehren	The guest **taught** me a funny word.
	milkshake ['mɪlkˌʃeɪk]	Milchmischgetränk; Milchshake	
	complaint [kəm'pleɪnt]	Beschwerde	**complaint** → to complain
	in my opinion [ɪn 'maɪ‿əˌpɪnjən]	meiner Meinung nach	**In my opinion** she is right.
	to **be wrong** [biː 'rɒŋ]	unrecht haben; sich irren	I **was wrong** about Paul. He's nice.
p. 77	**adjective** ['ædʒɪktɪv]	Adjektiv; Eigenschaftswort	**adjectives**: furious, confident, sad, …
p. 78	**to her place** [tʊ 'hɜː ˌpleɪs]	zu sich nach Hause	She invited me **to her place**.
	to kiss [kɪs]	küssen	I wouldn't **kiss** a spider.
p. 79	**coin** [kɔɪn]	Münze	
	time travel ['taɪm ˌtrævl]	Zeitreise	He has invented a **time travel** machine.

Station 2

Shopping

special offer [ˌspeʃl‿'ɒfə]	Sonderangebot	**brand** [brænd]	Marke
customer ['kʌstəmə]	Kunde; Kundin	**exact** [ɪg'zækt]	exakt; genau
to **repeat** [rɪ'piːt]	wiederholen	to **change one's mind** [ˌtʃeɪndʒ wʌnz 'maɪnd]	seine Meinung ändern
to **run out of** [ˌrʌn‿'aʊt‿əv]	ausgehen *(Ware)*		

V

p. 80	**actually** ['æktʃuəli]	eigentlich; tatsächlich; wirklich	**Actually**, I like your new dress.
	raspberry ['rɑ:zbri]	Himbeere	
	jam [dʒæm]	Marmelade; Konfitüre	I like raspberry **jam** on my toast.
	tasty ['teɪsti]	lecker; schmackhaft	This jam is **tastier** than that jam.
	jar [dʒɑ:]	Glas	**Jars** are made of glass.
	sliced bread [ˌslaɪst 'bred]	in Scheiben geschnittenes Brot	In England you buy **sliced bread**.
	healthy ['helθi]	gesund	This bread is **healthier** than that bread.
	loaf *(sg)* [ləʊf], **loaves** *(pl)* [ləʊvz]	Brotlaib	I'd like one **loaf** of farmer's bread, please.
	to post [pəʊst]	aufgeben *(einen Brief)*; abschicken *(einen Brief)*	I have to **post** this to my aunt.
	letter ['letə]	Brief; Buchstabe	We don't write **letters**, we write e-mails.
	stamp [stæmp]	Briefmarke	
	niece [ni:s]	Nichte	Sarah is her aunt's **niece**.
	less [les]	weniger	**less** ↔ more
	I have to get going. [aɪ ˌhæv tə get 'gəʊɪŋ]	Ich muss gehen.	Ganze Sätze am besten als Einheit lernen.
	to owe [əʊ]	schulden	How much do I **owe** you?
	to get [get]	*hier:* verstehen	Sorry, I didn't **get** that.
	wallet ['wɒlɪt]	Brieftasche; Geldbörse	Sorry, can you pay? I forgot my **wallet**.
p. 81	**to check** [tʃek]	überprüfen; kontrollieren	Can you **check** my homework, please?
	left [left]	übrig	I don't have any money **left**.
	tissue ['tɪʃu:]	Taschentuch	**tissue** → 
	mineral water ['mɪnrl ˌwɔ:tə]	Mineralwasser	I drink juice with **mineral water**.
	peanut butter [ˌpi:nʌt 'bʌtə]	Erdnussbutter	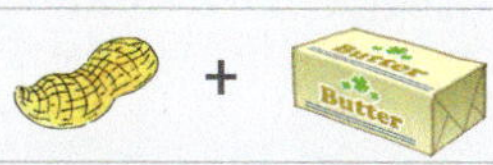
p. 83	**to go out** [ˌgəʊ_'aʊt]	ausgehen	I can't **go out** today.
	assistant [ə'sɪstnt]	Verkäufer; Verkäuferin	The **assistant** helped me in the shop.

Reading corner

p. 84	**disaster** [dɪ'zɑ:stə]	Katastrophe; Desaster; Unglück	My holiday was a **disaster**.
	to hit [hɪt]	gegen etw. fahren	The car **hit** the bike.

iceberg ['aɪsbɜ:g]	Eisberg	R айсберг 
to sink [sɪŋk], **sank** [sæŋk], **sunk** [sʌŋk]	untergehen; sinken	The Titanic hit an iceberg and **sank**.
after ['ɑ:ftə]	danach; später	Two days **after** there were more facts.
shipyard ['ʃɪpjɑ:d]	Werft	It was made in a Belfast **shipyard**.
shortly ['ʃɔ:tli]	kurz	It happened **shortly** after the start.
midnight ['mɪdnaɪt]	Mitternacht	**Midnight** is at twelve o'clock at night.
to fill [fɪl]	(sich) füllen	The ship **filled** with water.
very first ['veri fɜ:st]	allererste	It was her **very first** trip to England.
voyage ['vɔɪɪdʒ]	Reise; Fahrt	The **voyage** started on April 15th.
crew [kru:]	Crew; Besatzung; Mannschaft	The **crew** is the team who works on a ship.
on board ['ɒn bɔ:d]	an Bord	Achtung Schreibweise! on board
to survive [sə'vaɪv]	überleben	**to survive** ↔ to die
Turkish bath [ˌtɜ:kɪʃ 'bɑ:θ]	Dampfbad	There were **Turkish baths** on the Titanic.
gymnasium [dʒɪm'neɪziəm]	*hier:* Fitnessraum	**gymnasium** ≠ Gymnasium
ship builder ['ʃɪp ˌbɪldə]	Schiffsbauer; Schiffsbauerin	The **ship's builders** said the ship was safe.
not possibly [nɒt 'pɒsəbli]	unmöglich	It could **not possibly** sink.
half *(sg)* [hɑ:f], **halves** *(pl)* [hɑ:vz]	(die) Hälfte	**half** a lemon 
p. 85 **Dr** ['dɒktə]	Dr. *(Anrede)*	My doctor is **Dr** Smith.
however [haʊ'evə]	jedoch	**However**, we found out he was wrong.
to save [seɪv]	retten; bergen	The dog **saved** the people.
to be lucky [bi: 'lʌki]	Glück haben	Some people **were lucky**.
according to [ə'kɔ:dɪŋ tə]	laut; gemäß	**According to** the report it sank fast.
to bark [bɑ:k]	bellen	The dog **barked** loudly.
sinking ['sɪŋkɪŋ]	Untergang	The **sinking** of the Titanic was a disaster.
full [fʊl]	voll	Some lifeboats weren't **full**.
law [lɔ:]	Gesetz	The **law** has now been changed.

Film corner

p. 87	**court** [kɔ:t]	Spielfeld	You play tennis and basketball on a **court**.
	bench [benʃ]	Bank; Sitzbank	
	to **be sorry** [bi: 'sɒri]	leid tun	I **was sorry** when I heard what happened.

Checkpoint

author ['ɔ:θə]	Autor; Autorin	headteacher [ˌhed'ti:tʃə]	Schulleiter; Schulleiterin
introduction [ˌɪntrə'dʌkʃn]	Einleitung; Einführung	to take place [ˌteɪk 'pleɪs]	stattfinden

Speaking skills

p. 92	**upper** ['ʌpə]	obere	In the **upper** left corner there is a bird.
	corner ['kɔ:nə]	Ecke	Turn left at the **corner**.
	at the top [æt ðə 'tɒp]	oben	I can see a museum **at the top**.
	in the background [ɪn ðə 'bækgraʊnd]	im Hintergrund	The tree is **in the background**.
	in the middle [ɪn ðə 'mɪdl]	in der Mitte	The car is **in the middle** of the road.
	lower ['ləʊə]	untere	In the **lower** left corner there is a man.
	at the bottom [æt ðə 'bɒtəm]	unten	The sea is **at the bottom** of the picture.
	in the foreground [ɪn ðə 'fɔ:graʊnd]	im Vordergrund	The dog is **in the foreground**.
p. 93	**van** [væn]	Lieferwagen; Transporter	

Word bank: **Giving advice**

I have a good idea.

That's great.

Think positive.

That's good news.

That's a good idea.

That sounds good.

That's nice.

That's bad news.

That's terrible.

That's horrible.

That's a bad idea.

That sounds awful.

That's not very nice.

Suggestions:

Why don't you …
You can always …
Maybe you should …
How about you …
If I were you, I would …

If you told your mum / dad, …
If you talked to your mum's / dad's friend, …
If you …
Call me later.
Let's speak soon.

Word bank: Shopping

a bottle of

water

juice

ketchup

milk

lemonade

a bar of

chocolate

a can of

pet food

tomatoes

peaches

a jar of

jam

honey

peanut butter

a box of

tea bags

eggs

a bag of

flour

crisps

nuts

apples

a packet of

tissues

biscuits

tea

candles

sugar

a loaf of

bread

Where is …, please?
Where can I find …, please?
Have you got …, please?
Can you repeat that, please?
Sorry, I didn't understand / hear you.

How much is …, please?
Have you got this in a bigger size / box, please?
Have you got a different flavour, please?
Are these / Is this on special offer?
Could I have a …, please?

Unit 5 Welcome to Ireland

Way in

p. 94	**republic** [rɪ'pʌblɪk]	Republik	Ireland is called the green **republic**.
	euro ['jʊərəʊ]	Euro *(Währung)*	R евро T euro
	unlike [ʌn'laɪk]	anders als; im Gegensatz zu	**unlike** ↔ like
	heart [hɑ:t]	Herz	
	the Irish [ði 'aɪrɪʃ]	die Iren	Music is special to **the Irish**.
	Irish ['aɪrɪʃ]	irisch; Irisch	There are many famous **Irish** bands.
	rock [rɒk]	Rock *(Musik)*	R рок T rock
	pop [pɒp]	Pop *(Musik)*	I prefer **pop** music.
	pub [pʌb]	Kneipe; Gasthaus	People often play music in **pubs**.
	classical ['klæsɪkl]	klassisch *(Musik)*	I think **classical** music is the best.
	youth *(no pl)* [ju:θ]	Jugend-; Jugend	There are lots of **youth** groups in my town.
	orchestra ['ɔ:kɪstrə]	Orchester	R оркестр T orkestra
p. 95	**singing** ['sɪŋɪŋ]	Gesangs-	He is the winner of the **singing** prize.
	musical ['mju:zɪkl]	Musik-; musikalisch	**musical** → music
	style [staɪl]	Stil	My favourite **style** is rock music.
	hip hop ['hɪp hɒp]	Hip-Hop *(Musik)*	Keith's favourite style is **hip hop**.
	acting ['æktɪŋ]	Schauspielen; Schauspielerei	There are courses in **acting** and dancing.
	parade [pə'reɪd]	Parade; Umzug	R парад
	all around the world [ɔ:l‿əˌraʊnd ðə 'wɜ:ld]	in aller Welt	People **all around the world** like the music.
p. 94	**dancer** ['dɑ:nsə]	Tänzer; Tänzerin	**dancer** → to dance
p. 95	**to care (for)** ['keə (fɔ:)]	sich kümmern (um)	He **cares for** old people.
	sign language ['saɪn ˌlæŋgwɪdʒ]	Gebärdensprache; Zeichensprache	Keith knows **sign language**.
	with special needs [wɪð ˌspeʃl 'ni:dz]	mit Behinderung	He helps children **with special needs**.
	guitar [gɪ'tɑ:]	Gitarre	

Station 1

In the bathroom

towel ['taʊəl]	Handtuch	**shower gel** ['ʃaʊə ˌdʒel]	Duschgel
shampoo [ʃæm'pu:]	Shampoo	**body lotion** ['bɒdi ˌləʊʃn]	Körperlotion
toothbrush ['tu:θbrʌʃ]	Zahnbürste	**hair gel** ['heə ˌdʒel]	Haargel
nail scissors *(pl)* ['neɪl ˌsɪzəz]	Nagelschere	**soap** [səʊp]	Seife
comb ['kəʊm]	Kamm	**perfume** ['pɜ:fju:m]	Parfüm
toothpaste ['tu:θpeɪst]	Zahnpasta	**mirror** ['mɪrə]	Spiegel
hairdryer ['heəˌdraɪə]	Fön	**hairbrush** ['heəbrʌʃ]	Haarbürste

p. 96	to **take off** [ˌteɪk‿'ɒf]	ausziehen	You don't have to **take off** your shoes.
	fridge [frɪdʒ]	Kühlschrank	
	to **help oneself** [ˌhelp wʌn'self]	sich bedienen	**Help yourself** to food and drinks.
	completely [kəm'pli:tli]	völlig	That's **completely** wrong!
	what else [ˌwɒt‿'els]	was noch; was sonst	**What else** can we do?
	around [ə'raʊnd]	gegen; ungefähr um	We meet for dinner **around** 6:30 p.m.
	traditional [trə'dɪʃnl]	traditionell	I would like a **traditional** breakfast.
	on weekdays [ɒn 'wi:kdeɪz]	unter der Woche; an Werktagen	**On weekdays** I have toast with jam.
	cereal ['sɪəriəl]	Müsli; Cornflakes	I eat **cereal** for breakfast.
	sweet [swi:t]	süß	Leo likes a **sweet** breakfast.
	over there [ˌəʊvə 'ðeə]	da drüben	There are some towels **over there**.
	to **introduce** [ˌɪntrə'dju:s]	vorstellen	Let me **introduce** you to my sister Maddy.
	to **practise** ['præktɪs]	üben; trainieren	Today I have to **practise** with the band.
	grand [grænd]	großartig	I'm sure it will be **grand**.
	adaptor [ə'dæptə]	Adapter	I can't find my **adaptor**.
	ours [aʊəz]	unsere	This room is for you and me. It's **ours**.
	to **ring** [rɪŋ], **rang** [ræŋ], **rung** [rʌŋ]	klingeln; läuten	Just a moment, the phone is **ringing**.
	to **share** [ʃeə]	teilen	I'll **share** my room with you.
	to **make oneself at home** [ˌmeɪk wʌnself ət 'həʊm]	sich wie zu Hause fühlen	Just **make yourself at home**.

	to **prepare** [prɪ'peə]	zubereiten; (sich) vorbereiten	Mum is **preparing** a snack for us.
	to **join** [dʒɔɪn]	sich anschließen	**Join** us when you're ready.
p. 97	**ID** [ˌaɪ'diː]	Ausweis; Personalausweis	You need your **ID** to visit another country.
	charger ['tʃɑːdʒə]	Ladegerät	I need a **charger** for my phone.
	personal ['pɜːsnl]	persönlich	I have lots of **personal** things in my bag.
	raincoat ['reɪnkəʊt]	Regenmantel	I have a blue **raincoat**. 
	map [mæp]	Stadtplan; Landkarte	
p. 98	**German** ['dʒɜːmən]	deutsch; aus Deutschland	I like **German** hip hop.
	rapper ['ræpə]	Rapper; Rapperin	Listen to this new German **rapper**.
	project ['prɒdʒekt]	Projekt	R проект T proje
	to **wash** [wɒʃ]	(sich) waschen; spülen	I **wash** my hair with shampoo. 
	hair [heə]	Haar; Haare	
	cupboard ['kʌbəd]	Schrank	We always put the towels in the **cupboard**.
	to **let** [let], **let** [let], **let** [let]	lassen	**Let** me know if you can't find him.
p. 99	**theirs** [ðeəz]	ihre	This is Dave's and Ann's room. It's **theirs**.
	partner ['pɑːtnə]	Partner; Partnerin	Ask what your **partner** is doing.

Station 2

Public transport

timetable ['taɪmˌteɪbl]	Fahrplan	**station** ['steɪʃn]	Bahnhof; Haltestelle; Station
tram [træm]	Straßenbahn	to **get on** [ˌget‿'ɒn]	einsteigen
to **change** [tʃeɪndʒ]	umsteigen	**daily** ['deɪli]	täglich
line [laɪn]	Linie	**weekly** ['wiːkli]	wöchentlich
on time [ɒn 'taɪm]	pünktlich	**monthly** ['mʌnθli]	monatlich
fare [feə]	Fahrpreis	**return ticket** [rɪ'tɜːn ˌtɪkɪt]	Hin- und Rückfahrkarte
valid ['vælɪd]	gültig	**annual** ['ænjuəl]	jährlich
single ticket ['sɪŋgl ˌtɪkɪt]	einfache Fahrkarte		

p. 100	**striking** ['straɪkɪŋ]	bemerkenswert; auffallend	He is a **striking** actor.
	move [muːv]	Bewegung	We will learn lots of new **moves**.
	dance [dɑːns]	Tanz	**dance** → to dance → dancer
	drumming ['drʌmɪŋ]	Trommeln-	Let's try the **drumming** workshop.

	rhythm ['rɪðm]	Rhythmus	Practise great **rhythms**!
	to **perform** [pə'fɔ:m]	auftreten; aufführen	We will **perform** at the Big Bang Festival!
	I can't wait [aɪ ˌkɑ:nt 'weɪt]	ich kann es kaum erwarten	**I can't wait** to go on holiday.
	that's why ['ðæts waɪ]	deswegen	**That's why** I want to talk to you.
	journey ['dʒɜ:ni]	Fahrt; Reise	It's a long **journey** to London from here.
	before [bɪ'fɔ:]	schon einmal	I've been here **before**.
	public transport [ˌpʌblɪk 'trænspɔ:t]	öffentliche Verkehrsmittel	**public transport**: buses, trams, trains
	homepage ['həʊmpeɪdʒ]	Homepage	Let's look at the **homepage**.
	helpful ['helpfl]	hilfreich; nützlich	**helpful** → to help
	Fair enough. [ˌfeər‿ɪ'nʌf]	Na schön.	Ganze Sätze am besten als Einheit lernen.
	by [baɪ]	bis (spätestens)	We must leave **by** 8:30 a.m.
	mustn't ['mʌsnt]	nicht dürfen	You **mustn't** forget to buy a ticket.
	driver ['draɪvə]	Fahrer; Fahrerin	Don't talk to the **driver**!
	cent [sent]	Cent *(Währung)*	100 **cents** = 1 euro
p. 102	**step** [step]	Schritt	You must learn the new **steps**.
	to **push** [pʊʃ]	schubsen; drängeln	Don't **push** other people!
	seat [si:t]	Sitz; Sitzplatz	Don't put your feet on the **seats**!
p. 103	to **travel** ['trævl]	fahren	Dogs **travel** free.

Reading corner

p. 104	**gold** [gəʊld]	Gold	My jewellery is made of **gold**.
	to **rhyme** [raɪm]	(sich) reimen	'Niamh' **rhymes** with 'leave'.
	to **explain** [ɪk'spleɪn]	erklären	I always have to **explain** my name.
	area ['eəriə]	Gegend; Gebiet; Areal	There were no jobs in the **area**.
	holiday ['hɒlədeɪ]	Feiertag	St Patrick's Day is a **holiday** for the Irish.
	in fact [ɪn 'fækt]	eigentlich; tatsächlich; genau genommen	**In fact** it is my favourite holiday.
	whole [həʊl]	ganz	The **whole** city is green.
	shamrock ['ʃæmrɒk]	Kleeblatt	
	rainbow ['reɪnbəʊ]	Regenbogen	
	gold [gəʊld]	golden; Gold-	The sweets are in **gold** paper.
	national ['næʃnl]	National-; national	Look! There is the **national** team.
	flower ['flaʊə]	Blume	

	pot [pɒt]	Topf	The flower is in a **pot**.
	to **be homesick** [bi: 'həʊmsɪk]	Heimweh haben	It made me **be homesick**.
	call [kɔ:l]	Anruf; Ruf	They didn't answer my **calls**.
p. 105	to **stare** [steə]	starren	to see – to look – to **stare**
	to **cheer sb up** [ˌtʃɪər‿'ʌp]	jmdn. aufheitern; jmdn. aufmuntern	Dad tried to **cheer me up**.
	poem ['pəʊɪm]	Gedicht	I read a nice **poem** about summer.
	fable ['feɪbl]	Fabel; Märchen	A **fable** is a kind of story.
	once [wʌns]	einst; einmal	at a time in the past
	to foretell [fɔ:'tel]	vorhersagen	She **foretold** my life.
	wealth [welθ]	Reichtum	My **wealth** is my family and friends.
	though [ðəʊ]	jedoch	He tried but he wasn't very good, **though**.
	miserable ['mɪzrəbl]	elend; armselig; jämmerlich	I feel **miserable** today.
	to **feel sorry for** [ˌfi:l 'sɒri fə]	Mitleid haben mit; bedauern	Niamh **felt sorry for** herself.
	I couldn't believe my eyes. [aɪ ˌkʊdnt bɪˌli:v maɪ‿'aɪz]	Ich traute meinen Augen nicht.	Ganze Sätze am besten als Einheit lernen.
	dressed [drest]	angezogen; verkleidet	They were all **dressed** in green clothes.
	I couldn't help but … [ˌaɪ kʊdnt 'help bʌt]	Ich konnte nicht anders als …	**I couldn't help but** laugh.
	to **scream** [skri:m]	schreien; kreischen	Don't **scream** so loud.
	to bet [bet], **bet** [bet], **bet** [bet]	wetten (auf)	I **bet** he was happy.
	to rush [rʌʃ]	eilen; sich beeilen; stürzen	I **rushed** into my room.
	to **grab** [græb]	schnappen; greifen; ergreifen	Lucy was angry and she **grabbed** her bag.
	outfit ['aʊtfɪt]	Outfit; Kleidung	I grabbed my Paddy's Day **outfit**.
	Off we went. ['ɒf wi went]	Nichts wie weg.	Ganze Sätze am besten als Einheit lernen.
	beginning [bɪ'gɪnɪŋ]	Anfang; Beginn	**beginning** ↔ end
	wonderful ['wʌndəfl]	wunderbar	**Wonderful!** = Great! = Fantastic!

Film corner

p. 107	to **impress** [ɪm'pres]	beeindrucken	We **impressed** our English teacher.
	pineapple ['paɪnæpl]	Ananas	
	wherever [weə'revə]	wo(hin) auch immer; egal wo(hin); überall wo(hin)	I go **wherever** the wind takes me.

Word bank: Things for a trip

Word bank: Public transport

airport

plane

helicopter

station / stop

underground

train

bus

tram

other transport

skateboard

taxi

car

boat

motorbike / moped

bike / bicycle

ferry

You should take …
Use the … line.
Travel northbound / southbound / westbound / eastbound.
Then …
It's … stops.
It stops at …

You must / have to buy …
You needn't / don't have to …
It costs …
You can buy a single ticket / a return ticket.
Change buses / trains at …

Instructions

Arbeitsanweisungen mit Operatoren

Act the dialogue • the role play.	**Spielt** den Dialog • das Rollenspiel.
Add more words.	**Ergänze** mehr Wörter.
Answer the questions.	**Beantworte** die Fragen.
Ask a partner.	**Frage** eine Partnerin/einen Partner.
Check the sentences.	**Überprüfe** die Sätze.
Choose one of the tasks • the right answer.	**Wähle** eine der Aufgaben • die richtige Antwort **aus**.
Collect ideas.	**Sammle** Ideen.
Compare with your partner.	**Vergleicht** zu zweit.
Complete the sentences • the dialogue.	**Vervollständige** die Sätze • den Dialog.
Copy the list.	**Schreibe** die Liste **ab**.
Correct the wrong sentences.	**Verbessere** die falschen Sätze.
Decide on the best order.	**Entscheide dich für** die beste Reihenfolge.
Describe the picture.	**Beschreibe** das Bild.
Discuss in groups.	**Besprecht euch** in Gruppen.
Draw a picture.	**Zeichne** ein Bild.
Exchange your lists.	**Tauscht** eure Listen aus.
Explain the rules.	**Erkläre** die Regeln.
Finish the sentences.	**Vervollständige** die Sätze.
Give feedback.	**Gib** Rückmeldung.
Give reasons.	**Gib Gründe an.**
Guess.	**Überlege.**
Interview your partner.	**Interviewe** deine Partnerin/deinen Partner.
Label the picture.	**Beschrifte** das Bild.
Listen to the dialogue.	**Höre** dir den Dialog **an**.
Look at the photos • pictures (again).	**Schau** dir die Fotos • Bilder (noch einmal) **an**.
Make a list • a chart • a mind map.	**Erstelle** eine Liste • eine Tabelle • ein Wörternetz.
Make notes.	**Mache** dir **Stichpunkte**.
Make up more verses.	**Denke dir** weitere Strophen **aus**.
Match the sentences with the pictures.	**Ordne** den Bildern die richtigen Sätze **zu**.
Name the place.	**Nenne** den Ort.
Plan your role play.	**Plant** euer Rollenspiel.
Practise with a partner.	**Übe** mit einer Partnerin/einem Partner.
Present your profile to the class.	**Stelle** dein Profil deiner Klasse **vor**.
Put in the right verbs.	**Setze** die richtigen Verben **ein**.
Put the words **in the right order**.	**Bringe** die Wörter **in die richtige Reihenfolge**.
Read the story **again**.	**Lies** die Geschichte **noch einmal**.
Record your dialogue.	**Nehmt** euren Dialog **auf**.

Rewrite the sentences.	**Schreibe** die Sätze **um**.
Say how you feel.	**Sage**, wie du dich fühlst.
Show your text to a partner.	**Zeige** deinen Text einer Partnerin/einem Partner.
Sort the words **into groups**.	**Sortiere** die Wörter **in Gruppen**.
Take notes.	**Mache** dir **Notizen**.
Talk about the photos.	**Rede** über die Fotos.
Tell the class.	**Erzähle** es der Klasse.
Think about the story.	**Denke über** die Geschichte **nach**.
Think of a number.	**Denke** dir eine Nummer **aus**.
Use your own ideas.	**Benutze** deine eigenen Ideen.
Watch the film.	**Schau** den Film **an**.
Write a poem • a heading • a draft.	**Schreibe** ein Gedicht • einen Titel • einen Entwurf.

Classroom phrases

You and your teacher

I'm sorry I'm late.	Tut mir leid, dass ich mich verspätet habe.
I'm sorry I don't have my exercise book.	Tut mir leid, ich habe mein Heft nicht dabei.
What's the homework?	Was haben wir als Hausaufgabe auf?
Can you help me, please?	Können Sie / Kannst du mir bitte helfen?
Can you say that again, please?	Können Sie / Kannst du das bitte wiederholen?
Can I go to the toilet, please?	Kann ich bitte auf Toilette gehen?
Mr / Mrs / Miss ..., I don't feel well.	Herr / Frau ..., mir geht es nicht gut.
What page is it, please?	Auf welcher Seite ist das?
What's the German / English word for ...?	Was ist das deutsche / englische Wort für ...?
How do you spell ...?	Wie schreibt man ...?
What does that mean?	Was heißt / bedeutet das?
Sorry, I don't understand/ I don't know.	Tut mir leid, ich verstehe das nicht/ ich weiß es nicht.

Working together

Can we work in pairs / groups?	Können wir zu zweit / in Gruppen arbeiten?
Do you want to work with me / us?	Willst du / Wollt ihr mit mir / uns arbeiten?
Let's make a / draw a ...	Lass(t) uns ein ... machen / zeichnen.
Whose turn is it? – It's my / your turn.	Wer ist dran? – Ich bin dran. / Du bist dran.

Your teacher can say ...

Turn to page ...	Schlagt Seite ... auf.
Look at the board.	Schaut an die Tafel.
Put your hands up, please!	Meldet euch, bitte!
Try again!	Versuche es noch einmal.

List of irregular verbs

Hier findest du alle unregelmäßigen Verben, die im Buch vorkommen. Die Liste enthält jeweils alle drei Formen, auch wenn sie noch nicht alle in den Units vorgekommen sind.

infinitive	simple past	past participle	German
be [bi:]	was, were [wɒz, wɜ:]	been [bi:n]	sein
beat [bi:t]	beat [bi:t]	beaten ['bi:tn]	schlagen; besiegen
become [bɪ'kʌm]	became [bɪ'keɪm]	become [bɪ'kʌm]	werden
bleed [bli:d]	bled [bled]	bled [bled]	bluten
break [breɪk]	broke [brəʊk]	broken ['brəʊkn]	brechen
bring [brɪŋ]	brought [brɔ:t]	brought [brɔ:t]	bringen; mitbringen
build [bɪld]	built [bɪlt]	built [bɪlt]	bauen
burn [bɜ:n]	burned/burnt [bɜ:nt]	burned/burnt [bɜ:nt]	brennen
buy [baɪ]	bought [bɔ:t]	bought [bɔ:t]	kaufen
choose [tʃu:z]	chose [tʃəʊz]	chosen ['tʃəʊzn]	auswählen; wählen
come [kʌm]	came [keɪm]	come [kʌm]	kommen
cost [kɒst]	cost [kɒst]	cost [kɒst]	kosten
cut [kʌt]	cut [kʌt]	cut [kʌt]	(sich) schneiden
do [du:]	did [dɪd]	done [dʌn]	machen; tun
draw [drɔ:]	drew [dru:]	drawn [drɔ:n]	zeichnen
dream [dri:m]	dreamed/dreamt [dremt]	dreamed/dreamt [dremt]	träumen
drink [drɪŋk]	drank [dræŋk]	drunk [drʌŋk]	trinken
eat [i:t]	ate [eɪt]	eaten ['i:tn]	essen
fall [fɔ:l]	fell [fel]	fallen ['fɔ:ln]	fallen; hinfallen
feed [fi:d]	fed [fed]	fed [fed]	füttern; ernähren
feel [fi:l]	felt [felt]	felt [felt]	(sich) fühlen
fight [faɪt]	fought [fɔ:t]	fought [fɔ:t]	kämpfen; streiten
find [faɪnd]	found [faʊnd]	found [faʊnd]	finden
fly [flaɪ]	flew [flu:]	flown [fləʊn]	fliegen
forget [fə'get]	forgot [fə'gɒt]	forgotten [fə'gɒtn]	vergessen
freeze [fri:z]	froze [frəʊz]	frozen ['frəʊzn]	frieren; gefrieren
get [get]	got [gɒt]	got [gɒt]	bekommen; werden
give [gɪv]	gave [geɪv]	given ['gɪvn]	geben
go [gəʊ]	went [went]	gone [gɒn]	gehen; fahren
grow up [ˌgrəʊ‿'ʌp]	grew up [ˌgru:‿'ʌp]	grown up [ˌgrəʊn‿'ʌp]	aufwachsen
hang [hæŋ]	hung [hʌŋ]	hung [hʌŋ]	hängen
have [hæv]	had [hæd]	had [hæd]	haben; besitzen
hear [hɪə]	heard [hɜ:d]	heard [hɜ:d]	hören
hide [haɪd]	hid [hɪd]	hidden ['hɪdn]	verstecken
hit [hɪt]	hit [hɪt]	hit [hɪt]	schlagen; treffen
hold [həʊld]	held [held]	held [held]	halten; festhalten
hurt [hɜ:t]	hurt [hɜ:t]	hurt [hɜ:t]	verletzen; weh tun
keep [ki:p]	kept [kept]	kept [kept]	halten

infinitive	simple past	past participle	German
know [nəʊ]	knew [nju:]	known [nəʊn]	wissen; kennen
lay [leɪ]	laid [leɪd]	laid [leɪd]	legen; (den Tisch) decken
leave [li:v]	left [left]	left [left]	verlassen; lassen; abfahren
lend [lend]	lent [lent]	lent [lent]	leihen; verleihen
lose [lu:z]	lost [lɒst]	lost [lɒst]	verlieren
make [meɪk]	made [meɪd]	made [meɪd]	machen; tun; bilden
mean [mi:n]	meant [ment]	meant [ment]	bedeuten; meinen
meet [mi:t]	met [met]	met [met]	kennen lernen; (sich) treffen
pay [peɪ]	paid [peɪd]	paid [peɪd]	bezahlen
put [pʊt]	put [pʊt]	put [pʊt]	setzen; legen; stellen
read [ri:d]	read [red]	read [red]	lesen
ride [raɪd]	rode [rəʊd]	ridden ['rɪdn]	fahren; reiten
ring [rɪŋ]	rang [ræŋ]	rung [rʌŋ]	klingeln; läuten
run [rʌn]	ran [ræn]	run [rʌn]	laufen; rennen
say [seɪ]	said [sed]	said [sed]	sagen; sprechen
see [si:]	saw [sɔ:]	seen [si:n]	sehen
sell [sel]	sold [səʊld]	sold [səʊld]	verkaufen
send [send]	sent [sent]	sent [sent]	schicken; senden
show [ʃəʊ]	showed [ʃəʊd]	shown [ʃəʊn]	zeigen
sing [sɪŋ]	sang [sæŋ]	sung [sʌŋ]	singen
sink [sɪŋk]	sank [sæŋk]	sunk [sʌŋk]	untergehen; sinken
sit [sɪt]	sat [sæt]	sat [sæt]	sitzen
sleep [sli:p]	slept [slept]	slept [slept]	schlafen
smell [smel]	smelled/smelt [smelt]	smelled/smelt [smelt]	riechen
speak [spi:k]	spoke [spəʊk]	spoken ['spəʊkn]	sprechen
spell [spel]	spelled/spelt [spelt]	spelled/spelt [spelt]	buchstabieren
spend [spend]	spent [spent]	spent [spent]	ausgeben; verbringen
stand [stænd]	stood [stʊd]	stood [stʊd]	stehen
sweep [swi:p]	swept [swept]	swept [swept]	fegen
swim [swɪm]	swam [swæm]	swum [swʌm]	schwimmen
take [teɪk]	took [tʊk]	taken ['teɪkn]	nehmen; mitnehmen
tell [tel]	told [təʊld]	told [təʊld]	erzählen; sagen
think [θɪŋk]	thought [θɔ:t]	thought [θɔ:t]	denken; glauben
throw [θrəʊ]	threw [θru:]	thrown [θrəʊn]	werfen
understand [ˌʌndə'stænd]	understood [ˌʌndə'stʊd]	understood [ˌʌndə'stʊd]	verstehen
wake up [weɪk‿'ʌp]	woke up [wəʊk‿'ʌp]	woken up [ˌwəʊkn‿'ʌp]	aufwachen
wear [weə]	wore [wɔ:]	worn [wɔ:n]	tragen
win [wɪn]	won [wʌn]	won [wʌn]	gewinnen; siegen
write [raɪt]	wrote [rəʊt]	written ['rɪtn]	schreiben

Dictionary

Im *Dictionary* kannst du Wörter nachschlagen!

Im *Dictionary* sind alle wichtigen Wörter aus deinem Buch enthalten. Die Wörter stehen in alphabetischer Reihenfolge. Englische Wörter schlägst du ab S. 221 nach, deutsche Wörter ab S. 264.

Die Abkürzungen geben an, wo das Wort zum ersten Mal im Buch erscheint.

across	[ə'krɒs]	über	III	U1	11
englisches Wort	Aussprache	deutsche Übersetzung	Band 3	Unit 1	Seite

Die mit einem Sternchen (*) gekennzeichneten Verben sind unregelmäßige Verben (→ *List of irregular verbs*, S. 219 – 220).

Manche Wörter haben verschiedene Bedeutungen. Am besten liest du alle, bevor du dich für eine entscheidest.

practice ['præktɪs] Training; Übung I[1]
to **accept** [ək'sept] akzeptieren <III U4, 86>[3]
*to **spend** [spend] ausgeben; verbringen II[1]
actually ['æktʃuəli] tatsächlich; wirklich; eigentlich III U5, 105[2]
address [ə'dres] Adresse II[2]

1 Lernwortschatz für alle: schwarz; 2 Differenzierungswortschatz: blau; 3 kein Lernwortschatz: < >

A

a [ə] ein, eine I
a **bit** [ə 'bɪt] ein bisschen; ein wenig II
a **few** [ə 'fju:] ein paar; wenige; einige III U1, 20
a **little** [ə 'lɪtl] ein bisschen II
a **lot** [ə 'lɒt] viel I; sehr II
a **lot of** [ə 'lɒt_əv] viel(e); eine Menge I
a **pair of** [ə 'peər_əv] ein Paar II
a/one **hundred** ['hʌndrəd] einhundert; hundert I
a/one **thousand** [ə/wʌn 'θaʊznd] eintausend; tausend II
a five minute **walk** [ə 'faɪv mɪnɪt ˌwɔ:k] fünf Minuten zu Fuß III U1, 12
a.m. [ˌeɪ'em] vormittags *(Uhrzeit)* II
about [ə'baʊt] ungefähr; circa; etwa II
to be **about** [bi: ə'baʊt] gehen um; handeln von III U1, 31
about [ə'baʊt] über I
out and **about** [ˌaʊt_ən_ə'baʊt] unterwegs I
from **above** [ˌfrəm ə'bʌv] von oben <III U1, 28>
above [ə'bʌv] oben; oberhalb <III U5, 139>
to **abseil** ['æbseɪl] sich abseilen II
accent ['æksnt] Akzent <III ZI, 9>
to **accept** [ək'sept] akzeptieren <III U4, 86>
accident ['æksɪdnt] Unfall III U2, 38
according to [ə'kɔ:dɪŋ tə] laut; gemäß III U4, 85
stomach **ache** ['stʌmək ˌeɪk] Bauchweh; Bauchschmerzen II
across [ə'krɒs] über III U1, 11; quer <III U4, 91>
to **act** [ækt] spielen II
acting workshop ['æktɪŋ ˌwɜ:kʃɒp] Schauspielworkshop II
acting ['æktɪŋ] Schauspielen; Schauspielerei III U5, 95
Action! ['ækʃn] Achtung, Aufnahme! <III U1, 27>
activity [æk'tɪvəti] Aktivität I
activity centre [æk'tɪvəti ˌsentə] Jugendzentrum III U2, 34
actor ['æktə] Schauspieler; Schauspielerin II
actually ['æktʃuəli] eigentlich; tatsächlich; wirklich III U4, 80
AD (= Anno Domini) [ˌeɪ'di:] nach Christus III U2, 42
adaptor [ə'dæptə] Adapter III U5, 96
to **add** [æd] hinzufügen <I>; II
address [ə'dres] Adresse II
adjective ['ædʒɪktɪv] Adjektiv; Eigenschaftswort III U4, 77
adult ['ædʌlt] Erwachsene; Erwachsener III U4, 75
adventure [əd'ventʃə] Abenteuer I
adverb ['ædvɜ:b] Adverb <III U2, 36>
advert ['ædvɜ:t] Anzeige II

... looking at an advert. [ˌlʊkɪŋ ət‿ən 'ædvɜ:t] ... schaut sich eine Anzeige an. II
advertisement [əd'vɜ:tɪsmənt] Anzeige; Werbespot II
advice [əd'vaɪs] Rat; Ratschlag III U2, 51
afraid [ə'freɪd] ängstlich II
to be afraid [bi: ə'freɪd] sich fürchten; Angst haben II
after ['ɑ:ftə] nach I; danach; später III U4, 84
after that ['ɑ:ftə ðæt] danach I
after it's gone [ˌɑ:ftə ɪts 'gɒn] nachdem sie (die Kohle) weg ist III U1, 20
afternoon [ˌɑ:ftə'nu:n] Nachmittag I
in the afternoon [ˌɪn ði ˌɑ:ftə'nu:n] nachmittags I
again [ə'gen] wieder; noch einmal II
then again [ˌðen ə'gen] andererseits III U1, 16
against [ə'genst] gegen II
age [eɪdʒ] Alter I
ago [ə'gəʊ] vor II
to **agree** [ə'gri:] zustimmen II
to **agree** (on) [ə'gri:] sich einigen (auf) <III U1, 26>
to **agree** (with) [ə'gri:] einer Meinung sein (mit) III U3, 58
agreement [ə'gri:mənt] Vereinbarung <III U5, 139>
air [eə] Luft III U3, 55
airport ['eəpɔ:t] Flughafen II
alarm clock [ə'lɑ:m ˌklɒk] Wecker I
alien ['eɪliən] Außerirdischer; Außerirdische I
alive [ə'laɪv] am Leben <III U1, 17>; III U1, 22
all [ɔ:l] alle I; ganz II
all alone [ˌɔ:l‿ə'ləʊn] ganz allein I
all day [ˌɔ:l 'deɪ] den ganzen Tag III U3, 58
all over [ˌɔ:l‿'əʊvə] überall I
all the time [ˌɔ:l ðə 'taɪm] die ganze Zeit III U2, 33
all around the world [ɔ:l‿əˌraʊnd ðə 'wɜ:ld] in aller Welt III U5, 95
all right [ˌɔ:l 'raɪt] in Ordnung; alles klar II
allergic to [ə'lɜ:dʒɪk tə] allergisch gegen II
allergy ['ælədʒi] Allergie II
almost ['ɔ:lməʊst] fast; beinahe III U1, 12
alone [ə'ləʊn] allein I
all alone [ˌɔ:l‿ə'ləʊn] ganz allein I
along [ə'lɒŋ] entlang I
alphabet ['ælfəbet] Alphabet I
already [ɔ:l'redi] schon; bereits II
also ['ɔ:lsəʊ] auch I
aluminium [ˌæljə'mɪniəm] Aluminium III U3, 55
always ['ɔ:lweɪz] immer I
am [æm] bin I
amazing [ə'meɪzɪŋ] unglaublich; toll; erstaunlich II
ambition [æm'bɪʃn] Ziel III U3, 54
ambulance ['æmbjələns] Krankenwagen III U2, 38
among [ə'mʌŋ] unter; inmitten III U3, 54
an [ən] ein, eine I
and [ænd] und I
And you? [ænd 'ju:] Und du? I
angle ['æŋgl] Winkel <III U3, 67>
Anglo-Saxon [ˌæŋgləʊ'sæksn] angelsächsisch <III U1, 130>
the **Anglo-Saxons** [ði ˌæŋgləʊ'sæksnz] die Angelsachsen <III U1, 131>
angry ['æŋgri] wütend; zornig; verärgert; böse II
animal ['ænɪml] Tier I
animal rescue shelter [ˌænɪml 'reskju: ˌʃeltə] Tierheim I
ankle ['æŋkl] Fußgelenk; Fußknöchel II
announcement [ə'naʊnsmənt] Durchsage; Ankündigung II
annoyed [ə'nɔɪd] verärgert III U4, 77
annual ['ænjuəl] jährlich III U5, 101
another [ə'nʌðə] ein anderer; noch ein; ein andere II
answer ['ɑ:nsə] Antwort II
to **answer** ['ɑ:nsə] antworten; beantworten I
to answer the phone [ˌɑ:nsə ðə 'fəʊn] ans Telefon gehen III U2, 45
isn't answering his mobile [ɪznt 'ɑ:nsərɪŋ hɪz ˌməʊbaɪl] geht nicht an sein Handy I
antenna [æn'tenə] Antenne III U3, 67
antique [æn'ti:k] Antiquität <III U1, 30>
any ['eni] irgendein; irgendwelche II
not ... any [ˌnɒt ... eni] kein II
Any idea? [ˌeni aɪ'dɪə] Irgendeine Idee? I
any ['eni] jede III U1, 21
anything ['eniθɪŋ] irgendetwas II
Anything else? ['eniθɪŋ ˌels] Darf es sonst noch etwas sein? I
anything to drink ['eniθɪŋ tə 'drɪŋk] etwas zu trinken II
anyway ['eniweɪ] trotzdem; jedenfalls III U2, 34
anywhere ['eniweə] irgendwo <III U5, 112>
apostrophe [ə'pɒstrəfi] Apostroph <III U1, 23>
to **appear** [ə'pɪə] auftauchen; erscheinen III U2, 42
apple ['æpl] Apfel <III U3, 66>
apple crumble [ˌæpl 'krʌmbl] Apfelauflauf *(mit Streuseln bedeckt)* II
April ['eɪprl] April I
archer ['ɑ:tʃə] Bogenschütze; Bogenschützin <III U1, 130>
archive ['ɑ:kaɪv] Archiv II
are [ɑ:] bist; sind I
are required [rɪ'kwaɪəd] werden gebeten <III U4, 86>
Are you ready? [ˌɑ: ju: 'redi] Bist du fertig? I
Are you serious? [ˌɑ: ju 'sɪəriəs] Im Ernst? III U3, 58
... are 99p. [ɑ: 'naɪntinaɪn ˌpens] ... kosten 99 Pence. I
area ['eəriə] Gegend; Gebiet; Areal III U5, 104
argument ['ɑ:gjəmənt] Auseinandersetzung; Streit II
arm [ɑ:m] Arm I
armour ['ɑ:mə] Rüstung III U2, 43

army ['ɑ:mi] Armee; Heer III U1, 11
around [ə'raʊnd] herum; umher I
around the house [ə'raʊnd ðə haʊs] im Haus I
to get around [ˌget ə'raʊnd] herumkommen III U1, 16
to turn around [ˌtɜ:n‿ə'raʊnd] (sich) umdrehen III U1, 22
around [ə'raʊnd] gegen; ungefähr um III U5, 96
to **arrive** [ə'raɪv] ankommen II
arrow ['ærəʊ] Pfeil <III U1, 131>
Art [ɑ:t] Kunst I
article ['ɑ:tɪkl] Artikel; Bericht *(in einer Zeitung)* <III U2, 133>
make-up **artist** ['meɪkʌp ˌɑ:tɪst] Maskenbildner; Maskenbildnerin; Visagist; Visagistin <III U4, 87>
as [æz] so <III U4, 137>
as [æz] als III U3, 54
as [æz] wie II
as … as [əz … əz] so … wie II
to **ask** [ɑ:sk] fragen I
to ask about ['ɑ:sk‿əˌbaʊt] sich erkundigen nach; fragen nach II
to ask for ['ɑ:sk fɔ:] bitten um II
asking the way ['ɑ:skɪŋ ðə ˌweɪ] nach dem Weg fragen I
*to be **asleep** [bi: ə'sli:p] schlafen III U1, 25
to fall asleep [ˌfɔ:l‿ə'sli:p] einschlafen III U1, 25
assistant [ə'sɪstnt] Verkäufer; Verkäuferin III U4, 83
shop assistant ['ʃɒp‿əˌsɪstnt] Verkäufer; Verkäuferin II
association football ['əsəʊsieɪʃn ˌfʊtbɔ:l] **Assoziationsfußball** *(offizieller Name des Fußballs)* <III U1, 24>
at [æt] an; in; um; bei; auf I
at break [ət 'breɪk] in der Pause I
at home [ət 'həʊm] zu Hause I
at last [ət 'lɑ:st] endlich; zu guter Letzt II
at least [ət 'li:st] wenigstens; mindestens III U4, 76
at school [ət 'sku:l] in der Schule I
at the bottom [æt ðə 'bɒtəm] unten III U4, 92
at the end of the road [ət ði: 'end‿əv ðə ˌrəʊd] am Ende der Straße I
at the front of [ət ðə 'frʌnt‿əv] an der Spitze (von); im vorderen Bereich II
at the seaside [ət ðə 'si:saɪd] am Meer I
at the top [æt ðə 'tɒp] oben III U4, 92
at the weekend [ˌət ðə 'wi:kend] am Wochenende I
ate [eɪt] simple past von *to eat* II
athletics [æθ'letɪks] Leichtathletik <III U2, 193>
to **attach** [ə'tætʃ] verbinden III U3, 67
*to pay **attention** to [ˌpeɪ‿ə'tenʃn tʊ] beachten <III U2, 51>
attic ['ætɪk] Dachboden I
audition [ɔ:'dɪʃn] Vorspielen; Vorsprechen; Vorsingen; Vortanzen II
August ['ɔ:gəst] August I
in August [ɪn 'ɔ:gəst] im August I
aunt [ɑ:nt] Tante II
author ['ɔ:θə] Autor; Autorin <III U4, 88>
available [ə'veɪləbl] erhältlich; verfügbar <III U3, 68>
avalanche ['ævlɑ:nʃ] Lawine <III U3, 72>
to **avoid** [ə'vɔɪd] vermeiden; meiden; aus dem Weg gehen; ausweichen <III U4, 89>
awake [ə'weɪk] bei Bewusstsein; wach III U2, 38
away [ə'weɪ] weg; entfernt II
awful ['ɔ:fl] schrecklich; furchtbar I

B

baby ['beɪbi] Baby II
back [bæk] Rückseite <III U5, 109>
in the back [ɪn ðə 'bæk] (nach) hinten; Rücken <III U5, 110>
back street ['bæk stri:t] Hinterhof <III U1, 17>
back [bæk] zurück I
back home [bæk 'həʊm] zu Hause II
to get back [ˌget‿'bæk] zurückkommen <III U2, 132>
background ['bækgraʊnd] Hintergrund III U4, 92
in the background [ɪn ðə 'bækgraʊnd] im Hintergrund III U4, 92
backseat ['bæksi:t] Rücksitz <III U1, 17>
bad [bæd] schlecht I
badly ['bædli] sehr; schwer III U1, 21
badminton ['bædmɪntən] Badminton <III U2, 193>
bag [bæg] Tasche; Tüte; Sack I
tea bag ['ti: ˌbæg] Teebeutel <III U4, 209>
bagpipes *(pl)* ['bægpaɪps] Dudelsack III U3, 53
pasta **bake** [ˌpæstə 'beɪk] Nudelauflauf II
baker ['beɪkə] Bäcker; Bäckerin III U2, 50
baker's ['beɪkəz] Bäckerei III U1, 13
ball [bɔ:l] Ball II
cannon ball ['kænən ˌbɔ:l] Kanonenkugel II
balloon [bə'lu:n] Luftballon I
hot air balloon [ˌhɒt‿'eə bəˌlu:n] Heißluftballon <III U2, 44>
banana [bə'nɑ:nə] Banane I
band [bænd] Band; Musikgruppe II
pipe band ['paɪp bænd] *Band aus Dudelsackspielern und Trommlern* <III U3, 135>
to start a band [ˌstɑ:t‿ə 'bænd] eine Band gründen II
bandage ['bændɪdʒ] Verband III U2, 39
bar of chocolate [bɑ:r‿əv 'tʃɒklət] Tafel Schokolade I
barbecue ['bɑ:bɪkju:] Grill; Grillparty I
bargain ['bɑ:gɪn] Schnäppchen II
to **bark** [bɑ:k] bellen III U4, 85
basic ['beɪsɪk] Grund- <III U5, 110>
laundry **basket** ['lɔ:ndri ˌbɑ:skɪt] Wäschekorb <III U4, 86>

basketball ['bɑ:skɪtbɔ:l] Basketball II
bat [bæt] Fledermaus I
Turkish **bath** [ˌtɜ:kɪʃ 'bɑ:θ] Dampfbad III U4, 84
bathroom ['bɑ:θrʊm] Badezimmer; Bad I
batter ['bætə] Bierteig <III U3, 66>
battle ['bætl] Schlacht; Kampf III U1, 11
battleship ['bætlʃɪp] Schlachtschiff <III U4, 90>
BC (= before Christ) [ˌbi:'si:] vor Christus <III U5, 138>
*to **be** [bi:] sein I
to be about [bi: ə'baʊt] gehen um; handeln von III U1, 31
to be afraid [bi: ə'freɪd] sich fürchten; Angst haben II
to be asleep [bi: ə'sli:p] schlafen III U1, 25
to be born [bi: 'bɔ:n] geboren werden III U3, 52
to be called [bi: 'kɔ:ld] heißen; genannt werden II
to be fed up (with) [bi: fed‿'ʌp (wɪð)] die Nase voll haben (von); sauer sein III U4, 76
to be good at [bi: 'gʊd‿ət] gut sein in/bei I
to be homesick [bi: 'həʊmsɪk] Heimweh haben III U5, 104
to be included [bi: ɪn'klu:dɪd] enthalten sein III U2, 34
to be interested in [bi: 'ɪntrəstɪd‿ɪn] sich interessieren für; interessiert sein an III U1, 12
to be located [bi: ləʊ'keɪtɪd] liegen III U2, 33
to be lucky [bi: 'lʌki] Glück haben III U4, 85
to be made of [bi: 'meɪd‿əv] hergestellt sein aus III U1, 20
to be on fire [bi: ɒn 'faɪə] brennen II
to be right [bi: 'raɪt] recht haben II
to be scared [bi: 'skeəd] Angst haben; erschrocken sein II
to be sick [bi: 'sɪk] sich übergeben I
to be sorry [bi: 'sɒri] leid tun III U4, 87
to be stuck [bi: 'stʌk] feststecken; nicht weg können I
to be up to [bi: 'ʌp tə] vorhaben III U3, 67
to be worth [bi: 'wɜ:θ] wert sein III U1, 12
to be wrong [bi: 'rɒŋ] unrecht haben; sich irren III U4, 76
Be careful! [bi: 'keəfl] Sei vorsichtig! I
beach [bi:tʃ] Strand I
to go beach combing [gəʊ 'bi:tʃ ˌkəʊmɪŋ] den Strand nach Strandgut absuchen II
kidney **bean** ['kɪdni ˌbi:n] Kidneybohne II
bear [beə] Bär I
*to **beat** [bi:t] besiegen; schlagen III U3, 62
beat [bi:t] simple past von *to beat* III U3, 62
beaten ['bi:tn] past participle von *to beat* III U3, 62
beautiful ['bju:tɪfl] schön; hübsch I
became [bɪ'keɪm] simple past von *to become* II
because [bɪ'kɒz] weil; da I
because of [bɪ'kɒz‿əv] wegen III U2, 37
That's because … [ˌðæts bɪ'kɒz] Das liegt daran, dass … III U1, 20
*to **become** [bɪ'kʌm] werden II
become [bɪ'kʌm] past participle von *to become* II
bed [bed] Bett I
bed and breakfast (B & B) [ˌbed‿ən 'brekfəst] Frühstückspension III U3, 58
to go to bed [ˌgəʊ tə 'bed] ins Bett gehen I
bedroom ['bedrʊm] Schlafzimmer; Kinderzimmer I
beef [bi:f] Rindfleisch II
been [bi:n] past particple von *to be* II
before [bɪ'fɔ:] vorher; zuvor II; schon einmal III U5, 100
before that [bɪ'fɔ: ðæt] davor III U3, 54
before [bɪ'fɔ:] bevor; bis zu II
*to **begin** [bɪ'gɪn] beginnen; anfangen <III U5, 139>
beginning [bɪ'gɪnɪŋ] Anfang; Beginn III U5, 105
behind [bɪ'haɪnd] hinter II
from behind [ˌfrəm bɪ'haɪnd] von hinten I
to **believe** [bɪ'li:v] glauben II
I couldn't believe my eyes [aɪ ˌkʊdnt bɪˌli:v maɪ‿'aɪz] Ich traute meinen Augen nicht. III U5, 105
bell [bel] Glocke II
bench [benʃ] Bank; Sitzbank III U4, 87
beside [bɪ'saɪd] neben <III U1, 184>
best [best] beste II
best ever score [best ˌevə 'skɔ:] das beste Ergebnis II
to like … best [ˌlaɪk 'best] am meisten mögen; am liebsten mögen I
Best wishes, [ˌbest 'wɪʃɪz] Viele Grüße, I
the **best** [ðə 'best] die besten II
*to **bet** [bet] wetten (auf) III U5, 105
bet [bet] simple past, past participle von *to bet* III U5, 105
better ['betə] besser I
between [bɪ'twi:n] zwischen II
bicycle ['baɪsɪkl] Fahrrad <III U5, 216>
big [bɪg] groß I
big wheel [ˌbɪg 'wi:l] Riesenrad II
bike [baɪk] Fahrrad I
bill [bɪl] Rechnung III U3, 59
to pay the bill [ˌpeɪ ðə 'bɪl] die Rechnung bezahlen III U3, 59
billion ['bɪliən] Milliarde II
biography [baɪ'ɒgrəfi] Biografie <III U3, 54>
Biology [baɪ'ɒlədʒi] Biologie I
bird [bɜ:d] Vogel I
bird watching ['bɜ:d ˌwɒtʃɪŋ] Vogelbeobachtung III U3, 61
birthday ['bɜ:θdeɪ] Geburtstag I
Happy birthday! [ˌhæpi 'bɜ:θdeɪ] Alles Gute zum Geburtstag! I

biscuit ['bɪskɪt] Keks II
dog biscuit ['dɒg ˌbɪskɪt] Hundekeks II
a **bit** [ə 'bɪt] ein bisschen; ein wenig II
black [blæk] schwarz I
blackboard ['blækbɔːd] Tafel <III U2, 49>
blanket ['blæŋkɪt] Decke <III U2, 132>
to **blaze** [bleɪz] brennen; lodern <III U1, 17>
bled [bled] simple past, past participle von *to bleed* III U2, 38
*to **bleed** [bliːd] bluten III U2, 38
to **blind** [blaɪnd] blenden <III U1, 17>
blog [blɒg] Blog; Internettagebuch II
blouse [blaʊz] Bluse I
blue [bluː] blau I
blue cheese [ˌbluː 'tʃiːs] Schimmelkäse II
the blue one [ðə 'bluː‿wʌn] der blaue II
board [bɔːd] Tafel I
on board ['ɒn bɔːd] an Bord III U4, 84
boat [bəʊt] Boot II
boat trip ['bəʊt ˌtrɪp] Bootsfahrt; Schiffsfahrt II
bodhran ['baʊrɑːn] *schottisch-irische Trommel* <III U5, 107>
body ['bɒdi] Körper III U5, 97
body language ['bɒdi ˌlæŋgwɪdʒ] Körpersprache <III U1, 25>
body lotion ['bɒdi ˌləʊʃn] Körperlotion III U5, 97
bodyguard ['bɒdigɑːd] Leibwächter; Leibwächterin <III U3, 134>
Bonfire night ['bɒnfaɪə ˌnaɪt] *Festtag am 5. November in England* I
book [bʊk] Buch; Heft I
exercise book ['eksəsaɪz ˌbʊk] Übungsheft I
to **book** [bʊk] buchen; reservieren <III U2, 44>
to **bookmark** ['bʊkmɑːk] zu … hinzufügen II
boot [buːt] Stiefel II
border ['bɔːdə] Grenze III U1, 10
boring ['bɔːrɪŋ] langweilig I

*to be **born** [biː 'bɔːn] geboren werden III U3, 52
to **borrow** ['bɒrəʊ] ausleihen II
boss [bɒs] Boss; Chef II
both [bəʊθ] beide III U3, 54
both … and … ['bəʊθ … ənd] sowohl … als auch … <III U1, 130>
bottle ['bɒtl] Flasche I
bottle bank ['bɒtl bæŋk] Altglascontainer II
bottom ['bɒtəm] unterer Teil; Boden; Grund III U4, 92
at the bottom [æt ðə 'bɒtəm] unten III U4, 92
bought [bɔːt] simple past von *to buy* I; past participle von *to buy* II
bowl [bəʊl] Schale; Schälchen; Schüssel II
box [bɒks] Box; Kiste; Schachtel I
telephone box ['telɪfəʊn ˌbɒks] Telefonzelle II
boy [bɔɪ] Junge I
branch [brɑːnʃ] Zweig; Ast <III U5, 112>
brand [brænd] Marke III U4, 81
brave [breɪv] tapfer; mutig III U3, 63
sliced **bread** [ˌslaɪst 'bred] in Scheiben geschnittenes Brot III U4, 80
bread [bred] Brot II
break [breɪk] Pause I
at break [ət 'breɪk] in der Pause I
break of dawn [ˌbreɪk‿əv 'dɔːn] Tagesanbruch <III U5, 101>
to take a break [ˌteɪk‿ə 'breɪk] Pause machen II
*to **break** [breɪk] brechen; zerbrechen II
breakfast ['brekfəst] Frühstück I
bed and breakfast (B & B) [ˌbed‿ən 'brekfəst] Frühstückspension III U3, 58
to have breakfast [ˌhæv 'brekfəst] frühstücken I
to **breathe** [briːð] atmen III U1, 22
brick [brɪk] Stein; Ziegelstein II
brick by brick [ˌbrɪk baɪ 'brɪk] Stein für Stein II
bridge [brɪdʒ] Brücke II

briefcase ['briːfkeɪs] Aktenkoffer; Aktentasche III U2, 45
fire **brigade** ['faɪə brɪˌgeɪd] Feuerwehr <III U2, 38>
brilliant ['brɪliənt] toll I
*to **bring** [brɪŋ] bringen; mitbringen II
British ['brɪtɪʃ] britisch II
brochure ['brəʊʃə] Broschüre; Prospekt III U1, 31
broke [brəʊk] simple past von *to break* II
broken ['brəʊkn] past participle von *to break* II
broken ['brəʊkn] gebrochen; kaputt <III U1, 28>
brother ['brʌðə] Bruder I
brother-in-law ['brʌðər‿ɪn lɔː] Schwager <III U1, 130>
brought [brɔːt] simple past von *to bring* II
brown [braʊn] braun I
bruise [bruːz] Bluterguss; blauer Fleck <III U2, 194>
brush [brʌʃ] Pinsel <III U1, 29>
speech **bubble** ['spiːtʃ ˌbʌbl] Sprechblase <III U2, 47>
bucket of water ['bʌkɪt‿əv ˌwɔːtə] Eimer Wasser I
buffet ['bʊfeɪ] Büfett III U3, 58
*to **build** [bɪld] bauen II
builder ['bɪldə] Bauarbeiter; Bauarbeiterin II
ship builder ['ʃɪp ˌbɪldə] Schiffsbauer; Schiffsbauerin III U4, 84
building ['bɪldɪŋ] Gebäude II
built [bɪlt] simple past, past participle von *to build* II
light **bulb** ['laɪt ˌbʌlb] Glühbirne III U3, 57
burger ['bɜːgə] Hamburger II
burglar ['bɜːglə] Einbrecher; Einbrecherin I
*to **burn** [bɜːn] verbrennen; brennen III U2, 39
to burn down [bɜːn 'daʊn] niederbrennen; verbrennen II

burnt [bɜ:nt] simple past, past participle von *to burn* III U2, 39

bus [bʌs] Bus I

bus stop ['bʌs ˌstɒp] Bushaltestelle II

on the bus [ˌɒn ðə 'bʌs] im Bus II

business ['bɪznɪs] Geschäft <III U4, 137>

busy ['bɪzi] beschäftigt; arbeitsreich I; belebt <III U1, 30>; voller Menschen <III U5, 107>

a busy day [ə ˌbɪzi 'deɪ] ein ausgefüllter Tag I

but [bʌt] aber I

butcher's ['bʊtʃəz] Metzgerei III U1, 13

butter ['bʌtə] Butter I

peanut butter [ˌpi:nʌt 'bʌtə] Erdnussbutter III U4, 81

*to **buy** [baɪ] kaufen I

I can buy ... [aɪ kən 'baɪ] Ich kann ... kaufen. I

by [baɪ] von II; vorbei <III U1, 17>; <III U5, 107>; bis (spätestens) III U5, 100

by *(train)* [baɪ] mit *(dem Zug)* I

by the end [ˌbaɪ ði 'end] am Schluss II

by yourself [baɪ 'jɔ:self] allein II

Bye. [baɪ] Tschüss. I

C

cabbage ['kæbɪdʒ] Kohl; Kraut II

caber ['keɪbə] Baumstamm <III U3, 134>

caber toss ['keɪbə ˌtɒs] Baumstammwerfen <III U3, 134>

cache [kæʃ] Cache *(Geheimschatz)* I

cache box ['kæʃ ˌbɒks] *Schatzkiste beim Geocaching* I

café ['kæfeɪ] Café I

cafeteria [kæfə'tɪəriə] Cafeteria; Mensa I

cage [keɪdʒ] Käfig I

cake [keɪk] Kuchen I

to make a cake [ˌmeɪk‿ə 'keɪk] einen Kuchen backen I

calculator ['kælkjəleɪtə] Rechner; Taschenrechner I

calendar ['kæləndə] Kalender <III U2, 133>

call [kɔ:l] Anruf; Ruf III U5, 104

phone call ['fəʊn ˌkɔ:l] Telefonanruf I

to **call** [kɔ:l] rufen; anrufen I; nennen III U1, 16

to be called [bi: 'kɔ:ld] heißen; genannt werden II

to call out [ˌkɔ:l‿'aʊt] laut sagen <III U4, 91>

Call me ... ['kɔ:l ˌmi] Nenne mich ... I

caller ['kɔ:lə] Anrufer; Anruferin II

calm [kɑ:m] ruhig; friedlich <III U4, 77>

came [keɪm] simple past von *to come* I

camel ['kæml] Kamel I

camera ['kæmrə] Fotoapparat; Kamera <III U1, 27>

camera operator ['kæmrə ˌɒpreɪtə] Kameramann; Kamerafrau <III U4, 87>

camp [kæmp] Camp; Lager II

camper ['kæmpə] Wohnmobil <III U3, 202>

camping ['kæmpɪŋ] Camping; Zelten III U2, 36

to go camping [ˌgəʊ 'kæmpɪŋ] campen gehen; zelten II

campsite ['kæmpsaɪt] Campingplatz; Zeltplatz III U3, 58

can [kæn] Dose I

can't [kɑ:nt] nicht können I

can [kæn; kən] können I

Can you say that again, please? [kæn ju: 'seɪ ðæt ˌəgen pli:s] Könntest du das bitte wiederholen? I

Can you tell me the way to ...? [kæn ju: 'tel mi ðə ˌweɪ tə] Kannst du mir sagen, wie ich nach ... komme? I

I can't wait [aɪ ˌkɑ:nt 'weɪt] ich kann es kaum erwarten III U5, 100

I **can't find** ... [ˌaɪ kɑ:nt 'faɪnd] Ich kann ... nicht finden. I

canary [kə'neəri] Kanarienvogel III U1, 20

candle ['kændl] Kerze I

cannon ['kænən] Kanone II

cannon ball ['kænən ˌbɔ:l] Kanonenkugel II

cannot ['kænɒt] nicht können III U2, 45

canoeing [kə'nu:ɪŋ] Kanufahren I

cap [kæp] Kappe; Mütze I

capital (city) ['kæpɪtl (sɪti)] Hauptstadt III U2, 33

capital letter [ˌkæpɪtl 'letə] Großbuchstabe <III U5, 99>

captain ['kæptɪn] Kapitän; Kapitänin I

caption ['kæpʃn] Untertitel; Bildunterschrift <II>

car [kɑ:] Auto I

car park ['kɑ: ˌpɑ:k] Parkplatz <III U4, 86>

caravan ['kærəvæn] Wohnwagen III U3, 59

static caravan ['stætɪk ˌkærəvæn] Mobilheim *(großer, fest stehender Wohnwagen)* <III U3, 202>

card [kɑ:d] Karte; Spielkarte I

cardboard ['kɑ:dbɔ:d] Pappe; Karton III U3, 55

to **care** (for) ['keə (fɔ:)] sich kümmern (um) III U5, 95

careful ['keəfl] vorsichtig; sorgfältig II

Be careful! [bi: 'keəfl] Sei vorsichtig! I

caretaker ['keəˌteɪkə] Hausmeister; Hausmeisterin I

carnival ['kɑ:nɪvl] Karneval; Fasching I

carpenter ['kɑ:pəntə] Zimmermann; Zimmerin; Tischler; Tischlerin II

carpet ['kɑ:pɪt] Teppich I

carrot ['kærət] Karotte II

to **carry** ['kæri] tragen; befördern II

pencil **case** ['pensl ˌkeɪs] Federmäppchen I

cash [kæʃ] (mit) Bargeld II

cast [kɑ:st] Gips III U2, 39
castle ['kɑ:sl] Schloss; Burg II
cat [kæt] Katze I
***to catch** [kætʃ] fangen II
category ['kætəgri] Kategorie <III U4, 91>
catering college ['keɪtərɪŋ ˌkɒlɪdʒ] Hotelfachschule II
Catholic ['kæθlɪk] katholisch; Katholik; Katholikin III U4, 74
caught [kɔ:t] simple past, past participle von *to catch* II
to **cause** [kɔ:z] verursachen <III U4, 136>
'cause (= because) [kɒz] weil <III U5, 101>
cautious ['kɔ:ʃəs] vorsichtig; behutsam III U4, 77
cave [keɪv] Höhle II
CD [ˌsi:'di:] CD I
ceiling ['si:lɪŋ] Zimmerdecke I
to **celebrate** ['seləbreɪt] feiern I
Celt [kelt] Kelte; Keltin <III U5, 138>
Celtic ['keltɪk] keltisch <III U5, 138>
cent [sent] Cent *(Währung)* III U5, 100
centimetre (cm) ['sentɪˌmi:tə] Zentimeter (cm) I
centre ['sentə] Zentrum; Mitte; Center III U1, 12
  activity **centre** [æk'tɪvəti ˌsentə] Jugendzentrum III U2, 34
  city **centre** [ˌsɪti 'sentə] Stadtzentrum; Stadtmitte III U1, 16
  shopping **centre** ['ʃɒpɪŋ ˌsentə] Einkaufszentrum I
  in the **centre** of [ˌɪn ðə 'sentər‿əv] in der Mitte von III U1, 17
century ['senʃri] Jahrhundert III U1, 25
cereal ['sɪəriəl] Müsli; Cornflakes III U5, 96
certain ['sɜ:tn] bestimmte <III U1, 31>
chain [tʃeɪn] Kette <III U3, 61>
chair [tʃeə] Stuhl I
chalk [tʃɔ:k] Kreide <III U1, 28>
chamber of horrors [ˌtʃeɪmbər‿əv 'hɒrəz] Kammer des Schreckens <III U1, 30>
chance [tʃɑ:ns] Chance; Gelegenheit II
change [tʃeɪndʒ] Münzgeld; Wechselgeld II
  Here's your **change**. [ˌhɪəz jɔ: 'tʃeɪndʒ] Hier ist dein Wechselgeld. I
to **change** [tʃeɪndʒ] wechseln II; verändern; (sich) ändern III U3, 54; umsteigen III U5, 100
  to **change** one's mind [ˌtʃeɪndʒ wʌnz 'maɪnd] seine Meinung ändern <III U2, 44>; III U4, 81
chant [tʃɑ:nt] Sprechgesang <I>
character ['kærəktə] Charakter; Figur <III U5, 112>
characteristic [ˌkærəktə'rɪstɪk] typisches Merkmal; typisch <III U5, 110>
charades [ʃə'rɑ:dz] Scharaden <II>
charger ['tʃɑ:dʒə] Ladegerät III U5, 97
charity ['tʃærɪti] Wohltätigkeitsorganisation <III U2, 132>
chart [tʃɑ:t] Diagramm; Tabelle <I>
video **chat** ['vɪdiəʊ ˌtʃæt] Video-Chat III U3, 67
to **chat** [tʃæt] chatten; plaudern II
cheap [tʃi:p] billig II
spell **check** ['spel ˌtʃek] Rechtschreibprüfprogramm <III U4, 89>
to **check** [tʃek] überprüfen; kontrollieren III U4, 81
  to **check** in [ˌtʃek‿'ɪn] einchecken III U3, 59
  to **check** out [ˌtʃek‿'aʊt] auschecken III U3, 59
checked ['tʃekt] kariert <III U4, 90>
checklist ['tʃeklɪst] Checkliste <I>
checkpoint ['tʃekpɔɪnt] Überprüfung <I>
cheeky ['tʃi:ki] frech III U2, 34
to **cheer** sb up [ˌtʃɪər‿'ʌp] jmdn. aufheitern; jmdn. aufmuntern III U5, 105
cheese [tʃi:z] Käse I
  blue **cheese** [ˌblu: 'tʃi:s] Schimmelkäse II
cheesecake ['tʃi:skeɪk] Käsekuchen II
chef [ʃef] Koch; Köchin II
  head **chef** ['hed ʃef] Chefkoch II
chewing gum ['tʃu:ɪŋ ˌgʌm] Kaugummi I
chic [ʃɪk] schick; elegant I
chicken ['tʃɪkɪn] Huhn I
child [tʃaɪld] Kind II
children *(pl)* ['tʃɪldrn] Kinder II
chilli ['tʃɪli] Chili II
china ['tʃaɪnə] Porzellan III U3, 55
the **Chinese** [ðə 'tʃaɪni:z] die Chinesen <III U1, 24>
chips *(pl)* [tʃɪps] Pommes frites I
chocolate ['tʃɒklət] Schokolade I
***to choose** [tʃu:z] auswählen; wählen II
chorus ['kɔ:rəs] Refrain <I>
chose [tʃəʊz] simple past von *to choose* II
chosen ['tʃəʊzn] past participle von *to choose* II
Christianity [ˌkrɪsti'ænəti] Christentum <III U5, 138>
Christmas ['krɪsməs] Weihnachten I
chronological [ˌkrɒnə'lɒdʒɪkl] chronologisch <III U3, 57>
church [tʃɜ:tʃ] Kirche II
cinema ['sɪnəmə] Kino I
circle ['sɜ:kl] Kreis; Ring III U1, 10
city ['sɪti] Stadt; Großstadt II
  city centre [ˌsɪti 'sentə] Stadtzentrum; Stadtmitte III U1, 16
clan [klæn] Clan; Stamm <III U3, 134>
to **clap** [klæp] klatschen <I>
class [klɑ:s] Unterricht I; Klasse III U2, 36
classical ['klæsɪkl] klassisch *(Musik)* III U5, 94
classmate ['klɑ:smeɪt] Klassenkamerad; Klassenkameradin; Mitschüler; Mitschülerin <II>
classroom ['klɑ:srʊm] Klassenzimmer I
to **clean** [kli:n] sauber machen; putzen I
clean [kli:n] sauber I
to **clear** the table [ˌklɪə ðə 'teɪbl] den Tisch abräumen II

clear [klɪə] klar; deutlich <III U2, 37>
clever ['klevə] schlau; klug; intelligent I
to **click** [klɪk] klicken I
climb [klaɪm] Steigflug <III U3, 73>
to **climb** [klaɪm] besteigen; steigen; klettern III U2, 34
rock **climber** ['rɒk ˌklaɪmə] Kletterer; Kletterin <III U3, 72>
rock **climbing** ['rɒk ˌklaɪmɪŋ] Klettern I
clock [klɒk] Uhr II
alarm clock [ə'lɑːm ˌklɒk] Wecker I
clock tower ['klɒk ˌtaʊə] Uhrenturm II
o'clock [ə'klɒk] Uhr *(Zeitangabe bei vollen Stunden)* I
to **close** [kləʊz] schließen; zumachen I
Close the window. ['kləʊz ðə ˌwɪndəʊ] Schließe das Fenster. I
close [kləʊs] genau <III U1, 31>; eng; nahe <III U5, 110>
clothes *(pl)* [kləʊðz] Kleider *(Pl.)*; Kleidung I
cloud [klaʊd] Wolke III U2, 42
cloudy ['klaʊdi] wolkig I
club [klʌb] Klub; Verein II
clue [kluː] Hinweis; Spur I
coach [kəʊtʃ] Trainer; Trainerin <III U2, 36>
coal [kəʊl] Kohle III U1, 16
coast [kəʊst] Küste III U2, 33
on the coast [ˌɒn ðə 'kəʊst] an der Küste III U1, 17
roller **coaster** ['rəʊlə ˌkəʊstə] Achterbahn II
coastguard ['kəʊstgɑːd] Küstenwache <III U2, 38>
coat [kəʊt] Jacke I
coconut ['kəʊkənʌt] Kokosnuss II
code [kəʊd] Code <III U2, 48>
coffee ['kɒfi] Kaffee <III U3, 68>
coin [kɔɪn] Münze III U4, 79
coke [kəʊk] Cola I
cold [kəʊld] kalt I
to get cold [ˌget 'kəʊld] frieren III U3, 60

collar ['kɒlə] Halsband I
to **collect** [kə'lekt] sammeln I
catering **college** ['keɪtərɪŋ ˌkɒlɪdʒ] Hotelfachschule II
colour ['kʌlə] Farbe I
full of colour [ˌfʊl‿əv 'kʌlə] mit Farbe bedeckt <III U1, 29>
What colour is …? [ˌwɒt 'kʌlə ɪz] Welche Farbe hat …? I
colourful ['kʌləfl] bunt II
comb ['kəʊm] Kamm III U5, 97
combination [ˌkɒmbɪ'neɪʃn] Kombination II
*to **come** [kʌm] kommen I
to come to life [ˌkʌm tə 'laɪf] lebendig werden <III U3, 70>
to come up [ˌkʌm‿'ʌp] bevorstehen III U3, 58
Come on! [ˌkʌm‿'ɒn] Komm jetzt! I; Komm schon! III U1, 22
comedy ['kɒmədi] Komödie III U2, 50
comfortable ['kʌmftəbl] angenehm; bequem III U3, 58
comic ['kɒmɪk] Comic(heft) II
comic strip ['kɒmɪk strɪp] Comic <III U3, 52>
comment ['kɒment] Kommentar II
to put a comment [ˌpʊt‿ə 'kɒment] einen Kommentar schreiben <I>
company ['kʌmpəni] Gesellschaft; Firma II
to **compare** [kəm'peə] vergleichen I
to **compete** (against) [kəm'piːt] konkurrieren (gegen); sich messen (mit) <III U3, 134>
competition [ˌkɒmpə'tɪʃn] Wettbewerb II
competitive [kəm'petɪtɪv] wettkampforientiert; leistungsorientiert III U2, 35
competitor [kəm'petɪtə] Mitbewerber; Mitbewerberin; Teilnehmer; Teilnehmerin <III U3, 134>
to **complain** [kəm'pleɪn] sich beschweren; sich beklagen III U4, 76
complaint [kəm'pleɪnt] Beschwerde III U4, 76

to **complete** [kəm'pliːt] vervollständigen I
complete [kəm'pliːt] vollständig <III U3, 135>
completely [kəm'pliːtli] völlig III U5, 96
computer [ˌkəm'pjuːtə] Computer I
computer science [kəmˌpjuːtə 'saɪəns] Informatik <III U2, 47>
to **concentrate** ['kɒnsntreɪt] (sich) konzentrieren <III U1, 31>
concert ['kɒnsət] Konzert II
conclusion [kən'kluːʒn] Schlussfolgerung; Schluss III U2, 50
concrete ['kɒŋkriːt] Beton III U3, 55
condition [kən'dɪʃn] Bedingung <III U2, 45>
confident ['kɒnfɪdnt] selbstsicher; selbstbewusst III U4, 77
conflict ['kɒnflɪkt] Auseinandersetzung; Konflikt <III U4, 87>
confused [kən'fjuːzd] verwirrt; wirr III U1, 25
Congratulations! [ˌkəŋgrætjʊ'leɪʃnz] Glückwunsch! II
to **connect** [kə'nekt] verbinden III U3, 67
connecting [kə'nektɪŋ] verbindend <II>
connective [kə'nektɪv] Bindewort <III U4, 89>
conquest ['kɒŋkwest] Eroberung <III U1, 130>
content ['kɒntent] Inhalt III U2, 50
to **control** [kən'trəʊl] kontrollieren <III U1, 17>
conversation [ˌkɒnvə'seɪʃn] Konversation; Gespräch; Unterhaltung III U2, 32
convincing [kən'vɪnsɪŋ] überzeugend III U2, 42
to **cook** [kʊk] kochen II
cooking ['kʊkɪŋ] Kochen II
to **cool** [kuːl] kühlen III U2, 39
cool [kuːl] cool; super; kühl I
to keep cool [ˌkiːp 'kuːl] Ruhe bewahren <III U1, 27>

copy ['kɒpi] Kopie II; Abschrift <III U2, 51>
to copy ['kɒpi] kopieren II; abschreiben <III U2, 35>
cork [kɔ:k] Kork <III U3, 71>
corner ['kɔ:nə] Ecke III U4, 92
corner shop ['kɔ:nə ˌʃɒp] Tante-Emma-Laden I
film corner ['fi:lm ˌkɔ:nə] Filmecke <I>
Cornish ['kɔ:nɪʃ] Cornish; aus Cornwall II
to correct [kə'rekt] verbessern I
correct [kə'rekt] richtig; korrekt <III U1, 25>
corridor ['kɒrɪdɔ:] Gang; Flur II
cost [kɒst] Preis; Kosten <III U1, 30>
***to cost** [kɒst] kosten III U4, 75
cost [kɒst] simple past, past participle von *to cost* III U4, 75
costume ['kɒstju:m] Kostüm I
cosy ['kəʊzi] gemütlich III U3, 58
cottage ['kɒtɪdʒ] Häuschen III U3, 53
holiday cottage ['hɒlədeɪ ˌkɒtɪdʒ] Ferienhäuschen <III U3, 202>
cotton ['kɒtn] Baumwolle III U3, 55
to cough [kɒf] husten III U1, 21
could [kʊd] konnte III U1, 21; könnten III U3, 58
countdown ['kaʊntdaʊn] Countdown <I>
country ['kʌntri] ländliche Gegend; Land I
in the country [ɪn ðə 'kʌntri] auf dem Land I
countryside ['kʌntrɪsaɪd] Land; Landschaft III U1, 16
course [kɔ:s] Kurs III U2, 32
main course [ˌmeɪn 'kɔ:s] Hauptgericht II
of **course** [əv 'kɔ:s] natürlich; selbstverständlich I
court [kɔ:t] Spielfeld III U4, 87
cousin ['kʌzn] Cousin; Cousine II
to cover ['kʌvə] überziehen <III U3, 66>
cow [kaʊ] Kuh III U1, 16

Crack the code. ['kræk ðə ˌkəʊd] Knacke den Code. <I>
crazy ['kreɪzi] verrückt I
to drive sb crazy [ˌdraɪv ... 'kreɪzi] jmdn. verrückt machen III U4, 76
ice **cream** [ˌaɪs 'kri:m] Eiscreme; Eis I
to create [kri'eɪt] machen <III U2, 49>; schaffen; erschaffen <III U3, 67>
creative [kri'eɪtɪv] kreativ <III U1, 28>
credit card ['kredɪt ˌka:d] Kreditkarte <III U4, 86>
crew [kru:] Crew; Besatzung; Mannschaft III U4, 84
cricket ['krɪkɪt] Kricket II
crime [kraɪm] Verbrechen <III U4, 77>
financial **crisis** [faɪˌnænʃl 'kraɪsɪs] Wirtschaftskrise <III U5, 139>
crisp [krɪsp] Kartoffelchip I
crisp [krɪsp] knusprig, kross <III U3, 66>
crocodile ['krɒkədaɪl] Krokodil I
to cross [krɒs] überqueren III U1, 12
crowd [kraʊd] Menschenmenge II
to cry [kraɪ] weinen; rufen; schreien <III U4, 77>
CU (See you!) ['si: ˌju] Bis später! II
cuddly ['kʌdli] knuddelig III U2, 39
cuddly toy ['kʌdli ˌtɔɪ] Kuscheltier III U2, 39
cuju ['tsuju] Cuju *(asiatischer Vorgänger des Fußballs)* <III U1, 24>
culture ['kʌltʃə] Kultur <I>
cup [kʌp] Tasse II
cupboard ['kʌbəd] Schrank III U5, 98
curry ['kʌri] Curry II
custard ['kʌstəd] Vanillesauce II
customer ['kʌstəmə] Kunde; Kundin III U4, 80
cut [kʌt] Schnittverletzung <III U2, 194>
***to cut** [kʌt] (sich) schneiden II
to cut in half [ˌkʌt‿ɪn 'ha:f] halbieren <III U1, 29>
to cut out ['kʌt‿aʊt] ausschneiden <III U1, 29>
cut [kʌt] simple past, past participle von *to cut* II

cut-out ['kʌt‿aʊt] ausgeschnitten <III U1, 29>
cute [kju:t] niedlich; süß I
cycling ['saɪklɪŋ] Radfahren III U3, 61

D

dad [dæd] Papa I
daily ['deɪli] täglich III U5, 101
dance [da:ns] Tanz III U5, 100
to dance [da:ns] tanzen I
dancer ['da:nsə] Tänzer; Tänzerin III U5, 94
dancing ['da:nsɪŋ] Tanzen; Tanz- <III U3, 135>
danger ['deɪndʒə] Gefahr <III U2, 132>
dangerous ['deɪndʒrəs] gefährlich III U2, 34
the **dark** [ðə 'da:k] Dunkelheit III U1, 20
dark [da:k] dunkel I
darkness ['da:knəs] Dunkelheit <III U5, 101>
date [deɪt] Datum I
daughter ['dɔ:tə] Tochter I
break of **dawn** [ˌbreɪk‿əv 'dɔ:n] Tagesanbruch <III U5, 101>
day [deɪ] Tag I
a day off [ə ˌdeɪ‿'ɒf] ein freier Tag III U2, 39
all day [ˌɔ:l 'deɪ] den ganzen Tag III U3, 58
in the old days [ɪn ði 'əʊld ˌdeɪz] früher III U2, 43
lucky day [ˌlʌki 'deɪ] Glückstag II
one day [wʌn 'deɪ] eines Tages III U1, 21
a busy day [ə ˌbɪzi 'deɪ] ein ausgefüllter Tag I
four hours a day [ˌaʊəz‿ə 'deɪ] vier Stunden täglich I
dead [ded] tot III U1, 22
deadly ['dedli] tod-; tödlich III U1, 20
deaf [def] gehörlos; schwerhörig; taub III U3, 54
Dear ..., [dɪə] Liebe/Lieber ..., *(Anrede in Briefen)* I

debit card ['debɪt ˌkɑ:d] EC-Karte <III U4, 86>

December [dɪ'sembə] Dezember I

to **decide** [dɪ'saɪd] (sich) entscheiden III U3, 58

*to make a **decision** [ˌmeɪk‿ə dɪ'sɪʒn] eine Entscheidung treffen <III U5, 113>

to **decode** [ˌdi:'kəʊd] entschlüsseln <III U2, 48>

deep [di:p] tief <III U3, 70>

deep fried [ˌdi:p'fraɪd] frittiert; in Fett ausgebacken <III U3, 66>

definition [ˌdefɪ'nɪʃn] Definition <III U3, 59>

delicious [dɪ'lɪʃəs] köstlich II

department [dɪ'pɑ:tmənt] Abteilung II

department store [dɪ'pɑ:tmənt ˌstɔ:] Kaufhaus II

to **describe** [dɪ'skraɪb] beschreiben <I>

design [dɪ'zaɪn] Design; Gestaltung <III U3, 69>

Design Technology (DT) [dɪˌzaɪn tek'nɒlədʒi, ˌdi:'ti:] Technik I

to **design** [dɪ'zaɪn] entwerfen; gestalten <III U1, 29>; <III U3, 69>

desk [desk] Schreibtisch <III U2, 49>

information desk [ɪnfə'meɪʃn ˌdesk] Information II

dessert [dɪ'zɜ:t] Nachspeise II

detail ['di:teɪl] Detail; Einzelheit <II>

language **detectives** ['læŋgwɪdʒ ˌdɪtektɪvz] Sprachdetektive <I>

detector [dɪ'tektə] Detektor III U3, 54

dialogue ['daɪəlɒg] Dialog; Gespräch <III U2, 34>

diamond ['daɪəmənd] Diamant <II>

diary ['daɪəri] Tagebuch I

dictionary ['dɪkʃnri] Wörterbuch <III U2, 35>

did [dɪd] simple past von *to do* I

to **die** [daɪ] sterben III U1, 21

difference ['dɪfrns] Unterschied <III U2, 40>

different ['dɪfrnt] anders; unterschiedlich I

difficult ['dɪfɪklt] schwierig III U2, 35

dining room ['daɪnɪŋ ˌrʊm] Esszimmer I

dinner ['dɪnə] Abendessen II

dinosaur ['daɪnəsɔ:] Dinosaurier <III U3, 70>

to **dip** [dɪp] tunken <III U1, 29>

direct [dɪ'rekt] direkt <III U5, 112>

directions *(pl)* [dɪ'rekʃnz] Anweisungen; Wegbeschreibung <III U1, 10>

director [dɪ'rektə] Regisseur; Regisseurin II

dirty ['dɜ:ti] dreckig; schmutzig I

to **disagree** [ˌdɪsə'gri:] anderer Meinung sein; nicht einverstanden sein II

disagreement [ˌdɪsə'gri:mnt] Meinungsverschiedenheit; Streit <III U4, 136>

disaster [dɪ'zɑ:stə] Katastrophe; Desaster; Unglück III U4, 84

to **discover** [dɪ'skʌvə] entdecken <III U1, 30>

to **discuss** [dɪ'skʌs] diskutieren <III U1, 17>

dish [dɪʃ] Gericht; Speise II

distance ['dɪstns] Entfernung; Distanz III U1, 17

to **divide** [dɪ'vaɪd] teilen <III U3, 71>

*to **do** [du:] machen; tun I

to do homework [ˌdu: 'həʊmwɜ:k] Hausaufgabe(n) machen I

to do the right thing [ˌdu: ðə 'raɪt θɪŋ] das Richtige tun III U2, 38

to do the shopping [ˌdu: ðə 'ʃɒpɪŋ] Einkäufe machen; Besorgungen machen II

to do the washing up [ˌdu: ðə 'wɒʃɪŋ‿ʌp] abspülen II

dos and don'ts [ˌdu:z‿ən 'dəʊnts] Verhaltensregeln <III U2, 44>

doctor ['dɒktə] Arzt; Ärztin II

document ['dɒkjəmənt] Dokument <III U5, 215>

dog [dɒg] Hund I

dog biscuit ['dɒg ˌbɪskɪt] Hundekeks II

dolphin ['dɒlfɪn] Delfin <III U2, 45>

dome [dəʊm] Kuppel II

dos and don'ts [ˌdu:z‿ən 'dəʊnts] Verhaltensregeln <III U2, 44>

Don't talk. [ˌdəʊnt 'tɔ:k] Sei still.; Rede nicht. I

done [dʌn] past participle von *to do* II

door [dɔ:] Tür I

doorbell ['dɔ:bel] Türklingel I

to **double-check** [ˌdʌbl'tʃek] genau nachprüfen <III U3, 73>

down [daʊn] deprimiert III U4, 77

down [daʊn] entlang; herunter; hinunter III U1, 12

to **download** [ˌdaʊn'ləʊd] herunterladen II

Dr ['dɒktə] Dr. *(Anrede)* III U4, 85

draft [drɑ:ft] Entwurf <II>

drafting ['drɑ:ftɪŋ] Formulieren <III U5, 113>

drama ['drɑ:mə] Theater II; Drama III U2, 51

drank [dræŋk] simple past von *to drink* II

*to **draw** [drɔ:] zeichnen II

drawing ['drɔ:ɪŋ] Zeichnen <III U1, 28>

drawn [drɔ:n] past participle von *to draw* II

dreadful ['dredfl] furchtbar III U4, 77

dream [dri:m] Traum I

*to **dream** [dri:m] träumen III U1, 25

dreamt [dremt] simple past, past participle von *to dream* III U1, 25

dress [dres] Kleid I

fancy dress [ˌfænsi 'dres] Verkleidung; Kostüm I

dressed [drest] angezogen; verkleidet III U5, 105

to get dressed [ˌget 'drest] sich anziehen II

drew [dru:] simple past von *to draw* II

drink [drɪŋk] Getränk II

*to **drink** [drɪŋk] trinken II

anything to drink ['eniθɪŋ tə 'drɪŋk] etwas zu trinken II

*to **drive** [draɪv] treiben <III U5, 138>

to drive sb crazy [ˌdraɪv ... 'kreɪzi] jmdn. verrückt machen III U4, 76

driver ['draɪvə] Fahrer; Fahrerin III U5, 100

lorry driver ['lɒri ˌdraɪvə] LKW-Fahrer; LKW-Fahrerin II

to **drown** [draʊn] ertrinken <III U5, 138>

drum [drʌm] Trommel <III U5, 107>

drumming ['drʌmɪŋ] Trommel- III U5, 100

drunk [drʌŋk] past participle von *to drink* II

to **dry** [draɪ] trocknen <III U1, 29>

dry [draɪ] trocken III U2, 35

duke [dju:k] Herzog <III U1, 130>

dumpling ['dʌmplɪŋ] Kloß II

duration [djʊ'reɪʃn] Dauer <III U1, 30>

during ['djʊərɪŋ] während III U1, 11

on **duty** [ɒn 'dju:ti] im Dienst <III U3, 68>

DVD [ˌdi:vi:'di:] DVD I

E

each [i:tʃ] jeder <I>

each other [ˌi:tʃ‿'ʌðə] einander; sich; sich gegenseitig III U2, 34

each [i:tʃ] pro Stück II

ear [ɪə] Ohr II

early ['ɜ:li] früh I

earlier ['ɜ:liə] früher I

early settler [ˌɜ:li 'setlə] früher Siedler; frühe Siedlerin <III U5, 138>

east [i:st] Osten III U1, 10

eastbound ['i:stbaʊnd] in Richtung Osten <III U5, 216>

easy ['i:zi] einfach; leicht I

*to **eat** [i:t] essen I

eaten ['i:tn] past participle von *to eat* II

economy [ɪ'kɒnəmi] Wirtschaft <III U5, 139>

editing ['edɪtɪŋ] Kontrolle <III U5, 113>

egg [eg] Ei I

scrambled egg [ˌskræmbld‿'eg] Rührei II

Eid [i:d] Eid *(muslimisches Fest)* I

eight [eɪt] acht I

eighteen [ˌeɪ'ti:n] achtzehn I

eighty ['eɪti] achtzig I

not ... **either** [nɒt ... 'aɪðə] auch nicht III U3, 58

electricity [ˌelɪk'trɪsəti] Strom; Elektrizität III U3, 53

elephant ['elɪfənt] Elefant I

eleven [ɪ'levn] elf I

what **else** [ˌwɒt‿'els] was noch; was sonst III U5, 96

e-mail ['i:meɪl] E-Mail I

embarrassed [ɪm'bærəst] verlegen II

emergency [ɪ'mɜ:dʒənsi] Notfall III U2, 38

emergency call [ɪ'mɜ:dʒənsi ˌkɔ:l] Notruf III U2, 38

emergency service [ɪ'mɜ:dʒənsi ˌsɜ:vɪs] Notdienst; Rettungsdienst III U2, 38

to **emigrate** ['emɪgreɪt] auswandern <III U5, 139>

empire ['empaɪə] Reich; Kaiserreich III U1, 10

end [end] Ende; Schluss II

at the end of the road [ət ði: 'end‿əv ðə ˌrəʊd] am Ende der Straße I

by the end [ˌbaɪ ði 'end] am Schluss II

in the end [ɪn ði 'end] schließlich; zum Schluss II

to **end** [end] enden <II>; beenden <III U5, 113>

ending ['endɪŋ] Schluss; Ende III U2, 45

happy ending [ˌhæpi 'endɪŋ] Happy End <III U5, 113>

enemy ['enəmi] Feind; Feindin III U2, 50

fire **engine** ['faɪər‿ˌendʒɪn] Feuerwehrauto II

steam engine ['sti:m‿ˌendʒɪn] Dampfmaschine III U3, 57

engineer [ˌendʒɪ'nɪə] Ingenieur; Ingenieurin; Techniker; Technikerin II

English ['ɪŋglɪʃ] englisch; Englisch; aus England I

the **English** [ði 'ɪŋglɪʃ] die Engländer III U1, 11

to **enjoy** [ɪn'dʒɔɪ] genießen II; mögen III U2, 50

to enjoy oneself [ɪn'dʒɔɪ] Spaß haben; sich amüsieren III U2, 34

enough [ɪ'nʌf] genug; genügend III U2, 34

entry ['entri] Eintrag <III U3, 73>

entry form ['entri ˌfɔ:m] Anmeldeformular II

equipment [ɪ'kwɪpmənt] Ausrüstung III U2, 34

er [ɜ:] äh I

Victorian **era** [vɪkˌtɔ:riən 'ɪərə] viktorianisches Zeitalter III U1, 25

eraser [ɪ'reɪzə] Radiergummi I

escalator ['eskəleɪtə] Rolltreppe II

to **escape** [ɪ'skeɪp] entkommen; fliehen; entfliehen; flüchten <III U3, 72>

especially [ɪ'speʃli] besonders; vor allem II

euro ['jʊərəʊ] Euro *(Währung)* III U5, 94

European [ˌjʊərə'pi:ən] europäisch <III U5, 139>

even ['i:vn] noch; sogar II

evening ['i:vnɪŋ] Abend I

in the evenings [ɪn ði 'i:vnɪŋz] abends III U4, 76

event [ɪ'vent] Ereignis; Veranstaltung <III U2, 131>; <III U4, 88>

ever ['evə] jemals II

every ['evri] jeder I

everyone ['evriwʌn] jeder I; zusammen; alle II

everything ['evriθɪŋ] alles II

exact [ɪg'zækt] exakt; genau <III U2, 49>; III U4, 81

exam [ɪg'zæm] Examen; Prüfung <III U5, 112>

example [ɪg'zɑ:mpl] Beispiel <III U2, 51>

for example [fər‿ɪg'zɑ:mpl] zum Beispiel <III U1, 24>

excellent ['ekslnt] exzellent; hervorragend <III U5, 110>

except [ɪk'sept] außer III U2, 42
exchange [ɪks'tʃeɪndʒ] Austausch <III U5, 106>
to **exchange** [ɪks'tʃeɪndʒ] tauschen; austauschen <III U2, 41>
excited [ɪk'saɪtɪd] aufgeregt; begeistert II
exciting [ɪk'saɪtɪŋ] spannend; aufregend I
excuse [ɪk'skju:s] Entschuldigung; Ausrede <III U2, 39>
Excuse me! [ɪk'skju:z mi] Entschuldigung! I
exercise ['eksəsaɪz] Übung I
exercise book ['eksəsaɪz ˌbʊk] Übungsheft I
exhausted [ɪg'zɔ:stɪd] erschöpft III U2, 35
exhibition [ˌeksɪ'bɪʃn] Ausstellung III U3, 53
to **expect** [ɪk'spekt] erwarten III U2, 45
expensive [ɪk'spensɪv] teuer II
experiment [ɪk'sperɪmənt] Versuch II
expert ['ekspɜ:t] Experte; Expertin <III U1, 28>
to **explain** [ɪk'spleɪn] erklären III U5, 104
to **explode** [ɪk'spləʊd] explodieren III U1, 20
to **explore** [ɪk'splɔ:] erkunden; erforschen II
explosion [ɪk'spləʊʒn] Explosion III U1, 20
to **express** [ɪk'spres] ausdrücken <III U3, 60>
extra ['ekstrə] Extra; Zusatz <III U5, 215>
extra ['ekstrə] zusätzlich; Zusatz- II
extra activities ['ekstrə ˌæktɪvətiz] Zusatzaktivitäten <I>
eye [aɪ] Auge II
I couldn't believe my eyes. [aɪ ˌkʊdnt bɪˌli:v maɪ‿'aɪz] Ich traute meinen Augen nicht. III U5, 105
I spy with my little eye … [aɪ spaɪ wɪð ˌmaɪ lɪtl 'aɪ] Ich sehe was, was du nicht siehst … I

F

fable ['feɪbl] Fabel; Märchen III U5, 105
fabric paint ['fæbrɪk ˌpeɪnt] Stofffarbe <III U1, 29>
face [feɪs] Gesicht <III U1, 25>
to **face** [feɪs] sich gegenüber stehen <III U5, 110>
fact [fækt] Fakt; Tatsache II
in fact [ɪn 'fækt] eigentlich; tatsächlich; genau genommen III U5, 104
factory ['fæktri] Fabrik; Werk III U1, 16
fair [feə] gerecht; fair <III U1, 24>
Fair enough. [ˌfeər‿ɪ'nʌf] Na schön. III U5, 100
*to **fall** [fɔ:l] fallen I
to fall (over) [ˌfɔ:l‿'əʊvə] fallen; hinfallen; umfallen III U2, 38
to fall apart [ˌfɔ:l‿ə'pɑ:t] zusammenbrechen <III U4, 77>
to fall asleep [ˌfɔ:l‿ə'sli:p] einschlafen III U1, 25
to fall in love (with) [ˌfɔ:l‿ɪn 'lʌv] sich verlieben (in) III U2, 50
to fall off [ˌfɔ:l‿'ɒf] fallen; herunterfallen III U2, 40
false [fɔ:ls] falsch <II>
family ['fæmli] Familie I
host family ['həʊst fæmli] Gastfamilie <III U5, 94>
famine ['fæmɪn] Hungersnot <III U5, 139>
famous ['feɪməs] berühmt I
fan [fæn] Fan I
fancy dress [ˌfænsi 'dres] Verkleidung; Kostüm I
fantastic [fæn'tæstɪk] fantastisch; großartig II
fantasy ['fæntəsi] Fantasie; Fantasy II
far [fɑ:] weit III U1, 12
fare [feə] Fahrpreis III U5, 100
farewell speech [feə'wel spi:tʃ] Abschiedsrede II
farm [fɑ:m] Bauernhof I
wind farm ['wɪnd fɑ:m] Windpark III U3, 53
farmer ['fɑ:mə] Landwirt; Landwirtin; Bauer; Bäuerin I
fashionable ['fæʃnəbl] modisch II
fast [fɑ:st] schnell II
fast food [ˌfɑ:st 'fu:d] Fastfood I
fast food restaurant [ˌfɑ:st fu:d 'restrɒnt] Fastfood-Restaurant I
the fastest [ðə 'fɑ:stɪst] der/die/das schnellste I
fat [fæt] fett; dick <III U5, 112>
father ['fɑ:ðə] Vater I
It's my **fault**. [ɪts ˌmaɪ 'fɔ:lt] Es ist meine Schuld. II
favourite ['feɪvrɪt] Lieblings- I
fear [fɪə] Angst; Furcht <III U4, 77>
feature ['fi:tʃə] Merkmal <III U1, 31>
February ['februri] Februar I
fed [fed] simple past von *to feed* I; past participle von *to feed* II
*to be **fed** up (with) [bi: fed‿'ʌp (wɪð)] die Nase voll haben (von); sauer sein III U4, 76
*to **feed** [fi:d] füttern I
feedback ['fi:dbæk] Feedback; Rückmeldung <II>
*to **feel** [fi:l] (sich) fühlen II
to feel sorry for [ˌfi:l 'sɒri fə] Mitleid haben mit; bedauern III U5, 105
to make sb feel like sth [ˌmeɪk … 'fi:l laɪk] jmdm. das Gefühl geben, etw. zu sein III U2, 43
feeling ['fi:lɪŋ] Gefühl <III U4, 87>
fell [fel] simple past von *to fall* I
felt [felt] simple past von *to feel* II
felt-tip [ˌfelt'tɪp] Filzstift I
female ['fi:meɪl] weiblich <III U1, 24>
ferry ['feri] Fähre <III U5, 216>
festival ['festɪvl] Festival; Fest III U5, 100
a **few** [ə 'fju:] ein paar; wenige; einige III U1, 20
science **fiction** [ˌsaɪəns 'fɪkʃn] Science-Fiction I
fifteen [ˌfɪf'ti:n] fünfzehn I
fifty ['fɪfti] fünfzig I
fight [faɪt] Kampf; Streit III U2, 50

*to **fight** [faɪt] kämpfen; (sich) streiten III U1, 11
fighting ['faɪtɪŋ] Kämpfen; Kämpfe <III U4, 134>
file [faɪl] Datei II
to **fill** [fɪl] (sich) füllen III U4, 84
film [fɪlm] Film I
film corner ['fi:lm ˌkɔ:nə] Filmecke <I>
film maker ['fɪlm ˌmeɪkə] Filmemacher; Filmemacherin <III U5, 107>
to **film** [fɪlm] filmen; drehen <III U1, 26>
finally ['faɪnli] schließlich; zum Schluss II
financial crisis [faɪˌnænʃl 'kraɪsɪs] Wirtschaftskrise <III U5, 139>
*to **find** [faɪnd] finden; herausfinden I
to find out [ˌfaɪnd‿'aʊt] herausfinden I
I can't find … [ˌaɪ kɑ:nt 'faɪnd] Ich kann … nicht finden. I
fine [faɪn] schön; gut; in Ordnung II
I'm fine. [ˌaɪm 'faɪn] Mir geht es gut. II
finger ['fɪŋgə] Finger III U2, 39
fingerprint ['fɪŋgəprɪnt] Fingerabdruck II
to **finish** ['fɪnɪʃ] beenden; enden; aufhören; fertigstellen; vervollständigen II
fire [faɪə] Feuer I
to be on fire [bi: ɒn 'faɪə] brennen II
fire brigade ['faɪə brɪˌgeɪd] Feuerwehr <III U2, 38>
fire engine ['faɪər‿ˌendʒɪn] Feuerwehrauto II
fired ['faɪəd] gefeuert; hinausgeworfen III U1, 23
first [fɜ:st] zuerst; als Erstes; erste I
first name [ˌfɜ:st 'neɪm] Vorname <III U1, 131>; <III U3, 67>
very first ['veri fɜ:st] allererste III U4, 84
fish *(sg)* [fɪʃ], **fish** *(pl)* [fɪʃ] Fisch I
to **fit** [fɪt] passen II
fit [fɪt] fit; in Form III U2, 34
five [faɪv] fünf I
fizzy ['fɪzi] sprudelnd <III U3, 71>
flag [flæg] Flagge; Fahne II
flame [fleɪm] Flamme III U1, 20
flamingo [flə'mɪŋgəʊ] Flamingo I
flare [fleə] Leuchtsignal; Leuchtfackel <III U5, 101>
flat [flæt] Wohnung I
holiday flat ['hɒlədeɪ ˌflæt] Ferienwohnung <III U3, 202>
flavour ['fleɪvə] Geschmack; Geschmacksrichtung; Sorte <III U4, 209>
flew [flu:] simple past von *to fly* II
flight [flaɪt] Flug II
flip flop ['flɪp flɒp] Flipflop <III U2, 44>
floor [flɔ:] Fußboden I; Stockwerk II
flour [flaʊə] Mehl II
flower ['flaʊə] Blume III U5, 104
flown [fləʊn] past participle von *to fly* II
fluent ['flu:ənt] fließend; flüssig III U2, 33
*to **fly** [flaɪ] fliegen II; wehen <III U1, 30>
flyer ['flaɪə] Flyer; Faltblatt II
flying ['flaɪɪŋ] Fliegen <III U1, 30>
foggy ['fɒgi] neblig I
folder ['fəʊldə] Ordner; Mappe <III U2, 46>
to **follow** ['fɒləʊ] folgen <III U2, 49>; befolgen <III U4, 79>
food [fu:d] Essen; Nahrung; Lebensmittel I
fast food [ˌfɑ:st 'fu:d] Fastfood I
fast food restaurant [ˌfɑ:st fu:d 'restrɒnt] Fastfood-Restaurant I
food stall ['fu:d ˌstɔ:l] Essensstand II
foot *(sg)* [fʊt], **feet** *(pl)* [fi:t] Fuß I
on foot [ɒn 'fʊt] zu Fuß I
football ['fʊtbɔ:l] Fußball I
association football ['əsəʊsieɪʃn ˌfʊtbɔ:l] Assoziationsfußball *(offizieller Name des Fußballs)* <III U1, 24>
football association ['fʊtbɔ:l ˌəsəʊsieɪʃn] Fußballverband <III U1, 24>
I can play football. [ˌaɪ kən ˌpleɪ 'fʊtbɔ:l] Ich kann Fußball spielen. I
for [fɔ:] für I; seit <III U2, 133>; lang <III U5, 138>
for a start [ˌfɔ:r‿ə 'stɑ:t] zunächst III U3, 58
for five months [fə 'faɪv ˌmʌnθs] fünf Monate lang I
for fun [fə 'fʌn] zum Spaß III U2, 43
for service [fə 'sɜ:vɪs] um bedient zu werden <III U4, 86>
foreground ['fɔ:graʊnd] Vordergrund III U4, 92
in the foreground [ɪn ðə 'fɔ:graʊnd] im Vordergrund III U4, 92
forest ['fɒrɪst] Wald <III U5, 112>
to **foretell** [fɔ:'tel] vorhersagen III U5, 105
forever [fə'revə] für immer; ewig II
*to **forget** [fə'get] vergessen I
forgot [fə'gɒt] simple past von *to forget* I
forgotten [fə'gɒtn] past participle von *to forget* II
I must have forgotten it. [aɪ ˌmʌst hæv fə'gɒtn‿ɪt] Ich muss es vergessen haben. II
fork [fɔ:k] Gabel II
form [fɔ:m] Form <III U1, 23>
entry form ['entri ˌfɔ:m] Anmeldeformular II
to **form** [fɔ:m] bilden <III U1, 14>
forty ['fɔ:ti] vierzig I
fought [fɔ:t] simple past, past participle von *to fight* III U1, 11
found [faʊnd] simple past von *to find* I
four [fɔ:] vier I
fourteen [ˌfɔ:'ti:n] vierzehn I
fourth [fɔ:θ] vierte I
free [fri:] kostenlos III U4, 75
free range [ˌfri: 'reɪndʒ] Freiland- II
free time [ˌfri: 'taɪm] Freizeit I

free-time [ˌfriːˈtaɪm] Freizeit- <III U2, 32>
*to **freeze** [friːz] frieren; gefrieren III U3, 58
freeze frame [ˈfriːz ˌfreɪm] Standbild <I>
French [frentʃ] Französisch I
French [frenʃ] französisch <III U1, 130>
fresh [freʃ] frisch II
Friday [ˈfraɪdeɪ] Freitag I
fridge [frɪdʒ] Kühlschrank III U5, 96
fried [fraɪd] (in der Pfanne) gebraten II
deep fried [ˌdiːpˈfraɪd] frittiert; in Fett ausgebacken <III U3, 66>
friend [frend] Freund; Freundin I
to make friends [ˌmeɪk ˈfrendz] Freundschaften schließen I
to see friends [siː ˈfrendz] Freunde treffen I
That's what friends are for! [ˌðæts wɒt ˌfrendz‿ɑː ˈfɔː] Dafür sind Freunde da! II
friendly [ˈfrendli] freundlich; nett III U1, 12
frisbee [ˈfrɪzbi] Frisbee; Frisbeescheibe I
from [frɒm] aus; von I
from behind [ˌfrəm bɪˈhaɪnd] von hinten I
I'm from … [ˈaɪm ˌfrɒm] Ich komme aus … I
It's two hours from here. [ɪts tuː ˈaʊəz frɒm ˌhɪə] Es ist zwei Stunden von hier entfernt. I
Where are you from? [ˌweər‿ə ju ˈfrɒm] Woher kommst du? I
to the **front** [tʊ ðə ˈfrʌnt] nach vorn <III U5, 110>
at the front of [ət ðə ˈfrʌnt‿əv] an der Spitze (von); im vorderen Bereich II
in front of [ɪn ˈfrʌnt‿əv] vor; davor II
front [frʌnt] vordere <III U5, 111>
froze [frəʊz] simple past von *to freeze* III U3, 58
frozen [ˈfrəʊzn] past participle von *to freeze* III U3, 58
fruit [fruːt] Frucht; Obst I
to **fry** [fraɪ] frittieren <III U3, 66>
full [fʊl] voll III U4, 85
full service [ˌfʊl ˈsɜːvɪs] Komplettservice <III U3, 68>
full stop [ˌfʊl ˈstɒp] Punkt <III U1, 23>
full of colour [ˌfʊl‿əv ˈkʌlə] mit Farbe bedeckt <III U1, 29>
fun [fʌn] Freude; Spaß I
for fun [fə ˈfʌn] zum Spaß III U2, 43
is more fun [ɪz ˈmɔː ˌfʌn] macht mehr Spaß I
fundraising [ˈfʌndˌreɪzɪŋ] Spendenaktionen <III U2, 132>
funnel [ˈfʌnl] Trichter <III U3, 71>
funny [ˈfʌni] lustig; witzig I; merkwürdig; seltsam II
furious [ˈfjʊəriəs] wütend III U4, 77
future [ˈfjuːtʃə] Zukunft III U2, 42

G

gallery [ˈgæləri] Galerie <III U2, 49>
game [geɪm] Spiel I
gamer [ˈgeɪmə] Spieler *(Computer)*; Spielerin *(Computer)* II
garage [ˈgærɑːʒ] Werkstatt; Tankstelle <III U3, 68>
garden [ˈgɑːdn] Garten I
garlic [ˈgɑːlɪk] Knoblauch II
gas [gæs] Gas III U1, 20
gate [geɪt] Tor III U2, 42
gave [geɪv] simple past von *to give* II
gel [dʒel] Gel III U5, 97
hair gel [ˈheə ˌdʒel] Haargel III U5, 97
shower gel [ˈʃaʊə ˌdʒel] Duschgel III U5, 97
general [ˈdʒenrl] allgemein <III U4, 93>
gently [ˈdʒentli] sanft <III U4, 86>
geocaching [ˈdʒiəʊkæʃɪŋ] Geocaching I
Geography [dʒiˈɒgrəfi] Geografie; Erdkunde I
German [ˈdʒɜːmən] Deutsch I
German [ˈdʒɜːmən] deutsch; aus Deutschland III U5, 98
*to **get** [get] bekommen; werden I; holen II; verstehen III U4, 80
to get a job wrong [ˌget‿ə dʒɒb ˈrɒŋ] einen Auftrag vermasseln III U2, 50
to get around [ˌget əˈraʊnd] herumkommen III U1, 16
to get back [ˌget‿ˈbæk] zurückkommen <III U2, 132>
to get cold [ˌget ˈkəʊld] frieren III U3, 60
to get dressed [ˌget ˈdrest] sich anziehen II
to get in [ˈget‿ɪn] hereinkommen I
to get into trouble [ˌget‿ɪntə ˈtrʌbl] in Schwierigkeiten geraten <III U2, 132>
to get lost [get lɒst] sich verirren I
to get married [ˌget ˈmærɪd] heiraten II
to get off [ˌget‿ˈɒf] aussteigen II
to get on [ˌget‿ˈɒn] einsteigen III U5, 101
to get on one's nerves [ˌget‿ɒn wʌnz ˈnɜːvz] auf die Nerven gehen III U1, 16
to get out [ˌget ˈaʊt] herauskommen III U2, 43
to get ready [ˌget ˈredi] sich vorbereiten; sich fertig machen <III U1, 27>; <III U2, 44>
to get started [ˌget ˈstɑːtɪd] anfangen <III U5, 110>
to get stuck [ˌget ˈstʌk] stecken bleiben <III U4, 83>
to get there [ˈget‿ðeə] hinkommen III U2, 42
to get to [ˈget tʊ] hinkommen zu; gelangen <III U2, 132>
to get to know [ˌget tə ˈnəʊ] kennen lernen II
to get up [ˌget‿ˈʌp] aufstehen I
I have to get going. [aɪ ˌhæv tə get ˈgəʊɪŋ] Ich muss gehen. III U4, 80
ghost [gəʊst] Geist II

giant [dʒaɪənt] Riese III U4, 75
giant [dʒaɪənt] Riesen-; riesig III U4, 74
giraffe [dʒɪ'rɑ:f] Giraffe I
girl [gɜ:l] Mädchen I
gist [dʒɪst] das Wesentliche <III U1, 21>
*to **give** [gɪv] geben I
to give a talk [ˌgɪv‿ə 'tɔ:k] einen Vortrag halten <III U1, 19>
to give reasons [ˌgɪv 'ri:znz] Gründe nennen; Gründe angeben III U2, 51
to give sth a miss [ˌgɪv sʌmθɪŋ‿ə 'mɪs] auf etw. verzichten; etw. bleiben lassen III U2, 50
to give up [ˌgɪv‿'ʌp] aufgeben III U3, 54
glad [glæd] froh II
glass [glɑ:s] Glas II
glove [glʌv] Handschuh <III U2, 44>
to **glow** [gləʊ] leuchten <III U5, 101>
glue stick ['glu: ˌstɪk] Klebestift <III U3, 71>
glue [glu:] Klebstoff I; kleben <III U3, 71>
*to **go** [gəʊ] gehen; fahren I
to go beach combing [gəʊ 'bi:tʃ ˌkəʊmɪŋ] den Strand nach Strandgut absuchen II
to go camping [ˌgəʊ 'kæmpɪŋ] campen gehen; zelten II
to go on [ˌgəʊ‿'ɒn] hineingehen II; weitergehen <III U5, 113>
to go on a night walk [ˌgəʊ ɒn‿ə 'naɪt wɔ:k] eine Nachtwanderung machen I
to go out [ˌgəʊ‿'aʊt] ausgehen III U4, 83
to go quiet [ˌgəʊ 'kwaɪət] still werden III U1, 20
to go shopping [ˌgəʊ 'ʃɒpɪŋ] einkaufen gehen II
to go sightseeing [gəʊ 'saɪtsi:ɪŋ] eine Besichtigungstour machen II
to go swimming [ˌgəʊ 'swɪmɪŋ] schwimmen gehen I
to go to bed [ˌgəʊ tə 'bed] ins Bett gehen I
I have to get going. [aɪ ˌhæv tə get 'gəʊɪŋ] Ich muss gehen. III U4, 80
goat [gəʊt] Ziege III U1, 16
god [gɒd] Gott <III U1, 28>
goggles *(pl)* ['gɒglz] Schutzbrille <III U2, 44>
gold [gəʊld] Gold III U5, 104
gold [gəʊld] golden; Gold- III U5, 104
gone [gɒn] past participle von *to go* II
gonna (= going to) ['gɒnə] werden <III U4, 77>
good [gʊd] gut I
to be good at [bi: 'gʊd‿ət] gut sein in/bei I
Good morning. [ˌgʊd 'mɔ:nɪŋ] Guten Morgen. II
good luck [ˌgʊd 'lʌk] viel Glück II
Goodbye. [gʊd'baɪ] Auf Wiedersehen. I
gooey ['gu:i] zähflüssig <III U3, 66>
got [gɒt] simple past von *to get* I
got lost [gɒt 'lɒst] simple past von *to get lost* I
got off [ˌgɒt‿'ɒf] simple past von *to get off* II
*to have **got** [hæv 'gɒt] besitzen; haben II
GPS *(Global Positioning System)* [ˌdʒi:pi:'es] GPS I
gr8 (great) [greɪt] großartig; toll II
to **grab** [græb] schnappen; greifen; ergreifen III U5, 105
grammar ['græmə] Grammatik <I>
grand [grænd] großartig III U5, 96
grandad ['grændæd] Opa III U4, 75
great-great-grandad [ˌgreɪt greɪt 'grændæd] Ururopa I
grandfather ['grænˌfɑ:ðə] Großvater II
grandma ['grænmɑ:] Oma II
grandmother ['grænˌmʌðə] Großmutter III U3, 67
grandparent ['grænˌpeərənt] Großelternteil <III U4, 87>
grandparents *(pl)* ['grænˌpeərənts] Großeltern II
grass [grɑ:s] Gras I
grave [greɪv] Grab III U1, 11
great [greɪt] großartig; toll I; groß; riesig <III U5, 139>
green [gri:n] grün I
greengrocer's ['gri:nˌgrəʊsəz] Obst- und Gemüseladen III U1, 13
grew [gru:] simple past von *to grow* <III U5, 139>
grew up [ˌgru:‿'ʌp] simple past von *to grow up* III U3, 54
grey [greɪ] grau I
grid [grɪd] Gitter; Raster <III U4, 90>
ground [graʊnd] Boden; Erdboden III U3, 64
group [gru:p] Gruppe I
tutor group ['tju:tə ˌgru:p] Klasse *(in einer englischen Schule)* I
*to **grow** [grəʊ] wachsen <III U5, 139>
to grow up [ˌgrəʊ‿'ʌp] aufwachsen III U3, 54
grown up [ˌgrəʊn‿'ʌp] past participle von *to grow up* III U3, 54
guarded ['gɑ:dɪd] vorsichtig; zurückhaltend III U4, 77
guess [ges] Vermutung <III U1, 28>
have a guess [ˌhæv‿ə 'ges] rate mal <III U1, 28>
to **guess** [ges] erraten; raten; überlegen II
Guess what? [ges 'wɒt] Weißt du was? I
guest [gest] Gast III U2, 33
guestbook ['gestbʊk] Gästebuch <I>
guide [gaɪd] Führer; Führerin II
guinea pig ['gɪni ˌpɪg] Meerschweinchen I
guitar [gɪ'tɑ:] Gitarre III U5, 95
guys [gaɪz] Leute II
gymnasium [dʒɪm'neɪziəm] Fitnessraum III U4, 84

H

had [hæd] simple past von *to have* I; past participle von *to have* II

had to ['hæd tə] simple past von *to have to* II
haggis ['hægɪs] Haggis *(schottisches Gericht aus Schafsinnereien)* <III U3, 66>
hair [heə] Haar; Haare III U5, 98
hair gel ['heə ˌdʒel] Haargel III U5, 97
hair straightener ['heə ˌstreɪtnə] Haarglätter I
hairbrush ['heəbrʌʃ] Haarbürste III U5, 97
haircut ['heəkʌt] Haarschnitt II
to have a haircut ['heəkʌt] sich die Haare schneiden lassen II
hairdresser ['heəˌdresə] Friseur; Friseurin II
hairdryer ['heəˌdraɪə] Fön III U5, 97
half [hɑ:f] die Hälfte <III U3, 71>
to cut in half [ˌkʌt‿ɪn 'hɑ:f] halbieren <III U1, 29>
half past (two) [ˌhɑ:f 'pɑ:st] halb (drei) I
half *(sg)* [hɑ:f], halves *(pl)* [hɑ:vz] (die) Hälfte III U4, 84
half a million [ˌhɑ:f‿ə 'mɪljən] eine halbe Million III U1, 16
half [hɑ:f] halb III U1, 16
hall [hɔ:l] Flur; Diele; Korridor II
town hall [ˌtaʊn 'hɔ:l] Rathaus II
ham [hæm] Schinken II
hammer throw ['hæmə ˌθrəʊ] Hammerwurf <III U3, 135>
hand [hænd] Hand I
handball ['hændbɔ:l] Handball <III U2, 193>
*to **hang** [hæŋ] hängen II
to **happen** ['hæpn] geschehen; passieren II
What happened? [ˌwɒt 'hæpnd] Was ist geschehen?; Was ist passiert? I
happy ['hæpi] glücklich I
happy ending [ˌhæpi 'endɪŋ] Happy End <III U5, 113>
Happy birthday! [ˌhæpi 'bɜ:θdeɪ] Alles Gute zum Geburtstag! I
harbour ['hɑ:bə] Hafen II
hard [hɑ:d] hart; schwer; schwierig II
harp [hɑ:p] Harfe <III U5, 107>
hat [hæt] Hut II
to **hate** [heɪt] hassen; nicht mögen I
Have you finished yet? [ˌhæv ju: 'fɪnɪʃt jet] Seid ihr schon fertig? II
*to **have** [hæv] haben I; essen II
to have a haircut ['heəkʌt] sich die Haare schneiden lassen II
to have a look [ˌhæv‿ə 'lʊk] anschauen II
to have breakfast [ˌhæv 'brekfəst] frühstücken I
to have to ['hæv tə] müssen II
have you got [ˌhæv ju: 'gɒt] hast du II
have a guess [ˌhæv‿ə 'ges] rate mal <III U1, 28>
Have you ever been to …? [hæv ju 'evə ˌbi:n tə] Warst du schon in …? II
*to **have** got [hæv 'gɒt] besitzen; haben II
he [hi:] er I
head [hed] Kopf II
head chef ['hed ʃef] Chefkoch II
head first ['hed fɜ:st] kopfüber III U1, 18
headache ['hedeɪk] Kopfschmerzen; Kopfweh II
heading ['hedɪŋ] Überschrift; Titel <III U1, 22>
headline ['hedlaɪn] Schlagzeile <II>
headteacher [ˌhed'ti:tʃə] Schulleiter; Schulleiterin <III U4, 88>
healthy ['helθi] gesund III U4, 80
*to **hear** [hɪə] hören I
heard [hɜ:d] simple past von *to hear* I; past participle von *to hear* II
heart [hɑ:t] Herz III U5, 94
heavy ['hevi] schwer; stark II
height [haɪt] Höhe II
held [held] simple past, past participle von *to hold* III U2, 43
helicopter ['helɪkɒptə] Helikopter; Hubschrauber I
Hello. [hə'ləʊ] Hallo. I
Hello there. [hə'ləʊ ˌðeə] Hallo.; Grüß dich. I
helm [helm] Steuermann <III U2, 132>
helmet ['helmət] Helm III U1, 12
help [help] Hilfe II
to **help** [help] helfen I
to help oneself [ˌhelp wʌn'self] sich bedienen III U5, 96
Help yourselves! [ˌhelp jɔ:'selvz] Bedient euch!; Bedienen Sie sich! II
How can I help you? [ˌhaʊ kæn aɪ 'help‿ju] Was kann ich für dich tun? I
I couldn't help but … [ˌaɪ kʊdnt 'help bʌt] Ich konnte nicht anders als … III U5, 105
helpful ['helpfl] hilfreich; nützlich III U5, 100
her [hɜ:] ihr, ihre; sie I
here [hɪə] hier I
Here you are. [ˌhɪə ju‿'ɑ:] Bitte schön. I
Here's your change. [ˌhɪəz jɔ: 'tʃeɪndʒ] Hier ist dein Wechselgeld. I
hero *(sg)* ['hɪərəʊ], heroes *(pl)* ['hɪərəʊz] Held III U3, 52
hers [hɜ:z] ihre II
herself [hɜ:'self] sie selbst; sich selbst III U2, 156
Hi. [haɪ] Hi.; Hallo. I
to say hi to [ˌseɪ 'haɪ tə] grüßen; Grüße ausrichten I
hid [hɪd] simple past von *to hide* III U2, 50
hidden ['hɪdn] past participle von *to hide* III U2, 50
*to **hide** [haɪd] verstecken <III U2, 49>; (sich) verstecken III U2, 50
hiding place ['haɪdɪŋ ˌpleɪs] Versteck <III U2, 49>
high [haɪ] hoch; groß I
high jump ['haɪ ˌdʒʌmp] Hochsprung <III U2, 193>
high school ['haɪ ˌsku:l] High School *(weiterführende Schule, Oberstufe)* <III U2, 133>

highlight ['haɪlaɪt] Highlight; Höhepunkt <III U5, 138>

highlighted ['haɪlaɪtɪd] hervorgehoben <III U1, 31>

to **hike** [haɪk] wandern II

hiking ['haɪkɪŋ] Wandern III U3, 58

hill [hɪl] Berg; Hügel <III U1, 28>

him [hɪm] ihm; ihn I

himself [hɪm'self] sich (selbst); er selbst III U2, 35

hip hop ['hɪp hɒp] Hip-Hop *(Musik)* III U5, 95

his [hɪz] sein I; seins; seiner II

historical [hɪ'stɒrɪkl] historisch; geschichtlich <III U1, 10>

History ['hɪstri] Geschichte I

history ['hɪstri] Geschichte III U1, 12

hit [hɪt] Hit; Treffer <III U3, 73>

*to **hit** [hɪt] treffen; schlagen II; (sich) stoßen; anstoßen III U2, 40; gegen etw. fahren III U4, 84

hit [hɪt] simple past, past participle von *to hit*

hobby ['hɒbi] Hobby III ZI 9

*to **hold** [həʊld] halten; festhalten III U2, 43

Hold them up. [ˌhəʊld ðəm‿'ʌp] Halte sie hoch. I

hole [həʊl] Loch I

holiday ['hɒlədeɪ] Ferien; Urlaub I; Feiertag III U5, 104

holiday cottage ['hɒlədeɪ ˌkɒtɪdʒ] Ferienhäuschen <III U3, 202>

holiday flat ['hɒlədeɪ ˌflæt] Ferienwohnung <III U3, 202>

home [həʊm] Zuhause; Heim; nach Hause I

at home [ət 'həʊm] zu Hause I

back home [bæk 'həʊm] zu Hause II

to make oneself at home [ˌmeɪk wʌnself ət 'həʊm] sich wie zu Hause fühlen III U5, 96

homepage ['həʊmpeɪdʒ] Homepage III U5, 100

*to be **homesick** [bi: 'həʊmsɪk] Heimweh haben III U5, 104

homework ['həʊmwɜ:k] Hausaufgabe(n) I

to do homework [ˌdu: 'həʊmwɜ:k] Hausaufgabe(n) machen I

honest ['ɒnɪst] ehrlich III U4, 77

honey ['hʌni] Honig <III U4, 209>

hood [hʊd] Kapuze <III U1, 17>

Hooray! [hʊ'reɪ] Hurra! III U3, 65

to **hoover** ['hu:və] staubsaugen II

hop [hɒp] Sprung; Hüpfer <III U5, 111>

to **hope** [həʊp] hoffen I

hopeful ['həʊpfl] hoffnungsvoll III U4, 77

horrible ['hɒrəbl] schrecklich; furchtbar III U4, 76

chamber of **horrors** [ˌtʃeɪmbər‿əv 'hɒrəz] Kammer des Schreckens <III U1, 30>

horse [hɔ:s] Pferd I

horse riding ['hɔ:s ˌraɪdɪŋ] Reiten I

hospital ['hɒspɪtl] Hospital; Krankenhaus I

host family ['həʊst fæmli] Gastfamilie <III U5, 94>

youth **hostel** ['ju:θ ˌhɒstl] Jugendherberge III U3, 59

hot [hɒt] heiß I

hot air balloon [ˌhɒt‿'eə bəˌlu:n] Heißluftballon <III U2, 44>

hotel [həʊ'tel] Hotel II

hour [aʊə] Stunde I

40 kilometres an hour [kɪ'lɒmɪtəz‿ən‿'aʊə] 40 Kilometer pro Stunde I

house [haʊs] Haus I

around the house [ə'raʊnd ðə haʊs] im Haus I

how [haʊ] wie I

How about …? [ˌhaʊ‿ə'baʊt] Wie wäre es mit …? II

How are you? [ˌhaʊ‿'ɑ: jə] Wie geht es dir? I

How can I help you? [ˌhaʊ kæn aɪ 'help‿ju] Was kann ich für dich tun? I

How do I get there? [ˌhaʊ du aɪ 'get ðeə] Wie komme ich dahin? III U1, 12

how many [ˌhaʊ 'meni] wie viele II

how much [ˌhaʊ 'mʌtʃ] wie sehr III U3, 58

How much (is/are) …? [ˌhaʊ 'mʌtʃ‿ɪz/ɑ:] Wie viel (kostet/kosten) …? I

How old are you? [haʊ‿'əʊld‿ə ˌju:] Wie alt bist du? I

How to … ['haʊ tə] Wie man … II

however [haʊ'evə] jedoch III U4, 85

huge [hju:dʒ] riesig; riesengroß III U1, 17; gewaltig <III U3, 72>

human ['hju:mən] menschlich III U3, 54

a/one **hundred** ['hʌndrəd] einhundert; hundert I

hung [hʌŋ] simple past, past participle von *to hang* II

hungry ['hʌŋgri] hungrig I

hurling ['hɜ:lɪŋ] Hurling *(ähnliche Sportart wie Hockey)* <III U3, 135>

to **hurry** ['hʌri] sich beeilen II

*to **hurt** [hɜ:t] weh tun; verletzen II

hurt [hɜ:t] simple past, past participle von *to hurt* II

hurt [hɜ:t] verletzt II

I

I [aɪ] ich I

I can buy … [aɪ kən 'baɪ] Ich kann … kaufen. I

I can play football. [ˌaɪ kən ˌpleɪ 'fʊtbɔ:l] Ich kann Fußball spielen. I

I can't find … [ˌaɪ kɑ:nt 'faɪnd] Ich kann … nicht finden. I

I can't wait [aɪ ˌkɑ:nt 'weɪt] ich kann es kaum erwarten III U5, 100

I don't know! [ˌaɪ ˌdəʊnt 'nəʊ] Ich weiß (es) nicht! I

I don't like [aɪ ˌdəʊnt 'laɪk] ich mag nicht; gefällt mir nicht I

I have … [aɪ 'hæv] Ich habe … I

I like [aɪ 'laɪk] ich mag I

I wouldn't like (to) … [aɪ 'wʊdnt laɪk (tə)] Ich möchte nicht …; Ich würde nicht gerne … I

I'd like (to) … (= I would like to) [aɪd 'laɪk (tə)] Ich möchte …; Ich würde gerne … I

I'd love to … (= I would love to) [aɪd 'lʌv tə] Ich würde sehr gern … III U3, 58
I'd rather [aɪd 'rɑ:ðə] ich würde lieber III U1, 25
I'm from … ['aɪm ˌfrɒm] Ich komme aus … I
I'm sorry. [aɪm 'sɒrɪ] Es tut mir leid.; Entschuldigung. I
I've (I have) got [ˌaɪv 'gɒt] ich habe II
ice skating ['aɪs ˌskeɪtɪŋ] Schlittschuhlaufen <III U2, 193>
ice cream [ˌaɪs 'kri:m] Eiscreme; Eis I
iceberg ['aɪsbɜ:g] Eisberg III U4, 84
ID [ˌaɪ'di:] Ausweis; Personalausweis III U5, 97
idea [aɪ'dɪə] Idee; Ahnung I
Any idea? [ˌeni aɪ'dɪə] Irgendeine Idee? I
No idea! [ˌnəʊ‿aɪ'dɪə] Keine Ahnung! I
identity card [aɪ'dentəti ˌkɑ:d] Ausweis; Personalausweis <III U5, 215>
if [ɪf] wenn; falls II
ill [ɪl] krank; schlecht II
imperative [ɪm'perətɪv] Imperativ <III U3, 69>
important [ɪm'pɔ:tnt] wichtig; einflussreich II
impossible [ɪm'pɒsəbl] unmöglich III U3, 62
to **impress** [ɪm'pres] beeindrucken III U5, 107
in [ɪn] in I; drinnen II
in fact [ɪn 'fækt] eigentlich; tatsächlich; genau genommen III U5, 104
in need [ɪn 'ni:d] bedürftig; in Not <III U4, 77>
in the background [ɪn ðə 'bækgraʊnd] im Hintergrund III U4, 92
in the foreground [ɪn ðə 'fɔ:graʊnd] im Vordergrund III U4, 92
in the middle [ɪn ðə 'mɪdl] in der Mitte III U4, 92
in vain [ɪn 'veɪn] umsonst; vergeblich <III U5, 101>
in August [in 'ɔ:gəst] im August I
in front of [ɪn 'frʌnt‿əv] vor; davor II
in my opinion [ɪn 'maɪ‿əˌpɪnjən] meiner Meinung nach III U4, 76
in the afternoon [ˌɪn ði ˌɑ:ftə'nu:n] nachmittags I
in the centre of [ˌɪn ðə 'sentər‿əv] in der Mitte von III U1, 17
in the country [ɪn ðə 'kʌntri] auf dem Land I
in the end [ɪn ði 'end] schließlich; zum Schluss II
in the evenings [ɪn ði 'i:vnɪŋz] abends III U4, 76
in the south of [ˌɪn ðə 'saʊθ‿əv] im Süden von III U1, 10
in the world [ɪn ðə 'wɜ:ld] auf der Welt II
in time [ɪn 'taɪm] rechtzeitig I
to **include** [ɪn'klu:d] enthalten <III U3, 66>
*to be **included** [bi: ɪn'klu:dɪd] enthalten sein III U2, 34
including [ɪn'klu:dɪŋ] einschließlich <III U1, 131>
Indian ['ɪndiən] indisch I
Indian ['ɪndiən] indisch II
indoor [ˌɪn'dɔ:] Hallen-; Innen- III U2, 34
Industrial Revolution [ɪnˌdʌstriəl revl'u:ʃn] industrielle Revolution III U1, 11
industry ['ɪndəstri] Industrie III U1, 11
information *(no pl)* [ˌɪnfə'meɪʃn] Information; Informationen I
information desk [ɪnfə'meɪʃn ˌdesk] Information II
IT (**Information** Technology) [ˌaɪ'ti:, ɪnfəˌmeɪʃn tek'nɒlədʒi] Informatik; Informationstechnik I
informative [ɪn'fɔ:mətɪv] informativ <III U1, 27>
ingredient [ɪn'gri:diənt] Zutat II
inhabitant [ɪn'hæbɪtnt] Einwohner; Einwohnerin; Bewohner; Bewohnerin III U1, 16
injection [ɪn'dʒekʃn] Spritze III U2, 39
injury ['ɪndʒri] Verletzung III U2, 38
ink [ɪŋk] Tinte <III U3, 71>
insect ['ɪnsekt] Insekt III U3, 58
inside [ˌɪn'saɪd] in, innen in; im Innern III U1, 31
inside [ˌɪn'saɪd] in … hinein II
instantly ['ɪnstəntli] sofort <III U5, 112>
institution [ˌɪnstɪ'tju:ʃn] Einrichtung; Organisation; Institution <III U2, 132>
instructions *(pl)* [ɪn'strʌkʃnz] Anleitung <III U1, 29>
instructor [ɪn'strʌktə] Lehrer; Lehrerin III U2, 34
instrument ['ɪnstrəmənt] Instrument <III U5, 107>
intelligent [ɪn'telɪdʒnt] intelligent; klug; vernünftig III U4, 77
interest (in) ['ɪntrəst (ɪn)] Interesse (an) <III U4, 83>
*to be **interested** in [bi: 'ɪntrəstɪd‿ɪn] sich interessieren für; interessiert sein an III U1, 12
interesting ['ɪntrəstɪŋ] interessant I
internet ['ɪntənet] Internet II
to surf the internet [ˌsɜ:f ði 'ɪntənet] im Internet surfen II
interview ['ɪntəvju:] Interview; Befragung II
to **interview** ['ɪntəvju:] interviewen; befragen I
into ['ɪntə] in; drin <III U1, 17>
to **introduce** [ˌɪntrə'dju:s] vorstellen III U5, 96
introduction [ˌɪntrə'dʌkʃn] Einleitung; Einführung III U2, 50
to **invade** [ɪn'veɪd] einmarschieren (in); eindringen (in) III U1, 11
to **invent** [ɪn'vent] erfinden III U3, 54
invention [ɪn'venʃn] Erfindung III U3, 54
inventor [ɪn'ventə] Erfinder; Erfinderin III U3, 52

p pen • b bed • t ten • d dad • k cat • g grey • tʃ chair • dʒ joke • f fan • v very • θ three • ð the

invitation [ˌɪnvɪ'teɪʃn] Einladung I
to **invite** [ɪn'vaɪt] einladen I
Irish ['aɪrɪʃ] irisch; Irisch III U5, 94
the **Irish** [ði 'aɪrɪʃ] die Iren III U5, 94
is [ɪz] ist I
Is something wrong? [ɪz 'sʌmθɪŋ rɒŋ] Stimmt etwas nicht? II
… is £1.25. [ɪz 'wʌn paʊnd twentiˌfaɪv] … kostet ein Pfund fünfundzwanzig. I
island ['aɪlənd] Insel II
isn't it? ['ɪzntˬɪt] nicht wahr?; stimmt's? II
it [ɪt] es I
it isn't up to you [ɪtˬɪzntˬʌp tə 'ju:] es ist nicht deine Sache <III U1, 17>
It says … [ɪt 'sez] Hier steht …; Es heißt … <III U5, 112>
It'll be great fun. [ˌɪtl bɪ 'greɪt fʌn] Es wird großen Spaß machen. I
It's me. [ɪts 'mi:] Ich bin es. I
It's time to go. [ɪts ˌtaɪm tə 'gəʊ] Es ist Zeit zu gehen. I
It's two hours from here. [ɪts tu: 'aʊəz frɒm ˌhɪə] Es ist zwei Stunden von hier entfernt. I
IT (Information Technology) [ˌaɪ'ti:, ɪnfəˌmeɪʃn tek'nɒlədʒi] Informatik; Informationstechnik I
Italian [ɪ'tæliən] italienisch; Italiener; Italienerin; Italienisch II
its [ɪts] ihr; sein III U3, 52
itself [ɪt'self] (sich) selbst III U2, 156

J

jacket ['dʒækɪt] Jacke II
jacket potato [ˌdʒækɪt pə'teɪtəʊ] Ofenkartoffel II
jam [dʒæm] Marmelade; Konfitüre III U4, 80
Jamaican [dʒə'meɪkən] jamaikanisch II
January ['dʒænjuri] Januar I
jar [dʒɑ:] Glas III U4, 80
javelin ['dʒævlɪn] Speerwerfen <III U2, 193>
jealous ['dʒeləs] eifersüchtig; neidisch II
jeans *(pl)* [dʒi:nz] Jeans I
jerk [dʒɜ:k] *in Gewürzen mariniertes und über Holzfeuer gegrilltes Essen* II
jeweller's ['dʒu:ələz] Juwelierladen III U1, 13
jewellery ['dʒu:əlri] Schmuck II
job [dʒɒb] Job I; Aufgabe; Tätigkeit; Arbeit; Beruf II
jogging ['dʒɒgɪŋ] Joggen <III U2, 193>
to **join** [dʒɔɪn] Mitglied werden in <III U2, 133>; sich anschließen III U5, 96
joke [dʒəʊk] Witz I
to **joke** [dʒəʊk] Witze machen; scherzen III U2, 34
journey ['dʒɜ:ni] Fahrt; Reise III U5, 100
to **joust** [dʒaʊst] einen Turnierzweikampf austragen; turnieren III U2, 43
jousting ['dʒaʊstɪŋ] Turnierzweikampf III U2, 43
judge [dʒʌdʒ] Juror; Jurorin II
to **judge** [dʒʌdʒ] beurteilen; bewerten <III U4, 77>
juice [dʒu:s] Saft II
July [dʒʊ'laɪ] Juli I
on 7th July [ɒn ðə 'sevnθ əv ˌdʒʊlaɪ] am 7. Juli I
jumble sale ['dʒʌmbl ˌseɪl] Flohmarkt II
high **jump** ['haɪ ˌdʒʌmp] Hochsprung <III U2, 193>
long jump ['lɒŋ ˌdʒʌmp] Weitsprung <III U2, 193>
to **jump** [dʒʌmp] zusammenzucken; erschrecken; III U2, 42; springen <III U5, 112>
June [dʒu:n] Juni I
just [dʒʌst] gerade (eben); soeben; nur II

K

kayak ['kaɪæk] Kajak <III U2, 132>
kayaking ['kaɪækɪŋ] Kajakfahren <III U2, 132>
*to **keep** [ki:p] halten II; behalten <III U5, 112>
to keep cool [ˌki:p 'ku:l] Ruhe bewahren <III U1, 27>
to keep in touch [ˌki:p ɪn 'tʌtʃ] in Verbindung bleiben II
to keep out [ˌki:pˬ'aʊt] draußen halten III U3, 62
to keep quiet [ˌki:p 'kwaɪət] ruhig sein <III U5, 109>
to keep safe [ˌki:p 'seɪf] schützen III U2, 34
to keep up (with) [ˌki:pˬ'ʌp] mithalten (mit); Schritt halten (mit) <III U5, 112>
kept [kept] simple past, past participle von *to keep* II
ketchup ['ketʃʌp] Ketchup II
key [ki:] Schlüssel <III U2, 48>
keyword ['ki:ˌwɜ:d] Stichwort; Schlüsselbegriff <III U1, 31>
to **kick** [kɪk] schießen; treten III U2, 36
kid [kɪd] Kind II
kidney bean ['kɪdni ˌbi:n] Kidneybohne II
to **kill** [kɪl] töten III U1, 20
kilogram (kg) ['kɪləgræm] Kilogramm (kg) I
7 kilograms a day [ˌkɪləgræmzˬə 'deɪ] sieben Kilogramm täglich I
kilometre (km) [kɪ'lɒmɪtə] Kilometer (km) I
40 kilometres an hour [kɪ'lɒmɪtəzˬənˬ'aʊə] 40 Kilometer pro Stunde I
kilt [kɪlt] Schottenrock; Kilt III U3, 53
kind [kaɪnd] Art; Sorte III U3, 53
kind [kaɪnd] freundlich; nett II
king [kɪŋ] König III U1, 11
kiss [kɪs] Kuss II
to **kiss** [kɪs] küssen III U4, 78
kitchen ['kɪtʃɪn] Küche I
knee [ni:] Knie III U2, 39
knife *(sg)* [naɪf], **knives** *(pl)* [naɪvz] Messer II
knight [naɪt] Ritter III U2, 42
*to **know** [nəʊ] wissen; kennen I

to get to know [ˌget tə ˈnəʊ] kennen lernen II
I don't know! [ˌaɪ ˌdəʊnt ˈnəʊ] Ich weiß (es) nicht! I
I know my way around here. [aɪ ˌnəʊ maɪ ˈweɪ əraʊnd ˌhɪə] Ich kenne mich hier aus. III U1, 12

L

to **label** [ˈleɪbl] beschriften <III U2, 43>
lace [leɪs] Schnürsenkel <III U1, 17>
ladder [ˈlædə] Leiter I
lady [ˈleɪdi] Dame; Frau II
laid [leɪd] simple past, past participle von *to lay* II
lake [leɪk] See III U3, 53
lamb [læm] Lamm II
lamp [læmp] Lampe I
land [lænd] Land II
to **land** [lænd] landen <III U3, 134>
landlord [ˈlændlɔːd] Eigentümer II
language [ˈlæŋgwɪdʒ] Sprache II
body language [ˈbɒdi ˌlæŋgwɪdʒ] Körpersprache <III U1, 25>
language detectives [ˈlæŋgwɪdʒ ˌdɪtektɪvz] Sprachdetektive <I>
language tip [ˌlæŋgwɪdʒ ˈtɪp] Grammatikhinweis <I>
sign language [ˈsaɪn ˌlæŋgwɪdʒ] Gebärdensprache; Zeichensprache III U5, 95
laptop [ˈlæptɒp] Laptop I
large [lɑːdʒ] groß II
lasagne [ləˈzænjə] Lasagne II
last [lɑːst] letzte I
at last [ət ˈlɑːst] endlich; zu guter Letzt II
late [leɪt] (zu) spät I
later [ˈleɪtə] später I
to **laugh** [lɑːf] lachen II
LOL (**Laugh** out loud!) [ˈlɑːf aʊt ˌlaʊd] Laut lachen! II
laundry basket [ˈlɔːndri ˌbɑːskɪt] Wäschekorb <III U4, 86>
law [lɔː] Gesetz III U4, 85
*to **lay** [leɪ] legen; decken II
to lay the table [ˌleɪ ðə ˈteɪbl] den Tisch decken II
lead [liːd] Leine I
*to **lead** [liːd] anführen; leiten <III U2, 133>
leader [ˈliːdə] Anführer; Anführerin; Führer; Führerin III U1, 11
leaf *(sg)* [liːf], **leaves** *(pl)* [liːvz] Blatt <III U5, 112>
to **learn** [lɜːn] lernen II
to learn about sth [ˌlɜːn əˈbaʊt] etwas erfahren über III U1, 12
at **least** [ət ˈliːst] wenigstens; mindestens III U4, 76
leather [ˈleðə] Leder III U3, 55
*to **leave** [liːv] lassen; verlassen; abfahren II
to leave out [ˌliːv‿ˈaʊt] weglassen <III U5, 113>
leaving [ˈliːvɪŋ] Abschieds- II
left [left] simple past, past participle von *to leave* II
left [left] links III U1, 12; übrig III U4, 81
to the left [tə ðə ˈleft] nach links <III U5, 110>
to turn left [ˌtɜːn ˈleft] (nach) links abbiegen I
on the left [ɒn ðə ˈleft] auf der linken Seite; links I
leg [leg] Bein II
legend [ˈledʒənd] Legende; Sage <III U3, 134>
lemon [ˈlemən] Zitrone II
lemonade [ˌleməˈneɪd] Limonade II
*to **lend** [lend] leihen; verleihen II
lent [lent] simple past von *to lend* II
less [les] weniger III U4, 80
lesson [ˈlesn] Schulstunde; Unterricht I
*to **let** [let] lassen III U5, 98
to let go [ˌlet ˈgəʊ] loslassen <III U3, 135>
let us [ˈlet ˌʌs] lass(t) uns <III U2, 44>
let's [lets] lass uns I
Let's see … [ˌlets ˈsiː] Lass mal sehen …; Also … I
let [let] simple past, past participle von *to let* III U5, 98
letter [ˈletə] Buchstabe; Brief III U4, 80
capital letter [ˌkæpɪtl ˈletə] Großbuchstabe <III U5, 99>
lettuce [ˈletɪs] Kopfsalat II
library [ˈlaɪbri] Bibliothek; Bücherei III U1, 15
life *(sg)* [laɪf], **lives** *(pl)* [laɪvz] Leben I
to come to life [ˌkʌm tə ˈlaɪf] lebendig werden <III U3, 70>
lifeboat [ˈlaɪfbəʊt] Rettungsboot III U2, 33
to **lift** [lɪft] heben; hochheben; anheben <III U5, 111>
light [laɪt] Licht <III U1, 17>
light bulb [ˈlaɪt ˌbʌlb] Glühbirne III U3, 57
traffic light [ˈtræfɪk ˌlaɪt] (Verkehrs-)Ampel <III U1, 184>
*to **light** up [ˌlaɪt‿ˈʌp] (sich) erhellen; anzünden <III U5, 101>
light [laɪt] leicht; hell <III U3, 201>
lighting [ˈlaɪtɪŋ] Beleuchtung <III U3, 67>
to **like** [laɪk] mögen I
to like … best [ˌlaɪk ˈbest] am meisten mögen; am liebsten mögen I
would like [wʊd ˈlaɪk] würde(n) gern; hätte(n) gern II
I don't like [aɪ ˌdəʊnt ˈlaɪk] ich mag nicht; gefällt mir nicht I
I like [aɪ ˈlaɪk] ich mag I
I wouldn't like (to) … [aɪ ˈwʊdnt laɪk (tə)] Ich möchte nicht …; Ich würde nicht gerne … I
I'd like (to) … (= I would like to) [aɪd ˈlaɪk (tə)] Ich möchte …; Ich würde gerne … I
Would you like (to) …? [ˌwʊd jə ˈlaɪk (tə)] Möchtest du? I
like [laɪk] wie I
like this [laɪk ˈðɪs] so; auf diese Weise I; ähnlich; so <III U3, 58>
What must you be like? [wɒt ˌmʌst ju ˈbiː laɪk] Wie musst du sein? III U2, 37
line [laɪn] Zeile; Linie II
lines [laɪnz] Text II

lion ['laɪən] Löwe I
list [lɪst] Liste II
shopping list ['ʃɒpɪŋ ˌlɪst] Einkaufszettel I
to **listen** (to) ['lɪsn] zuhören; anhören; hören I
listener ['lɪsənə] Zuhörer; Zuhörerin II
listening ['lɪsnɪŋ] Hörverstehen <I>
little ['lɪtl] klein II
a little [ə 'lɪtl] ein bisschen II
to **live** [lɪv] wohnen; leben I
liver ['lɪvə] Leber <III U3, 66>
living room ['lɪvɪŋ ˌrʊm] Wohnzimmer I
loaf *(sg)* [ləʊf], **loaves** *(pl)* [ləʊvz] Brotlaib III U4, 80
local ['ləʊkl] hiesig; lokal; örtlich III U3, 58
*to be **located** [bi: ləʊ'keɪtɪd] liegen III U2, 33
location [ləʊ'keɪʃn] Drehort; Lage III U2, 50
loch [lɒk] See *(in Schottland)* III U3, 53
to **lock** [lɒk] abschließen I
LOL (Laugh out loud!) ['lɑ:f aʊt ˌlaʊd] Laut lachen! II
lonely ['ləʊnli] einsam III U4, 76
long [lɒŋ] lang I
long jump ['lɒŋ ˌdʒʌmp] Weitsprung <III U2, 193>
*to have a **look** [ˌhæv‿ə 'lʊk] anschauen II
to **look** [lʊk] schauen; nachschauen I; aussehen; sehen II
to look after [ˌlʊk‿'ɑ:ftə] aufpassen; hüten II
to look at ['lʊk‿ət] anschauen I
to look for ['lʊk fə] suchen nach II
to look up [ˌlʊk‿'ʌp] aufschauen; nachschauen II
Look at you. ['luk‿ət ju:] Schaut euch an. I
Look … [lʊk] Schau mal …; Schau … nach. I
… looking at an advert. [ˌlʊkɪŋ ət‿ən 'ædvɜ:t] … schaut sich eine Anzeige an. II
lookout point ['lʊkaʊt ˌpɔɪnt] Aussichtspunkt II
loose [lu:s] locker; lose II
lorry driver ['lɒri ˌdraɪvə] LKW-Fahrer; LKW-Fahrerin II
*to **lose** [lu:z] verlieren II
lost [lɒst] simple past von *to lose* II; past participle von *to lose* III U3, 62
*to get **lost** [get lɒst] sich verirren I
a **lot** [ə 'lɒt] viel I; sehr II
a lot of [ə 'lɒt‿əv] viel(e); eine Menge I
lots of ['lɒts‿əv] viel; jede Menge I
body **lotion** ['bɒdi ˌləʊʃn] Körperlotion III U5, 97
lots [lɒts] viel; jede Menge III U2, 43
loud [laʊd] laut III U2, 35
*to fall in **love** (with) [ˌfɔ:l‿ɪn 'lʌv] sich verlieben (in) III U2, 50
to **love** [lʌv] lieben; gern mögen I
I'd love to … (= I would love to) [aɪd 'lʌv tə] Ich würde sehr gern … III U3, 58
lovely ['lʌvli] schön; herrlich; hübsch II
low [ləʊ] niedrig II
lower ['ləʊə] untere III U4, 92
good **luck** [ˌgʊd 'lʌk] viel Glück II
luckily ['lʌkɪli] glücklicherweise II
lucky day [ˌlʌki 'deɪ] Glückstag II
to be lucky [bi: 'lʌki] Glück haben III U4, 85
lucky number [ˌlʌki 'nʌmbə] Glückszahl I
luminous ['lu:mɪnəs] leuchtend <III U5, 101>
lunch [lʌnʃ] Mittagessen I
packed lunch [ˌpækt 'lʌnʃ] Lunchpaket; Vesper II
lunchtime ['lʌnʃtaɪm] Mittagszeit; Mittagspause I
lyrics *(pl)* ['lɪrɪks] Liedtext <II>

M

machine [mə'ʃi:n] Automat; Maschine II
payment machine ['peɪmənt ˌməʃi:n] Bezahlautomat II
made [meɪd] simple past von *to make* I; past participle von *to make* II
magazine [ˌmægə'zi:n] Zeitschrift I
magic ['mædʒɪk] Magie; Zauberei II
magic ['mædʒɪk] magisch; Zauber- II
magical ['mædʒɪkl] zauberhaft; magisch <III U3, 68>
main [meɪn] Haupt- <III U1, 21>
main course [ˌmeɪn 'kɔ:s] Hauptgericht II
*to **make** [meɪk] erstellen; machen; tun; bilden I
to be made of [bi: 'meɪd‿əv] hergestellt sein aus III U1, 20
to make a cake [ˌmeɪk‿ə 'keɪk] einen Kuchen backen I
to make a decision [ˌmeɪk‿ə dɪ'sɪʒn] eine Entscheidung treffen <III U5, 113>
to make a reservation [ˌmeɪk‿ə 'rezəveɪʃn] reservieren III U3, 59
to make friends [ˌmeɪk 'frendz] Freundschaften schließen I
to make oneself at home [ˌmeɪk wʌnself ət 'həʊm] sich wie zu Hause fühlen III U5, 96
to make sb feel like sth [ˌmeɪk … 'fi:l laɪk] jmdm. das Gefühl geben, etw. zu sein III U2, 43
to make sense [ˌmeɪk 'sens] Sinn ergeben; einleuchten <III U5, 113>
to make sure [ˌmeɪk 'ʃɔ:] dafür sorgen; sich versichern III U2, 35
to make up [ˌmeɪk‿'ʌp] erfinden; sich ausdenken <III U1, 18>
It's made with … [ˌɪts 'meɪd wɪð] Es wird aus … gemacht. II
she was making [ˌʃi: wəz 'meɪkɪŋ] sie machte II
film maker ['fɪlm ˌmeɪkə] Filmemacher; Filmemacherin <III U5, 107>
make-up artist ['meɪkʌp ˌɑ:tɪst] Maskenbildner; Maskenbildnerin; Visagist; Visagistin <III U4, 87>
mama ['mæmə] Mama II

man *(sg)* [mæn], **men** *(pl)* [men] Mann I
many ['meni] viele II
how many [ˌhaʊ 'meni] wie viele II
map [mæp] Stadtplan; Landkarte III U5, 97; Karte; Plan <III U1, 13>
mind map ['maɪnd ˌmæp] Wörternetz <I>
March [mɑ:tʃ] März I
to **march** [mɑ:tʃ] marschieren <III U3, 135>
to **mark** [mɑ:k] markieren; kennzeichnen III U1, 10
market ['mɑ:kɪt] Markt II
*to get **married** [ˌget 'mærɪd] heiraten II
mascot ['mæskət] Maskottchen <III U5, 109>
mashed potatoes [ˌmæʃt pə'teɪtəʊz] Kartoffelbrei II
match [mætʃ] Spiel I
to **match** [mætʃ] zuordnen I
material [mə'tɪəriəl] Material; Stoff III U3, 56
Maths [mæθs] Mathe I
It doesn't **matter**. [ɪt ˌdʌznt 'mætə] Es ist egal. II
won't matter [ˌwəʊnt 'mætə] wird nicht von Bedeutung sein; wird nichts ausmachen <III U5, 101>
May [meɪ] Mai I
may [meɪ] vielleicht; können; dürfen II
maybe ['meɪbi] vielleicht I
mayonnaise [ˌmeɪə'neɪz] Mayonnaise II
me [mi:] mich; ich; mir I
It's me. [ɪts 'mi:] Ich bin es. I
meal [mi:l] Essen; Mahlzeit II
*to **mean** [mi:n] bedeuten; meinen III U2, 33
meaning ['mi:nɪŋ] Bedeutung <III U3, 73>
meant [ment] simple past, past participle von *to mean* III U2, 33
meat [mi:t] Fleisch I
mechanic [mə'kænɪk] Mechaniker; Mechanikerin <III U3, 68>
mediation [ˌmi:'di'eɪʃn] Sprachmittlung <I>
medicine ['medsn] Medikamente; Medizin III U2, 39
*to **meet** [mi:t] kennen lernen; treffen I
meeting ['mi:tɪŋ] Treffen; Treff- <III U1, 30>
meeting point ['mi:tɪŋ ˌpɔɪnt] Treffpunkt <III U1, 30>
member ['membə] Mitglied <III U1, 30>; <III U2, 132>
menu ['menju:] Speisekarte II
mess [mes] Unordnung; Durcheinander I
message ['mesɪdʒ] Botschaft; Nachricht; SMS II
text message ['tekst ˌmesɪdʒ] SMS II
met [met] simple past von *to meet* I
metal ['metl] Metall III U3, 54
method ['meθəd] Methode II
metre ['mi:tə] Meter I
Miaow! [ˌmi:'aʊ] Miau! I
microwave ['maɪkrəweɪv] Mikrowelle II
middle ['mɪdl] Mitte III U2, 33
in the middle [ɪn ðə 'mɪdl] in der Mitte III U4, 92
midnight ['mɪdnaɪt] Mitternacht III U4, 84
mild [maɪld] mild I
mile [maɪl] Meile II
milk [mɪlk] Milch I
to **milk** [mɪlk] melken III U1, 16
milkshake ['mɪlkˌʃeɪk] Milchmischgetränk; Milchshake III U4, 76
million ['mɪljən] Million III U1, 11
half a million [ˌhɑ:f‿ə 'mɪljən] eine halbe Million III U1, 16
mind [maɪnd] Geist; Verstand <III U1, 17>
mind map ['maɪnd ˌmæp] Wörternetz <I>
Never **mind.** [ˌnevə 'maɪnd] Macht nichts.; Schon gut.; Mach dir nichts draus. II
mine [maɪn] Bergwerk III U1, 16
mine [maɪn] meins; meine II
of mine [əv 'maɪn] von mir II
miner ['maɪnə] Bergarbeiter; Bergarbeiterin III U1, 20
mineral water ['mɪnrl ˌwɔ:tə] Mineralwasser III U4, 81
prime **minister** [ˌpraɪm 'mɪnɪstə] Premierminister; Premierministerin; Ministerpräsident; Ministerpräsidentin <III U5, 139>
minute ['mɪnɪt] Minute II
mirror ['mɪrə] Spiegel <III U3, 201>; III U5, 97
miserable ['mɪzrəbl] elend; armselig; jämmerlich III U5, 105
miss [mɪs] kein Treffer <III U4, 91>
to give sth a miss [ˌgɪv sʌmθɪŋ‿ə 'mɪs] auf etw. verzichten; etw. bleiben lassen III U2, 50
to **miss** [mɪs] verpassen; vermissen II
mistake [mɪ'steɪk] Fehler <III U1, 23>
to **mix** [mɪks] mischen <III U2, 46>
mixed [mɪkst] gemischt <III U4, 137>
mobile (phone) ['məʊbaɪl (ˌfəʊn)] Handy; Mobiltelefon I
modern ['mɒdn] modern I
moment ['məʊmənt] Moment; Augenblick II
Monday ['mʌndeɪ] Montag I
money ['mʌni] Geld I
monkey ['mʌŋki] Affe I
monster ['mɒnstə] Ungeheuer; Monster III U3, 58
month [mʌnθ] Monat I
monthly ['mʌnθli] monatlich III U5, 101
monument ['mɒnjəmənt] Denkmal II
mood [mu:d] Stimmung; Laune <III U1, 25>
moon [mu:n] Mond <III U5, 101>
moped ['məʊped] Moped <III U5, 216>
more [mɔ:] mehr I
is more fun [ɪz 'mɔ: ˌfʌn] macht mehr Spaß I
morning ['mɔ:nɪŋ] Morgen; Vormittag I
Good morning. [gʊd 'mɔ:nɪŋ] Guten Morgen. II

mosque [mɒsk] Moschee II
most [məʊst] die meisten; die Mehrheit I; am meisten II
mother ['mʌðə] Mutter I
motorbike ['məʊtəbaɪk] Motorrad I
motorship ['məʊtəʃɪp] Motorboot <III U4, 91>
mountain ['maʊntɪn] Berg III U1, 17
in the mountains [ˌɪn ðə 'maʊntɪnz] in den Bergen III U1, 17
mouse *(sg)* [maʊs], **mice** *(pl)* [maɪs] Maus I
moussaka [mu'sɑ:kə] Moussaka II
mouth [maʊθ] Mund II
move [mu:v] Bewegung III U5, 100
to move [mu:v] (sich) bewegen III U2, 39
to move in [ˌmu:v‿'ɪn] einziehen <III U3, 71>
to move (house) [mu:v] umziehen II
movie ['mu:vi] Film I
Mr ['mɪstə] Herr *(Anrede)* I
Mrs ['mɪsɪz] Frau *(Anrede)* I
Ms [mɪz] Frau *(Anrede)* I
much [mʌtʃ] viel I
so much ['səʊ ˌmʌtʃ] so sehr III U4, 76
too much [ˌtu: 'mʌtʃ] zu sehr II
how much [ˌhaʊ 'mʌtʃ] wie sehr III U3, 58
How much (is/are) ...? [ˌhaʊ 'mʌtʃ‿ɪz/ɑ:] Wie viel (kostet/kosten) ...? I
mud [mʌd] Schlamm; Matsch III U1, 18
muddy ['mʌdi] schlammig I
mum [mʌm] Mama I
mural ['mjʊərəl] Wandgemälde III U4, 74
murderer ['mɜ:drə] Mörder; Mörderin III U2, 50
museum [mju:'zi:əm] Museum II
music ['mju:zɪk] Musik I
musical ['mju:zɪkl] Musical <III U3, 73>
musical ['mju:zɪkl] Musik-; musikalisch III U5, 95
musician [mju:'zɪʃn] Musiker; Musikerin <III U3, 135>
Muslim ['mʊzlɪm] Muslim; Muslimin I
must [mʌst] müssen I
must not/never [ˌmʌst 'nɒt/'nevə] nicht/nie dürfen III U3, 63
I must have forgotten it. [aɪ ˌmʌst hæv fə'gɒtn‿ɪt] Ich muss es vergessen haben. II
mustard ['mʌstəd] Senf II
mustn't ['mʌsnt] nicht dürfen III U5, 100
my [maɪ] mein, meine I
My name is ... [maɪ 'neɪm‿ɪz] Ich heiße ... I
myself [maɪ'self] selbst; selber III U2, 34
mystery ['mɪstri] Rätsel; Geheimnis I

N

to nag [næg] nörgeln; meckern III U4, 76
nail [neɪl] Nagel III U5, 97
nail scissors *(pl)* ['neɪl ˌsɪzəz] Nagelschere III U5, 97
name [neɪm] Name I
first name [ˌfɜ:st 'neɪm] Vorname <III U1, 131>; <III U3, 67>
napkin ['næpkɪn] Serviette II
narrator [nə'reɪtə] Erzähler; Erzählerin I
national ['næʃnl] National-; national III U5, 104
nature ['neɪtʃə] Natur III U3, 53
naughty ['nɔ:ti] frech; böse III U2, 43
near [nɪə] nah III U1, 15
near [nɪə] in der Nähe von I
with special **needs** [wɪð ˌspeʃl 'ni:dz] mit Behinderung III U5, 95
to need [ni:d] brauchen I
needn't ['ni:dnt] nicht brauchen; nicht müssen I
neighbour ['neɪbə] Nachbar; Nachbarin III U3, 67
*to get on one's **nerves** [ˌget‿ɒn wʌnz 'nɜ:vz] auf die Nerven gehen III U1, 16
nervous ['nɜ:vəs] nervös; aufgeregt II
netball ['netbɔ:l] Korbball I
never ['nevə] nie; niemals I
Never mind. [ˌnevə 'maɪnd] Macht nichts.; Schon gut.; Mach dir nichts draus. II
new [nju:] neu I
news [nju:z] Neuigkeit(en); Nachricht(en) II
newsagent's ['nju:zˌeɪdʒnts] Zeitschriftenladen III U1, 13
newspaper ['nju:sˌpeɪpə] Zeitung II
next [nekst] nächste I; als Nächstes II
next to ['nekst tə] neben I
nice [naɪs] schön; nett I; lecker; gut III U3, 58
Nice to meet you. [ˌnaɪs tə 'mi:t ju:] Nett, dich kennen zu lernen. I
nickname ['nɪkneɪm] Spitzname <III U1, 131>
niece [ni:s] Nichte III U4, 80
night [naɪt] Nacht I
night walk [ˌnaɪt 'wɔ:k] Nachtwanderung I
that night [ˌðæt 'naɪt] an jenem Abend; in jener Nacht II
nine [naɪn] neun I
nineteen [ˌnaɪn'ti:n] neunzehn I
ninety ['naɪnti] neunzig I
no [nəʊ] kein, keine; nein I
No idea! [ˌnəʊ‿aɪ'dɪə] Keine Ahnung! I
no one ['nəʊ wʌn] niemand I
no vacancies [ˌnəʊ 'veɪknsiz] kein Zimmer frei <III U4, 86>
No way! [ˌnəʊ 'weɪ] Auf keinen Fall!; Was?!; Echt?! III U3, 58
No way am I doing that again! [ˌnəʊ 'weɪ əm aɪ ˌdu:ɪŋ ðæt ə'gen] Das mache ich auf keinen Fall noch mal! III U2, 34
nobody ['nəʊbədi] niemand III U3, 58
noise [nɔɪz] Geräusch I
noisy ['nɔɪzi] laut III U1, 16
non [nɒn] nicht <III U4, 86>
the **Normans** [ðə 'nɔ:mənz] die Normannen III U1, 11
Norman ['nɔ:mən] normannisch <III U1, 130>

north [nɔ:θ] Norden III U1, 10
to the north of [ˌtə ðə 'nɔ:θ‿əv] nördlich von III U1, 17
northbound ['nɔ:θbaʊnd] in Richtung Norden <III U5, 216>
northeast [ˌnɔ:θ'i:st] Nordosten III U1, 19
northern ['nɔ:ðən] nördlich III U1, 11
northwest [ˌnɔ:θ'west] Nordwesten III U1, 16
northwest of [ˌnɔ:θ'west‿əv] nordwestlich III U4, 75
nose [nəʊz] Nase I
not [nɒt] nicht I
not … any [ˌnɒt … eni] kein II
not at all [ˌnɒt‿ət‿'ɔ:l] überhaupt nicht; gar nicht II
not … any more [ˌnɒt … eni 'mɔ:] nicht mehr III U4, 76
not … either [nɒt … 'aɪðə] auch nicht III U3, 58
not … yet [nɒt … 'jet] noch nicht II
not possibly [nɒt 'pɒsəbli] unmöglich III U4, 84
note [nəʊt] Geldschein II; Notiz <III U1, 23>
nothing ['nʌθɪŋ] nichts III U1, 21
to **notice** ['nəʊtɪs] bemerken; wahrnehmen III U1, 20
noun [naʊn] Nomen; Hauptwort <I>
November [nə'vembə] November I
now [naʊ] jetzt; nun I; heutzutage II
right now [ˌraɪt 'naʊ] jetzt gerade III U2, 38
nowadays ['naʊədeɪz] heutzutage <III U1, 24>
out of **nowhere** [aʊt‿əv 'nəʊweə] aus dem Nichts <III U5, 112>
number ['nʌmbə] Nummer; Zahl I
lucky number [ˌlʌki 'nʌmbə] Glückszahl I
ordinal number [ˌɔ:dɪnəl 'nʌmbə] Ordinalzahl <I>
phone number ['fəʊn ˌnʌmbə] Telefonnummer III U2, 38
nurse [nɜ:s] Krankenschwester; Krankenpfleger II
nut [nʌt] Nuss I

O

o'clock [ə'klɒk] Uhr *(Zeitangabe bei vollen Stunden)* I
oat [əʊt] Hafer III U3, 53
oatmeal ['əʊtmi:l] Haferflocken <III U3, 66>
object ['ɒbdʒɪkt] Objekt; Gegenstand <III U3, 55>
October [ɒk'təʊbə] Oktober I
odd [ɒd] seltsam; komisch <III U5, 112>
the odd one out [ˌɒd wʌn‿'aʊt] das Wort, das nicht in die Gruppe passt <III U5, 101>
of [ɒv] von I
of course [əv 'kɔ:s] natürlich; selbstverständlich I
of mine [əv 'maɪn] von mir II
off [ɒf] von … weg <III U2, 132>
a day off [ə ˌdeɪ‿'ɒf] ein freier Tag III U2, 39
Off we went. ['ɒf wi went] Nichts wie weg. III U5, 105
offer ['ɒfə] Angebot <III U3, 68>
special offer [ˌspeʃl‿'ɒfə] Sonderangebot III U4, 80
office ['ɒfɪs] Büro II
post office ['pəʊst‿ˌɒfɪs] Postamt I
police officer [pə'li:s‿ɒfɪsə] Polizeibeamter; Polizeibeamtin I
officially [ə'fɪʃli] offiziell <III U5, 108>
often ['ɒfn] oft; häufig I
oh [əʊ] null *(bei Uhrzeiten und Telefonnummern)* I
oil [ɔɪl] Öl <III U3, 66>
sunflower oil ['sʌnflaʊər‿ɔɪl] Sonnenblumenöl <III U3, 71>
OK [əʊ'keɪ] okay I
old [əʊld] alt I
in the old days [ɪn ði 'əʊld ˌdeɪz] früher III U2, 43
How old are you? [haʊ‿'əʊld‿ə ju:] Wie alt bist du? I
old-looking ['əʊldˌlʊkɪŋ] alt aussehend <III U2, 48>
on [ɒn] auf; an I
on board ['ɒn bɔ:d] an Bord III U4, 84
on duty [ɒn 'dju:ti] im Dienst <III U3, 68>
on time [ɒn 'taɪm] pünktlich III U5, 100
on weekdays [ɒn 'wi:kdeɪz] unter der Woche; an Werktagen III U5, 96
to try on [ˌtraɪ‿'ɒn] anprobieren II
on foot [ɒn 'fʊt] zu Fuß I
on purpose [ɒn 'pɜ:pəs] absichtlich II
on 7th July [ɒn ðə 'sevnθ əv ˌdʒʊlaɪ] am 7. Juli I
on the bus [ˌɒn ðə 'bʌs] im Bus II
on the left [ɒn ðə 'left] auf der linken Seite; links I
on the right [ɒn ðə 'raɪt] auf der rechten Seite; rechts I
on the way [ˌɒn ðə ˌ'weɪ] auf dem Weg; unterwegs I
on Tuesday [ˌɒn 'tju:zdeɪ] am Dienstag I
on Wednesdays [ɒn 'wenzdeɪz] mittwochs I
once [wʌns] einst; einmal III U5, 105
once more ['wʌns ˌmɔ:] noch einmal II
one [wʌn] eins I
a/one hundred ['hʌndrəd] einhundert; hundert I
one day [wʌn 'deɪ] eines Tages III U1, 21
one(s) [wʌn(z)] *Platzhalter für ein Nomen* III U3, 54
the blue one [ðə 'blu:‿wʌn] der blaue II
onion ['ʌnjən] Zwiebel II
online [ˌɒn'laɪn] online II
only ['əʊnli] einzige III U3, 54
only ['əʊnli] nur I
onto ['ɒntə] auf … hinauf <III U1, 29>
to **open** ['əʊpn] öffnen; aufmachen I
open ['əʊpn] offen; geöffnet III U1, 22
operation [ˌɒpr'eɪʃn] Operation III U2, 39
operator ['ɒpreɪtə] Vermittlung III U2, 38

camera operator ['kæmrə ˌɒpreɪtə] Kameramann; Kamerafrau <III U4, 87>
opinion [ə'pɪnjən] Meinung III U2, 50
in my opinion [ɪn 'maɪ‿əˌpɪnjən] meiner Meinung nach III U4, 76
opposite ['ɒpəzɪt] Gegenteil <II>
opposite ['ɒpəzɪt] gegenüber I
optimistic [ˌɒptɪ'mɪstɪk] optimistisch III U4, 77
option ['ɒpʃn] Möglichkeit; Wahl; Option <III U3, 58>
or [ɔ:] oder I
orange ['ɒrɪndʒ] Orange I
orange ['ɒrɪndʒ] orange I
orchestra ['ɔ:kɪstrə] Orchester III U5, 94
order ['ɔ:də] Reihenfolge <III U2, 47>
to **order** ['ɔ:də] bestellen II
ordinal number [ˌɔ:dɪnəl 'nʌmbə] Ordinalzahl <I>
to **organize** ['ɔ:gənaɪz] organisieren II
other ['ʌðə] andere; weitere I
each other [ˌi:tʃ‿'ʌðə] einander; sich; sich gegenseitig III U2, 34
others ['ʌðəz] anderen II
the others [ðiˌ'ʌðəz] die anderen I
our [aʊə] unser, unsere I
ours [aʊəz] unsere III U5, 96
ourselves [ˌaʊə'selvz] selbst; selber III U2, 156
out [aʊt] heraus II
to go out [ˌgəʊ‿'aʊt] ausgehen III U4, 83
to keep out [ˌki:p‿'aʊt] draußen halten III U3, 62
out and about [ˌaʊt‿ən‿ə'baʊt] unterwegs I
out of ['aʊt‿əv] aus … heraus II
outdoor [ˌaʊt'dɔ:] Freiluft-; Outdoor- III U2, 34
outfit ['aʊtfɪt] Outfit; Kleidung III U5, 105
outside [ˌaʊt'saɪd] Außenseite <III U3, 71>
outside [ˌaʊt'saɪd] draußen; im Freien II
oven ['ʌvn] Backofen II

over ['əʊvə] über III U2, 32
over there [ˌəʊvə 'ðeə] da drüben; dort drüben II
to **owe** [əʊ] schulden III U4, 80
to **own** [əʊn] besitzen II
own [əʊn] eigene II
owner ['əʊnə] Besitzer; Besitzerin <III U5, 112>

P

p.m. [ˌpi:'em] nachmittags *(Uhrzeit)* II
to **pack** [pæk] packen; einpacken II
to pack up ['pæk‿ʌp] packen; einpacken II
packed lunch [ˌpækt 'lʌnʃ] Lunchpaket; Vesper II
packet ['pækɪt] Packung; Tüte I
paddle ['pædl] Paddel <III U2, 193>
page [peɪdʒ] Seite I
paid [peɪd] simple past, past participle von *to pay* II
fabric **paint** ['fæbrɪk ˌpeɪnt] Stofffarbe <III U1, 29>
paint [peɪnt] Farbe <III U1, 29>
to **paint** [peɪnt] streichen; anmalen; malen II
pair [peə] Paar <III U2, 41>
a pair of [ə 'peər‿əv] ein Paar II
palace ['pælɪs] Palast <III U1, 30>
pancake ['pænkeɪk] Pfannkuchen II
to **panic** ['pænɪk] panisch werden II
pantomime ['pæntəmaɪm] Weihnachtstheaterstück II
paper ['peɪpə] Papier III U3, 55
paperchase ['peɪpəˌtʃeɪs] Schnitzeljagd <III U2, 49>
parade [pə'reɪd] Parade; Umzug III U5, 95
Pardon? ['pɑ:dn] Wie bitte? I
parents *(pl)* ['peərnts] Eltern II
park [pɑ:k] Park I
theme park ['θi:m ˌpɑ:k] Freizeitpark I; Themenpark II
parrot ['pærət] Papagei I
part [pɑ:t] Rolle; Teil II
to take part (in) [ˌteɪk 'pɑ:t] teilnehmen (an) II

partner ['pɑ:tnə] Partner; Partnerin III U5, 99
party ['pɑ:ti] Party; Feier I
to **pass** [pɑ:s] reichen II
to pass on [ˌpɑ:s‿'ɒn] weitergeben <III U1, 10>
passenger ['pæsndʒə] Passagier; Passagierin II
passport ['pɑ:spɔ:t] Pass <III U5, 215>
past [pɑ:st] Vergangenheit III U1, 16
simple past [ˌsɪmpl 'pɑ:st] einfache Vergangenheit <III U2, 41>
past [pɑ:st] nach *(bei Uhrzeitangaben)* II; vorbei (an) III U1, 12
half past (two) [ˌhɑ:f 'pɑ:st] halb (drei) I
pasta ['pæstə] Pasta; Nudeln II
pasta bake [ˌpæstə 'beɪk] Nudelauflauf II
to **paste** [peɪst] einfügen II
pasty ['pæsti] Pastete II
patient ['peɪʃnt] Patient; Patientin II
patient ['peɪʃnt] geduldig III U2, 35
patron saint [ˌpeɪtrn 'seɪnt] Schutzheiliger; Schutzheilige <III U5, 138>
pattern ['pætn] Muster <III U1, 29>
patterned ['pætənd] gemustert II
pay phone ['peɪ fəʊn] Münztelefon III U3, 67
*to **pay** [peɪ] bezahlen II
to pay attention to [ˌpeɪ‿ə'tenʃn tʊ] beachten <III U2, 51>
to pay back [ˌpeɪ 'bæk] zurückzahlen II
to pay the bill [ˌpeɪ ðə 'bɪl] die Rechnung bezahlen III U3, 59
payment machine ['peɪmənt ˌməʃi:n] Bezahlautomat II
PE (Physical Education) [ˌpi:'i:, ˌfɪzɪkl edʒʊ'keɪʃn] Sportunterricht I
peace [pi:s] Frieden III U3, 65
peach [pi:tʃ] Pfirsich I
peanut ['pi:nʌt] Erdnuss <III U3, 71>
peanut butter [ˌpi:nʌt 'bʌtə] Erdnussbutter III U4, 81
pen [pen] Füller; Stift I
pence *(pl)* [pens], **penny** *(sg)* ['peni] Pence *(brit. Währungseinheit)* I

... are 99p. [ɑː 'naɪntinaɪn ˌpens] ... kosten 99 Pence. I

pencil ['pensl] Bleistift; Buntstift I

pencil case ['pensl ˌkeɪs] Federmäppchen I

pencil sharpener ['pensl ˌʃɑːpnə] Anspitzer I

penguin ['peŋgwɪn] Pinguin I

people ['piːpl] Volk <III U5, 138>

people *(pl)* ['piːpl] Leute; Menschen I

pepper ['pepə] Pfeffer II

per [pɜː] pro <III U2, 132>

percent (%) [pə'sent] Prozent <III U4, 86>

present **perfect** [ˌpreznt 'pɜːfɪkt] das Perfekt <III U2, 41>

perfect ['pɜːfɪkt] perfekt <III U2, 45>

to **perform** [pə'fɔːm] auftreten; aufführen III U5, 100

perfume ['pɜːfjuːm] Parfüm III U5, 97

person ['pɜːsn] Person; Mensch II

personal ['pɜːsnl] persönlich III U5, 97

personality [ˌpɜːsn'æləti] Persönlichkeit <III U5, 113>

to **persuade** [pə'sweɪd] überreden <III U3, 61>

pet [pet] Haustier I

pet shop ['pet ˌʃɒp] Tierhandlung III U1, 13

petrol ['petrl] Benzin <III U3, 68>

mobile **(phone)** ['məʊbaɪl (ˌfəʊn)] Handy; Mobiltelefon I

phone [fəʊn] Telefon II

to answer the phone [ˌɑːnsə ðə 'fəʊn] ans Telefon gehen III U2, 45

pay phone ['peɪ fəʊn] Münztelefon III U3, 67

phone call ['fəʊn ˌkɔːl] Telefonanruf I

phone number ['fəʊn ˌnʌmbə] Telefonnummer III U2, 38

to **phone** [fəʊn] anrufen; telefonieren II

photo ['fəʊtəʊ] Foto I

to take a photo [ˌteɪk‿ə 'fəʊtəʊ] ein Foto machen I

to take photos [ˌteɪk 'fəʊtəʊz] fotografieren; Fotos machen II

phrase [freɪz] Redewendung; Ausdruck <III U1, 17>; Satz <III U3, 54>

PE (**Physical** Education) [ˌpiː'iː, ˌfɪzɪkl edʒʊ'keɪʃn] Sportunterricht I

to **pick** up [ˌpɪk‿'ʌp] aufheben II; aufgreifen <III U1, 31>

picnic ['pɪknɪk] Picknick I

picture ['pɪktʃə] Bild II

pie [paɪ] Kuchen; Pastete II

piece [piːs] Stück II

a piece of [ə 'piːs‿əv] ein Stück <III U1, 29>

pierogi [pjɜ'rɔgi] Pirogge II

pig [pɪg] Schwein <III U1, 131>

guinea pig ['gɪni ˌpɪg] Meerschweinchen I

pinch [pɪntʃ] Prise II

pineapple ['paɪnæpl] Ananas III U5, 107

pink [pɪŋk] pink; rosa I

pipe [paɪp] Rohr III U3, 67

pipe band ['paɪp bænd] *Band aus Dudelsackspielern und Trommlern* <III U3, 135>

pirate ['paɪrət] Seeräuber; Seeräuberin; Pirat; Piratin I

pizza ['piːtsə] Pizza I

place [pleɪs] Platz; Stelle; Ort I

to take place [ˌteɪk 'pleɪs] stattfinden <III U3, 134>; <III U4, 89>; <III U5, 112>

to her place [tʊ 'hɜː ˌpleɪs] zu sich nach Hause III U4, 78

to **place** [pleɪs] stellen <III U5, 110>

plain [pleɪn] schlicht; einfach II

plan [plæn] Plan II

to **plan** [plæn] planen III U3, 58

plane [pleɪn] Flugzeug II

plank [plæŋk] Brett; Planke II

plant [plɑːnt] Pflanze I

plantain ['plænteɪn] Kochbanane II

plaster ['plɑːstə] Pflaster III U2, 39

plastic ['plæstɪk] Plastik; Kunststoff III U3, 54

plate [pleɪt] Teller II

play [pleɪ] Theaterstück II

role play ['rəʊl ˌpleɪ] Rollenspiel <II>

to **play** [pleɪ] spielen I

I can play football. [ˌaɪ kən ˌpleɪ 'fʊtbɔːl] Ich kann Fußball spielen. I

I'm playing [aɪm 'pleɪɪŋ] ich spiele gerade II

player ['pleɪə] Spieler; Spielerin II

playground ['pleɪgraʊnd] Schulhof; Pausenhof; Spielplatz I

please [pliːz] bitte I

plot [plɒt] Handlung <III U5, 113>

pocket ['pɒkɪt] Tasche; Hosentasche II

podcast ['pɒdkɑːst] Podcast <I>

poem ['pəʊɪm] Gedicht III U5, 105

lookout **point** ['lʊkaʊt ˌpɔɪnt] Aussichtspunkt II

meeting point ['miːtɪŋ ˌpɔɪnt] Treffpunkt <III U1, 30>

point of view [ˌpɔɪnt‿əv 'vjuː] Standpunkt; Perspektive <III U2, 133>

starting point ['stɑːtɪŋ ˌpɔɪnt] Ausgangspunkt <III U5, 101>

turning point ['tɜːnɪŋ ˌpɔɪnt] Wendepunkt <III U2, 45>

to **point** (at) [ˌpɔɪnt‿'ət] zeigen (auf) I

poison ['pɔɪzn] Gift <III U2, 194>

pole [pəʊl] Pfahl; Stange <III U3, 134>

police [pə'liːs] Polizei III U2, 38

police officer [pə'liːs‿ɒfɪsə] Polizeibeamter; Polizeibeamtin I

polite [pə'laɪt] höflich II

polystyrene [ˌpɒlɪ'staɪriːn] Styropor <III U3, 71>

swimming **pool** ['swɪmɪŋ ˌpuːl] Schwimmbad I

poor [pɔː] arm I

pop [pɒp] Pop *(Musik)* III U5, 94

popcorn ['pɒpkɔːn] Popcorn I

popular ['pɒpjələ] beliebt III U2, 33

population *(no pl)* [ˌpɒpjə'leɪʃn] Bevölkerung; Einwohner; Einwohnerzahl III U4, 74

pork [pɔːk] Schweinefleisch II

porridge ['pɒrɪdʒ] Haferbrei III U3, 53

position [pə'zɪʃn] Position <III U5, 110>

positive ['pɒzətɪv] positiv III U4, 76

possessive pronoun [pəˈsesɪv ˌprəʊnaʊn] Possessivpronomen <III U5, 99>
possible [ˈpɒsəbl] möglich <III U5, 110>
not **possibly** [nɒt ˈpɒsəbli] unmöglich III U4, 84
post office [ˈpəʊst‿ɒfɪs] Postamt I
to **post** [pəʊst] aufgeben *(einen Brief)*; abschicken *(einen Brief)* III U4, 80
postcard [ˈpəʊstkɑːd] Postkarte I
poster [ˈpəʊstə] Poster I
postman [ˈpəʊsmən] Postbote <III U2, 133>
pot [pɒt] Topf III U5, 104
potato *(sg)* [pəˈteɪtəʊ], **potatoes** *(pl)* [pəˈteɪtəʊz] Kartoffel II
jacket potato [ˌdʒækɪt pəˈteɪtəʊ] Ofenkartoffel II
mashed potatoes [ˌmæʃt pəˈteɪtəʊz] Kartoffelbrei II
pound [paʊnd] Pfund *(brit. Währungseinheit)* I
… is £1.25. [ɪz ˈwʌn paʊnd twentiˌfaɪv] … kostet ein Pfund fünfundzwanzig. I
power [ˈpaʊə] Energie; Kraft; Macht III U3, 53
practice [ˈpræktɪs] Training; Übung I
to **practise** [ˈpræktɪs] üben; trainieren III U5, 96
to **prefer** [prɪˈfɜː] vorziehen II
I prefer working [aɪ prɪˈfɜː ˌwɜːkɪŋ] ich arbeite lieber II
to **prepare** [prɪˈpeə] zubereiten; (sich) vorbereiten III U5, 96
preposition [ˌprepəˈzɪʃn] Präposition <III U4, 93>
present [ˈpreznt] Geschenk I
simple present [ˌsɪmpl ˈpreznt] Gegenwart; Präsens <III U2, 51>
present perfect [ˌpreznt ˈpɜːfɪkt] das Perfekt <III U2, 41>
present progressive [ˌpreznt prəˈgresɪv] Verlaufsform der Gegenwart <III U4, 93>
to **present** [prɪˈzent] vorstellen I; präsentieren <III U1, 27>
presentation [ˌpreznˈteɪʃn] Präsentation; Vortrag <III U5, 105>
presenter [prɪˈzentə] Moderator; Moderatorin <III U1, 26>
to **press** [pres] drücken; pressen <III U1, 29>
pretty [ˈprɪti] hübsch II
prewriting [priːˈraɪtɪŋ] vor dem Schreiben <III U5, 113>
price [praɪs] Preis II
prime minister [ˌpraɪm ˈmɪnɪstə] Premierminister; Premierministerin; Ministerpräsident; Ministerpräsidentin <III U5, 139>
to **print** [prɪnt] drucken <III U1, 29>
prison [ˈprɪzn] Gefängnis II
private [ˈpraɪvɪt] Privat-; private <III U4, 86>
prize [praɪz] Preis II
probably [ˈprɒbəbli] wahrscheinlich III U1, 21
problem [ˈprɒbləm] Problem I
process [ˈprəʊsəs] Prozess <III U5, 139>
to **produce** [prəˈdjuːs] hervorbringen; produzieren III U3, 52
product [ˈprɒdʌkt] Produkt <III U3, 68>
production [prəˈdʌkʃn] Produktion; Herstellung <III U4, 87>
profile [ˈprəʊfaɪl] Profil; Steckbrief <III U2, 133>; <III U3, 55>
programme [ˈprəʊgræm] Programm; Sendung I
present **progressive** [ˌpreznt prəˈgresɪv] Verlaufsform der Gegenwart <III U4, 93>
project [ˈprɒdʒekt] Projekt III U5, 98
possessive **pronoun** [pəˈsesɪv ˌprəʊnaʊn] Possessivpronomen <III U5, 99>
prop [prɒp] Requisit III U2, 45
to **protect** [prəˈtekt] schützen III U3, 53
Protestant [ˈprɒtɪstnt] protestantisch; Protestant; Protestantin III U4, 74
proud (of) [ˈpraʊd‿əv] stolz (auf) II
proud (of) [praʊd (əv)] stolz (auf) III U3, 65
to **prove** [pruːv] beweisen <III U3, 70>
pub [pʌb] Kneipe; Gasthaus III U5, 94
public transport [ˌpʌblɪk ˈtrænspɔːt] öffentliche Verkehrsmittel III U5, 100
published [ˈpʌblɪʃt] veröffentlicht <III U3, 72>
pudding [ˈpʊdɪŋ] Nachspeise; Pudding II
to **pull** [pʊl] ziehen I
punctuation [ˌpʌŋktʃuˈeɪʃn] Zeichensetzung; Interpunktion <III U5, 113>
purple [ˈpɜːpl] lila; violett I
purpose [ˈpɜːpəs] Ziel; Absicht; Zweck <III U4, 137>
on purpose [ɒn ˈpɜːpəs] absichtlich II
to **push** [pʊʃ] schieben; drücken I; schubsen; drängeln III U5, 102
*to **put** [pʊt] setzen; legen; stellen I
to put a comment [ˌpʊt‿ə ˈkɒment] einen Kommentar schreiben <I>
to put in [ˌpʊt‿ˈɪn] einsetzen I
to put in the right order [ˌpʊt‿ɪn ðə ˈraɪt ɔːdə] in die richtige Reihenfolge bringen I
to put on [ˌpʊt‿ˈɒn] anlegen; anziehen III U2, 39
to put up [ˌpʊt‿ˈʌp] hochhalten <III U2, 132>; aufhängen <III U5, 112>
Put your hands up. [ˈpʊt jɔː ˌhændz‿ʌp] Meldet euch. I
put [pʊt] simple past von *to put* I
puzzle [ˈpʌzl] Rätsel; Puzzle <I>

Q

quarter [ˈkwɔːtə] Viertel <III U3, 71>
quarter past [ˈkwɔːtə pɑːst] Viertel nach I
quarter to [ˈkwɔːtə tə] Viertel vor I
queen [kwiːn] Königin III U1, 31
question [ˈkwestʃən] Frage I
queue [kjuː] Warteschlange II
quick [kwɪk] schnell II
quiet [ˈkwaɪət] ruhig; leise; still III U1, 16
to go quiet [ˌgəʊ ˈkwaɪət] still werden III U1, 20

to keep quiet [ˌkiːp ˈkwaɪət] ruhig sein <III U5, 109>
quite [kwaɪt] ziemlich III U2, 34
quiz [kwɪz] Quiz; Rätsel <I>
quote [kwəʊt] Zitat <III U2, 133>

R

raccoon [rəˈkuːn] Waschbär I
race [reɪs] Wettrennen; Rennen I
racket [ˈrækɪt] Schläger <III U2, 193>
radio [ˈreɪdiəʊ] Radio II
rafting [ˈrɑːftɪŋ] Rafting III U2, 33
rain [reɪn] Regen III U3, 52
to **rain** [reɪn] regnen I
rainbow [ˈreɪnbəʊ] Regenbogen III U5, 104
raincoat [ˈreɪnkəʊt] Regenmantel III U5, 97
rainy [ˈreɪni] regnerisch I
ran [ræn] simple past von *to run* III U4, 75
rang [ræŋ] simple past von *to ring* III U5, 96
rap [ræp] Rap <I>
to **rap** [ræp] rappen II
rapper [ˈræpə] Rapper; Rapperin III U5, 98
raspberry [ˈrɑːzbri] Himbeere III U4, 80
to **rate** [reɪt] bewerten; einstufen III U2, 51
I'd **rather** [aɪd ˈrɑːðə] ich würde lieber III U1, 25
rating [ˈreɪtɪŋ] Bewertung <III U2, 51>
RE (Religious Education) [ˌɑːˈriː, rɪˌlɪdʒəs ˌedʒʊˈkeɪʃn] Religionsunterricht I
*to **read** [riːd] lesen I
reader [ˈriːdə] Leser; Leserin <III U3, 69>
reading [ˈriːdɪŋ] Lesen <I>
reading corner [ˈriːdɪŋ ˌkɔːnə] Leseecke <I>
ready [ˈredi] fertig; bereit I
to get ready [ˌget ˈredi] sich vorbereiten; sich fertig machen <III U1, 27>; <III U2, 44>
Are you ready? [ˌɑː juː ˈredi] Bist du fertig? I
real [rɪəl] echt; richtig; wirklich II
really [ˈrɪəli] wirklich I; echt II
reason [ˈriːzn] Grund III U2, 51
to give reasons [ˌgɪv ˈriːznz] Gründe nennen; Gründe angeben III U2, 51
receipt [rɪˈsiːt] Quittung II
recipe [ˈresɪpi] Rezept II
to **record** [rɪˈkɔːd] aufnehmen <III U2, 43>
recording [rɪˈkɔːdɪŋ] Aufnahme <III U2, 43>
recording studio [rɪˈkɔːdɪŋ ˌstjuːdiəʊ] Tonstudio I
recyclable [ˌriːˈsaɪkləbl] wiederverwertbar; recycelbar <III U3, 201>
red [red] rot I
registration [ˌredʒɪˈstreɪʃn] Überprüfung der Anwesenheit I
registration [ˌrədʒɪˈstreɪʃn] Anmeldung II
to **relax** [rɪˈlæks] entspannen; locker lassen <III U5, 110>
relaxed [rɪˈlækst] entspannt; locker; gelassen II
relaxing [rɪˈlæksɪŋ] entspannend; erholsam III U2, 34
religion [rɪˈlɪdʒn] Religion <III U4, 136>
RE (**Religious Education**) [ˌɑːˈriː, rɪˌlɪdʒəs ˌedʒʊˈkeɪʃn] Religionsunterricht I
to **remember** [rɪˈmembə] sich merken; sich erinnern (an) II
rent [rent] Miete II
to **rent** [rent] mieten III U3, 58
to **repair** [rɪˈpeə] reparieren III U3, 67
to **repeat** [rɪˈpiːt] wiederholen III U4, 80
to **reply** [rɪˈplaɪ] antworten; erwidern <III U5, 112>
report [rɪˈpɔːt] Bericht <I>
reporter [rɪˈpɔːtə] Reporter; Reporterin III U2, 42
republic [rɪˈpʌblɪk] Republik III U5, 94
are **required** [rɪˈkwaɪəd] werden gebeten <III U4, 86>
animal **rescue** shelter [ˌænɪml ˈreskjuː ˌʃeltə] Tierheim I
rescue [ˈreskjuː] Rettung <III U2, 132>
to **rescue** [ˈreskjuː] retten <III U2, 132>
rescued [ˈreskjuːd] gerettet <III U2, 133>
reservation [ˌrezəˈveɪʃn] Reservierung III U3, 59
to make a reservation [ˌmeɪk‿ə ˈrezəveɪʃn] reservieren III U3, 59
the **rest** [ðə ˈrest] der Rest <III U1, 29>; <III U5, 113>
restaurant [ˈrestrɒnt] Restaurant II
fast food restaurant [ˌfɑːst fuːd ˈrestrɒnt] Fastfood-Restaurant I
result [rɪˈzʌlt] Ergebnis II
return ticket [rɪˈtɜːn ˌtɪkɪt] Hin- und Rückfahrkarte III U5, 101
review [rɪˈvjuː] Kritik III U2, 50
revising [rɪˈvaɪzɪŋ] Überarbeitung <III U5, 113>
Industrial **Revolution** [ɪnˌdʌstriəl revlˈuːʃn] industrielle Revolution III U1, 11
to **rhyme** [raɪm] (sich) reimen III U5, 104
rhythm [ˈrɪðm] Rhythmus III U5, 100
rice [raɪs] Reis II
rich [rɪtʃ] reich III U3, 54
ridden [ˈrɪdn] past participle von *to ride* II
ride [raɪd] Fahrt; Ritt II
*to **ride** [raɪd] fahren; reiten II
horse **riding** [ˈhɔːs ˌraɪdɪŋ] Reiten I
right [raɪt] richtig; korrekt I; rechts III U1, 12
to be right [biː ˈraɪt] recht haben II
to do the right thing [ˌduː ðə ˈraɪt θɪŋ] das Richtige tun III U2, 38
to the right [tə ðə ˈraɪt] nach rechts <III U5, 110>
to turn right [ˌtɜːn ˈraɪt] (nach) rechts abbiegen I
all right [ɔːl ˈraɪt] in Ordnung; alles klar II
on the right [ɒn ðə ˈraɪt] auf der rechten Seite; rechts I

You're right. [jɔː‿'raɪt] Du hast recht. I
right now [ˌraɪt 'naʊ] jetzt gerade III U2, 38
right there [ˌraɪt 'ðeə] genau vor dir <III U5, 112>
right [raɪt] also II
*to **ring** [rɪŋ] klingeln; läuten III U5, 96
*to **rise** onto the toes [ˌraɪz ɒntʊ ðə 'təʊz] sich auf die Zehenspitzen stellen <III U5, 110>
river ['rɪvə] Fluss I
road [rəʊd] Straße I
rock [rɒk] Fels; Stein III U2, 38
rock climber ['rɒk ˌklaɪmə] Kletterer; Kletterin <III U3, 72>
rock climbing ['rɒk ˌklaɪmɪŋ] Klettern I
rock [rɒk] Rock *(Musik)* III U5, 94
space **rocket** ['speɪs ˌrɒkɪt] Raumschiff <III U1, 30>
rode [rəʊd] simple past von *to ride* II
role [rəʊl] Rolle <III U5, 107>
role play ['rəʊl ˌpleɪ] Rollenspiel <II>
roller coaster ['rəʊlə ˌkəʊstə] Achterbahn II
the **Romans** [ðə 'rəʊmənz] die Römer III U1, 10
romance ['rəʊmæns] Liebesgeschichte III U2, 51
roof [ruːf] Dach II
room [ruːm] Zimmer; Raum I; Platz <III U5, 110>
root word [ˌruːt 'wɜːd] Stammwort <III U3, 73>
rope [rəʊp] Seil I
round [raʊnd] Runde <III U5, 111>
royal ['rɔɪəl] königlich II
rubber ['rʌbə] Gummi III U3, 55
rubbish ['rʌbɪʃ] Müll; Abfall II
rugby ['rʌgbi] Rugby III U2, 34
to **ruin** ['ruːɪn] ruinieren; zerstören II
rule [ruːl] Regel III U2, 34
ruler ['ruːlə] Lineal I
run [rʌn] Lauf <III U2, 133>
*to **run** [rʌn] rennen; laufen I; betreiben; leiten; führen III U4, 75
to run about ['rʌn‿əˌbaʊt] herumrennen II
to run away [ˌrʌn‿ə'weɪ] weglaufen III U2, 50
to run out of [ˌrʌn‿'aʊt‿əv] ausgehen *(Ware)* III U4, 81
run [rʌn] past participle von *to run* III U4, 75
rung [rʌŋ] past participle von *to ring* III U5, 96
to **rush** [rʌʃ] eilen; sich beeilen; stürzen III U5, 105
to rush down [rʌʃ 'daʊn] hinuntereilen II

S

sad [sæd] traurig III U3, 65
safe [seɪf] in Sicherheit; sicher III U1, 22
to keep safe [ˌkiːp 'seɪf] schützen III U2, 34
safety ['seɪfti] Sicherheit <III U2, 132>
said [sed] simple past von *to say* I
to **sail** [seɪl] segeln <III U1, 130>
sailing ship ['seɪlɪŋ ʃɪp] Segelboot <III U4, 91>
patron **saint** [ˌpeɪtrn 'seɪnt] Schutzheiliger; Schutzheilige <III U5, 138>
salad ['sæləd] Salat II
sale [seɪl] Schlussverkauf; Ausverkauf II; Verkauf <III U2, 133>
jumble sale ['dʒʌmbl ˌseɪl] Flohmarkt II
salt [sɔːlt] Salz II
the **same** [ðə 'seɪm] derselbe; gleich II
sandal ['sændl] Sandale <III U2, 44>
sandwich ['sænwɪdʒ] Sandwich; belegtes Brot I
sang [sæŋ] simple past von *to sing* II
sank [sæŋk] simple past von *to sink* III U4, 84
satnav ['sætnæv] Navi I
Saturday ['sætədeɪ] Samstag I
sauce [sɔːs] Soße II
sausage ['sɒsɪdʒ] Wurst; Bratwurst II
sausage roll [ˌsɒsɪdʒ 'rəʊl] Blätterteig mit Wurstfüllung II
to **save** [seɪv] speichern II; retten; bergen III U4, 85
saw [sɔː] simple past von *to see* I
saxophone ['sæksəfəʊn] Saxofon I
*to **say** [seɪ] nachsprechen; nennen; sagen; sprechen I
to say hi to [ˌseɪ 'haɪ tə] grüßen; Grüße ausrichten I
to say sorry [ˌseɪ 'sɒri] sich entschuldigen II
It says … [ɪt 'sez] Hier steht …; Es heißt … <III U5, 112>
to **scan** [skæn] scannen; nach Details durchsuchen <III U1, 31>
to **scare** [skeə] erschrecken II
*to be **scared** [biː 'skeəd] Angst haben; erschrocken sein II
scarf *(sg)* [skɑːf], **scarves** *(pl)* [skɑːvz] Schal; Tuch I
scary ['skeəri] gruselig; beängstigend I
scene [siːn] Szene II
school [skuːl] Schule I
at school [ət 'skuːl] in der Schule I
high school ['haɪ ˌskuːl] High School *(weiterführende Schule, Oberstufe)* <III U2, 133>
school life ['skuː‿ˌlaɪf] Schulalltag <I>
school trip [ˌskuːl 'trɪp] Klassenfahrt I
Science [saɪəns] Wissenschaft; Naturwissenschaft I
computer science [kəmˌpjuːtə 'saɪəns] Informatik <III U2, 47>
science fiction [ˌsaɪəns 'fɪkʃn] Science-Fiction I
scissors *(pl)* ['sɪzəz] Schere <III U3, 71>
scissors *(pl)* ['sɪzəz] Schere III U5, 97
nail scissors *(pl)* ['neɪl ˌsɪzəz] Nagelschere III U5, 97
scone [skɒn] Scone *(eine Art süßes Brötchen)* II
score [skɔː] Punktestand II
best ever score [best ˌevə 'skɔː] das beste Ergebnis II

Scot [skɒt] Schotte; Schottin III U3, 53
Scottish ['skɒtɪʃ] schottisch III U3, 52
scrambled egg [ˌskræmbld‿'eg] Rührei II
to **scream** [skri:m] schreien; kreischen III U5, 105
script [skrɪpt] Drehbuch; Skript <III U1, 27>
scriptwriter ['skrɪptˌraɪtə] Drehbuchautor; Drehbuchautorin <III U4, 87>
sea [si:] Meer I
seal [si:l] Seehund; Robbe <III U2, 45>
search [sɜ:tʃ] Suche <III U3, 73>
to **search** [sɜ:tʃ] durchsuchen <III U3, 65>
  to search for ['sɜ:tʃ fə] suchen nach <III U1, 31>
seasick ['si:sɪk] seekrank <III U2, 132>
at the **seaside** [ət ðə 'si:saɪd] am Meer I
seat [si:t] Sitz; Sitzplatz III U5, 102
second ['seknd] Sekunde II
second ['seknd] zweite I
secret ['si:krət] Geheimnis II
secret ['si:krət] geheim II
section ['sekʃn] Abschnitt <III U1, 21>
*to **see** [si:] sehen I
  CU (See you!) ['si: ˌju] Bis später! II
  to see friends [si: 'frendz] Freunde treffen I
  Let's see ... [ˌlets 'si:] Lass mal sehen ...; Also ... I
  See you later. [ˌsi: jə 'leɪtə] Tschüss.; Bis bald. I
  See you soon! ['si: ˌju ˌsu:n] Bis bald! I
  See you. ['si: ˌju:] Tschüss.; Bis bald. I
to **seem** [si:m] scheinen III U4, 76
seen [si:n] past participle von *to see* II
to **seize** [si:z] ergreifen <III U5, 101>
self [self] sich; selbst III U2, 34
*to **sell** [sel] verkaufen III U1, 12
*to **send** [send] schicken; senden I
*to make **sense** [ˌmeɪk 'sens] Sinn ergeben; einleuchten <III U5, 113>

sent [sent] simple past von *to send* I; past participle von *to send* II
sentence ['sentəns] Satz <I>
to **separate** ['sepreɪt] trennen <III U4, 137>
separate ['seprət] getrennt; separat; verschieden <III U4, 136>
September [sep'tembə] September I
series *(no pl)* ['sɪəri:z] Serie <III U4, 137>
serious ['sɪəriəs] schwer; ernst III U2, 38
  Are you serious? [ˌɑ: ju 'sɪəriəs] Im Ernst? III U3, 58
to **serve** [sɜ:v] servieren <III U3, 66>
service ['sɜ:vɪs] Dienst III U2, 38
  emergency service [ɪ'mɜ:dʒnsi ˌsɜ:vɪs] Notdienst; Rettungsdienst III U2, 38
  full service [ˌfʊl 'sɜ:vɪs] Komplettservice <III U3, 68>
  for service [fə 'sɜ:vɪs] um bedient zu werden <III U4, 86>
*to **set free** [set 'fri:] freilassen <III U4, 77>
  to set off [ˌset‿'ɒf] auslösen <III U3, 72>
setting ['setɪŋ] Schauplatz <III U5, 112>
to **settle (in)** ['setl (ɪn)] besiedeln; sich niederlassen (in) <III U4, 136>
early **settler** [ˌɜ:li 'setlə] früher Siedler; frühe Siedlerin <III U5, 138>
seven ['sevn] sieben I
seventeen [ˌsevn'ti:n] siebzehn I
seventy ['sevnti] siebzig I
shampoo [ʃæm'pu:] Shampoo III U5, 96
shamrock ['ʃæmrɒk] Kleeblatt III U5, 104
to **share** [ʃeə] teilen III U5, 96
shark [ʃɑ:k] Hai I
pencil **sharpener** ['pensl ˌʃɑ:pnə] Anspitzer I
she [ʃi:] sie I
sheep *(sg)* [ʃi:p], **sheep** *(pl)* [ʃi:p] Schaf I

sheet of paper ['ʃi:t‿əv ˌpeɪpə] Blatt Papier <III U4, 90>
shelf *(sg)* [ʃelf], **shelves** *(pl)* [ʃelvz] Regal; Regalbrett I
animal rescue **shelter** [ˌænɪml 'reskju: ˌʃeltə] Tierheim I
shift [ʃɪft] Verlagerung <III U5, 111>
to **shift** your weight [ˌʃɪft jɔ: 'weɪt] sein Gewicht verlagern <III U5, 111>
*to **shine** [ʃaɪn] scheinen <III U5, 101>
ship [ʃɪp] Schiff I
  sailing ship ['seɪlɪŋ ʃɪp] Segelboot <III U4, 91>
  ship builder ['ʃɪp ˌbɪldə] Schiffsbauer; Schiffsbauerin III U4, 84
shipyard ['ʃɪpjɑ:d] Werft III U4, 84
shirt [ʃɜ:t] Hemd; Shirt I
T-shirt ['ti:ʃɜ:t] T-Shirt I
shoe [ʃu:] Schuh I
*to **shoot** [ʃu:t] abschießen <III U4, 91>
*to **shoot** (a film) [ˌʃu:t (ə 'fɪlm)] (einen Film) drehen <III U5, 107>
shop [ʃɒp] Laden; Geschäft I
  corner shop ['kɔ:nə ˌʃɒp] Tante-Emma-Laden I
  shop assistant ['ʃɒp‿əˌsɪstnt] Verkäufer; Verkäuferin II
  sports shop ['spɔ:ts ˌʃɒp] Sportgeschäft I
shopping ['ʃɒpɪŋ] Einkaufen I
  to do the shopping [ˌdu: ðə 'ʃɒpɪŋ] Einkäufe machen; Besorgungen machen II
  to go shopping [ˌgəʊ 'ʃɒpɪŋ] einkaufen gehen II
  shopping centre ['ʃɒpɪŋ ˌsentə] Einkaufszentrum I
  shopping list ['ʃɒpɪŋ ˌlɪst] Einkaufszettel I
short [ʃɔ:t] kurz II
shortly ['ʃɔ:tli] kurz III U4, 84
shorts *(pl)* [ʃɔ:ts] Shorts; kurze Hose I
should [ʃʊd] sollte III U2, 34
should [ʃʊd] sollte <III U1, 25>
shoulder ['ʃəʊldə] Schulter <III U5, 110>
shout [ʃaʊt] Schrei I
to **shout** [ʃaʊt] schreien; rufen II

show [ʃəʊ] Show; Wettbewerb I
talent show ['tælənt ˌʃəʊ] Talentwettbewerb I
TV show [ˌti: 'vi: ˌʃəʊ] Fernsehsendung II
*to **show** [ʃəʊ] zeigen II
shower ['ʃaʊə] Dusche III U5, 97
shower gel ['ʃaʊə ˌdʒel] Duschgel III U5, 97
sick [sɪk] krank III U1, 11
to be sick [bi: 'sɪk] sich übergeben I
side [saɪd] Seite I
sight [saɪt] Sehenswürdigkeit II
*to go **sightseeing** [gəʊ 'saɪtsi:ɪŋ] eine Besichtigungstour machen II
sign [saɪn] Schild; Zeichen III U2, 32
sign language ['saɪn ˌlæŋgwɪdʒ] Gebärdensprache; Zeichensprache III U5, 95
to **sign** [saɪn] unterschreiben; unterzeichnen <III U5, 139>
signal ['sɪgnl] Empfang; Signal; Zeichen III U3, 67
signal word ['sɪgnl ˌwɜ:d] Signalwort <III U2, 41>
silence ['saɪləns] Stille; Schweigen; Ruhe III U1, 20
silent ['saɪlənt] schweigsam; stumm III U1, 21
silk [sɪlk] Seide III U3, 55
silly ['sɪli] albern II; dumm; doof III U4, 76
similar ['sɪmɪlə] ähnlich <III U3, 135>; <III U4, 84>
similarity [ˌsɪmɪ'lærəti] Ähnlichkeit <III U1, 24>
simple ['sɪmpl] einfach III U3, 58
simple past [ˌsɪmpl 'pɑ:st] einfache Vergangenheit <III U2, 41>
simple present [ˌsɪmpl 'preznt] Gegenwart; Präsens <III U2, 51>
since [sɪns] seit <III U2, 132>; <III U3, 68>; seitdem <III U4, 136>
*to **sing** [sɪŋ] singen I
singer ['sɪŋə] Sänger; Sängerin I
singing ['sɪŋɪŋ] Gesangs- III U5, 95
single ['sɪŋgl] einzeln <III U1, 31>
single ticket ['sɪŋgl ˌtɪkɪt] einfache Fahrkarte III U5, 100
*to **sink** [sɪŋk] untergehen; sinken III U4, 84
sinking ['sɪŋkɪŋ] Untergang III U4, 85
siren ['saɪrən] Sirene; Martinshorn <III U1, 17>
sister ['sɪstə] Schwester I
*to **sit** [sɪt] sitzen I
Sit down. [ˌsɪt 'daʊn] Setz dich (hin). I
situation [ˌsɪtju'eɪʃn] Situation II
six [sɪks] sechs I
sixteen [ˌsɪk'sti:n] sechzehn I
sixty ['sɪksti] sechzig I
size [saɪz] Größe II
skateboard ['skeɪtbɔ:d] Skateboard III U2, 41
ice **skating** ['aɪs ˌskeɪtɪŋ] Schlittschuhlaufen <III U2, 193>
to **ski** [ski:] Ski fahren II
skiing ['ski:ɪŋ] Skifahren III U2, 32
skill [skɪl] Fertigkeit <I>
to **skim** [skɪm] überfliegen <III U1, 31>
skin [skɪn] Haut <III U2, 44>
skip [skɪp] Hüpfer; Sprung <III U5, 110>
skirt [skɜ:t] Rock I
sleep [sli:p] Schlaf <III U1, 17>; III U2, 39
*to **sleep** [sli:p] schlafen I
sleepover ['sli:pˌəʊvə] Übernachtung I
slept [slept] simple past, past participle von *to sleep* II
sliced bread [ˌslaɪst 'bred] in Scheiben geschnittenes Brot III U4, 80
slow [sləʊ] langsam III U2, 34
small [smɔ:l] klein I
smart [smɑ:t] schlau; klug; intelligent III U4, 77
smell [smel] Geruch III U1, 23
to **smile** [smaɪl] lächeln III U2, 36
smoke [sməʊk] Rauch III U2, 42
smuggler ['smʌglə] Schmuggler; Schmugglerin II
smurf [smɜ:f] Schlumpf I
snack [snæk] Snack; Imbiss I
snake [sneɪk] Schlange I
snow [snəʊ] Schnee <III U3, 72>
snowboarding ['snəʊbɔ:dɪŋ] Snowboarden <III U2, 193>
so much ['səʊ ˌmʌtʃ] so sehr III U4, 76
so [səʊ] deshalb; also I; so II
so that ['səʊ ðət] so dass <III U3, 134>
soap [səʊp] Seife III U5, 97
soccer *(AE)* ['sɒkə] Fußball <III U1, 24>
Social Studies ['səʊʃl ˌstʌdiz] Gesellschaftslehre; Sozialkunde I
sock [sɒk] Socke I
sofa ['səʊfə] Sofa II
software ['sɒftweə] Software II
solar ['səʊlə] Sonnen-; Solar-; solar III U3, 53
sold [səʊld] simple past, past participle von *to sell* III U1, 12
soldier ['səʊldʒə] Soldat; Soldatin III U3, 62
solid ['sɒlɪd] fest III U3, 55
solution [sə'lu:ʃn] Lösung <III U1, 28>
to **solve** [sɒlv] lösen I
some [sʌm] einige; ein paar I; etwas II
somebody ['sʌmbədi] jemand III U4, 76
somebody else [ˌsʌmbədi 'els] jemand anderes II
something ['sʌmθɪŋ] etwas I
sometimes ['sʌmtaɪmz] manchmal I
somewhere ['sʌmweə] irgendwo <III U3, 58>
son [sʌn] Sohn III U3, 64
song [sɒŋ] Lied I
soon [su:n] bald II
See you soon! ['si: ju ˌsu:n] Bis bald! I
sore [sɔ:] schmerzhaft; wund II
sore throat [ˌsɔ: 'θrəʊt] Halsschmerzen II
*to be **sorry** [bi: 'sɒri] leid tun III U4, 87
to feel sorry for [ˌfi:l 'sɒri fə] Mitleid haben mit; bedauern III U5, 105
Sorry. ['sɒri] Tut mir leid.; Entschuldigung. I

I'm sorry. [aɪm 'sɒri] Es tut mir leid.; Entschuldigung. I
Sorry about … ['sɒri ˌəbaʊt] Es tut mir leid wegen … I
sort [sɔ:t] Sorte; Art II
to **sort** [sɔ:t] sortieren <III U1, 17>
sound [saʊnd] Ton; Laut; Geräusch III U1, 21
sounds [saʊndz] Laute <I>
to **sound** [saʊnd] klingen II
soup [su:p] Suppe II
south [saʊθ] Süden III U1, 10
in the south of [ˌɪn ðə 'saʊθ‿əv] im Süden von III U1, 10
southbound ['saʊθbaʊnd] in Richtung Süden <III U5, 216>
southwest [ˌsaʊθ'west] Südwesten III U1, 19
souvenir [ˌsu:vn'ɪə] Souvenir; Andenken III U1, 12
souvenir shop ['su:vnɪə ˌʃɒp] Souvenirladen III U1, 12
space rocket ['speɪs ˌrɒkɪt] Raumschiff <III U1, 30>
spaghetti [spə'geti] Spaghetti II
*to **speak** [spi:k] sprechen II
speaking ['spi:kɪŋ] Sprechen <I>
special ['speʃl] besonders; speziell I
special offer [ˌspeʃl‿'ɒfə] Sonderangebot III U4, 80
with special needs [wɪð ˌspeʃl 'ni:dz] mit Behinderung III U5, 95
specific [spə'sɪfɪk] spezifisch; speziell <III U1, 31>
spectacular [spek'tækjələ] spektakulär III U4, 74
speech [spi:tʃ] Sprache; Rede III U3, 54
farewell speech [feə'wel spi:tʃ] Abschiedsrede II
speech bubble ['spi:tʃ ˌbʌbl] Sprechblase <III U2, 47>
*to **spell** [spel] buchstabieren I
spell check ['spel ˌtʃek] Rechtschreibprüfprogramm <III U4, 89>
spelling ['spelɪŋ] Rechtschreibung I
*to **spend** [spend] ausgeben *(Geld)*; verbringen *(Zeit)* II
spent [spent] simple past, past participle von *to spend* II
spice [spaɪs] Gewürz II
spicy ['spaɪsi] würzig; pikant II
spider ['spaɪdə] Spinne III U3, 63
splash [splæʃ] Platsch I
*to **split** [splɪt] teilen; spalten <III U5, 139>
spoke [spəʊk] simple past von *to speak* II
spoken ['spəʊkn] past participle von *to speak* II
spoon [spu:n] Löffel II
sport [spɔ:t] Sport I; Sportart III U2, 33
sports shop ['spɔ:ts ˌʃɒp] Sportgeschäft I
to **spot** [spɒt] sehen; erkennen <III U2, 132>
to **sprain** [spreɪn] verstauchen; verrenken III U2, 39
spring roll [ˌsprɪŋ 'rəʊl] Frühlingsrolle II
I **spy** with my little eye … [aɪ spaɪ wɪð ˌmaɪ lɪtl 'aɪ] Ich sehe was, was du nicht siehst … I
square [skweə] Platz II; Feld <III U4, 90>
squash [skwɒʃ] Squash <III U2, 193>
stadium ['steɪdiəm] Stadion II
stage [steɪdʒ] Bühne II
stairs *(pl)* [steəz] Treppe II
food **stall** ['fu:d ˌstɔ:l] Essensstand II
stallholder ['stɔ:lˌhəʊldə] Standinhaber; Standinhaberin II
stamp [stæmp] Stempel <III U1, 29>; Briefmarke III U4, 80
*to **stand** [stænd] stehen II
to stand for ['stænd fə] stehen für <III U2, 48>
star [stɑ:] Star I; Stern III U2, 50
You're a star. [ˌjɔ:r‿ə 'stɑ:] Du bist fantastisch. II
to **stare** [steə] starren III U5, 105
start [stɑ:t] Start; Anfang III U2, 51
for a start [ˌfɔ:r‿ə 'stɑ:t] zunächst III U3, 58
to **start** [stɑ:t] anfangen; beginnen; starten II; gründen III U3, 54
to start a band [ˌstɑ:t‿ə 'bænd] eine Band gründen II
starting point ['stɑ:tɪŋ ˌpɔɪnt] Ausgangspunkt <III U5, 101>
*to get **started** [ˌget 'stɑ:tɪd] anfangen <III U5, 110>
starter ['stɑ:tə] Vorspeise II
static caravan ['stætɪk ˌkærəvæn] Mobilheim *(großer, fest stehender Wohnwagen)* <III U3, 202>
station ['steɪʃn] Haltestelle; Station; Bahnhof III U5, 101
to **stay** [steɪ] übernachten; bleiben II
steam engine ['sti:m‿endʒɪn] Dampfmaschine III U3, 57
steel [sti:l] Stahl III U3, 55
steep [sti:p] steil <III U3, 73>
step [step] Schritt III U5, 102; Stufe II
stick [stɪk] Stock II
*to be **stuck** [bi: 'stʌk] feststecken; nicht weg können I
sticker ['stɪkə] Aufkleber II
sticky ['stɪki] klebrig <III U3, 66>
still [stɪl] immer noch; noch III U1, 21; dennoch III U1, 16
to **stir** [stɜ:] rühren; umrühren II
stocks [stɒks] Pranger III U2, 43
stomach ['stʌmək] Magen; Bauch II
stomach ache ['stʌmək ˌeɪk] Bauchweh; Bauchschmerzen II
stone [stəʊn] Stein III U1, 10
stone put ['stəʊn ˌpʊt] Steinwurf <III U3, 135>
stood [stʊd] simple past, past participle von *to stand* II
stop [stɒp] Haltestelle; Halt II
bus stop ['bʌs ˌstɒp] Bushaltestelle II
full stop [ˌfʊl 'stɒp] Punkt <III U1, 23>
Stop it! ['stɒp‿ɪt] Hör(t) auf! II
department **store** [dɪ'pɑ:tmənt ˌstɔ:] Kaufhaus II
storm [stɔ:m] Sturm I
story ['stɔ:ri] Geschichte I
straight [streɪt] gerade <III U5, 110>
straight on [streɪt‿'ɒn] geradeaus I

hair straightener ['heə ˌstreɪtnə] Haarglätter I
straightforward [ˌstreɪt'fɔ:wəd] aufrichtig; geradlinig III U4, 77
strange [streɪndʒ] merkwürdig; seltsam II
stranger ['streɪndʒə] Fremder; Fremde <III U1, 17>
straw [strɔ:] Trinkhalm II
strawberry ['strɔ:bri] Erdbeere II
stray [streɪ] Streuner; Streunerin <III U5, 112>
street [stri:t] Straße III U1, 15
back street ['bæk stri:t] Hinterhof <III U1, 17>
striking ['straɪkɪŋ] bemerkenswert; auffallend III U5, 100
comic **strip** ['kɒmɪk strɪp] Comic <III U3, 52>
strong [strɒŋ] stark III U2, 34
structure ['strʌktʃə] Aufbau; Struktur III U2, 51
*to get **stuck** [ˌget 'stʌk] stecken bleiben <III U4, 83>
to be stuck [bi: 'stʌk] feststecken; nicht weg können I
student ['stju:dnt] Schüler; Schülerin; Student; Studentin I
studio ['stju:diəʊ] Studio <III U5, 107>
recording studio [rɪ'kɔ:dɪŋ ˌstju:diəʊ] Tonstudio I
TV studio [ˌti:'vi: ˌstju:diəʊ] Fernsehstudio II
study skills [ˌstʌdi 'skɪlz] Fertigkeit Lern- und Arbeitstechniken <I>
style [staɪl] Stil III U5, 95
subject ['sʌbdʒɪkt] Schulfach I
submarine [ˌsʌbmr'i:n] U-Boot I
success [sək'ses] Erfolg III U3, 54
successful [sək'sesfl] erfolgreich III U3, 54
such as ['sʌtʃ‿əz] wie <III U1, 24>
suddenly ['sʌdnli] plötzlich; auf einmal II
sugar ['ʃʊgə] Zucker I
suit [su:t] Anzug <III U2, 44>
to **suit** [su:t] stehen; passen II
suitcase ['su:tkeɪs] Koffer II
trolley suitcase ['trɒli ˌsu:tkeɪs] Rollkoffer III U3, 57
to **sum up** [ˌsʌm‿'ʌp] zusammenfassen <III U1, 131>
summary ['sʌmri] Zusammenfassung <III U1, 25>
summer ['sʌmə] Sommer II
sun [sʌn] Sonne III U1, 11
to **sunbathe** ['sʌnbeɪð] sonnenbaden II
Sunday ['sʌndeɪ] Sonntag I
sunflower oil ['sʌnflaʊər‿ˌɔɪl] Sonnenblumenöl <III U3, 71>
sunglasses *(pl)* ['sʌnˌglɑ:sɪz] Sonnenbrille II
sunk [sʌŋk] past participle von *to sink* III U4, 84
sunny ['sʌni] sonnig I
super ['su:pə] super II
superman ['su:pəmæn] Superman I
supermarket ['su:pəˌmɑ:kɪt] Supermarkt II
sure [ʃʊə] sicher I
to make sure [ˌmeɪk 'ʃɔ:] dafür sorgen; sich versichern III U2, 35
sure of oneself ['ʃʊər‿əv ˌwʌnself] selbstsicher III U4, 77
to **surf** [sɜ:f] surfen; wellenreiten II
to surf the internet [ˌsɜ:f ði 'ɪntənet] im Internet surfen II
surfer ['sɜ:fə] Wellenreiter; Wellenreiterin; Surfer; Surferin <III U2, 45>
surfing ['sɜ:fɪŋ] Surfen; Wellenreiten III U2, 33
surname ['sɜ:neɪm] Nachname; Familienname <III U1, 131>
surprise [sə'praɪz] Überraschung I
to **surprise** [sə'praɪz] überraschen <III U1, 22>
surprised [sə'praɪzd] überrascht II
surprising [sə'praɪzɪŋ] überraschend <III U4, 137>
survey ['sɜ:veɪ] Umfrage II
to **survive** [sə'vaɪv] überleben III U4, 84
suspense [sə'spens] Spannung <III U3, 67>
swam [swæm] simple past von *to swim* II
sweater ['swetə] Pullover <III U5, 215>
sweatshirt ['swetʃɜ:t] Sweatshirt I
*to **sweep** [swi:p] fegen II; mitreißen <III U3, 72>
to sweep through [ˌswi:p 'θru:] durchziehen <III U3, 73>
sweet [swi:t] Süßigkeit; Bonbon I
sweet [swi:t] süß III U5, 96
swept [swept] simple past, past participle von *to sweep* II
*to **swim** [swɪm] schwimmen II
*to go **swimming** [ˌgəʊ 'swɪmɪŋ] schwimmen gehen I
swimming pool ['swɪmɪŋ ˌpu:l] Schwimmbad I
swimming things ['swɪmɪŋ ˌθɪŋz] Schwimmsachen <III U5, 215>
swimming ['swɪmɪŋ] schwimmend <III U3, 70>
*to **swing** [swɪŋ] schwingen; schwenken <III U3, 135>
sword [sɔ:d] Schwert III U2, 43
swum [swʌm] past participle von *to swim* II
symbol ['sɪmbl] Symbol <III U1, 28>
system ['sɪstəm] System <III U5, 100>

T

table ['teɪbl] Tisch I; Tabelle <III ZI, 9>
table tennis ['teɪbl ˌtenɪs] Tischtennis II
tablet ['tæblət] Tablette II
tactic ['tæktɪk] Taktik; Vorgehensweise III U3, 64
take [teɪk] Aufnahme <III U1, 27>
*to **take** [teɪk] nehmen; mitnehmen I; hinbringen II; dauern III U1, 10
to take a break [ˌteɪk‿ə 'breɪk] Pause machen II
to take a photo [ˌteɪk‿ə 'fəʊtəʊ] ein Foto machen I
to take a trip [ˌteɪk‿ə 'trɪp] eine Fahrt machen III U2, 34
to take notes [ˌteɪk 'nəʊts] sich Notizen machen I

to take off [ˌteɪk ˈɒf] wegnehmen <III U1, 29>; ausziehen III U5, 96
to take out [ˌteɪk ˈaʊt] herausnehmen I
to take part (in) [ˌteɪk ˈpɑːt] teilnehmen (an) II
to take photos [ˌteɪk ˈfəʊtəʊz] fotografieren; Fotos machen II
to take place [ˌteɪk ˈpleɪs] stattfinden <III U3, 134>; <III U4, 89>; <III U5, 112>
to take the dog for a walk [ˌteɪk ðə ˌdɒg fər ə ˈwɔːk] den Hund spazieren führen II
to take turns [ˌteɪk ˈtɜːnz] sich abwechseln <II>
Take care. [ˈteɪk ˌkeə] Macht's gut. I

takeaway [ˈteɪkəweɪ] Essen zum Mitnehmen II
takeaway [ˈteɪkəweɪ] zum Mitnehmen II
taken [ˈteɪkn] past participle von *to take* II
talent [ˈtælənt] Talent I
talent show [ˈtælənt ˌʃəʊ] Talentwettbewerb I
talented [ˈtæləntɪd] begabt; talentiert III U2, 35
talk [tɔːk] Gerede II; Vortrag; Rede <III U1, 19>
to give a talk [ˌgɪv ə ˈtɔːk] einen Vortrag halten <III U1, 19>
to **talk** (to) [ˈtɔːk tə] sprechen (mit); reden (mit) I
TTYL (**Talk** to you later!) [ˈtɔːk tə ju ˌleɪtə] Wir reden später! II
to talk about [ˈtɔːk əˌbaʊt] sprechen über II
Don't talk. [ˌdəʊnt ˈtɔːk] Sei still.; Rede nicht. I
tall [tɔːl] groß; hoch II
tapestry [ˈtæpɪstri] Wandteppich <III U1, 131>
task [tɑːsk] Aufgabe; Auftrag <I>
tasty [ˈteɪsti] lecker; schmackhaft III U4, 80
taught [tɔːt] simple past, past participle von *to teach* III U4, 76
taxi [ˈtæksi] Taxi II
tea bag [ˈtiː ˌbæg] Teebeutel <III U4, 209>
tea [tiː] Tee; (frühes) Abendessen I
*to **teach** [tiːtʃ] beibringen; unterrichten; lehren III U4, 76
teacher [ˈtiːtʃə] Lehrer; Lehrerin I
team [tiːm] Team; Mannschaft I
teamwork [ˈtiːmwɜːk] Teamwork II
tear [tɪə] Träne <III U4, 77>
teaspoon [ˈtiːspuːn] Teelöffel II
teaspoon *(tsp)* [ˈtiːspuːn] Teelöffel *(TL)* II
Design **Technology** (DT) [dɪˌzaɪn tekˈnɒlədʒi, ˌdiːˈtiː] Technik I
technology [tekˈnɒlədʒi] Technologie <III U1, 30>
teen [tiːn] Jugend-; Teenager; Jugendliche; Jugendlicher II
teenage [ˈtiːneɪdʒ] jugendlich <III U2, 132>
teenager [ˈtiːneɪdʒə] Teenager; Teenagerin; Jugendliche; Jugendlicher III U2, 33
telephone [ˈtelɪfəʊn] Telefon III U3, 54
telephone box [ˈtelɪfəʊn ˌbɒks] Telefonzelle II
*to **tell** [tel] erzählen; sagen I
ten [ten] zehn I
tennis [ˈtenɪs] Tennis I
tense [tens] Zeit; Zeitform <III U1, 14>
tent [tent] Zelt II
terrible [ˈterəbl] schrecklich; schlimm; furchtbar I
terrorism [ˈterɪzm] Terrorismus <III U4, 136>
test [test] Test; Klassenarbeit I
to **test** [test] testen; prüfen II
text [tekst] Text II
text message [ˈtekst ˌmesɪdʒ] SMS II
to **text** [tekst] eine SMS schreiben II
texter [ˈtekstə] SMS-Schreiber; SMS-Schreiberin II
than [ðæn] als II
Thank you. [ˈθæŋk ju] Danke. I
thanks [θæŋks] danke I
that [ðæt] so *(Betonung)* III U1, 12
that [ðæt] dass III U1, 21
so that [ˈsəʊ ðət] so dass <III U3, 134>
that [ðæt] das I
after that [ˈɑːftə ðət] danach I
that night [ˌðæt ˈnaɪt] an jenem Abend; in jener Nacht II
That's £2.24. [ðæts ˈtuː paʊndz ˌtwenti fɔː] Das macht zwei Pfund und 24 Pence. I
That's because … [ˌðæts bɪˈkɒz] Das liegt daran, dass … III U1, 20
That's not for me. [ˌðæts nɒt fə ˈmiː] Das ist nichts für mich. III U2, 34
that's why [ˈðæts waɪ] deswegen III U5, 100
the [ðə] der; die *(auch Pl.)*; das I
the same [ðə ˈseɪm] derselbe; gleich II
theatre [ˈθɪətə] Theater II
their [ðeə] ihr, ihre *(Pl.)* I
theirs [ðeəz] ihre III U5, 99
them [ðem; ðəm] sie *(Pl.)*; ihnen I
theme park [ˈθiːm ˌpɑːk] Freizeitpark I; Themenpark II
themselves [ðəmˈselvz] sich selbst; selber; sie selbst; selbst III U2, 156
then [ðen] dann; danach I; damals III U1, 10
then again [ˌðen əˈgen] andererseits III U1, 16
there [ðeə] da; dort I
over there [ˌəʊvə ˈðeə] da drüben; dort drüben II
there are [ðeər ˈɑː] da sind; es gibt I
there is [ðeə ˈɪz] da ist; dort ist; es gibt I
There's no money missing. [ðeəz nəʊ ˈmʌni mɪsɪŋ] Es fehlt kein Geld. I
these [ðiːz] diese (hier) II
they [ðeɪ] sie *(Pl.)* I
thing [θɪŋ] Sache; Ding I
*to **think** [θɪŋk] denken; glauben I
to think of [ˈθɪŋk əv] sich ausdenken; sich einfallen lassen <III U3, 68>

p pen • b bed • t ten • d dad • k cat • g grey • tʃ chair • dʒ joke • f fan • v very • θ three • ð the

I don't think so. [ˌaɪ dəʊnt 'θɪŋk səʊ] Ich glaube nicht. II
I think so. [aɪ 'θɪŋk səʊ] Ich glaube. II
third [θɜːd] dritte I
thirsty ['θɜːsti] durstig II
thirteen [θɜː'tiːn] dreizehn I
thirty ['θɜːti] dreißig I
this [ðɪs] das; dies I
like this [laɪk 'ðɪs] ähnlich; so <III U3, 58>
this way [ðɪs 'weɪ] in diese Richtung II
this way ['ðɪs weɪ] auf diese Weise <III U1, 28>; <III U5, 112>
those [ðəʊz] jene II
though [ðəʊ] jedoch III U5, 105
thought [θɔːt] simple past, past participle von *to think* II
a/one **thousand** [ə/wʌn 'θaʊznd] eintausend; tausend II
three [θriː] drei I
threw [θruː] simple past von *to throw* I
throat [θrəʊt] Hals II
sore throat [ˌsɔː 'θrəʊt] Halsschmerzen II
through [θruː] durch II
*to **throw** [θrəʊ] werfen I
Thursday ['θɜːzdeɪ] Donnerstag I
ticket ['tɪkɪt] Karte II; Fahrschein; Eintrittskarte; III U1, 15
return ticket [rɪ'tɜːn ˌtɪkɪt] Hin- und Rückfahrkarte III U5, 101
single ticket ['sɪŋgl ˌtɪkɪt] einfache Fahrkarte III U5, 100
to **tidy** (up) [ˌtaɪdi 'ʌp] aufräumen; in Ordnung bringen II
tiger ['taɪgə] Tiger I
tight [taɪt] eng; fest II
time [taɪm] Zeit; Uhrzeit I; Mal III U1, 21
all the time [ˌɔːl ðə 'taɪm] die ganze Zeit III U2, 33
free time [ˌfriː 'taɪm] Freizeit I
on time [ɒn 'taɪm] pünktlich III U5, 100
time travel ['taɪm ˌtrævl] Zeitreise III U4, 79
in time [ɪn 'taɪm] rechtzeitig I
It's time to go. [ɪts ˌtaɪm tə 'gəʊ] Es ist Zeit zu gehen. I
What time is it? [ˌwɒt 'taɪm‿ɪz‿ɪt] Wie spät ist es?; Wie viel Uhr ist es? I
timeline ['taɪmˌlaɪn] Zeitstrahl <III U3, 54>
timetable ['taɪmˌteɪbl] Stundenplan I; Fahrplan III U5, 100
tiny ['taɪni] klein; winzig III U1, 17
tip [tɪp] Tipp; Ratschlag II
tired [taɪəd] müde I
tissue ['tɪʃuː] Taschentuch III U4, 81
title ['taɪtl] Titel; Überschrift <II>
to [tʊ] bis II
to her place [tʊ 'hɜː ˌpleɪs] zu sich nach Hause III U4, 78
to the north of [ˌtə ðə 'nɔːθ‿əv] nördlich von III U1, 17
to [tuː; tʊ; tə] in; nach; zu; vor *(bei Uhrzeitangaben)* I
to [tuː] um zu <III U1, 24>
toast [təʊst] Toast II
today [tə'deɪ] heute I
toe [təʊ] Zeh <III U5, 110>
to rise onto the toes [ˌraɪz ɒntʊ ðə 'təʊz] sich auf die Zehenspitzen stellen <III U5, 110>
together [tə'geðə] zusammen; gemeinsam I
toilet ['tɔɪlət] Toilette I
toiletries ['tɔɪlɪtriz] Toilettenartikel; Hygieneartikel <III U5, 215>
told [təʊld] simple past von *to tell* I
tomato *(sg)* [tə'mɑːtəʊ], **tomatoes** *(pl)* [tə'mɑːtəʊz] Tomate II
tomorrow [tə'mɒrəʊ] morgen II
tongue twister ['tʌŋ ˌtwɪstə] Zungenbrecher <III U1, 13>
tonight [tə'naɪt] heute Abend; heute Nacht II
tonne [tʌn] Tonne II
too [tuː] auch I; zu II
too much [ˌtuː 'mʌtʃ] zu sehr II
took [tʊk] simple past von *to take* II
tool [tuːl] Werkzeug; Gerät II
tooth *(sg)* [tuːθ], **teeth** *(pl)* [tiːθ] Zahn III U2, 39
toothbrush ['tuːθbrʌʃ] Zahnbürste III U5, 96
toothpaste ['tuːθpeɪst] Zahnpasta III U5, 97
toothpick ['tuːθpɪk] Zahnstocher II
top [tɒp] Top; Oberteil II; oberer Teil; oberes Ende III U4, 92
at the top [æt ðə 'tɒp] oben III U4, 92
topic ['tɒpɪk] Thema <II>
torch [tɔːtʃ] Taschenlampe I
tornado [tɔː'neɪdəʊ] Tornado <III U3, 73>
caber **toss** ['keɪbə ˌtɒs] Baumstammwerfen <III U3, 134>
*to keep in **touch** [ˌkiːp ɪn 'tʌtʃ] in Verbindung bleiben II
to **touch** [tʌtʃ] berühren III U1, 20
tough [tʌf] hart III U2, 34
tour [tʊə] Tour; Fahrt; Reise <III U1, 30>
tourist ['tʊərɪst] Tourist; Touristin I
Tourist Information Centre ['tʊərɪst ɪnfə'meɪʃn ˌsentə] Touristeninformation I
to **tow away** ['təʊ ˌəweɪ] abschleppen <III U4, 86>
towel ['taʊəl] Handtuch III U5, 96
tower ['taʊə] Turm II
clock tower ['klɒk ˌtaʊə] Uhrenturm II
town [taʊn] Stadt I
town hall [ˌtaʊn 'hɔːl] Rathaus II
toy [tɔɪ] Spielzeug III U2, 39
cuddly toy ['kʌdli ˌtɔɪ] Kuscheltier III U2, 39
tractor ['træktə] Traktor I
tradition [trə'dɪʃn] Tradition III U3, 53
traditional [trə'dɪʃnl] traditionell III U5, 96
traffic light ['træfɪk ˌlaɪt] (Verkehrs-)Ampel <III U1, 184>
traffic ['træfɪk] Verkehr III U1, 16
train [treɪn] Zug I

trained [treɪnd] ausgebildet <III U1, 130>
trainer ['treɪnə] Turnschuh I
training ['treɪnɪŋ] Training III U2, 41
tram [træm] Straßenbahn III U5, 100
translation [trænz'leɪʃn] Übersetzung <III U3, 73>
transparent [træn'spærnt] durchsichtig <III U3, 71>
public **transport** [ˌpʌblɪk 'trænspɔ:t] öffentliche Verkehrsmittel III U5, 100
time **travel** ['taɪm ˌtrævl] Zeitreise III U4, 79
to **travel** ['trævl] reisen II; fahren III U5, 103
traveller ['trævlə] Reisender; Reisende <III U1, 17>
tray [treɪ] Tablett II
treasure ['treʒə] Schatz II
treat [tri:t] Leckerbissen <III U3, 66>
tree [tri:] Baum I
tribe [traɪb] Stamm; Volksstamm <III U1, 28>
trick [trɪk] Trick; Streich I; Kunststück III U2, 41
Trick or treat! [ˌtrɪk‿ə 'tri:t] Süßes, sonst gibt's Saures! I
trip [trɪp] Ausflug I; Trip; Fahrt III U2, 34; Reise III U3, 58
boat trip ['bəʊt ˌtrɪp] Bootsfahrt; Schiffsfahrt II
school trip [ˌsku:l 'trɪp] Klassenfahrt I
to take a trip [ˌteɪk‿ə 'trɪp] eine Fahrt machen III U2, 34
trolley suitcase ['trɒli ˌsu:tkeɪs] Rollkoffer III U3, 57
trouble ['trʌbl] Schwierigkeiten; Problem; Ärger III U2, 33
to get into trouble [ˌget‿ɪntə 'trʌbl] in Schwierigkeiten geraten <III U2, 132>
trousers *(pl)* ['traʊzəz] Hose I
truck [trʌk] Wagen; Karre III U1, 21
true [tru:] wahr II
truth [tru:θ] Wahrheit <III U4, 77>
to **try** [traɪ] probieren; versuchen II
to try on [ˌtraɪ‿'ɒn] anprobieren II
to try out [ˌtraɪ‿'aʊt] ausprobieren III U2, 43
T-shirt ['ti:ʃɜ:t] T-Shirt I
TTYL (Talk to you later!) ['tɔ:k tə ju ˌleɪtə] Wir reden später! II
tube [tju:b] Schlauch; Rohr III U3, 55
Tuesday ['tju:zdeɪ] Dienstag I
on Tuesday [ˌɒn 'tju:zdeɪ] am Dienstag I
tuna ['tju:nə] Thunfisch II
tunnel ['tʌnl] Tunnel III U1, 20
(wind) **turbine** [(wɪnd) 'tɜ:baɪn] Windrad III U3, 53
Turkish bath [ˌtɜ:kɪʃ 'bɑ:θ] Dampfbad III U4, 84
It's Holly's **turn.** [ɪts 'hɒliz ˌtɜ:n] Holly ist dran. II
to take turns [ˌteɪk 'tɜ:nz] sich abwechseln <II>
Your turn. [ˌjɔ: 'tɜ:n] Du bist dran. II
to **turn** [tɜ:n] abbiegen III U1, 12
to turn around [ˌtɜ:n‿ə'raʊnd] (sich) umdrehen III U1, 22
to turn left [ˌtɜ:n 'left] (nach) links abbiegen I
to turn right [ˌtɜ:n 'raɪt] (nach) rechts abbiegen I
turning point ['tɜ:nɪŋ ˌpɔɪnt] Wendepunkt <III U2, 45>
tutor ['tju:tə] Klassenlehrer; Klassenlehrerin I
tutor group ['tju:tə ˌgru:p] Klasse *(in einer englischen Schule)* I
TV [ˌti:'vi:] Fernseher; Fernsehen I
TV show [ˌti: 'vi: ˌʃəʊ] Fernsehsendung II
TV studio [ˌti:'vi: ˌstju:diəʊ] Fernsehstudio II
to watch TV [ˌwɒtʃ ti:'vi:] fernsehen I
tweet [twi:t] Pieps III U1, 22
twelve [twelv] zwölf I
twenty ['twenti] zwanzig I
twenty-one [ˌtwenti'wʌn] einundzwanzig I
to **twist** [twɪst] verdrehen; verzerren II
two [tu:] zwei I
type [taɪp] Sorte; Typ; Art III U1, 31
to **type** [taɪp] tippen <III U2, 47>
tyre [taɪə] Reifen III U3, 55

U

umbrella [ʌm'brelə] Regenschirm II
umpire ['ʌmpaɪə] Schiedsrichter; Schiedsrichterin <III U5, 109>
uncle ['ʌŋkl] Onkel I
uncomfortable [ʌn'kʌmftəbl] unbequem; unangenehm II
under ['ʌndə] unter I
underground ['ʌndəgraʊnd] U-Bahn II
underlined [ˌʌndə'laɪnd] unterstrichen <III U3, 73>
*to **understand** [ˌʌndə'stænd] verstehen II
understood [ˌʌndə'stʊd] simple past von *to understand* II
underwater [ˌʌndə'wɔ:tə] Unterwasser- <III U3, 70>
unemployment *(no pl)* [ˌʌnɪm'plɔɪmənt] Arbeitslosigkeit <III U4, 137>
unexpected [ˌʌnɪk'spektɪd] unerwartet <III U5, 113>
unfair [ʌn'feə] unfair III U1, 16
unfashionable [ʌn'fæʃnəbl] unmodisch II
unfriendly [ʌn'frendli] unfreundlich III U2, 35
unhappy [ʌn'hæpi] unglücklich II
unicorn ['ju:nɪkɔ:n] Einhorn <III U1, 28>
uniform ['ju:nɪfɔ:m] Uniform I
unit ['ju:nɪt] Lektion; Kapitel <I>
university [ˌju:nɪ'vɜ:səti] Universität III U3, 52
unlike [ʌn'laɪk] anders als; im Gegensatz zu III U5, 94
unpopular [ʌn'pɒpjələ] unpopulär; unbeliebt III U2, 35
unreal [ʌn'rɪəl] irreal <III U5, 101>
untied [ʌn'taɪd] nicht zugebunden <III U1, 17>

until [ʌn'tɪl] bis I
unusual [ʌn'ju:ʒl] ungewöhnlich <II>
up [ʌp] hinauf; oben II
to make up [ˌmeɪk‿'ʌp] erfinden; sich ausdenken <III U1, 18>
up to ['ʌp tə] bis zu <III U3, 134>
to **upload** ['ʌpləʊd] hochladen; ins Internet stellen II
upper ['ʌpə] obere III U4, 92
upset [ʌp'set] aufgebracht; bestürzt I
us [ʌs] wir; uns I
to **use** [ju:z] benutzen; verwenden II
used to (live) ['ju:st tə] (wohnte) früher III U1, 16
useful ['ju:sfl] nützlich; hilfreich III U2, 34
usually ['ju:ʒli] normalerweise; gewöhnlich II

V

no **vacancies** [ˌnəʊ 'veɪknsiz] kein Zimmer frei <III U4, 86>
in **vain** [ɪn 'veɪn] umsonst; vergeblich <III U5, 101>
valid ['vælɪd] gültig III U5, 100
van [væn] Lieferwagen; Transporter III U4, 93
vegetable (veg) ['vedʒtəbl] Gemüse II
vegetarian [ˌvedʒɪ'teəriən] Vegetarier; Vegetarierin I
veggie bean cake [ˌvedʒi 'bi:n keɪk] *vegetarisches Bohnengericht* II
vehicle ['vɪəkl] Fahrzeug <III U4, 86>
verb [vɜ:b] Verb <III U3, 60>
verse [vɜ:s] Vers; Strophe <III U1, 23>
version ['vɜ:ʃn] Version <III U1, 27>
very ['veri] sehr I
very first ['veri fɜ:st] allererste III U4, 84
vet [vet] Tierarzt; Tierärztin III U3, 55
Victorian era [vɪkˌtɔ:riən 'ɪərə] viktorianisches Zeitalter III U1, 25
video ['vɪdiəʊ] Video II
video chat ['vɪdiəʊ ˌtʃæt] Video-Chat III U3, 67
point of **view** [ˌpɔɪnt‿əv 'vju:] Standpunkt; Perspektive <III U2, 133>
viewing ['vju:ɪŋ] Hör-/Sehverstehen <I>
Viking ['vaɪkɪŋ] Wikinger; Wikingerin <III U5, 138>
Viking ['vaɪkɪŋ] Wikinger- III U1, 11
village ['vɪlɪdʒ] Dorf III U1, 16
violence *(no pl)* ['vaɪəlns] Gewalt <III U4, 137>
violent ['vaɪəlnt] gewaltsam; gewalttätig; brutal <III U4, 136>
visa ['vi:zə] Visum; Einreisebewilligung <III U5, 215>
visit ['vɪzɪt] Besuch III U1, 12
to **visit** ['vɪzɪt] besuchen II
visitor ['vɪzɪtə] Besucher; Besucherin II
vocabulary [və'kæbjəlri] Vokabular; Wortschatz II
voice [vɔɪs] Stimme III U1, 22
volunteer [ˌvɒlən'tɪə] Freiwilliger; Freiwillige; ehrenamtlicher Helfer; ehrenamtliche Helferin III U2, 33
voyage ['vɔɪɪdʒ] Reise; Fahrt III U4, 84

W

to **wait** [weɪt] warten II
to wait for ['weɪt fɔ:] warten auf II
I can't wait [aɪ ˌkɑ:nt 'weɪt] ich kann es kaum erwarten III U5, 100
waiter ['weɪtə] Kellner II
*to **wake** up [ˌweɪk‿'ʌp] aufwachen II
walk [wɔ:k] Spaziergang III U3, 61
to go on a night walk [ˌgəʊ ɒn‿ə 'naɪt wɔ:k] eine Nachtwanderung machen I
night walk [ˌnaɪt 'wɔ:k] Nachtwanderung I
to take the dog for a walk [ˌteɪk ðə ˌdɒg fər‿ə 'wɔ:k] den Hund spazieren führen II
a five minute walk [ə 'faɪv mɪnɪt ˌwɔ:k] fünf Minuten zu Fuß III U1, 12
to **walk** [wɔ:k] gehen I; laufen II
walking ['wɔ:kɪŋ] Wandern III U3, 61
wall [wɔ:l] Mauer; Wand II
wallet ['wɒlɪt] Brieftasche; Geldbörse III U4, 80
to **want** (to) [wɒnt (tə)] wollen I
wardrobe ['wɔ:drəʊb] Kleiderschrank I
warm [wɔ:m] warm I
to **warn** [wɔ:n] warnen III U1, 21
was [wɒz] simple past von *to be* I
to **wash** [wɒʃ] waschen <III U1, 29>; (sich) waschen; spülen III U5, 98
washable ['wɒʃəbl] waschbar <III U3, 201>
*to do the **washing** up [ˌdu: ðə 'wɒʃɪŋ‿ʌp] abspülen II
to **watch** [wɒtʃ] anschauen; ansehen I; aufpassen auf; zuschauen; beobachten II
to watch TV [ˌwɒtʃ ti:'vi:] fernsehen I
bird **watching** ['bɜ:d ˌwɒtʃɪŋ] Vogelbeobachtung III U3, 61
mineral **water** ['mɪnrl ˌwɔ:tə] Mineralwasser III U4, 81
water ['wɔ:tə] Wasser I
bucket of water ['bʌkɪt‿əv ˌwɔ:tə] Eimer Wasser I
waterproof ['wɔ:təpru:f] wasserfest <III U3, 71>
waterproofs ['wɔ:təpru:fs] Regenbekleidung <III U2, 193>
wave [weɪv] Welle I
to **wave** [weɪv] winken II
wax [wæks] Wachs <III U1, 30>
way [weɪ] Weg III U1, 12; Art und Weise III U3, 58
No way! [ˌnəʊ 'weɪ] Auf keinen Fall!; Was?!; Echt?! III U3, 58
way in [ˌweɪ 'ɪn] Einstieg <I>
asking the way ['ɑ:skɪŋ ðə ˌweɪ] nach dem Weg fragen I
Can you tell me the way to …? [kæn ju: 'tel mi ðə ˌweɪ tə] Kannst du mir sagen, wie ich nach … komme? I
I know my way around here. [aɪ ˌnəʊ maɪ 'weɪ əraʊnd ˌhɪə] Ich kenne mich hier aus. III U1, 12

No way am I doing that again! [ˌnəʊ ˈweɪ əm aɪ ˌduːɪŋ ðæt əˈgen] Das mache ich auf keinen Fall noch mal! III U2, 34
on the way [ˌɒn ðə ˌweɪ] auf dem Weg; unterwegs I
this way [ðɪs ˈweɪ] in diese Richtung II
this way [ˈðɪs weɪ] auf diese Weise <III U1, 28>; <III U5, 112>
way to go [ˈweɪ tə ˌgəʊ] super II
we [wiː; wi] wir I
weak [wiːk] schwach III U2, 35
wealth [welθ] Reichtum III U5, 105
*to **wear** [weə] tragen *(Kleidung)* I
weather [ˈweðə] Wetter I
web [web] Spinnennetz; Netz III U3, 63
website [ˈwebsaɪt] Website II
wedding [ˈwedɪŋ] Hochzeit II
Wednesday [ˈwenzdeɪ] Mittwoch I
on Wednesdays [ɒn ˈwenzdeɪz] mittwochs I
week [wiːk] Woche I
on **weekdays** [ɒn ˈwiːkdeɪz] unter der Woche; an Werktagen III U5, 96
weekend [ˈwiːkend] Wochenende I
at the weekend [ˌət ðə ˈwiːkend] am Wochenende I
weekly [ˈwiːkli] wöchentlich III U5, 101
to **weigh** [weɪ] wiegen II
to shift your **weight** [ˌʃɪft jɔː ˈweɪt] sein Gewicht verlagern <III U5, 111>
to **welcome** [ˈwelkəm] willkommen heißen <III U4, 136>
You're welcome. [jɔː ˈwelkəm] Gern geschehen. I
welcome (to) [ˈwelkəm (tʊ)] willkommen (bei/in) I
well [wel] gut II
Well done! [ˌwel ˈdʌn] Gut gemacht! I
well [wel] na ja I
welly [ˈweli] Gummistiefel I
Welsh [welʃ] Walisisch; walisisch; Waliser; Waliserin III U2, 32
went [went] simple past von *to go* I
were [wɜː] simple past von *to be* I

west [west] Westen III U1, 10
westbound [ˈwesbaʊnd] in Richtung Westen <III U5, 216>
wet [wet] nass I
what [wɒt] was I; welche II; wie III U1, 12
What a … [ˈwɒt‿ə] Was für ein/eine … I
What about you? [ˌwɒt‿əbaʊt ˈjuː] Und du? II
What about …? [ˈwɒt‿əˌbaʊt] Was ist mit …? I
What colour is …? [ˌwɒt ˈkʌlə ɪz] Welche Farbe hat …? I
what else [ˌwɒt‿ˈels] was noch; was sonst III U5, 96
What else can you …? [ˌwɒt‿ˈels kæn juː] Was kannst du noch …? <I>
What happened? [ˌwɒt ˈhæpnd] Was ist geschehen?; Was ist passiert? I
What must you be like? [wɒt ˌmʌst ju ˈbiː laɪk] Wie musst du sein? III U2, 37
what sth was like [ˌwɒt … ˈwɒz laɪk] wie etwas war III U1, 12
What time is it? [ˌwɒt ˈtaɪm‿ɪz‿ɪt] Wie spät ist es?; Wie viel Uhr ist es? I
What to … [ˈwɒt tə] Was man … II
What's your name? [ˌwɒts jə ˈneɪm] Wie heißt du? I
What's wrong? [ˌwɒts ˈrɒŋ] Was ist los?; Was stimmt nicht? II
wheel [wiːl] Rad II
big wheel [ˌbɪg ˈwiːl] Riesenrad II
wheelchair [ˈwiːltʃeə] Rollstuhl III U2, 43
when [wen] wenn; als II
when [wen] wann I
where [weə] wo; wohin; woher I
Where are you from? [ˌweər‿ə ju ˈfrɒm] Woher kommst du? I
wherever [weəˈrevə] wo(hin) auch immer; egal wo(hin); überall wo(hin) III U5, 107
which [wɪtʃ] welche II

which [wɪtʃ] die; der; dem; den; das III U3, 54
while [waɪl] während II
white [waɪt] weiß I
who [huː] wer I
Who is it? [ˌhuː ˈɪz‿ɪt] Wer ist da? I
Who's up there? [ˌhuz ʌp ˈðeə] Wer ist da oben? I
who [huː] die; welche II; der; dem; den III U3, 54
whole [həʊl] ganz III U5, 104
whom [huːm] wen; wem III U3, 64
whose [huːz] dessen; deren III U3, 54
why [waɪ] warum I
that's why [ˈðæts waɪ] deswegen III U5, 100
wide [waɪd] breit <III U3, 70>
wife *(sg)* [waɪf], **wives** *(pl)* [waɪvz] Ehefrau III U3, 54
wild [waɪld] wild III U3, 53
will [wɪl] werden II
*to **win** [wɪn] gewinnen; siegen I
wind [wɪnd] Wind I
wind farm [ˈwɪnd fɑːm] Windpark III U3, 53
window [ˈwɪndəʊ] Fenster I
Close the window. [ˈkləʊz ðə ˌwɪndəʊ] Schließe das Fenster. I
windowsill [ˈwɪndəʊsɪl] Fenstersims <III U1, 17>
windscreen wiper [ˈwɪnskriːn ˌwaɪpə] Scheibenwischer III U3, 57
windsurfing [ˈwɪndsɜːfɪŋ] Windsurfen <III U2, 193>
windy [ˈwɪndi] windig I
winner [ˈwɪnə] Sieger; Siegerin; Gewinner; Gewinnerin I
winter [ˈwɪntə] Winter I
windscreen **wiper** [ˈwɪnskriːn ˌwaɪpə] Scheibenwischer III U3, 57
wire [ˈwaɪə] Draht; Kabel III U3, 54
Best **wishes**, [ˌbest ˈwɪʃɪz] Viele Grüße, I
to **wish** [wɪʃ] wünschen III U1, 25
witch [wɪtʃ] Hexe I
with [wɪð] mit I
without [wɪˈðaʊt] ohne III U4, 76

woke up [ˌwəʊkˈʌp] simple past von *to wake up* II
woman *(sg)* [ˈwʊmən], **women** *(pl)* [ˈwɪmɪn] Frau I
women's national team [ˌwɪmɪnz ˈnæʃnl tiːm] Frauen-Nationalmannschaft <III U1, 24>
won [wʌn] simple past von *to win* I; past participle von *to win* II
won't (= will not) [wəʊnt] nicht werden II
It won't be long. [ɪt ˌwəʊnt bi ˈlɒŋ] Es wird nicht lange dauern. II
won't matter [ˌwəʊnt ˈmætə] wird nicht von Bedeutung sein; wird nichts ausmachen <III U5, 101>
wonderful [ˈwʌndəfl] wunderbar III U5, 105
wood [wʊd] Holz III U3, 54
wood [wʊd] Holz I; Wald III U2, 34
wool [wʊl] Wolle I
word [wɜːd] Wort <I>
root word [ˌruːt ˈwɜːd] Stammwort <III U3, 73>
signal word [ˈsɪgnl ˌwɜːd] Signalwort <III U2, 41>
work [wɜːk] Arbeit I
to **work** [wɜːk] arbeiten I; funktionieren II
workbook [ˈwɜːkbʊk] Arbeitsheft I
worker [ˈwɜːkə] Arbeiter; Arbeiterin II
workshop [ˈwɜːkʃɒp] Workshop II
acting workshop [ˈæktɪŋ ˌwɜːkʃɒp] Schauspielworkshop II
world [wɜːld] Welt II
all around the world [ɔːl‿əˌraʊnd ðə ˈwɜːld] in aller Welt III U5, 95
from around the world [frəm‿əˌraʊnd ðə ˈwɜːld] aus aller Welt <III U3, 134>
in the world [ɪn ðə ˈwɜːld] auf der Welt II
worn [wɔːn] past participle von *to wear* II
worried [ˈwʌrid] beunruhigt; besorgt II
to **worry** [ˈwʌri] sich Sorgen machen I
Don't worry. [ˌdəʊnt ˈwʌri] Mach dir keine Sorgen. II
worst [wɜːst] schlimmste; schlechteste III U1, 16
*to **be worth** [biː ˈwɜːθ] wert sein III U1, 12
would [wʊd] würde(n) II
would like [wʊd ˈlaɪk] würde(n) gern; hätte(n) gern II
I'd love to ... (= I would love to) [aɪd ˈlʌv tə] Ich würde sehr gern ... III U3, 58
Would you like (to) ...? [ˌwʊd jə ˈlaɪk (tə)] Möchtest du? I
I wouldn't like (to) ... [aɪ ˈwʊdnt laɪk (tə)] Ich möchte nicht ...; Ich würde nicht gerne ... I
wound [wuːnd] Wunde; Verletzung <III U2, 194>
wrap [ræp] Wrap II
*to **write** [raɪt] schreiben I
to write down [ˌraɪt ˈdaʊn] aufschreiben <III U1, 24>
writer [ˈraɪtə] Schriftsteller; Schriftstellerin II; Verfasser; Verfasserin; Autor; Autorin III U2, 50
writing [ˈraɪtɪŋ] Schreiben <I>
wrong [rɒŋ] falsch I
to be wrong [biː ˈrɒŋ] unrecht haben; sich irren III U4, 76
to get a job wrong [ˌget‿ə dʒɒb ˈrɒŋ] einen Auftrag vermasseln III U2, 50
Is something wrong? [ɪz ˈsʌmθɪŋ rɒŋ] Stimmt etwas nicht? II
What's wrong? [ˌwɒts ˈrɒŋ] Was ist los?; Was stimmt nicht? II
wrote [rəʊt] simple past von *to write* I

Y

yeah *(infml)* [jeə] ja II
year [jɪə] Jahr; Jahrgangsstufe; Klasse I
yellow [ˈjeləʊ] gelb I
yes [jes] ja I
yesterday [ˈjestədeɪ] gestern I
yet [jet] schon II
not ... yet [nɒt ... ˈjet] noch nicht II
yippee [jɪˈpiː] hurra II
yogurt [ˈjɒgət] Joghurt II
you [juː] du; Sie; ihr; euch; dich; dir; Ihnen I
You're right. [jɔːˈraɪt] Du hast recht. I
You're welcome. [jɔː ˈwelkəm] Gern geschehen. I
young [jʌŋ] jung II
your [jɔː] dein, deine; euer, eure; Ihr, Ihre I
yours [jɔːz] deine; eure; Ihre I
Yours, [jɔːz] Eure *(als Briefabschluss)* I
yourself [jɔːˈself] dich selbst II
by yourself [baɪ ˈjɔːself] allein II
yourselves [jɔːˈselvz] ihr/euch/Sie/sich (selbst); selber III U2, 156
Help yourselves! [ˌhelp jɔːˈselvz] Bedient euch!; Bedienen Sie sich! II
youth hostel [ˈjuːθ ˌhɒstl] Jugendherberge III U3, 59
youth *(no pl)* [juːθ] Jugend; Jugend-; III U5, 94
yummy [ˈjʌmi] lecker II

Z

zebra [ˈzebrə] Zebra I
zero [ˈzɪərəʊ] null I
zip line [ˈzɪp ˌlaɪn] Seilrutsche III U2, 32
zoo [zuː] Zoo; Tierpark I
zookeeper [ˌzuːˈkiːpə] Tierpfleger; Tierpflegerin I
to **zoom** in [ˈzuːm‿ɪn] heranzoomen <I>

Boys' names

Alan [ˈælən] III U5, 103
Alex [ˈælɪks] II
Ashley [ˈæʃli] III U4, 76
Barney [ˈbɑːni] I
Barry [ˈbæri] I
Bart [bɑːt] III U1, 21

Ben [ben] I
Bertie ['bɜ:ti] <III U5, 139>
Billy ['bɪli] III U1, 20
Brad [bræd] II
Conor ['kɒnə] III U5, 96
Dan [dæn] III U4, 80
Dave [deɪv] I
Desmond ['dezmənd] I
Dylan ['dɪlən] III ZI 9
Edward ['edwəd] <III U1, 130>
Frank [fræŋk] I
Fred [fred] I
George [dʒɔ:dʒ] III U4, 75
Hamid ['hæmɪd] I
Harold ['hærəld] <III U1, 130>
Harry ['hæri] III U3, 58
Howard ['haʊəd] <III U2, 132>
Ian ['i:ən] III U4, 80
Jahangir ['dʒəhæŋgɪr] I
Jake [dʒeɪk] III U3, 58
Jamie ['dʒeɪmi] I
Jay [dʒeɪ] I
Jim [dʒɪm] I
Jinsoo ['dʒɪnsu:] I
Joe [dʒəʊ] II
John [dʒɒn] <III U2, 133>
John [dʒɒn] III U4, 85
Jonas ['dʒəʊnəs] III U1, 20
Keith [ki:θ] III U5, 95
Leo ['li:əʊ] III U5, 96
Lewis ['lʊɪs] III ZI 9
Luke [lu:k] I
Malcolm ['mælkəm] <III U3, 134>
Mark [mɑ:k] III U2, 34
Marley ['mɑ:li] I
Max [mæks] <III U5, 112>
Nathan ['neɪθn] I
Nick [nɪk] II
Patrick ['pætrɪk] III ZI 9
Paul [pɔ:l] I
Peter ['pi:tə] I
Richard ['rɪtʃəd] III U2, 42
Rob [rɒb] I
Sam [sæm] I
Sean [ʃɔ:n] III U4, 87
Seb [seb] III U4, 79
Shahid ['ʃɑ:hɪd] I
Sherlock ['ʃɜ:lɒk] I
Sid [sɪd] I
Simon ['saɪmən] I
Spike [spaɪk] III U5, 99
Steve [sti:v] III U4, 79
Tom [tɒm] I
Toni ['təʊni] I
William ['wɪljəm] <III U1, 130>

Girls' names

Abby ['æbi] III U3, 58
Alicia [ə'lɪʃə] I
Alva ['ælvə] III U3, 67
Amber ['æmbə] I
Beth [beθ] III U2, 34
Billy ['bɪli] III U5, 104
Carol ['kærl] III U4, 79
Ciara ['kiərə] III U5, 107
Claire [kleə] I
Daisy ['deɪzi] III U1, 16
Dianne [daɪ'æn] <III U3, 59>
Ellie ['eli] III U2, 43
Emily ['emɪli] III ZI 9
Gwen [gwen] II
Hannah ['hænə] III U1, 16
Hayley ['heɪli] III U5, 107
Helen ['helɪn] III U5, 103
Holly ['hɒli] I
Irina [i'ri:nə] I
Jamila [dʒə'mi:lə] II
Janet ['dʒænɪt] I
Julie ['dʒu:li] III U4, 74
Kate [keɪt] I
Katie ['keɪti] III U3, 58
Kim [kɪm] III U2, 41
Laura ['lɔ:rə] I
Lisa ['li:sə] I
Lizzy ['lɪzi] I
Lucy ['lu:si] I
Maddy ['mædi] III U5, 96
Maggie ['mægi] III U4, 75
Maisie ['meɪzi] II
Mary ['meəri] I
Megan ['megən] III U2, 40
Mina ['mi:nə] II
Molly ['mɒli] II
Niamh [ni:v] III U5, 104
Nichola ['nɪklə] II
Nisha ['nɪʃə] III U5, 104
Olivia [ɒl'ɪviə] I
Pamela ['pæmələ] II
Parule ['pəru:l] I
Polly ['pɒli] II
Rachel ['reɪtʃl] I
Sally ['sæli] I
Sarah ['seərə] III U4, 74
Sharon ['ʃærən] III U1, 13
Sonya ['sɒnjə] III U5, 104
Sophie ['səʊfi] III ZI 9
Susan ['su:zn] <III U2, 133>
Violet ['vaɪələt] III U1, 25

Surnames

Adams ['ædəmz] III U2, 38
Ahern [ə'hɜ:n] <III U5, 139>
Archer ['ɑ:tʃə] <III U1, 131>
Azad ['æzæd] I
Becket ['bekɪt] III U2, 45
Brown [braʊn] III U4, 74
Burgess ['bɜ:dʒəs] II
Darcy ['dɑ:si] <III U1, 131>
Elliot ['eliət] I
Fox [fɒks] III U1, 20
Fraser ['freɪzə] I
Green [gri:n] II
Hanley ['hænli] III U5, 95
Hardy ['hɑ:di] II
Jenkins ['dʒeŋkɪnz] III U1, 12
Kapoor ['kæpɔ:] I
Kent [kent] III U2, 36
Link [lɪŋk] <III U2, 132>
MacGowan [mə'gaʊən] III U3, 61
McCane [mə'keɪn] II
Merchant ['mɜ:tʃnt] <III U2, 133>
Nair [neə] II
O'Brian [ə'braɪən] III U5, 96
Preston ['prestən] I
Reedman [ri:dmæn] II
Richardson ['rɪtʃədsn] I
Robbins ['rɒbɪnz] I
Safi ['sæfi] I
Simpson ['sɪmsən] III U4, 85
Smith [smɪθ] III U2, 42
Swindon ['swɪndən] I
Taylor ['teɪlə] <III U2, 133>

Thomas [ˈtɒməs] III U2, 38
Thompson [ˈtɒmpsn] III U4, 80
Warren [ˈwɒrn] I
Yeates [jeɪts] III U2, 42

Place names

Africa [ˈæfrɪkə] Afrika II
America [əˈmerɪkə] Amerika II
Australia [ɒsˈtreɪliə] Australien I
Ballyronan [ˌbælɪˈrəʊnən] *Ort in Nordirland* III U4, 80
Bannockburn [ˈbænəkbɜ:n] *Ort in Schottland* III U3, 64
Bavaria [bəˈveəriə] Bayern II
Belfast [belˈfɑ:st] *Hauptstadt von Nordirland* III U4, 74
Berlin [bɜ:ˈlɪn] Berlin II
Blackhorse [ˈblækhɔ:s] *Straßenbahnhaltestelle in Dublin* III U5, 101
Boston [ˈbɒstən] *Stadt in den USA* III U3, 54
Bramford [ˈbræmfəd] *Dorf in Nordengland* III U1, 16
Brighton [ˈbraɪtn] *Küstenstadt in Südostengland* III U1, 17
Bristol [ˈbrɪstl] *Stadt in Südwestengland* II
The **British Isles** [ðə ˌbrɪtɪʃ ˈaɪlz] die Britischen Inseln III ZI 8
Cambridge [ˈkeɪmbrɪdʒ] *Stadt in Ostengland* <III U1, 24>
Canada [ˈkænədə] Kanada III U3, 54
Cardiff [ˈkɑ:dɪf] *Hauptstadt von Wales* III U2, 33
Central Europe [ˌsentrl ˈjʊərəp] Mitteleuropa <III U5, 138>
Cork [kɔ:k] *Stadt in Irland* III U5, 95
Cornwall [ˈkɔ:nwɔ:l] *Grafschaft in Südwestengland* II
The **Czech Republic** [ðə ˌtʃek rɪˈpʌblɪk] Tschechien II
Denmark [ˈdenmɑ:k] Dänemark III U1, 11
Devon [ˈdevn] *Grafschaft in Südwestengland* I
Donegal [ˌdɒnɪˈgɔ:l] *Ort in Irland* III U5, 104
Dublin [ˈdʌblɪn] *Hauptstadt von Irland* III U4, 76
Edinburgh [ˈedɪnbrə] *Hauptstadt von Schottland* III U3, 52
England [ˈɪŋglənd] England I
Europe [ˈjʊərəp] Europa II
France [frɑ:ns] Frankreich II
Germany [ˈdʒɜ:məni] Deutschland I
Glasgow [ˈglɑ:zgəʊ] *Stadt in Schottland* III U3, 61
Goldenbridge [ˌgəʊldnˈbrɪdʒ] *Stadtteil von Dublin* III U5, 100
Great Britain [ˌgreɪt ˈbrɪtn] Großbritannien III ZI 8
Greenwich [ˈgrenɪdʒ] *Stadtteil im Südosten Londons* I
Hastings [ˈheɪstɪŋz] *Stadt in Südostengland* III U1, 11
India [ˈɪndiə] Indien I
Inverness [ˌɪnvəˈnes] *Ort in Nordschottland* III U3, 58
Isle of Skye [ˌaɪl‿əv ˈskaɪ] *Insel in Nordwestschottland* III U3, 61
Isle of Wight [ˌaɪl əv ˈwaɪt] *Insel südlich von England* II
Italy [ˈɪtəli] Italien II
Jamaica [dʒəˈmeɪkə] Jamaika II
Kingskerswell [ˌkɪŋkəˈswel] *Ort in Südengland* <III U5, 112>
Lisburn [ˈlɪzbɜ:n] *Stadt in Nordirland* III U4, 92
Liverpool [ˈlɪvəpu:l] *Stadt in Nordwestengland* III U1, 17
Llanberis [lænˈberɪs] *Ort in Wales* III U2, 36
Llandudno [lænˈdɪdnəʊ] *Küstenort in Wales* III U2, 38
London [ˈlʌndən] *Hauptstadt von England* I
Manchester [ˈmæntʃɪstə] *Stadt im Norden von England* II
Margate [ˈmɑ:geɪt] *Ausflugsort in England* I
Milltown [ˈmɪltaʊn] *Stadtteil von Dublin* III U5, 101
The **Netherlands** [ðə ˈneðələndz] die Niederlande II
New York [ˌnju: ˈjɔ:k] *Großstadt in den USA* III U4, 84
Newcastle [ˈnju:ˌkɑ:sl] *Stadt in Nordostengland* III U1, 16
Northampton [ˌnɔ:ˈθæmtən] *Stadt in Mittelengland* III U5, 104
Northern Ireland [ˌnɔ:ðn‿ˈaɪələnd] Nordirland III ZI 8
Norway [ˈnɔ:weɪ] Norwegen III U1, 11
Oxford [ˈɒksfəd] *Stadt in Südostengland* <III U1, 28>
Paris [ˈpærɪs] Paris II
Poland [ˈpəʊlənd] Polen II
Powys [ˈpəʊɪs] *Stadt in Wales* III U2, 34
Randalstown [ˈrændlztaʊn] *Ort in Nordirland* III U4, 75
The **Republic of Ireland** [ðə rɪˌpʌblɪk‿əv‿ˈaɪələnd] Irland III ZI 8
Rugby [ˈrʌgbi] *Stadt in Mittelengland* <III U1, 24>
Scotland [ˈskɒtlənd] Schottland III ZI 8
Senlac Hill [ˌsenlæk ˈhɪl] *Ort in der Nähe von Hastings* <III U1, 130>
Snowdonia [snəʊˈdəʊniə] *Nationalpark in Nordwales* <III U2, 44>
South Pole [ˈsaʊθ ˌpəʊl] Südpol II
Southampton [saʊˈθæmtən] *Hafenstadt in Südengland* III U4, 84
Spain [speɪn] Spanien II
Stamford Bridge [ˈstæmfəd ˌbrɪdʒ] *Ort in Nordengland* <III U1, 130>
Stirling [ˈstɜ:lɪŋ] *Ort in Schottland* III U3, 64
Turkey [ˈtɜ:ki] Türkei II
Uffington [ˈʌfɪŋtən] *Ort in der Nähe von Oxford* <III U1, 28>
UK [ˌju:ˈkeɪ] Vereinigtes Königreich von Großbritannien und Nordirland II
The **United Kingdom** [ðə ju:ˌnaɪtɪd ˈkɪŋdəm] Vereinigtes Königreich von Großbritannien und Nordirland III ZI 8
USA (United States of America) [ˌju:esˈeɪ (ju:ˌnaɪtɪd ˌsteɪts‿əv əˈmerɪkə)] USA (Vereinigte Staaten von Amerika) III U3, 54

Wales [weɪlz] Wales III ZI 8

York [jɔ:k] *Stadt in Nordengland* III U1, 11

Other names

Abbey Street ['æbi ˌstri:t] *Straße in Dublin* III U5, 100

Arsenal ['ɑ:snl] *Name einer Fußballmannschaft* <III U1, 24>

The **Baker** [ˌðə 'beɪkə] *Filmname* III U2, 50

Bayeux Tapestry [ˌbaɪjɜ: 'tæpɪstri] Bayeuxteppich <III U1, 131>

Alexander Graham **Bell** [ˌælɪgzɑ:ndə 'greɪəm bel] *Erfinder des Telefons* III U3, 54

Ben Nevis [ˌben 'nevɪs] *höchster Berg Schottlands* <III U3, 72>

Big Bang Festival [ˌbɪg bæŋ 'festɪvl] *Musikfest in Dublin* III U5, 100

Big Ben [ˌbɪg 'ben] *Sehenswürdigkeit in London* II

Bollywood ['bɒliwʊd] *indische Filmindustrie: Bombay + Hollywood* II

Bond Street ['bɒnd ˌstri:t] *Londoner Straßenname* II

Bram Stoker [ˌbræm 'stəʊkə] *irischer Schriftsteller* <III U5, 139>

Brandenburg Gate ['brændənbɜ:g ˌgeɪt] Brandenburger Tor II

Buckingham Palace [ˌbʌkɪŋəm 'pælɪs] Buckingham-Palast <III U1, 30>

Caldicot Castle ['kɑ:ldɪkɒt ˌkɑ:sl] *Burgruine in Wales* III U2, 42

Camden Market [ˌkæmdən 'mɑ:kɪt] *Markt im Londoner Stadtteil Camden* II

Captain Sparrow [ˌkæptɪn 'spærəʊ] *Filmfigur* II

Cats [kæts] *Musicalname* <III U3, 73>

The **Channel Tunnel** [ðə ˌtʃænl 'tʌnl] Ärmelkanaltunnel III ZI 8

Chelsea ['tʃelsi] *Name einer Fußballmannschaft* <III U1, 24>

Lewis **Clarke** [ˌlʊɪs 'klɑ:k] *Personenname* II

Connolly ['kɒnli] *Bahnhof in Dublin* III U5, 101

Cutty Sark [ˌkʌti 'sɑ:k] *Museumsschiff in Greenwich* I

Duke of Normandy [ˌdju:k‿əv 'nɔ:məndi] *Herzog der Normandie* <III U1, 130>

Edward I [ˌedwəd ðə 'fɜ:st] *König von England (1272–1307)* III U3, 62

Elizabeth Tower [ɪˌlɪzəbəθ 'taʊə] *Sehenswürdigkeit in London* II

European Union [ˌjʊərəpi:ən 'ju:njən] Europäische Union III U5, 94

George's Dock ['dʒɔ:dʒɪz ˌdɒk] *Hafen in Dublin* III U5, 101

Giant's Causeway [ˌdʒaɪənts 'kɔ:zweɪ] *Sehenswürdigkeit in Nordirland* III U4, 74

Glenbow Hotel [ˌglenbəʊ həʊ'tel] *Hotelname* III U2, 38

The **Globe Theatre** [ðə ˌgləʊb 'θɪətə] das Globe-Theater II

Good Friday [ˌgʊd 'fraɪdeɪ] Karfreitag <III U5, 139>

Green Park [ˌgri:n 'pɑ:k] *Park in London* <III U1, 30>

Greenwich Market ['grenɪdʒ ˌmɑ:kɪt] *überdachter Marktplatz in Greenwich* I

Greenwich Park ['grenɪdʒ ˌpɑ:k] *Park in Greenwich* I

Greenwich Shopping Park [ˌgrenɪdʒ 'ʃɒpɪŋ pɑ:k] *Einkaufszentrum in Greenwich* II

Hadrian's Wall [ˌheɪdriənz 'wɔ:l] *Sehenswürdigkeit in Nordengland* III U1, 10

Harley Street ['hɑ:li ˌstri:t] *Londoner Straßenname* II

Harrods ['hærədz] *Kaufhaus in London* II

Henry II [ˌhenri ðə 'seknd] *König von England (1154-1189)* <III U5, 138>

Henry the Eighth [ˌhenri ði 'eɪtθ] *Drama von Shakespeare* II

Henry VIII [ˌhenri ði 'eɪtθ] *König von England (1509-1547)* <III U5, 138>

High Road ['haɪ ˌrəʊd] *Straßenname* II

the **Highlands** [ˌðə 'haɪləndz] *Bergregion in Schottland* III U3, 58

Hollywell School ['hɒliwel ˌsku:l] *Schulname* <III U4, 88>

Hollywood ['hɒliwʊd] *Zentrum der amerikanischen Filmindustrie (in Los Angeles)* II

Hyde Park [ˌhaɪd 'pɑ:k] *Park in London* <III U1, 30>

Irish Sea ['aɪrɪʃ ˌsi:] Irische See III U5, 105

Ivar the Boneless [ˌaɪvə ðə 'bəʊnləs] *Wikingername* III U1, 11

Jedward ['dʒedwəd] *irische Popgruppe* <III U5, 101>

John Dunlop [ˌdʒɒn 'dʌnlɒp] *Erfinder der Gummireifen* III U3, 55

John Lewis ['dʒɒn ˌlu:ɪs] *Name einer Kaufhauskette* II

Kilkenny [kɪl'keni] *Tiername* III U1, 18

Lancelot ['lɑ:nsəlɒt] *Name eines Ritters* III U2, 42

Lionheart ['laɪənhɑ:t] Löwenherz III U2, 42

Loch Ness [ˌlɒk 'nes] *See in Schottland* III U3, 58

The **London Eye** [ðə ˌlʌndən‿'aɪ] *Riesenrad in London* II

London Underground ['lʌndən ˌʌndəgraʊnd] Londoner U-Bahn II

Lough Neagh [ˌlɒx 'neɪ] *See in Nordirland* III U4, 75

Madame Tussauds [ˌmædəm tʊ'sɔ:dz] *Wachsfigurenmuseum in London* <III U1, 30>

Manchester City [ˌmæntʃɪstə 'sɪti] *Name einer Fußballmannschaft* III U1, 16

Michael Collins [ˌmaɪkl 'kɒlɪnz] *irischer Unabhängigkeitskämpfer* <III U5, 139>

Mont Blanc [ˌmɒn 'blɒn] *höchster Berg in Europa* <III U3, 72>

Mount Snowdon [ˌmaʊnt 'snəʊdn] *höchster Berg in Wales* III U2, 32

Nano Nagle [ˌnænəʊ 'neɪgl] *irische Ordensschwester* <III U5, 139>

Nessie ['nesi] *Ungeheuer, das angeblich in Loch Ness wohnt* III U3, 58
Nessie's Nest [ˌnesiz 'nest] *Name einer Frühstückspension* III U3, 61
No Tree Hostel [ˌnəʊ tri: 'hɒstl] *Name einer Herberge* III U3, 61
Norman Conquest [ˌnɔ:mən 'kɒŋkwest] *Normannische Eroberung Englands* <III U1, 130>
Notting Hill Carnival [ˌnɒtɪŋ hɪl 'kɑ:nɪvl] *jährlicher Karneval im Londoner Stadtteil Notting Hill* I
The **O2** [ði 'əʊˌtu:] *Konzertarena in London* II
O'Connell Street [ə'kɒnl ˌstri:t] *Straße in Dublin* III U5, 100
Grace **O'Malley** [ˌgreɪs ə'mæli] *irische Piratin* <III U5, 139>
Oxford Street ['ɒksfəd ˌstri:t] *Einkaufsstraße in London* I
Paddy ['pædi] *Kosename für Patrick* III U5, 105
Phil Lynott [ˌfɪl 'laɪnət] *irischer Sänger und Songwriter* <III U5, 139>
Portobello Road Market [ˌpɔ:təbeləʊ rəʊd 'mɑ:kɪt] *Straßenmarkt in London* <III U1, 30>
Prince George Theatre [ˌprɪns dʒɔ:dʒ 'θɪətə] *Theater in London* II
Queen Victoria [ˌkwi:n vɪk'tɔ:riə] *Königin von England (1837-1901)* <III U1, 25>
Red Line ['red ˌlaɪn] *Straßenbahnlinie in Dublin* III U5, 100
Red Nose Day ['red nəʊz ˌdeɪ] *Spendenmarathon* I
River Humber [ˌrɪvə 'hʌmbə] *Fluss im Nordosten Englands* II
River Severn [ˌrɪvə 'sevn] *Fluss im Südwesten Englands* II
River Thames [ˌrɪvə 'temz] *Fluss in London* II
River Wye [ˌrɪvə 'waɪ] *Fluss in Wales* III U2, 34
RNLI (Royal National Lifeboat Institution) ['ɑ:r‿en el ˌaɪ] *britische Seenotrettungsorganisation* <III U2, 132>
Robert the Bruce ['rɒbət də ˌbru:s] *König von Schottland (1306-1329)* III U3, 52
Rushy Park Coal Mine [ˌrʌʃi pɑ:k 'kəʊl maɪn] *Name eines Kohlebergwerks* III U1, 20
Sackville Place ['sækvɪl ˌpleɪs] *Straßenname in Dublin* III U5, 100
Saint Patrick [snt 'pætrɪk] *Schutzheiliger von Irland* <III U5, 138>
Selfridges ['selfrɪdʒɪz] *Name einer Kaufhauskette* II
William **Shakespeare** [ˌwɪljəm 'ʃeɪkspɪə] *englischer Schriftsteller* II
The **Shambles** [ðə 'ʃæmblz] *Einkaufsstraße in York* III U1, 12
The **Shard** [ðə 'ʃɑ:d] *Name eines Gebäudes in London* II
South Kensington [saʊθ 'kenzɪŋtən] *Londoner U-Bahn-Haltestelle* <III U1, 30>
Spiderman ['spaɪdəmæn] Spiderman II
The **Spire** [ðə 'spaɪə] *Monument und Wahrzeichen von Dublin* III U5, 100
St Patrick's Cross [sn ˌpætrɪks 'krɒs] *Kreuz auf der nordirischen Flagge* <III U5, 108>
St Patrick's Day [sn 'pætrɪks ˌdeɪ] *Feiertag in Irland am 17. März* III U5, 95
St Paul's Cathedral [sənt 'pɔ:lz ˌkəθi:drəl] St.-Pauls-Kathedrale II
Stonehenge [ˌstəʊn'hendʒ] *Sehenswürdigkeit in Südwestengland* III U1, 10
The **Strand** [ðə 'strænd] *Straßenname in London* II
The **Busy Bookworm** [ðə ˌbɪzi 'bʊkwɜ:m] *Name einer Buchhandlung* III U1, 14
Thomas Tallis School [ˌtɒməs 'tælɪs ˌsku:l] *Schulname* I
Tigerboy III ['taɪgəˌbɔɪ 'θri:] *Filmname* III U4, 79
Titanic [taɪ'tænɪk] *Schiffsname* III U4, 75
Torch OneTwo ['tɔ:tʃ wʌnˌtu:] *Rappername* III U5, 98
The **Tower of London** [ðə ˌtaʊər‿əv 'lʌndən] *Sehenswürdigkeit in London* II
Union Flag [ˌju:njən 'flæg] *britische Flagge* <III U5, 108>
Victoria Station [vɪkˌtɔ:riə 'steɪʃn] *Londoner Bahnhof* III U5, 107
Viking Centre ['vaɪkɪŋ ˌsentə] *Wikingermuseum in York* III U1, 12
The **Voice of Ireland** [ðə ˌvɔɪs‿əv 'aɪələnd] *Name einer Fernsehsendung* III U5, 95
Emma **Watson** [ˌemə 'wɒtsn] *Schauspielerin* II
Wembley ['wembli] *Name eines Fußballstadions in London* II
Westminster Abbey ['westmɪnstər‿ˌæbi] *Kirche im Londoner Stadtteil Westminster* II
Westminster Cathedral ['westmɪnstə ˌkəθi:drəl] *Dom im Londoner Stadtteil Westminster* II
The **White Star Line** [ðə ˌwaɪt stɑ: 'laɪn] *Baufirma der Titanic* III U4, 84
Whitelee [ˌwaɪt'li:] *Name eines Windparks in Schottland* III U3, 53
William the Conqueror [ˌwɪljəm ðə 'kɒŋkrə] *englischer König* <III U1, 131>
Zip World ['zɪp ˌwɜ:ld] *Erlebniswelt in Nordwales* <III U2, 44>

A

abbiegen to turn III U1, 12
Abend evening I
  an jenem Abend that night II
  heute Abend tonight II
Abendessen dinner II
(frühes) **Abendessen** tea I
abends in the evenings III U4, 76
Abenteuer adventure I
aber but I
abfahren to leave II
Abfall rubbish II
den Tisch **abräumen** to clear the table II
abschicken *(einen Brief)* to post III U4, 80
Abschieds- leaving II
Abschiedsrede farewell speech II
abschließen to lock I
sich **abseilen** to abseil II
absichtlich on purpose II
abspülen to do the washing up II
Abteilung department II
acht eight I
Achterbahn roller coaster II
achtzehn eighteen I
achtzig eighty I
Adapter adaptor III U5, 96
Adjektiv adjective III U4, 77
Adresse address II
Affe monkey I
äh er I
Ahnung idea I
  Keine Ahnung! No idea! I
Aktenkoffer briefcase III U2, 45
Aktentasche briefcase III U2, 45
Aktivität activity I
albern silly II
alle all I; everyone II
allein alone I; by yourself II
  ganz allein all alone I
allererste very first III U4, 84
Allergie allergy II
allergisch gegen allergic to II
alles klar all right II
alles everything II
Alphabet alphabet I
als than II; as III U3, 54
als when II
Also … Let's see … I
also so I
also right II
alt old I
  Wie alt bist du? How old are you? I
Alter age I
Altglascontainer bottle bank II
Aluminium aluminium III U3, 55
am 7. Juli on 7th July I
  am Dienstag on Tuesday I
  am Ende der Straße at the end of the road I
  am Schluss by the end II
  am Wochenende at the weekend I
sich **amüsieren** to enjoy oneself III U2, 34
an on; at I
  an Bord on board III U4, 84
  an der Spitze (von) at the front of II
Ananas pineapple III U5, 107
Andenken souvenir III U1, 12
andere other I
  ein andere another II
  die anderen the others I
  anderer Meinung sein to disagree II
anderen others II
ein **anderer** another II
andererseits then again III U1, 16
seine Meinung **ändern** to change one's mind III U4, 81
  (sich) ändern to change III U3, 54
anders different I
anders als unlike III U5, 94
Anfang start III U2, 51; beginning III U5, 105
anfangen to start II
Anführer leader III U1, 11
Anführerin leader III U1, 11
angenehm comfortable III U3, 58
angezogen dressed III U5, 105
Angst haben to be scared; to be afraid II
ängstlich afraid II
anhören to listen (to) I
ankommen to arrive II
Ankündigung announcement II
anlegen to put on III U2, 39
anmalen to paint II
Anmeldeformular entry form II
Anmeldung registration II
anprobieren to try on II
Anruf call III U5, 104
anrufen to call I; to phone II
Anrufer caller II
Anruferin caller II
anschauen to watch; to look at I; to have a look II
sich **anschließen** to join III U5, 96
ansehen to watch I
Anspitzer pencil sharpener I
anstoßen to hit III U2, 40
Antenne antenna III U3, 67
Antwort answer II
antworten to answer I
Anzeige advert; advertisement II
anziehen to put on III U2, 39
  sich anziehen to get dressed II
April April I
Arbeit work I; job II
arbeiten to work I
Arbeiter worker II
Arbeiterin worker II
Arbeitsheft workbook I
arbeitsreich busy I
Archiv archive II
Areal area III U5, 104
Ärger trouble III U2, 33
Arm arm I
arm poor I
Armee army III U1, 11
armselig miserable III U5, 105
Art sort II; type III U1, 31; kind III U3, 53
  Art und Weise way III U3, 58
Arzt doctor II
Ärztin doctor II
atmen to breathe III U1, 22
auch too; also I
  auch nicht not … either III U3, 58
auf on; at I
  auf dem Weg on the way I
  auf der linken Seite on the left I

B

bereit ready I
bereits already II
Berg mountain III U1, 17
in den Bergen in the mountains III U1, 17
Bergarbeiter miner III U1, 20
Bergarbeiterin miner III U1, 20
bergen to save III U4, 85
Bergwerk mine III U1, 16
Beruf job II
berühmt famous I
berühren to touch III U1, 20
Besatzung crew III U4, 84
beschäftigt busy I
Beschwerde complaint III U4, 76
sich **beschweren** to complain III U4, 76
eine **Besichtigungstour** machen to go sightseeing II
besitzen to own; to have got II
besonders special I
besonders especially II
besorgt worried II
Besorgungen machen to do the shopping II
besser better I
beste best II
die besten the best II
besteigen to climb III U2, 34
bestellen to order II
bestürzt upset I
Besuch visit III U1, 12
besuchen to visit II
Besucher visitor II
Besucherin visitor II
Beton concrete III U3, 55
betreiben to run III U4, 75
Bett bed I
ins Bett gehen to go to bed I
beunruhigt worried II
Bevölkerung population *(no pl)* III U4, 74
bevor before II
bevorstehen to come up III U3, 58
(sich) **bewegen** to move III U2, 39
Bewegung move III U5, 100
bewerten to rate III U2, 51
Bewohner inhabitant III U1, 16
Bewohnerin inhabitant III U1, 16
bei **Bewusstsein** awake III U2, 38
Bezahlautomat payment machine II
bezahlen to pay II
Bibliothek library III U1, 15
Bild picture II
bilden to make I
billig cheap II
bin am I
Biologie Biology I
bis to II
bis zu before II
Bis bald! See you soon! I
Bis bald. See you later.; See you. I
bis (spätestens) by III U5, 100
bis until I
ein **bisschen** a little; a bit II
bitte please I
Bitte schön. Here you are. I
bitten um to ask for II
blau blue I
der blaue the blue one II
bleiben to stay II
etw. bleiben lassen to give sth a miss III U2, 50
in Verbindung bleiben to keep in touch II
Bleistift pencil I
Blog blog II
Blume flower III U5, 104
Bluse blouse I
bluten to bleed III U2, 38
Boden ground III U3, 64; bottom III U4, 92
Bonbon sweet I
Boot boat II
Bootsfahrt boat trip II
an **Bord** on board III U4, 84
böse angry II; naughty III U2, 43
Boss boss II
Botschaft message II
Box box I
Bratwurst sausage II
brauchen to need I
nicht brauchen needn't I
braun brown I
brechen to break II
brennen to be on fire II; to burn III U2, 39
Brett plank II
Brief letter III U4, 80
Briefmarke stamp III U4, 80
Brieftasche wallet III U4, 80
bringen to bring II
britisch British II
Broschüre brochure III U1, 31
Brot bread II
belegtes Brot sandwich I
Brotlaib loaf III U4, 80
Brücke bridge II
Bruder brother I
Buch book I
Bücherei library III U1, 15
Buchstabe letter III U4, 80
buchstabieren to spell I
Büfett buffet III U3, 58
Bühne stage II
bunt colourful II
Buntstift pencil I
Burg castle II
Büro office II
Bus bus I
im Bus on the bus II
Bushaltestelle bus stop II
Butter butter I

C

Cache *(Geheimschatz)* cache I
Café café I
Cafeteria cafeteria I
Camp camp II
campen gehen to go camping II
Camping camping III U2, 36
Campingplatz campsite III U3, 58
CD CD I
Cent *(Währung)* cent III U5, 100
Center centre III U1, 12
Chance chance II
chatten to chat II
Chef boss II
Chefkoch head chef II
Chili chilli II
nach **Christus** AD (= Anno Domini) III U2, 42

circa about II
Cola coke I
Comic(heft) comic II
Computer computer I
cool cool I
Cornflakes cereal III U5, 96
Cousin cousin II
Cousine cousin II
Crew crew III U4, 84
Curry curry II

D

da there I
da drüben over there II
da ist there is I
da sind there are I
da because I
Dach roof II
Dachboden attic I
damals then III U1, 10
Dame lady II
Dampfbad Turkish bath III U4, 84
Dampfmaschine steam engine III U3, 57
danach then; after that I; after III U4, 84
danke thanks I
Danke. Thank you. I
dann then I
das the I
das this; that I; which III U3, 54
Das ist nichts für mich. That's not for me. III U2, 34
dass that III U1, 21
Datei file II
Datum date I
dauern to take III U1, 10
davor before that III U3, 54
davor in front of II
decken to lay II
dein, deine your I
deine yours I
dem who; which III U3, 54
den who; which III U3, 54
denken to think I
Denkmal monument II
dennoch still III U1, 16
deprimiert down III U4, 77
der the I
der who; which III U3, 54
deren whose III U3, 54
derselbe the same II
Desaster disaster III U4, 84
deshalb so I
dessen whose III U3, 54
deswegen that's why III U5, 100
Detektor detector III U3, 54
Deutsch German I
deutsch German III U5, 98
aus **Deutschland** German III U5, 98
Dezember December I
dich you I
dich selbst yourself II
die *(auch Pl.)* the I
die who II; which III U3, 54
Diele hall II
Dienst service III U2, 38
Dienstag Tuesday I
am Dienstag on Tuesday I
dies this I
diese (hier) these II
Ding thing I
dir you I
Distanz distance III U1, 17
Donnerstag Thursday I
doof silly III U4, 76
Dorf village III U1, 16
dort there I
dort drüben over there II
dort ist there is I
Dose can I
Dr. *(Anrede)* Dr III U4, 85
Draht wire III U3, 54
Drama drama III U2, 51
drängeln to push III U5, 102
draußen outside II
draußen halten to keep out III U3, 62
dreckig dirty I
Drehort location III U2, 50
drei three I
dreißig thirty I
dreizehn thirteen I
drinnen in II
dritte third I
da **drüben** over there III U5, 96
drücken to push I
du you I
Dudelsack bagpipes *(pl)* III U3, 53
dumm silly III U4, 76
dunkel dark I
Dunkelheit the dark III U1, 20
durch through II
Durcheinander mess I
Durchsage announcement II
dürfen may II
nicht/nie dürfen must not/never III U3, 63
nicht dürfen mustn't III U5, 100
Darf es sonst noch etwas sein? Anything else? I
durstig thirsty II
Dusche shower III U5, 97
Duschgel shower gel III U5, 97
DVD DVD I

E

echt real II
Echt?! No way! III U3, 58
echt really II
Ecke corner III U4, 92
Es ist **egal.** It doesn't matter. II
egal wo(hin) wherever III U5, 107
Ehefrau wife, wives *(pl)* III U3, 54
ehrenamtliche Helferin volunteer III U2, 33
ehrenamtlicher Helfer volunteer III U2, 33
ehrlich honest III U4, 77
Ei egg I
Eid *(muslimisches Fest)* Eid I
eifersüchtig jealous II
eigene own II
Eigenschaftswort adjective III U4, 77
eigentlich actually III U4, 80; in fact III U5, 104
Eigentümer landlord II
eilen to rush III U5, 105
Eimer Wasser bucket of water I
ein, eine a; an I
ein bisschen a bit II
ein paar a few III U1, 20

ein wenig a bit II
einander each other III U2, 34
Einbrecher burglar I
Einbrecherin burglar I
einchecken to check in III U3, 59
eindringen (in) to invade III U1, 11
einfach easy I; plain II; simple III U3, 58
einfache Fahrkarte single ticket III U5, 100
einflussreich important II
einfügen to paste II
Einführung introduction III U2, 50
einhundert a/one hundred I
einige some I
einige a few III U1, 20
Einkäufe machen to do the shopping II
Einkaufen shopping I
einkaufen gehen to go shopping II
Einkaufszentrum shopping centre I
Einkaufszettel shopping list I
einladen to invite I
Einladung invitation I
Einleitung introduction III U2, 50
einmal once III U5, 105
noch einmal once more II
einmarschieren (in) to invade III U1, 11
einpacken to pack; to pack up II
eins one I
einsam lonely III U4, 76
einschlafen to fall asleep III U1, 25
einsetzen to put in I
einst once III U5, 105
einsteigen to get on III U5, 101
einstufen to rate III U2, 51
Eintrittskarte ticket III U1, 15
nicht **einverstanden** sein to disagree II
Einwohner inhabitant III U1, 16; population *(no pl)* III U4, 74
Einwohnerin inhabitant III U1, 16
Einwohnerzahl population *(no pl)* III U4, 74
einzige only III U3, 54
Eis ice cream I
Eisberg iceberg III U4, 84
Eiscreme ice cream I
Elefant elephant I
elegant chic I
Elektrizität electricity III U3, 53
elend miserable III U5, 105
elf eleven I
Eltern parents *(pl)* II
E-Mail e-mail I
Empfang signal III U3, 67
Ende end II; ending III U2, 45
am Ende der Straße at the end of the road I
oberes Ende top III U4, 92
enden to finish II
endlich at last II
Energie power III U3, 53
eng tight II
aus **England** English I
die **Engländer** the English III U1, 11
Englisch English I
englisch English I
entfernt away II
Entfernung distance III U1, 17
enthalten sein to be included III U2, 34
entlang down III U1, 12
entlang along I
(sich) **entscheiden** to decide III U3, 58
sich **entschuldigen** to say sorry II
Entschuldigung! Excuse me! I
Entschuldigung. Sorry.; I'm sorry. I
entspannend relaxing III U2, 34
entspannt relaxed II
er he I
Erdbeere strawberry II
Erdboden ground III U3, 64
Erdkunde Geography I
Erdnussbutter peanut butter III U4, 81
etwas **erfahren** über to learn about sth III U1, 12
erfinden to invent III U3, 54
Erfinder inventor III U3, 52
Erfinderin inventor III U3, 52
Erfindung invention III U3, 54
Erfolg success III U3, 54
erfolgreich successful III U3, 54
erforschen to explore II
Ergebnis result II
ergreifen to grab III U5, 105
erholsam relaxing III U2, 34
sich **erinnern** (an) to remember II
erklären to explain III U5, 104
erkunden to explore II
sich **erkundigen** nach to ask about II
ernst serious III U2, 38
Im Ernst? Are you serious? III U3, 58
erraten to guess II
erscheinen to appear III U2, 42
erschöpft exhausted III U2, 35
erschrecken to scare II; to jump III U2, 42
erschrocken sein to be scared II
erstaunlich amazing II
erste first I
erstellen to make I
als **Erstes** first I
Erwachsene adult III U4, 75
Erwachsener adult III U4, 75
erwarten to expect III U2, 45
ich kann es kaum erwarten I can't wait III U5, 100
erzählen to tell I
Erzähler narrator I
Erzählerin narrator I
es it I
es gibt there are; there is I
Es tut mir leid wegen ... Sorry about ... I
Es tut mir leid. I'm sorry. I
Essen food I; meal II
Essen zum Mitnehmen takeaway II
essen to eat I; to have II
Essensstand food stall II
Esszimmer dining room I
etwa about II
etwas something I; some II
euch you I
euer, **eure** your I
eure yours I
Eure *(als Briefabschluss)* Yours, I
Euro *(Währung)* euro III U5, 94
ewig forever II
exakt exact III U4, 81
explodieren to explode III U1, 20
Explosion explosion III U1, 20

F

Fabel fable III U5, 105
Fabrik factory III U1, 16
Fahne flag II
fahren to go I; to ride II; to travel III U5, 103
gegen etw. fahren to hit III U4, 84
Ski fahren to ski II
Fahrer driver III U5, 100
Fahrerin driver III U5, 100
einfache **Fahrkarte** single ticket III U5, 100
Fahrplan timetable III U5, 100
Fahrpreis fare III U5, 100
Fahrrad bike I
Fahrschein ticket III U1, 15
Fahrt ride II; trip III U2, 34; journey III U5, 100; voyage III U4, 84
eine Fahrt machen to take a trip III U2, 34
Fakt fact II
Das mache ich auf keinen **Fall** noch mal! No way am I doing that again! III U2, 34
fallen to fall I; to fall (over) III U2, 38; to fall off III U2, 40
falls if II
falsch wrong I
Faltblatt flyer II
Familie family I
Fan fan I
fangen to catch II
Fantasie fantasy II
fantastisch fantastic II
Du bist fantastisch. You're a star. II
Fantasy fantasy II
Farbe colour I
Fasching carnival I
fast almost III U1, 12
Fastfood fast food I
Fastfood-Restaurant fast food restaurant I
Februar February I
Federmäppchen pencil case I
fegen to sweep II
Feier party I
feiern to celebrate I
Feiertag holiday III U5, 104
Feind enemy III U2, 50
Feindin enemy III U2, 50
Fels rock III U2, 38
Fenster window I
Schließe das Fenster. Close the window. I
Ferien holiday I
Fernsehen TV I
fernsehen to watch TV I
Fernseher TV I
Fernsehsendung TV show II
Fernsehstudio TV studio II
fertig ready I
fertigstellen to finish II
Fest festival III U5, 100
fest tight II; solid III U3, 55
festhalten to hold III U2, 43
Festival festival III U5, 100
feststecken to be stuck I
Feuer fire I
Feuerwehrauto fire engine II
Film film; movie I
Filzstift felt-tip I
finden to find I
Ich kann … nicht finden. I can't find … I
Finger finger III U2, 39
Fingerabdruck fingerprint II
Firma company II
Fisch fish I
fit fit III U2, 34
Fitnessraum gymnasium III U4, 84
Flagge flag II
Flamingo flamingo I
Flamme flame III U1, 20
Flasche bottle I
Fledermaus bat I
Fleisch meat I
fliegen to fly II
fließend fluent III U2, 33
Flohmarkt jumble sale II
Flug flight II
Flughafen airport II
Flugzeug plane II
Flur hall; corridor II
Fluss river I
flüssig fluent III U2, 33
Flyer flyer II
Fön hairdryer III U5, 97
in **Form** fit III U2, 34
Foto photo I
ein Foto machen to take a photo I
Fotos machen to take photos II
fotografieren to take photos II
Frage question I
fragen to ask I
fragen nach to ask about II
nach dem Weg fragen asking the way I
Französisch French I
Frau woman I; lady II
Frau *(Anrede)* Mrs; Ms I
frech cheeky III U2, 34; naughty III U2, 43
ein **freier** Tag a day off III U2, 39
Freiland- free range II
Freiluft- outdoor III U2, 34
Freitag Friday I
Freiwillige volunteer III U2, 33
Freiwilliger volunteer III U2, 33
Freizeit free time I
Freizeitpark theme park I
Freude fun I
Freund friend I
Freunde treffen to see friends I
Freundin friend I
freundlich kind II; friendly III U1, 12
Freundschaften schließen to make friends I
Frieden peace III U3, 65
frieren to freeze III U3, 58; to get cold III U3, 60
Frisbee frisbee I
Frisbeescheibe frisbee I
frisch fresh II
Friseur hairdresser II
Friseurin hairdresser II
froh glad II
Frucht fruit I
früh early I
früher earlier I
früher in the old days III U2, 43
(wohnte) **früher** used to (live) III U1, 16
Frühlingsrolle spring roll II

Frühstück breakfast I
frühstücken to have breakfast I
Frühstückspension bed and breakfast (B & B) III U3, 58
sich wie zu Hause **fühlen** to make oneself at home III U5, 96
(sich) fühlen to feel II
führen to run III U4, 75
Führer guide II; leader III U1, 11
Führerin guide II; leader III U1, 11
(sich) **füllen** to fill III U4, 84
Füller pen I
fünf five I
fünfzehn fifteen I
fünfzig fifty I
funktionieren to work II
für for I
für immer forever II
furchtbar awful; terrible I; horrible III U4, 76; dreadful III U4, 77
sich **fürchten** to be afraid II
Fuß foot I
zu Fuß on foot I
Fußball football I
Fußboden floor I
Fußgelenk ankle II
Fußknöchel ankle II
füttern to feed I

G

Gabel fork II
Gang corridor II
ganz all II; whole III U5, 104
ganz allein all alone I
den **ganzen** Tag all day III U3, 58
gar nicht not at all II
Garten garden I
Gas gas III U1, 20
Gast guest III U2, 33
Gasthaus pub III U5, 94
Gebärdensprache sign language III U5, 95
Gebäude building II
geben to give I
jmdm. das Gefühl geben, etw. zu sein to make sb feel like sth III U2, 43
es gibt there are; there is I
Gebiet area III U5, 104
geboren werden to be born III U3, 52
(in der Pfanne) **gebraten** fried II
Geburtstag birthday I
Alles Gute zum Geburtstag! Happy birthday! I
Gedicht poem III U5, 105
geduldig patient III U2, 35
gefährlich dangerous III U2, 34
gefällt mir nicht I don't like I
Gefängnis prison II
gefeuert fired III U1, 23
gefrieren to freeze III U3, 58
jmdm. das **Gefühl** geben, etw. zu sein to make sb feel like sth III U2, 43
gegen against II; around III U5, 96
gegen etw. fahren to hit III U4, 84
Gegend area III U5, 104
im **Gegensatz** zu unlike III U5, 94
sich **gegenseitig** each other III U2, 34
gegenüber opposite I
geheim secret II
Geheimnis mystery I; secret II
gehen to go; to walk I
gehen um to be about III U1, 31
ins Bett gehen to go to bed I
geht nicht an sein Handy isn't answering his mobile I
Ich muss gehen. I have to get going. III U4, 80
Wie geht es dir? How are you? I
gehörlos deaf III U3, 54
Geist ghost II
Gel gel III U5, 97
gelassen relaxed II
gelb yellow I
Geld money I
Geldbörse wallet III U4, 80
Geldschein note II
Gelegenheit chance II
gemäß according to III U4, 85
gemeinsam together I
Gemüse vegetable (veg) II
Obst- und **Gemüseladen** greengrocer's III U1, 13
gemustert patterned II
gemütlich cosy III U3, 58
genannt werden to be called II
genau exact III U4, 81
genau genommen in fact III U5, 104
genießen to enjoy II
genug enough III U2, 34
genügend enough III U2, 34
Geocaching geocaching I
geöffnet open III U1, 22
Geografie Geography I
gerade (eben) just II
geradeaus straight on I
geradlinig straightforward III U4, 77
Gerät tool II
Geräusch noise I; sound III U1, 21
Gerede talk II
Gericht dish II
Gern geschehen. You're welcome. I
gern mögen to love I
hätte(n) **gern** would like II
würde(n) gern would like II
Ich würde nicht gerne … I wouldn't like (to) … I
Ich würde sehr gern … I'd love to … (= I would love to) III U3, 58
Geruch smell III U1, 23
Gesangs- singing III U5, 95
Geschäft shop I
geschehen to happen II
Was ist geschehen? What happened? I
Geschenk present I
Geschichte History; story I; history III U1, 12
Gesellschaft company II
Gesellschaftslehre Social Studies I
Gesetz law III U4, 85
Gespräch conversation III U2, 32
gestern yesterday I
gesund healthy III U4, 80
Getränk drink II
gewinnen to win I
Gewinner winner I
Gewinnerin winner I
gewöhnlich usually II
Gewürz spice II
Gips cast III U2, 39

Giraffe giraffe I
Gitarre guitar III U5, 95
Glas glass II; jar III U4, 80
glauben to think I; to believe II
Ich glaube nicht. I don't think so. II
Ich glaube. I think so. II
gleich the same II
Glocke bell II
Glück haben to be lucky III U4, 85
viel Glück good luck II
glücklich happy I
glücklicherweise luckily II
Glückstag lucky day II
Glückszahl lucky number I
Glückwunsch! Congratulations! II
Glühbirne light bulb III U3, 57
Gold gold III U5, 104
Gold- gold III U5, 104
golden gold III U5, 104
Grab grave III U1, 11
Gras grass I
grau grey I
greifen to grab III U5, 105
Grenze border III U1, 10
Grill barbecue I
Grillparty barbecue I
groß big; high I; tall; large II
großartig great I; fantastic II; grand III U5, 96
Größe size II
Großeltern grandparents *(pl)* II
Großmutter grandmother III U3, 67
Großstadt city II
Großvater grandfather II
grün green I
Grund reason III U2, 51; bottom III U4, 92
Gründe angeben to give reasons III U2, 51
Gründe nennen to give reasons III U2, 51
gründen to start III U3, 54
Gruppe group I
gruselig scary I
Grüße ausrichten to say hi to I
Viele Grüße, Best wishes, I
grüßen to say hi to I
Grüß dich. Hello there. I

gültig valid III U5, 100
Gummi rubber III U3, 55
Gummistiefel welly I
gut good I; fine II; nice III U3, 58
gut sein in/bei to be good at I
Guten Morgen. Good morning. II
Gut gemacht! Well done! I
Mir geht es gut. I'm fine. II
gut well II

H

Haar hair III U5, 98
Haarbürste hairbrush III U5, 97
Haare hair III U5, 98
sich die Haare schneiden lassen to have a haircut II
Haargel hair gel III U5, 97
Haarglätter hair straightener I
Haarschnitt haircut II
haben to have I
hast du have you got II
hätte(n) gern would like II
Spaß haben to enjoy oneself III U2, 34
Du hast recht. You're right. I
Ich habe … I have … I
Hafen harbour II
Hafer oat III U3, 53
Haferbrei porridge III U3, 53
Hai shark I
halb half III U1, 16
halb (drei) half past (two) I
eine **halbe** Million half a million III U1, 16
(die) **Hälfte** half III U4, 84
Hallen- indoor III U2, 34
Hallo. Hello.; Hi.; Hello there. I
Hals throat II
Halsband collar I
Halsschmerzen sore throat II
Halt stop II
halten to keep II; to hold III U2, 43
Halte sie hoch. Hold them up. I
Haltestelle stop II
Hamburger burger II
Hand hand I
handeln von to be about III U1, 31

Handtuch towel III U5, 96
Handy mobile (phone) I
hängen to hang II
hart hard II; tough III U2, 34
hassen to hate I
häufig often I
Hauptgericht main course II
Hauptstadt capital (city) III U2, 33
Haus house I
im Haus around the house I
nach Hause home I
sich wie zu Hause fühlen to make oneself at home III U5, 96
zu Hause at home I
zu sich nach Hause to her place III U4, 78
Hausaufgabe(n) homework I
Hausaufgabe(n) machen to do homework I
Häuschen cottage III U3, 53
Hausmeister caretaker I
Hausmeisterin caretaker I
Haustier pet I
Heer army III U1, 11
Heft book I
Heim home I
Heimweh haben to be homesick III U5, 104
heiraten to get married II
heiß hot I
heißen to be called II
Ich heiße … My name is … I
Wie heißt du? What's your name? I
Held hero III U3, 52
helfen to help I
ehrenamtliche **Helferin** volunteer III U2, 33
ehrenamtlicher Helfer volunteer III U2, 33
Helikopter helicopter I
Helm helmet III U1, 12
Hemd shirt I
heraus out II
aus … heraus out of II
herausfinden to find; to find out I
herauskommen to get out III U2, 43
herausnehmen to take out I
hereinkommen to get in I

hergestellt sein aus to be made of III U1, 20
Herr *(Anrede)* Mr I
herrlich lovely II
herum around I
herumkommen to get around III U1, 16
herumrennen to run about II
herunter down III U1, 12
herunterfallen to fall off III U2, 40
herunterladen to download II
hervorbringen to produce III U3, 52
Herz heart III U5, 94
heute today I
  heute Abend tonight II
  heute Nacht tonight II
heutzutage now II
Hexe witch I
Hi. Hi. I
hier here I
hiesig local III U3, 58
Hilfe help II
hilfreich useful III U2, 34; III U4, 76; helpful III U5, 100
Himbeere raspberry III U4, 80
hinauf up II
hinausgeworfen fired III U1, 23
hinbringen to take II
in … **hinein** inside II
hineingehen to go on II
Hin- und **Rückfahrkarte** return ticket III U5, 101
hinfallen to fall (over) III U2, 38
hinkommen to get there III U2, 42
hinter behind II
Hintergrund background III U4, 92
im **Hintergrund** in the background III U4, 92
hinunter down III U1, 12
hinuntereilen to rush down II
Hinweis clue I
hinzufügen to add II
  zu … hinzufügen to bookmark II
Hip-Hop *(Musik)* hip hop III U5, 95
Hobby hobby III ZI 9
hoch high I; tall II
hochladen to upload II
Hochzeit wedding II

hoffen to hope I
hoffnungsvoll hopeful III U4, 77
höflich polite II
Höhe height II
Höhle cave II
holen to get II
Holz wood I; wood III U3, 54
Homepage homepage III U5, 100
hören to listen (to); to hear I
Hose trousers *(pl)* I
  kurze Hose shorts *(pl)* I
Hosentasche pocket II
Hospital hospital I
Hotel hotel II
Hotelfachschule catering college II
hübsch beautiful I; pretty; lovely II
Hubschrauber helicopter I
Huhn chicken I
Hühnchen chicken II
Hund dog I
Hundekeks dog biscuit II
hundert a/one hundred I
hungrig hungry I
husten to cough III U1, 21
Hut hat II
hüten to look after II

I

ich I; me I
  Ich habe … I have … I
  Ich heiße … My name is … I
  Ich kann … kaufen. I can buy … I
  Ich kann … nicht finden. I can't find … I
  Ich komme aus … I'm from … I
  ich mag I like I
  ich mag nicht I don't like I
  Ich sehe was, was du nicht siehst … I spy with my little eye … I
  Ich weiß (es) nicht! I don't know! I
  ich würde lieber I'd rather III U1, 25
Idee idea I
  Irgendeine Idee? Any idea? I
ihm him I
ihn him I
Ihnen you I
ihnen them I

ihr you I; its III U3, 52
ihr, ihre her I
  ihr seid you're (= you are) I
Ihr, Ihre your I
ihr, ihre *(Pl.)* their I
Ihre yours I
ihre hers II; theirs III U5, 99
im August in August I
  im Freien outside II
  im Haus around the house I
  im Bus on the bus II
  Im Ernst? Are you serious? III U3, 58
  im Süden von in the south of III U1, 10
  im vorderen Bereich at the front of II
Imbiss snack I
immer always I
  für immer forever II
  immer noch still III U1, 21
in in; to; at I; inside III U1, 31
  in der Pause at break I
  in der Schule at school I
  in Form fit III U2, 34
  in … hinein inside II
  in der Mitte von in the centre of III U1, 17
  in Ordnung fine; all right II
indisch Indian I; Indian II
Industrie industry III U1, 11
industrielle Revolution Industrial Revolution III U1, 11
Informatik IT (Information Techno-logy) I
Information information *(no pl)* I; information desk II
Informationen information *(no pl)* I
Ingenieur engineer II
Ingenieurin engineer II
Inhalt content III U2, 50
inmitten among III U3, 54
innen in inside III U1, 31
Innen- indoor III U2, 34
im **Innern** inside III U1, 31
Insekt insect III U3, 58
Insel island II
intelligent clever I; smart; intelligent III U4, 77

V

interessant interesting I
sich **interessieren** für to be interested in III U1, 12
interessiert sein an to be interested in III U1, 12
Internet internet II
im Internet surfen to surf the internet II
ins Internet stellen to upload II
Internettagebuch blog II
Interview interview II
interviewen to interview I
die **Iren** the Irish III U5, 94
irgendein any II
Irgendeine Idee? Any idea? I
irgendetwas anything II
irgendwelche any II
Irisch Irish III U5, 94
irisch Irish III U5, 94
sich **irren** to be wrong III U4, 76
ist is I
Italiener Italian II
Italienerin Italian II
Italienisch Italian II
italienisch Italian II

J

ja yes I; yeah *(infml)* II
na ja well I
Jacke coat I; jacket II
Jahr year I
Jahrgangsstufe year I
Jahrhundert century III U1, 25
jährlich annual III U5, 101
jamaikanisch Jamaican II
jämmerlich miserable III U5, 105
Januar January I
Jeans jeans *(pl)* I
jede any III U1, 21
jedenfalls anyway III U2, 34
jeder every; everyone I
jedoch however III U4, 85; though III U5, 105
jemals ever II
jemand somebody III U4, 76
jemand anderes somebody else II
jene those II
jetzt now I
jetzt gerade right now III U2, 38
Job job I
Joghurt yogurt II
Jugend youth *(no pl)* III U5, 94
Jugend- teen II; youth *(no pl)* III U5, 94
Jugendherberge youth hostel III U3, 59
Jugendliche teen II; teenager III U2, 33
Jugendlicher teen II; teenager III U2, 33
Jugendzentrum activity centre III U2, 34
Juli July I
am 7. Juli on 7th July I
jung young II
Junge boy I
Juni June I
Juror judge II
Jurorin judge II
Juwelierladen jeweller's III U1, 13

K

Kabel wire III U3, 54
Käfig cage I
Kaiserreich empire III U1, 10
kalt cold I
Kamel camel I
Kamm comb III U5, 97
Kampf battle III U1, 11; fight III U2, 50
kämpfen to fight III U1, 11
Kanarienvogel canary III U1, 20
Kanone cannon II
Kanonenkugel cannon ball II
Kanufahren canoeing I
Kapitän captain I
Kapitänin captain I
Kappe cap I
Karneval carnival I
Karotte carrot II
Karre truck III U1, 21
Karte card I; ticket II
Kartoffel potato II
Kartoffelbrei mashed potatoes II
Kartoffelchip crisp I
Karton cardboard III U3, 55
Käse cheese I
Käsekuchen cheesecake II
Katastrophe disaster III U4, 84
Katholik Catholic III U4, 74
Katholikin Catholic III U4, 74
katholisch Catholic III U4, 74
Katze cat I
kaufen to buy I
Ich kann … kaufen. I can buy … I
Kaufhaus department store II
Kaugummi chewing gum I
kein, keine no I
Keine Ahnung! No idea! I
kein not … any II
Keks biscuit II
Kellner waiter II
kennen to know I
Ich kenne mich hier aus. I know my way around here. III U1, 12
kennen lernen to meet I; to get to know II
kennzeichnen to mark III U1, 10
Kerze candle I
Ketchup ketchup II
Kidneybohne kidney bean II
Kilogramm (kg) kilogram (kg) I
sieben Kilogramm täglich 7 kilograms a day I
Kilometer (km) kilometre (km) I
40 Kilometer pro Stunde 40 kilometres an hour I
Kilt kilt III U3, 53
Kind child; kid II
Kinder children *(pl)* II
Kinderzimmer bedroom I
Kino cinema I
Kirche church II
Kiste box I
alles **klar** all right II
Klasse year I; class III U2, 36
Klasse *(in einer englischen Schule)* tutor group I
Klassenarbeit test I
Klassenfahrt school trip I
Klassenlehrer tutor I
Klassenlehrerin tutor I
Klassenzimmer classroom I
klassisch *(Musik)* classical III U5, 94

Klebstoff glue I
Kleeblatt shamrock III U5, 104
Kleid dress I
Kleider *(Pl.)* clothes *(pl)* I
Kleiderschrank wardrobe I
Kleidung clothes *(pl)* I; outfit III U5, 105
klein small I; little II; tiny III U1, 17
Klettern rock climbing I
klettern to climb III U2, 34
klicken to click I
klingeln to ring III U5, 96
klingen to sound II
Kloß dumpling II
Klub club II
klug clever I; smart; intelligent III U4, 77
Kneipe pub III U5, 94
Knie knee III U2, 39
Knoblauch garlic II
knuddelig cuddly III U2, 39
Koch chef II
Kochbanane plantain II
Kochen cooking II
kochen to cook II
Köchin chef II
Koffer suitcase II
Kohl cabbage II
Kohle coal III U1, 16
Kokosnuss coconut II
Kombination combination II
kommen to come I
Ich komme aus ... I'm from ... I
Komm schon! Come on! III U1, 22
Woher kommst du? Where are you from? I
Kommentar comment II
Komödie comedy III U2, 50
Konfitüre jam III U4, 80
König king III U1, 11
Königin queen III U1, 31
königlich royal II
können can I; may II
nicht können can't I; cannot III U2, 45
nicht weg können to be stuck I
Ich kann ... nicht finden. I can't find ... I
Ich konnte nicht anders als ... I couldn't help but ... III U5, 105
Könntest du das bitte wiederholen? Can you say that again, please? I
konnte could III U1, 21
könnten could III U3, 58
kontrollieren to check III U4, 81
Konversation conversation III U2, 32
Konzert concert II
Kopf head II
Kopfsalat lettuce II
Kopfschmerzen headache II
kopfüber head first III U1, 18
Kopfweh headache II
Kopie copy II
kopieren to copy II
Korbball netball I
Körper body III U5, 97
Körperlotion body lotion III U5, 97
korrekt right I
Korridor hall II
kosten to cost III U4, 75
Wie viel (kostet/kosten) ...? How much (is/are) ...? I
... kosten 99 Pence. ... are 99p. I
... kostet ein Pfund fünfundzwanzig. ... is £1.25. I
kostenlos free III U4, 75
köstlich delicious II
Kostüm costume; fancy dress I
Kraft power III U3, 53
krank ill II; sick III U1, 11
Krankenhaus hospital I
Krankenpfleger nurse II
Krankenschwester nurse II
Krankenwagen ambulance III U2, 38
Kraut cabbage II
Kreis circle III U1, 10
kreischen to scream III U5, 105
Kricket cricket II
Kritik review III U2, 50
Krokodil crocodile I
Küche kitchen I
Kuchen cake I; pie II
einen Kuchen backen to make a cake I
Kuh cow III U1, 16
kühl cool I
kühlen to cool III U2, 39
Kühlschrank fridge III U5, 96
sich **kümmern** (um) to care (for) III U5, 95
Kunde customer III U4, 80
Kundin customer III U4, 80
Kunst Art I
Kunststoff plastic III U3, 54
Kunststück trick III U2, 41
Kuppel dome II
Kurs course III U2, 32
kurz short II; shortly III U4, 84
kurze Hose shorts *(pl)* I
Kuscheltier cuddly toy III U2, 39
Kuss kiss II
küssen to kiss III U4, 78
Küste coast III U2, 33
an der Küste on the coast III U1, 17

L

lächeln to smile III U2, 36
lachen to laugh II
Ladegerät charger III U5, 97
Laden shop I
Tante-Emma-Laden corner shop I
Lage location III U2, 50
Lager camp II
Lamm lamb II
Lampe lamp I
Land country I; land II; countryside III U1, 16
auf dem Land in the country I
Landkarte map III U5, 97
ländliche Gegend country I
Landschaft countryside III U1, 16
Landwirt farmer I
Landwirtin farmer I
lang long I
langsam slow III U2, 34
langweilig boring I
Laptop laptop I
Lasagne lasagne II
lassen to leave II; to let III U5, 98
lass uns let's I
laufen to run I; to walk II
Laut sound III U1, 21

laut noisy III U1, 16; loud III U2, 35
laut according to III U4, 85
läuten to ring III U5, 96
Leben life I
am Leben alive III U1, 22
leben to live I
Lebensmittel food I
lecker yummy II; nice III U3, 58; tasty III U4, 80
Leder leather III U3, 55
legen to put I; to lay II
lehren to teach III U4, 76
Lehrer teacher I; instructor III U2, 34
Lehrerin teacher I; instructor III U2, 34
leicht easy I
Es tut mir **leid** wegen … Sorry about … I
leid tun to be sorry III U4, 87
Es tut mir leid. I'm sorry. I
Tut mir leid. Sorry. I
leihen to lend II
Leine lead I
leise quiet III U1, 16
leistungsorientiert competitive III U2, 35
leiten to run III U4, 75
Leiter ladder I
lernen to learn II
kennen lernen to get to know II
lesen to read I
zu guter **Letzt** at last II
letzte last I
Leute people *(pl)* I; guys II
Liebe/Lieber …, *(Anrede in Briefen)* Dear …, I
lieben to love I
ich arbeite **lieber** I prefer working II
ich würde **lieber** I'd rather III U1, 25
Liebesgeschichte romance III U2, 51
Lieblings- favourite I
Lied song I
Lieferwagen van III U4, 93
liegen to be located III U2, 33
lila purple I
Limonade lemonade II
Lineal ruler I
Linie line II
links left III U1, 12
links on the left I
Liste list II
LKW-Fahrer lorry driver II
LKW-Fahrerin lorry driver II
Loch hole I
locker relaxed; loose II
Löffel spoon II
lokal local III U3, 58
lose loose II
lösen to solve I
Löwe lion I
Luft air III U3, 55
Luftballon balloon I
Lunchpaket packed lunch II
lustig funny I

M

machen to do; to make I
ein Foto machen to take a photo I
eine Nachtwanderung machen to go on a night walk I
Hausaufgabe(n) machen to do homework I
sich Notizen machen to take notes I
Es wird aus … gemacht. It's made with … II
Gut gemacht! Well done! I
Mach dir keine Sorgen. Don't worry. II
Mach dir nichts draus. Never mind. II
Macht nichts. Never mind. II
Macht's gut. Take care. I
sie machte she was making II
Macht power III U3, 53
Mädchen girl I
Magen stomach II
Magie magic II
magisch magic II
Mahlzeit meal II
Mai May I
Mal time III U1, 21
malen to paint II
Mama mum I; mama II
manchmal sometimes I
Mann man I
Mannschaft team I; crew III U4, 84
Märchen fable III U5, 105
Marke brand III U4, 81
markieren to mark III U1, 10
Markt market II
Marmelade jam III U4, 80
März March I
Maschine machine II
Material material III U3, 56
Mathe Maths I
Matsch mud III U1, 18
Mauer wall II
Mayonnaise mayonnaise II
meckern to nag III U4, 76
Medikamente medicine III U2, 39
Medizin medicine III U2, 39
Meer sea I
am Meer at the seaside I
Meerschweinchen guinea pig I
Mehl flour II
nicht **mehr** not … any more III U4, 76
mehr more I
die **Mehrheit** most I
Meile mile II
mein, meine my I
meine mine II
meiner Meinung nach in my opinion III U4, 76
meinen to mean III U2, 33
meins mine II
Meinung opinion III U2, 50
einer Meinung sein (mit) to agree (with) III U3, 58
seine Meinung ändern to change one's mind III U4, 81
anderer Meinung sein to disagree II
meiner Meinung nach in my opinion III U4, 76
am **meisten** most II
die **meisten** most I
Meldet euch. Put your hands up. I
melken to milk III U1, 16
eine **Menge** a lot of I
jede Menge lots of I; lots III U2, 43
Mensa cafeteria I
Mensch person II

Menschen people *(pl)* I
Menschenmenge crowd II
menschlich human III U3, 54
sich **merken** to remember II
merkwürdig strange; funny II
Messer knife II
Metall metal III U3, 54
Meter metre I
Methode method II
Metzgerei butcher's III U1, 13
Miau! Miaow! I
mich me I
Miete rent II
mieten to rent III U3, 58
Mikrowelle microwave II
Milch milk I
Milchmischgetränk milkshake III U4, 76
Milchshake milkshake III U4, 76
mild mild I
Milliarde billion II
Million million III U1, 11
  eine halbe Million half a million III U1, 16
mindestens at least III U4, 76
Mineralwasser mineral water III U4, 81
Minute minute II
mir me I
  von mir of mine II
mit with I
mit *(dem Zug)* by *(train)* I
mitbringen to bring II
Mitleid haben mit to feel sorry for III U5, 105
zum **Mitnehmen** takeaway II
mitnehmen to take I
Mittagessen lunch I
Mittagspause lunchtime I
Mittagszeit lunchtime I
Mitte centre III U1, 12; middle III U2, 33
  in der Mitte in the middle III U4, 92
  in der Mitte von in the centre of III U1, 17
Mitternacht midnight III U4, 84
Mittwoch Wednesday I
mittwochs on Wednesdays I
Mobiltelefon mobile (phone) I
modern modern I
modisch fashionable II
mögen to like I; to enjoy III U2, 50
  am liebsten mögen to like ... best I
  am meisten mögen to like ... best I
  gern mögen to love I
  nicht mögen to hate I
  ich mag I like I
  ich mag nicht I don't like I
  Ich möchte nicht ... I wouldn't like (to) ... I
  Ich möchte ... I'd like (to) ... (= I would like to) I
  Möchtest du? Would you like (to) ...? I
Moment moment II
Monat month I
monatlich monthly III U5, 101
Monster monster III U3, 58
Montag Monday I
Mörder murderer III U2, 50
Mörderin murderer III U2, 50
Morgen morning I
  Guten Morgen. Good morning. II
morgen tomorrow II
Moschee mosque II
Motorrad motorbike I
Moussaka moussaka II
müde tired I
Müll rubbish II
Mund mouth II
Münze coin III U4, 79
Münzgeld change II
Münztelefon pay phone III U3, 67
Museum museum II
Musik music I
Musik- musical III U5, 95
musikalisch musical III U5, 95
Musikgruppe band II
Müsli cereal III U5, 96
Muslimin Muslim I
Muslim Muslim I
müssen must I; to have to II
  nicht müssen needn't I
mutig brave III U3, 63
Mutter mother I
Mütze cap I

N

Na schön. Fair enough. III U5, 100
nach to; after I
  nach Hause home I
  nach dem Weg fragen asking the way I
nach *(bei Uhrzeitangaben)* past II
Nachbar neighbour III U3, 67
Nachbarin neighbour III U3, 67
nachdem sie (die Kohle) weg ist after it's gone III U1, 20
Nachmittag afternoon I
nachmittags in the afternoon I
nachmittags *(Uhrzeit)* p.m. II
Nachricht message II
Nachricht(en) news II
nachschauen to look I; to look up II
Nachspeise dessert; pudding II
nachsprechen to say I
nächste next I
als **Nächstes** next II
Nacht night I
  heute Nacht tonight II
  in jener Nacht that night II
Nachtwanderung night walk I
  eine Nachtwanderung machen to go on a night walk I
Nagel nail III U5, 97
Nagelschere nail scissors *(pl)* III U5, 97
nah near III U1, 15
in der **Nähe** von near I
Nahrung food I
Name name I
Nase nose I
  die Nase voll haben (von) to be fed up (with) III U4, 76
nass wet I
National- national III U5, 104
national national III U5, 104
Natur nature III U3, 53
natürlich of course I
Naturwissenschaft Science I
Navi satnav I

neben next to I
neblig foggy I
nehmen to take I
neidisch jealous II
nein no I
nennen to say I; to call III U1, 16
auf die Nerven gehen to get on one's nerves III U1, 16
nervös nervous II
nett nice I; kind II; friendly III U1, 12
Nett, dich kennen zu lernen. Nice to meet you. I
Netz web III U3, 63
neu new I
Neuigkeit(en) news II
neun nine I
neunzehn nineteen I
neunzig ninety I
nicht not I
auch nicht not ... either III U3, 58
nicht brauchen needn't I
nicht dürfen mustn't III U5, 100
nicht können can't I; cannot III U2, 45
nicht mögen to hate I
nicht müssen needn't I
nicht werden won't (= will not) II
nicht einverstanden sein to disagree II
nicht mehr not ... any more III U4, 76
nicht wahr? isn't it? II
Nichte niece III U4, 80
Nichts wie weg. Off we went. III U5, 105
nichts nothing III U1, 21
nie never I
niederbrennen to burn down II
niedlich cute I
niedrig low II
niemals never I
niemand nobody III U3, 58
niemand no one I
noch still III U1, 21; even II
noch ein another II
noch einmal again; once more II
noch nicht not ... yet II
Norden north III U1, 10
nördlich northern III U1, 11
nördlich von to the north of III U1, 17
Nordosten northeast III U1, 19
Nordwesten northwest III U1, 16
nordwestlich northwest of III U4, 75
nörgeln to nag III U4, 76
normalerweise usually II
die Normannen the Normans III U1, 11
Notdienst emergency service III U2, 38
Notfall emergency III U2, 38
sich Notizen machen to take notes I
Notruf emergency call III U2, 38
November November I
Nudelauflauf pasta bake II
Nudeln pasta II
null zero I
null *(bei Uhrzeiten und Telefonnummern)* oh I
Nummer number I
nun now I
nur only I; just II
Nuss nut I
nützlich useful III U2, 34; helpful III U5, 100

O

oben up II
oben at the top III U4, 92
obere upper III U4, 92
oberer Teil top III U4, 92
oberes Ende top III U4, 92
Oberteil top II
Obst fruit I
Obst- und Gemüseladen greengrocer's III U1, 13
oder or I
Ofenkartoffel jacket potato II
offen open III U1, 22
öffentliche Verkehrsmittel public transport III U5, 100
öffnen to open I
oft often I
ohne without III U4, 76
Ohr ear II
okay OK I
Oktober October I
Oma grandma II
Onkel uncle I
online online II
Opa grandad III U4, 75
Operation operation III U2, 39
optimistisch optimistic III U4, 77
Orange orange I
orange orange I
Orchester orchestra III U5, 94
in Ordnung bringen to tidy (up) II
in Ordnung fine; all right II
organisieren to organize II
Ort place I
örtlich local III U3, 58
Osten east III U1, 10
Outdoor- outdoor III U2, 34
Outfit outfit III U5, 105

P

ein Paar a pair of II
ein paar some I; a few III U1, 20
packen to pack; to pack up II
Packung packet I
panisch werden to panic II
Papa dad I
Papagei parrot I
Papier paper III U3, 55
Pappe cardboard III U3, 55
Parade parade III U5, 95
Parfüm perfume III U5, 97
Park park I
Partner partner III U5, 99
Partnerin partner III U5, 99
Party party I
Passagier passenger II
Passagierin passenger II
passen to suit; to fit II
passieren to happen II
Was ist passiert? What happened? I
Pasta pasta II
Pastete pasty; pie II
Patient patient II
Patientin patient II
Pause break I

in der Pause at break I
Pause machen to take a break II
Pausenhof playground I
Pence *(brit. Währungseinheit)* pence I
Das macht zwei Pfund und 24 Pence. That's £2.24. I
… kosten 99 Pence. … are 99p. I
Person person II
Personalausweis ID III U5, 97
persönlich personal III U5, 97
Pfannkuchen pancake II
Pfeffer pepper II
Pferd horse I
Pfirsich peach I
Pflanze plant I
Pflaster plaster III U2, 39
Pfund *(brit. Währungseinheit)* pound I
Das macht 2 Pfund und 24 Pence. That's £2.24. I
… kostet ein Pfund fünfundzwanzig. … is £1.25. I
Picknick picnic I
Pieps tweet III U1, 22
pikant spicy II
Pinguin penguin I
pink pink I
Pirat pirate I
Piratin pirate I
Pirogge pierogi II
Pizza pizza I
Plan plan II
planen to plan III U3, 58
Planke plank II
Plastik plastic III U3, 54
Platsch splash I
Platz place I; square II
plaudern to chat II
plötzlich suddenly II
Polizei police III U2, 38
Polizeibeamter police officer I
Polizeibeamtin police officer I
Pommes frites chips *(pl)* I
Pop *(Musik)* pop III U5, 94
Popcorn popcorn I
Porzellan china III U3, 55
positiv positive III U4, 76
Postamt post office I
Poster poster I
Postkarte postcard I
Pranger stocks III U2, 43
Preis prize; price II
Prise pinch II
pro Stück each II
probieren to try II
Problem problem I; trouble III U2, 33
produzieren to produce III U3, 52
Programm programme I
Projekt project III U5, 98
Prospekt brochure III U1, 31
Protestant Protestant III U4, 74
Protestantin Protestant III U4, 74
protestantisch Protestant III U4, 74
prüfen to test II
Pudding pudding II
Punktestand score II
pünktlich on time III U5, 100
putzen to clean I

Q

Quittung receipt II

R

Rad wheel II
Radfahren cycling III U3, 61
Radiergummi eraser I
Radio radio II
Rafting rafting III U2, 33
rappen to rap II
Rapper rapper III U5, 98
Rapperin rapper III U5, 98
Rat advice III U2, 51
raten to guess II
Rathaus town hall II
Ratschlag advice III U2, 51; tip II
Rätsel mystery I
Rauch smoke III U2, 42
Raum room I
Rechner calculator I
Rechnung bill III U3, 59
Du hast **recht**. You're right. I
recht haben to be right II
rechts right III U1, 12
rechts on the right I
Rechtschreibung spelling I
rechtzeitig in time I
Rede speech III U3, 54
reden (mit) to talk (to) I
Rede nicht. Don't talk. I
Regal shelf I
Regalbrett shelf I
Regel rule III U2, 34
Regen rain III U3, 52
Regenbogen rainbow III U5, 104
Regenmantel raincoat III U5, 97
Regenschirm umbrella II
Regisseur director II
Regisseurin director II
regnen to rain I
regnerisch rainy I
Reich empire III U1, 10
reich rich III U3, 54
reichen to pass II
Reichtum wealth III U5, 105
Reifen tyre III U3, 55
in die richtige **Reihenfolge** bringen to put in the right order I
(sich) **reimen** to rhyme III U5, 104
Reis rice II
Reise trip III U3, 58; voyage III U4, 84; journey III U5, 100
reisen to travel II
Reiten horse riding I
reiten to ride II
Religionsunterricht RE (Religious Education) I
rennen to run I
reparieren to repair III U3, 67
Reporter reporter III U2, 42
Reporterin reporter III U2, 42
Republik republic III U5, 94
Requisit prop III U2, 45
reservieren to make a reservation III U3, 59
Reservierung reservation III U3, 59
Restaurant restaurant II
Fastfood-Restaurant fast food restaurant I
retten to save III U4, 85
Rettungsboot lifeboat III U2, 33
Rettungsdienst emergency service III U2, 38

schrecklich awful; terrible I; horrible III U4, 76
Schrei shout I
schreiben to write I
eine SMS schreiben to text II
schreien to shout II; to scream III U5, 105
Schriftsteller writer II
Schriftstellerin writer II
Schritt step III U5, 102
schubsen to push III U5, 102
Schuh shoe I
Es ist meine **Schuld**. It's my fault. II
schulden to owe III U4, 80
Schule school I
in der Schule at school I
Schüler student I
Schülerin student I
Schulfach subject I
Schulhof playground I
Schulstunde lesson I
Schüssel bowl II
schützen to protect III U3, 53; to keep safe III U2, 34
schwach weak III U2, 35
schwarz black I
Schweigen silence III U1, 20
schweigsam silent III U1, 21
Schweinefleisch pork II
schwer heavy; hard II; badly III U1, 21; serious III U2, 38
schwerhörig deaf III U3, 54
Schwert sword III U2, 43
Schwester sister I
schwierig difficult III U2, 35; hard II
Schwierigkeiten trouble III U2, 33
Schwimmbad swimming pool I
schwimmen to swim II
schwimmen gehen to go swimming I
Science-Fiction science fiction I
Scone *(eine Art süßes Brötchen)* scone II
sechs six I
sechzehn sixteen I
sechzig sixty I
See lake III U3, 53
Seeräuber pirate I
Seeräuberin pirate I
sehen to see I; to look II
Ich sehe was, was du nicht siehst ... I spy with my little eye ... I
Lass mal sehen ... Let's see ... I
Sehenswürdigkeit sight II
sehr very I; a lot II; badly III U1, 21
so sehr so much III U4, 76
zu sehr too much II
Seide silk III U3, 55
Seife soap III U5, 97
Seil rope I
Seilrutsche zip line III U2, 32
sein to be I
Sei still. Don't talk. I
Seid ihr schon fertig? Have you finished yet? II
sein his I; its III U3, 52
seiner his II
seins his II
Seite page; side I
Sekunde second II
selber myself III U2, 34; ourselves; yourselves; themselves III U2, 156
ihr/euch/Sie/sich (**selbst**) yourselves III U2, 156
dich selbst yourself II
er selbst himself III U2, 35
sie selbst herself; themselves III U2, 156
selbst myself; self III U2, 34
selbstbewusst confident III U4, 77
selbstsicher confident; sure of oneself III U4, 77
selbstverständlich of course I
seltsam strange; funny II
senden to send I
Sendung programme I
Senf mustard II
September September I
Serviette napkin II
setzen to put I
Setz dich (hin). Sit down. I
Shampoo shampoo III U5, 96
Shirt shirt I
Shorts shorts *(pl)* I
Show show I
sich each other; self III U2, 34
sich (selbst) himself III U2, 35
sich gegenseitig each other III U2, 34
sich kümmern (um) to care (for) III U5, 95
sich selbst herself III U2, 156
sicher sure I; safe III U1, 22
in **Sicherheit** safe III U1, 22
Sie you I
sie her; she I
sie *(Pl.)* they; them I
sie selbst herself III U2, 156
sieben seven I
siebzehn seventeen I
siebzig seventy I
siegen to win I
Sieger winner I
Siegerin winner I
Signal signal III U3, 67
singen to sing I
sinken to sink III U4, 84
Situation situation II
Sitz seat III U5, 102
Sitzbank bench III U4, 87
sitzen to sit I
Sitzplatz seat III U5, 102
Skateboard skateboard III U2, 41
Ski fahren to ski II
Skifahren skiing III U2, 32
SMS message; text message II
eine SMS schreiben to text II
SMS-Schreiber texter II
SMS-Schreiberin texter II
Snack snack I
so like this I
so sehr so much III U4, 76
so so II
so ... wie as ... as II
Socke sock I
soeben just II
Sofa sofa II
Software software II
sogar even II
Sohn son III U3, 64
solar solar III U3, 53
Solar- solar III U3, 53
Soldat soldier III U3, 62
Soldatin soldier III U3, 62

sollte should III U2, 34
Sommer summer II
Sonderangebot special offer III U4, 80
Sonne sun III U1, 11
Sonnen- solar III U3, 53
sonnenbaden to sunbathe II
Sonnenbrille sunglasses *(pl)* II
sonnig sunny I
Sonntag Sunday I
Darf es **sonst** noch etwas sein? Anything else? I
Mach dir keine **Sorgen**. Don't worry. II
sich Sorgen machen to worry I
dafür **sorgen** to make sure III U2, 35
sorgfältig careful II
Sorte sort II; type III U1, 31; kind III U3, 53
Soße sauce II
Souvenir souvenir III U1, 12
Souvenirladen souvenir shop III U1, 12
Sozialkunde Social Studies I
Spaghetti spaghetti II
spannend exciting I
Spaß fun I
Spaß haben to enjoy oneself III U2, 34
zum Spaß for fun III U2, 43
Wie **spät** ist es? What time is it? I
später later I
(zu) spät late I
später after III U4, 84
den Hund **spazieren** führen to take the dog for a walk II
Spaziergang walk III U3, 61
speichern to save II
Speise dish II
Speisekarte menu II
spektakulär spectacular III U4, 74
speziell special I
Spiegel mirror III U5, 97
Spiel match; game I
spielen to play I; to act II
Spieler player II
Spieler *(Computer)* gamer II
Spielerin player II
Spielerin *(Computer)* gamer II
Spielfeld court III U4, 87
Spielkarte card I
Spielplatz playground I
Spielzeug toy III U2, 39
Spinne spider III U3, 63
Spinnennetz web III U3, 63
an der **Spitze** (von) at the front of II
Sport sport I
Sportart sport III U2, 33
Sportgeschäft sports shop I
Sportunterricht PE (Physical Education) I
Sprache language II; speech III U3, 54
sprechen to say I; to speak II
sprechen (mit) to talk (to) I
sprechen über to talk about II
Spritze injection III U2, 39
spülen to wash III U5, 98
Spur clue I
Stadion stadium II
Stadt town I; city II
Stadtmitte city centre III U1, 16
Stadtplan map III U5, 97
Stadtzentrum city centre III U1, 16
Stahl steel III U3, 55
Standinhaber stallholder II
Standinhaberin stallholder II
Star star I
stark heavy II
starren to stare III U5, 105
Start start III U2, 51
starten to start II
staubsaugen to hoover II
stehen to suit; to stand II
steigen to climb III U2, 34
Stein brick II; rock III U2, 38; stone III U1, 10
Stein für Stein brick by brick II
Stelle place I
stellen to put I
sterben to die III U1, 21
Stern star III U2, 50
Stiefel boot II
Stift pen I
Stil style III U5, 95
still quiet III U1, 16
still werden to go quiet III U1, 20
Sei still. Don't talk. I
Stille silence III U1, 20
Stimme voice III U1, 22
stimmt's? isn't it? II
Stock stick II
Stockwerk floor II
Stoff material III U3, 56
stolz (auf) proud (of) III U3, 65
(sich) **stoßen** to hit III U2, 40
Strand beach I
den Strand nach Strandgut absuchen to go beach combing II
Straße road I; street III U1, 15
Straßenbahn tram III U5, 100
Streich trick I
streichen to paint II
Streit argument II; fight III U2, 50
(sich) **streiten** to fight III U1, 11
Strom electricity III U3, 53
Struktur structure III U2, 51
Stück piece II
pro Stück each II
Student student I
Studentin student I
Stufe step II
Stuhl chair I
stumm silent III U1, 21
Stunde hour I
40 Kilometer pro Stunde 40 kilometres an hour I
Stundenplan timetable I
Sturm storm I
suchen nach to look for II
Süden south III U1, 10
im Süden von in the south of III U1, 10
Südwesten southwest III U1, 19
super cool I; super; way to go II
Superman superman I
Supermarkt supermarket II
Suppe soup II
Surfen surfing III U2, 33
surfen to surf II
im Internet surfen to surf the internet II
süß sweet III U5, 96; cute I
Süßes, sonst gibt's Saures! Trick or treat! I
Süßigkeit sweet I

Sweatshirt sweatshirt I
Szene scene II

T

Tablett tray II
Tablette tablet II
Tafel board I
Tafel Schokolade bar of chocolate I
Tag day I
ein freier Tag a day off III U2, 39
eines Tages one day III U1, 21
den ganzen Tag all day III U3, 58
ein ausgefüllter Tag a busy day I
Tagebuch diary I
täglich daily III U5, 101
vier Stunden täglich four hours a day I
Taktik tactic III U3, 64
Talent talent I
talentiert talented III U2, 35
Talentwettbewerb talent show I
Tante aunt II
Tanz dance III U5, 100
tanzen to dance I
Tänzer dancer III U5, 94
Tänzerin dancer III U5, 94
tapfer brave III U3, 63
Tasche bag I; pocket II
Taschenlampe torch I
Taschenrechner calculator I
Taschentuch tissue III U4, 81
Tasse cup II
Tätigkeit job II
Tatsache fact II
tatsächlich actually III U4, 80; in fact III U5, 104
taub deaf III U3, 54
tausend a/one thousand II
Taxi taxi II
Team team I
Teamwork teamwork II
Technik Design Technology (DT) I
Techniker engineer II
Technikerin engineer II
Tee tea I
Teelöffel teaspoon II
Teelöffel *(TL)* teaspoon *(tsp)* II
Teenager teen II; teenager III U2, 33
Teenagerin teenager III U2, 33
Teil part II
oberer Teil top III U4, 92
unterer Teil bottom III U4, 92
teilen to share III U5, 96
teilnehmen (an) to take part (in) II
Telefon phone II; telephone III U3, 54
ans Telefon gehen to answer the phone III U2, 45
Telefonanruf phone call I
telefonieren to phone II
Telefonnummer phone number III U2, 38
Telefonzelle telephone box II
Teller plate II
Tennis tennis I
Teppich carpet I
Test test I
testen to test II
teuer expensive II
Text lines; text II
Theater theatre; drama II
Theaterstück play II
Themenpark theme park II
Thunfisch tuna II
Tier animal I
Tierarzt vet III U3, 55
Tierärztin vet III U3, 55
Tierhandlung pet shop III U1, 13
Tierheim animal rescue shelter I
Tierpark zoo I
Tierpfleger zookeeper I
Tierpflegerin zookeeper I
Tiger tiger I
Tipp tip II
Tisch table I
den Tisch decken to lay the table II
Tischler carpenter II
Tischlerin carpenter II
Tischtennis table tennis II
Toast toast II
Tochter daughter I
tod- deadly III U1, 20
tödlich deadly III U1, 20
Toilette toilet I
toll great; brilliant I; amazing II
Tomate tomato II
Ton sound III U1, 21
Tonne tonne II
Tonstudio recording studio I
Top top II
Topf pot III U5, 104
Tor gate III U2, 42
tot dead III U1, 22
töten to kill III U1, 20
Tourist tourist I
Touristin tourist I
Touristeninformation Tourist Information Centre I
Tradition tradition III U3, 53
traditionell traditional III U5, 96
tragen to carry II
tragen *(Kleidung)* to wear I
trainieren to practise III U5, 96
Training practice I; training III U2, 41
Traktor tractor I
Transporter van III U4, 93
Ich **traute** meinen Augen nicht. I couldn't believe my eyes. III U5, 105
Traum dream I
träumen to dream III U1, 25
traurig sad III U3, 65
treffen to meet I; to hit II
Freunde treffen to see friends I
Treppe stairs *(pl)* II
treten to kick III U2, 36
Trick trick I
trinken to drink II
Trinkhalm straw II
Trip trip III U2, 34
trocken dry III U2, 35
Trommeln- drumming III U5, 100
trotzdem anyway III U2, 34
Tschüss. See you later.; Bye.; See you. I
T-Shirt T-shirt I
Tuch scarf I
tun to do; to make I
leid tun to be sorry III U4, 87
Tut mir leid. Sorry. I
Was kann ich für dich tun? How can I help you? I
Tunnel tunnel III U1, 20

vernünftig intelligent III U4, 77
verpassen to miss II
verrenken to sprain III U2, 39
verrückt crazy I
  jmdn. verrückt machen to drive sb crazy III U4, 76
sich **versichern** to make sure III U2, 35
verstauchen to sprain III U2, 39
(sich) **verstecken** to hide III U2, 50
verstehen to understand II; to get III U4, 80
Versuch experiment II
versuchen to try II
vervollständigen to complete I; to finish II
verwenden to use II
verwirrt confused III U1, 25
verzerren to twist II
auf etw. **verzichten** to give sth a miss III U2, 50
Vesper packed lunch II
Video video II
Video-Chat video chat III U3, 67
viel a lot; much; lots of I; lots III U2, 43
viel(e) a lot of I
  viel Glück good luck II
  Viele Grüße, Best wishes, I
viele many II
wie **viele** how many II
vielleicht maybe I; may II
vier four I
vierte fourth I
Viertel nach quarter past I
  Viertel vor quarter to I
vierzehn fourteen I
vierzig forty I
viktorianisches Zeitalter Victorian era III U1, 25
violett purple I
Vogel bird I
Vogelbeobachtung bird watching III U3, 61
Vokabular vocabulary II
voll full III U4, 85
völlig completely III U5, 96
von from; of I; by II
  von hinten from behind I
  nördlich von to the north of III U1, 17
vor ago; in front of II
vor *(bei Uhrzeitangaben)* to I
  vor allem especially II
vorbei (an) past III U1, 12
(sich) **vorbereiten** to prepare III U5, 96
Vordergrund foreground III U4, 92
  im Vordergrund in the foreground III U4, 92
Vorgehensweise tactic III U3, 64
vorhaben to be up to III U3, 67
vorher before II
vorhersagen to foretell III U5, 105
Vormittag morning I
vormittags *(Uhrzeit)* a.m. II
vorsichtig careful II; cautious; guarded III U4, 77
  Sei vorsichtig! Be careful! I
Vorsingen audition II
Vorspeise starter II
Vorspielen audition II
Vorsprechen audition II
vorstellen to present I; to introduce III U5, 96
Vortanzen audition II
vorziehen to prefer II

W

wach awake III U2, 38
Wagen truck III U1, 21
wählen to choose II
wahr true II
während during III U1, 11
während while II
wahrnehmen to notice III U1, 20
wahrscheinlich probably III U1, 21
Wald wood III U2, 34
Waliser Welsh III U2, 32
Waliserin Welsh III U2, 32
Walisisch Welsh III U2, 32
walisisch Welsh III U2, 32
Wand wall II
Wandern hiking III U3, 58; walking III U3, 61
wandern to hike II
Wandgemälde mural III U4, 74
wann when I
warm warm I
warnen to warn III U1, 21
warten to wait II
  warten auf to wait for II
Warteschlange queue II
warum why I
was what I
  was noch what else III U5, 96
  Was für ein/eine … What a … I
  Was ist los? What's wrong? II
  Was ist mit …? What about …? I
  Was ist passiert? What happened? I
  Was kann ich für dich tun? How can I help you? I
  Was man … What to … II
  was sonst what else III U5, 96
  Was stimmt nicht? What's wrong? II
Was?! No way! III U3, 58
Waschbär raccoon I
(sich) **waschen** to wash III U5, 98
Wasser water I
  Eimer Wasser bucket of water I
Website website II
Wechselgeld change II
  Hier ist dein Wechselgeld. Here's your change. I
wechseln to change II
Wecker alarm clock I
Weg way III U1, 12
  auf dem Weg on the way I
weg away II
  nicht weg können to be stuck I
wegen because of III U2, 37
weglaufen to run away III U2, 50
weh tun to hurt II
Weihnachten Christmas I
Weihnachtstheaterstück pantomime II
weil because I
Art und **Weise** way III U3, 58
  auf diese Weise like this I
weiß white I
weit far III U1, 12
weitere other I
welche which; what; who II

Welle wave I
Wellenreiten surfing III U2, 33
wellenreiten to surf II
Welt world II
auf der Welt in the world II
in aller Welt all around the world III U5, 95
wem whom III U3, 64
wen whom III U3, 64
ein **wenig** a bit II
wenige a few III U1, 20
weniger less III U4, 80
wenigstens at least III U4, 76
wenn when; if II
wer who I
Wer ist da oben? Who's up there? I
Wer ist da? Who is it? I
Werbespot advertisement II
werden to get I; will; to become II
genannt werden to be called II
nicht werden won't (= will not) II
Ich würde gerne … I'd like (to) … (= I would like to) I
Ich würde nicht gerne … I wouldn't like (to) … I
werfen to throw I
Werft shipyard III U4, 84
Werk factory III U1, 16
an **Werktagen** on weekdays III U5, 96
Werkzeug tool II
wert sein to be worth III U1, 12
Westen west III U1, 10
Wettbewerb show I; competition II
wetten (auf) to bet III U5, 105
Wetter weather I
wettkampforientiert competitive III U2, 35
wichtig important II
wie like I
so … wie as … as II
wie as II
wie how I; what III U1, 12
Wie alt bist du? How old are you? I
Wie bitte? Pardon? I
wie etwas war what sth was like III U1, 12
Wie geht es dir? How are you? I
Wie heißt du? What's your name? I
Wie man … How to … II
Wie musst du sein? What must you be like? III U2, 37
wie sehr how much III U3, 58
Wie spät ist es? What time is it? I
Wie viel (kostet/kosten) …? How much (is/are) …? I
Wie viel Uhr ist es? What time is it? I
wie viele how many II
Wie wäre es mit …? How about …? II
wieder again II
wiederholen to repeat III U4, 80
Könntest du das bitte wiederholen? Can you say that again, please? I
Auf **Wiedersehen**. Goodbye. I
wiegen to weigh II
Wikinger- Viking III U1, 11
wild wild III U3, 53
willkommen (bei/in) welcome (to) I
Wind wind I
windig windy I
Windpark wind farm III U3, 53
Windrad (wind) turbine III U3, 53
winken to wave II
Winter winter I
winzig tiny III U1, 17
wir we; us I
wirklich real II
wirklich really I; actually III U4, 80
wirr confused III U1, 25
wissen to know I
Ich weiß (es) nicht! I don't know! I
Weißt du was? Guess what? I
Wissenschaft Science I
Witz joke I
Witze machen to joke III U2, 34
witzig funny I
wo where I
wo(hin) auch immer wherever III U5, 107
Woche week I
unter der Woche on weekdays III U5, 96
Wochenende weekend I
am Wochenende at the weekend I
wöchentlich weekly III U5, 101
woher where I
Woher kommst du? Where are you from? I
wohin where I
wohnen to live I
Wohnung flat I
Wohnwagen caravan III U3, 59
Wohnzimmer living room I
Wolke cloud III U2, 42
wolkig cloudy I
Wolle wool I
wollen to want (to) I
Workshop workshop II
Wortschatz vocabulary II
Wrap wrap II
wund sore II
wunderbar wonderful III U5, 105
wünschen to wish III U1, 25
würde(n) would II
würde(n) gern would like II
Wurst sausage II
würzig spicy II
wütend angry II; furious III U4, 77

Z

Zahl number I
Zahn tooth III U2, 39
Zahnbürste toothbrush III U5, 96
Zahnpasta toothpaste III U5, 97
Zahnstocher toothpick II
Zauber- magic II
Zauberei magic II
Zebra zebra I
zehn ten I
Zeichen sign III U2, 32; signal III U3, 67
Zeichensprache sign language III U5, 95
zeichnen to draw II
zeigen to show II
Zeile line II
Zeit time I
die ganze Zeit all the time III U2, 33
viktorianisches **Zeitalter** Victorian era III U1, 25
Zeitreise time travel III U4, 79

Zeitschrift magazine I
Zeitschriftenladen newsagent's III U1, 13
Zeitung newspaper II
Zelt tent II
Zelten camping III U2, 36
zelten to go camping II
Zeltplatz campsite III U3, 58
Zentimeter (cm) centimetre (cm) I
Zentrum centre III U1, 12
zerbrechen to break II
zerstören to ruin II
Ziege goat III U1, 16
Ziegelstein brick II
ziehen to pull I
Ziel ambition III U3, 54
ziemlich quite III U2, 34
Zimmer room I
Zimmerdecke ceiling I
Zimmerin carpenter II
Zimmermann carpenter II
Zitrone lemon II
Zoo zoo I
zornig angry II
zu too II
zu to I
zu Fuß on foot I
zu Hause at home I; back home II
zu sehr too much II
zubereiten to prepare III U5, 96
Zucker sugar I
zuerst first I
Zug train I
Zuhause home I
zuhören to listen (to) I
Zuhörer listener II
Zuhörerin listener II
Zukunft future III U2, 42
zum Schluss finally II
zum Spaß for fun III U2, 43
zumachen to close I
zunächst for a start III U3, 58
zuordnen to match I
zurück back I
zurückhaltend guarded III U4, 77
zurückzahlen to pay back II
zusammen together I
zusammen everyone II
zusammenzucken to jump III U2, 42
Zusatz- extra II
zusätzlich extra II
zuschauen to watch II
zustimmen to agree II
Zutat ingredient II
zuvor before II
zwanzig twenty I
zwei two I
zweite second I
Zwiebel onion II
zwischen between II
zwölf twelve I

Lösungen Zoom in (Seite 8)

1. England, Wales, Scotland, Northern Ireland and the Republic of Ireland; 2. England;
3. The Republic of Ireland; 4. Scotland;
5. Northern Ireland; 6. Scotland 7. London;
8. The Republic of Ireland; 9. England

Bildquellennachweis

Cover.1 plainpicture GmbH (Jim Erickson), Hamburg; **Cover.2** Getty Images RF (Vetta/peter zelei), München; **2.1** plainpicture GmbH (Robert Harding), Hamburg; **3.1** Mauritius Images (Alamy), Mittenwald; **3.2** Getty Images (The Image Bank/Victoria Snowber), München; **4.1** plainpicture GmbH (Cultura), Hamburg; **4.2** Getty Images (Joe Daniel Price), München; **5.1** Alamy Images (GL Archive), Abingdon, Oxon; **9.1** plainpicture GmbH (Bias), Hamburg; **9.2** plainpicture GmbH (Design Pics/Wayne Hutchinson), Hamburg; **9.3** plainpicture GmbH (Westend61/lyzs), Hamburg; **9.4** plainpicture GmbH (Design Pics/The Irish Image Collection), Hamburg; **9.5** Corbis (Lola Akinmade Akerstrom/National Geographic Creative), Berlin; **9.6** Thinkstock (Jessica Hunnicutt), München; **9.7** iStockphoto (Guillermo Perales Gonzalez), Calgary, Alberta; **9.8** iStockphoto (kati1313), Calgary, Alberta; **9.9** Thinkstock (Brian Doty), München; **9.10** iStockphoto (jcarter), Calgary, Alberta; **10.1** plainpicture GmbH (Arcaid), Hamburg; **10.2** plainpicture GmbH (Robert Harding), Hamburg; **11.1** Getty Images (Iconica/Arctic-Images), München; **11.2** Alamy Images (Carolyn Clarke), Abingdon, Oxon; **11.3** Getty Images, München; **12.1** Alamy Images (Simon Dack), Abingdon, Oxon; **12.2** plainpicture GmbH (Robert Harding), Hamburg; **12.3** Alamy Images (Steve Morgan), Abingdon, Oxon; **12.4** shutterstock.com (Alastair Wallace), New York, NY; **16.1** plainpicture GmbH (alt6/Suzanne Rochette), Hamburg; **16.2** shutterstock.com (Julija Sapic), New York, NY; **19.1** Getty Images (Photodisc), München; **19.2** Klett-Archiv (Thomas Weccard), Stuttgart; **24.1** Corbis (Imaginechina), Berlin; **24.2** Getty Images (E+), München; **25.1** February Films, London; **25.2** February Films, London; **25.3** February Films, London; **27.1** Weccard, Thomas, Ludwigsburg; **28.1** Corbis (David Parker// Science Photo Library), Berlin; **29.1** Saal, Katharina, Fürstenfeldbruck; **29.2** Saal, Katharina, Fürstenfeldbruck; **29.3** Saal, Katharina, Fürstenfeldbruck; **29.4** Saal, Katharina, Fürstenfeldbruck; **30.1** Corbis (Steven Vidler), Berlin; **30.2** Mauritius Images (Alamy), Mittenwald; **30.3** Getty Images (Brendan Hoffman), München; **30.4** Mauritius Images (Alamy), Mittenwald; **32.1** Getty Images (Cultura), München; **32.2** Mauritius Images (Alamy), Mittenwald; **33.1** Getty Images (Robert Harding), München; **33.2** Mauritius Images (Alamy), Mittenwald; **33.3** Corbis (Andrew Fox), Berlin; **34.1** Getty Images (Cultura), München; **36.1** Alamy Images (John Robertson), Abingdon, Oxon; **37.1** shutterstock.com (Elena Elisseeva), New York, NY; **37.2** Thinkstock/ iStock/Wojciech Gajda, Getty Images RF/PhotoDisc, shutterstock/Worytko Pawel; **39.1** shutterstock.com (PathDoc), New York, NY; **41.1** Weccard, Thomas, Ludwigsburg; **42.1** Fotolia.com (BasPhoto), New York; **42.2** Getty Images (Cultura), München; **43.1** Alamy Images (James Davies), Abingdon, Oxon; **43.2** Alamy Images (Cultura Creative), Abingdon, Oxon; **44.1** Corbis, Berlin; **45.1** February Films, London; **46.1** Corbis (Ed Bock), Berlin; **46.2** Corbis (Ed Bock), Berlin; **46.3** Corbis (Ed Bock), Berlin; **46.4** Corbis (Ed Bock), Berlin; **46.5** Corbis (Ed Bock), Berlin; **46.6** Corbis (Ed Bock), Berlin; **46.7** Corbis (Ed Bock), Berlin; **47.1** Corbis (Ed Bock), Berlin; **47.2** Corbis (Ed Bock), Berlin; **47.3** Corbis (Ed Bock), Berlin; **47.4** Corbis (Ed Bock), Berlin; **47.5** Corbis (Ed Bock), Berlin; **47.6** Corbis (Ed Bock), Berlin; **47.7** Corbis (Ed Bock), Berlin; **52.1** Getty Images (John Lawson/ Moment), München; **52.2** Getty Images (AWL Images), München; **53.1** CC-BY-SA-4.0 (Rosser1954/keine Änderungen), Mountain View; **53.2** Getty Images (2010 Billy Currie), München; **53.3** Getty Images (The Image Bank/Victoria Snowber), München; **54.1** Thinkstock (Photos.com), München; **56.1** Thinkstock (Dorling Kindersley RF), München; **57.1** Thinkstock (istock/ bandit2523), München; **57.2** Thinkstock (iStock/Digital Paws Inc.), München; **57.3** Fotolia.com (Africa Studio), New York; **57.4** Fotosearch Stock Photography (Eclecti Collection RF), Waukesha, WI; **57.5** Fotolia.com (Diogo Barbosa), New York; **58.1** Avenue Images GmbH (Banana Stock), Hamburg; **60.1** Thinkstock (Eli Franssens), München; **61.1** Thinkstock (iStock/ Nastco), München; **61.2** Klett-Archiv, Stuttgart; **61.3** Thinkstock (istock/ffolas), München; **61.4** Thinkstock (istock/Juliane Jacobs), München; **61.5** Thinkstock (istock/andreusK), München; **61.6** Thinkstock (iStock/JaySi), München; **66.1** Mauritius Images (Alamy), Mittenwald; **66.2** Mauritius Images (Hüttner + Consorten), Mittenwald; **66.3** shutterstock.com (Gencay M. Emin), New York, NY; **66.4** Thinkstock (iStockphoto), München; **66.5** shutterstock.com (Gencay M. Emin), New York, NY; **66.6** Thinkstock (iStockphoto), München; **67.1** iStockphoto (davincidig), Calgary, Alberta; **68.1** Thinkstock (Smitt), München; **68.2** Fotolia.com (laralova), New York; **70.1** Corbis (VO TRUNG DUNG/CORBIS SYGMA), Berlin; **72.1** shutterstock.com (John A Cameron), New York, NY; **72.2** Alamy Images (Alex Ekins Adventure Photography), Abingdon, Oxon; **72.3** dreamstime.com (Micka), Brentwood, TN; **73.1** PONS GmbH, Stuttgart, Stuttgart; **74.1** Getty Images (John Molloy), München; **74.2** plainpicture GmbH (Design Pics), Hamburg; **74.3** plainpicture GmbH (Cultura), Hamburg; **75.1** Corbis (Jon Boyes/incamerastock), Berlin; **75.2** plainpicture GmbH (Stockwerk/Dirk Kugelmeier), Hamburg; **75.3** Corbis (Hugh Rooney/http://www. eyeubiquitous. com/ Eye Ubiquitous), Berlin; **76.1** Getty Images (John Molloy), München; **76.2** Getty Images (Stockbyte), München; **87.1** February Films, London; **87.2** February Films, London; **87.3** February Films, London; **88.1** Fotolia.com (sharynos), New York; **89.1** Klett-Archiv (Peter Nierhoff), Stuttgart; **94.1** Getty Images (Joe Daniel Price), München; **94.2** Alamy Images (imageBROKER), Abingdon, Oxon; **95.1** shutterstock.com (TDC Photography), New York, NY; **95.2** plainpicture GmbH (Hero Images), Hamburg; **95.3** iStockphoto (Carmine Salvatore), Calgary, Alberta; **96.1** shutterstock.com (Tracy Whiteside), New York, NY; **96.2** shutterstock.com (RyFlip), New York, NY; **100.1** plainpicture GmbH (Westend61), Hamburg; **101.1** TRANSDEV Ireland, Dublin; **102.1** Thinkstock (Steeve ROCHE), München; **103.1** Thinkstock (istock/worac), München; **106.1** Picture-Alliance (Jens Kalaene/dpa), Frankfurt; **108.1** shutterstock.com (Aleksandar Mijatovic), New York, NY; **108.2** Thinkstock (iStockphoto), München; **108.3** shutterstock.com (ruskpp), New York, NY; **108.4** shutterstock.com (Gencay M. Emin), New York, NY; **108.5** shutterstock.com (Jim Barber), New York, NY; **108.6** Thinkstock (iStockphoto), München; **110.1** Corbis (Robbie Jack), Berlin; **110.2** Thinkstock (darkbird77), München; **110.3** Thinkstock (darkbird77), München; **111.1** Thinkstock (darkbird77), München;

München; 117.2 Picture-Alliance (Everett Collection), Frankfurt; **117.3** Thinkstock (istock/passigatti), München; **117.4** iStockphoto (davincidig), Calgary, Alberta; **117.5** Thinkstock (istock/NatalyaAksenova), München; **117.6** Thinkstock (istock/TimZillion), München; **117.7** Thinkstock (istock/thumb), München; **117.8** Thinkstock (istock/rvlsoft), München; **120.1** Thinkstock (iStock Editorial/IR_ Stone), München; **120.2** Fotolia.com (Calin Bocian), New York; **120.3** shutterstock.com (Anneka), New York, NY; **120.4** Corbis (Steve Raymer/National Geographic Creative), Berlin; **120.5** shutterstock.com (Ilaszlo), New York, NY; **121.1** Thinkstock (iStock/Nastco), München; **121.2** Thinkstock (istock/ffolas), München; **121.3** Thinkstock (istock/Juliane Jacobs), München; **121.4** Thinkstock (istock/ andreusK), München; **121.5** Thinkstock (iStock/JaySi), München; **126.1** TRANSDEV Ireland, Dublin; **127.1** Thinkstock (istock/worac), München; **129.1** Alamy Images (GL Archive), Abingdon, Oxon; **130.1** Mauritius Images (Matthew Horwood/Alamy), Mittenwald; **130.2** Mauritius Images (Jack Sullivan/Alamy), Mittenwald; **131.1** Getty Images (Moment), München; **131.2** plainpicture GmbH (Thorsten Rother), Hamburg; **131.3** Fotolia.com (PT Images), New York; **131.4** Mauritius Images (Phil Rees/Alamy), Mittenwald; **132.1** Getty Images (Stockbyte), München; **132.2** Getty Images (Stockbyte), München; **133.1** Getty Images (The Image Bank), München; **133.2** iStockphoto (Liz Leyden), Calgary, Alberta; **133.3** Getty Images (Moment Open), München; **134.1** shutterstock. com (VanderWolf Images), New York, NY; **134.2** Getty Images (Stockbyte), München; **134.3** Getty Images (Christopher Pillitz), München; **135.1** Corbis (Artur Widak/NurPhoto), Berlin; **135.2** Mauritius Images (Marco Secchi/Alamy), Mittenwald; **136.1** Getty Images (Matt Cardy), München; **136.2** Mauritius Images (Brickley Pix/Alamy), Mittenwald; **136.3** Getty Images (Universal Images Group), München; **136.4** Getty Images (Hulton Fine Art Collection), München; **136.5** Alamy Images (imageBROKER/Dr. Wilfried Bahnmüller), Abingdon, Oxon; **137.1** Mauritius Images (Ian Shipley IRE/Alamy), Mittenwald; **137.2** Alamy Images (jeremy sutton-hibbert), Abingdon, Oxon; **137.3** plainpicture GmbH (STOCK4B), Hamburg; **137.4** Getty Images (Cultura), München; **138.1** Klett-Archiv (Axel Reis), Stuttgart; **138.2** Klett-Archiv, Stuttgart; **138.3** Klett-Archiv (Axel Reis), Stuttgart; **138.4** Klett-Archiv (Axel Reis), Stuttgart; **138.5** Klett-Archiv (Axel Reis), Stuttgart; **139.1** Klett-Archiv (Axel Reis), Stuttgart; **139.2** Klett-Archiv (Axel Reis), Stuttgart; **139.3** Klett-Archiv (Axel Reis), Stuttgart; **139.4** Klett-Archiv (Axel Reis), Stuttgart; **139.5** Klett-Archiv, Stuttgart; **139.6** Klett-Archiv (Axel Reis), Stuttgart; **139.7** Klett-Archiv (Axel Reis), Stuttgart; **139.8** Klett-Archiv (Axel Reis), Stuttgart; **140.1** Thinkstock (Brand X Pictures/Jupiterimages), München; **140.2** Thinkstock (istock/Krzysztof Slusarczyk), München; **140.3** shutterstock.com (Leemonton), New York, NY; **140.4** Thinkstock (iStockphoto), München; **141.1** Thinkstock (iStock/blueringmedia), München; **141.2** Thinkstock (iStock/graphicsdunia4you), München; **146.1** Alamy Images (Ivy Close Images), Abingdon, Oxon; **174.1** dreamstime.com (Indos82), Brentwood, TN; **175.1** shutterstock.com (ensiferum), New York, NY; **181.1** picturemaxx.net (RF), München; **181.2** Thinkstock (Medioimages/Photodisc), München; **181.3** Getty Images RF (Photodisc), München; **181.4** Thinkstock (iStockphoto), München; **187.1** Thinkstock (iStock/Michael Braun), München; **187.2** Thinkstock (Comstock), München; **187.3** Fotolia.com (Steve Lovegrove), New York; **187.4** Thinkstock (Lifesize), München; **187.5** Thinkstock (istockphoto), München; **187.6** Fotolia.com (Ints), New York; **187.7** Thinkstock (iStockphoto), München; **187.8** shutterstock.com (RF/McNally), New York, NY; **187.9** February Films (Elke Bock), London; **187.10** shutterstock.com, New York, NY; **187.11** Corbis RF (RF), Berlin; **187.12** Thinkstock (Comstock), München; **187.13** Fotolia.com (philippe Devanne), New York; **187.14** Thinkstock (mavrek), München; **187.15** iStockphoto (Liz Leyden), Calgary, Alberta; **187.16** Avenue Images GmbH (Image Source), Hamburg; **187.17** Avenue Images GmbH (Fancy RF), Hamburg; **187.18** shutterstock.com (Stefan Schurr), New York, NY; **187.19** dreamstime.com (Denyskuvaiev), Brentwood, TN; **187.20** Corbis (Gary Kufner), Berlin; **187.21** Getty Images RF (PhotoDisc), München; **187.22** Avenue Images GmbH (Ingram Publishing), Hamburg; **187.23** iStockphoto (Webphotographeer), Calgary, Alberta; **187.24** Thinkstock (iStockphoto), München; **187.25** creativ collection Verlag GmbH, Freiburg; **187.26** Avenue Images GmbH (image source), Hamburg; **187.27** Ingram Publishing, Tattenhall Chester; **187.28** Thinkstock (iStock/Ljupco), München; **187.29** Fotolia.com (mustgo), New York; **187.30** shutterstock.com (Cathleen A Clapper), New York, NY; **187.31** Thinkstock (Jupiterimages), München; **194.1** Klett-Archiv (Wolfgang Schaar, Grafing), Stuttgart; **195.1** shutterstock.com (Anneka), New York, NY; **195.2** iStockphoto (onfilm), Calgary, Alberta; **195.3** picturemaxx. net (RF), München; **195.4** Thinkstock (Medioimages/Photodisc), München; **195.5** Getty Images RF (Photodisc), München; **195.6** Thinkstock (iStockphoto), München; **207.1** shutterstock.com (Pack), New York, NY; **208.1** Thinkstock (iStockphoto), München; **208.2** iStockphoto (Lorraine Boogich), Calgary, Alberta; **208.3** iStockphoto (ollo), Calgary, Alberta; **208.4** shutterstock.com (Jordan Tan), New York, NY; **208.5** Fotolia.com (ang17a), New York; **208.6** Fotolia.com (david hughes), New York; **208.7** Avenue Images GmbH (Banana Stock), Hamburg; **208.8** Corbis RF, Berlin; **208.9** dreamstime.com, Brentwood, TN; **208.10** iStockphoto (Nick free), Calgary, Alberta; **208.11** panthermedia.net (dieschu), München; **208.12** Fotolia.com (godfer), New York; **208.13** shutterstock.com (William Attard McCarthy), New York, NY; **U00/Vorsatz hinten.1** Visit York, York

Sollte es in einem Einzelfall nicht gelungen sein, den korrekten Rechteinhaber ausfindig zu machen, so werden berechtigte Ansprüche selbstverständlich im Rahmen der üblichen Regelungen abgegolten.

Textquellennachweis

S. 17: The City, GOSLING, JAKE NATHAN/Sheeran, Edward Christopher © BDI Music Limited/Sony ATV Music Publishing (UK) Limited, Platz Musikverlage GmbH, Hamburg/Sony/ATV Music Publishing, (Germany) GmbH, Berlin

S. 77: Let your tears fall, FURLER, SIA KATE/Kurstin, Gregory Allen © EMI April Music Inc/EMI Music Publishing Ltd/Kurstin Music, EMI Music Publishing Germany GmbH, Berlin

S. 101: Luminous, Gustafsson, Johan/Haeggstam, Fredrik Folke Alexander/Lundberg, Sebastian Per Emil © Universal Music Publishing AB, Universal Music Publishing GmbH, Berlin

S. 112: The magic water stone, Clare Treleaven © Ernst Klett Verlag GmbH, Stuttgart 2014

S. 142–145: Siobhan Dowd, The London Eye Mystery, Corgi Yearling (Verlag) © Siobhan Dowd, 2007

VisitYork
visityork.org
Key to City Centre Map & Car Parking
Main roads
Car Park access routes
Restricted vehicle access
Visitor Information Centre
Place of Interest
Fairfax House
City wall
Riverboat pick-up points
Toilets
PARK&RIDE
City of York Council operated car park
Piccadilly CAR PARK
Other/private car parks
Post Offices are located at Lendal, Micklegate and Colliergate
Mini Bus & Mobile Home Parking
Charges - apply 08.00hrs up to 24.00hrs
Pay & Display
Up to 2 hours – £3.80
2-5 hours – £6.00
5-12 hours – £9.50
Alternative parking at Park & Ride sites. See Car Parking Information
York Railway Station
York Minster
Minster Quarter
Dean's Park
Museum Gardens
War Memorial Gardens
River Ouse
National Railway Museum
Clifford's Tower
York Castle Museum
JORVIK
Shambles Market
The Shambles
York Art Gallery (re-opening Summer 2015)
Yorkshire Museum
York Theatre Royal
Treasurer's House
Monkgate Bar-Richard III Experience
Micklegate Bar-Henry VII Experience
Quilt Museum (closed from 31st October)
York's Chocolate Story
National Centre for Early Music
York Barbican Centre
Fairfax House
Merchant Adventurers' Hall
Barley Hall
Holy Trinity Church
Bedern Hall
Mansion House
City Screen
Roman Bathhouse
Original Ghost Walk
Opera House
Friargate Theatre
York Dungeon
Army Museum
York Brewery
Bar Convent Trust
Register Office
King's Manor
Yorkwalk
Yorkboat
Left luggage
Union Terrace CAR PARK
Bootham Row CAR PARK
Marygate CAR PARK
Esplanade CAR PARK
Monk Bar CAR PARK
Foss Bank CAR PARK
Piccadilly CAR PARK
Castle CAR PARK
Castle Mills CAR PARK
St. George's Field CAR PARK
Nunnery Lane CAR PARK
© Copyright Visit York www.visityork.
Produced by FWT 10.3.15 www.fwt.co